DISORDERLY CONDUCT

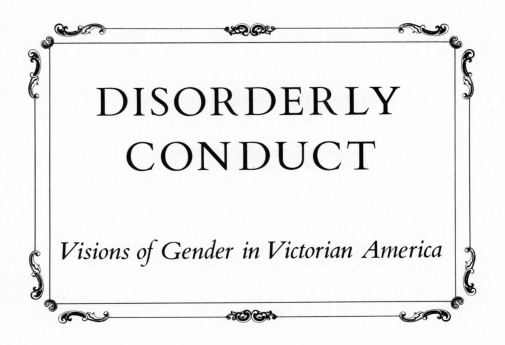

DISORDERLY CONDUCT

Visions of Gender in Victorian America

Carroll Smith-Rosenberg

Alfred A. Knopf　New York 1985

Library of Congress Cataloging in Publication Data

Smith-Rosenberg, Carroll.
Disorderly conduct.
Bibliography: p. _45365_
1. Women—United States—History—19th century—Addresses, essays, lectures. 2. Women—United States—Social conditions—Addresses, essays, lectures. 3. Middle classes—United States—History—Addresses, essays, lectures. 4. Sex role—United States—History—Addresses, essays, lectures. I. Title.
HQ1419.S58   1985   305.4'0973   84-48821
ISBN 0-394-53545-6

Manufactured in the United States of America
FIRST EDITION

For
Angela Haug and Carroll Abbott Smith

Contents

DISORDERLY CONDUCT

Preface

To gather together the essays one has written over a twelve-year period and mold them into a coherent volume of description and analysis is an arresting experience, psychologically as well as intellectually, requiring that one step momentarily outside oneself and become a critical reviewer. One's intellectual progress unfolds as if it belonged to another person. Works are carefully scrutinized—will those once esteemed now embarrass? Old essays seem like old snapshots, freezing a moment of intellectual development within a specific time frame. One endlessly asks: "How ever did I get from there to here?" Or like some latter-day Alice: What vials of change—theoretical and methodological—did I consume? What tiny doors did I slip through to find new gardens of historical experiences? And so the rediscovery of one's past enriches all future work.

Gradually, I have isolated the factors—intellectual and political—that shaped my training and helped me to formulate new approaches. Interpretive threads, seemingly spun in isolation, have woven themselves into perceptible analytic patterns. As I review these patterns, the give-and-take between my ideas and those of my colleagues, mentors, and students stands out boldly. My place within the larger discipline becomes clearer.

But on a far broader scale, there is the sudden awareness of how external forces have shaped my work. To my surprise, my intellectual enthusiasms and new directions echo the work of others with whom I have not knowingly communicated or shared ideas. The suspicion we have all entertained at one time or another seems eerily confirmed: Scholarship follows a rhythm of its own, external to the individual practitioners of the art, a rhythm which sweeps us along, without conscious consultation, until the discipline as a whole is transformed. When do these radical breaks appear? How have we experienced them in our own intellectual development?

These questions are especially critical for workers in new scholarly fields, innovators and iconoclasts. Wedded to new methods and techniques, we tend to labor outside regular professional channels. If we are women scholars insisting upon women's centrality to the reconstruction of our past and to an understanding of social and economic processes, we experience the double marginality of our subject and our gender. To insist on the legitimacy of both is to assume the role of perpetual rebel and iconoclast. For us, therefore, it is crucial to understand the external factors that brought us into existence and the forces that maintain our intellectual vitality. Seen from this perspective my personal hegira assumes a political cast.

An almost irresistible temptation to revise seizes a person beginning to compile a collection of previously published essays: as an older scholar and a critical reader of my younger self, I was strongly tempted to reinterpret and update these older pieces. But if a retrospective collection is to illustrate the path an individual—and, far more significantly, that individual as representative of general scholarly trends—has taken over time, then the previously published essays must remain as originally conceived. The only change I have imposed upon them is to prune material that became redundant when the essays were brought together. My objective has been to bind the individual essays into a cohesive explication of women's and men's experiences and interactions, beginning with the industrial revolution and extending through the First World War. In addition to the essays that have already appeared, I have included four new essays. One was conceived some years ago ("The Abortion Movement and the AMA, 1850–1880"); the two other essays ("The Cross and the Pedestal: Women, Anti-Ritualism, and the Emergence of the American Bourgeoisie" and "The New Woman as Androgyne: Social Disorder and Gender Crisis, 1870–1936") represent my present research and analytic interests.

The fourth essay, "Hearing Women's Words: A Feminist Reconstruction of History," is perhaps the most ambitious in intent. It explores the interconnectedness of women's and of contemporary social history. Women's history constitutes one of the most expansive and revolutionary forces within the New Social History. To look back over the past decade is to explore the ways in which an examination of women's past has transformed the conceptual framework and methodological approaches of contemporary social history. The study of women, moreover, has underscored the importance of a whole new field of scholarly exploration— analysis of social experience and the ways in which individuals and social groups give voice to that experience.

People speak with a multitude of voices. Political beliefs, sexual practices, medical doctrines, religious dogmas, food rituals, all constitute symbolic languages, reflective of social relationships. If we can learn to decode these languages we will begin to hear ancient voices discussing the social and economic experiences that informed their lives. The different ways in which formal ideologies and informal conventions, the distribution of power, the fragmenting force of economic and institutional change, affected women and men across and within class will become clear. Few analytic problems could be more challenging. Students of women in history, anthropology, literary criticism, have been among the first to insist upon such a decoding. In doing so, they have obliterated the artificial boundaries scholars have erected between words and the world that speaks them, myths and the structure of power. It is this new feminist vision that "Hearing Women's Words" addresses in the hope of bridging analytic visions and traditional disciplinary divides.

Historians depend on libraries, manuscript collections, state and local historical societies, corporate archivists. We are greedy exploiters of the directors, curators, and staff of these invaluable institutions. Without these guardians and organizers of The Book and The Word, we could not exist. It gives me great pleasure to acknowledge the invaluable assistance and wise suggestions of the many who have helped make these essays possible. Their numbers are legion. I am especially indebted to Gordon Marshall of the Library Company and to Peter Parker of the Historical Society of Pennsylvania, to Sandra Chafee, Women in Medicine Archives of the Medical College of Pennsylvania, to David Heaney, now emeritus director of the Rare Book Division, Free Library of Philadelphia, and to the staff of the College of Physicians of Philadelphia. I am indebted as well to William Joyce, formerly director of manuscripts, American Antiquarian Society, and now director of manuscripts, New York Public Library, and to all the staff of the American Antiquarian Society. Patricia King and Barbara Hamer of the Schlesinger Library at Radcliffe College have aided me on countless occasions, always with patience and insight. The director of the archives of Mount Holyoke College has given generously of her time, as has her staff. Betty Bright Lowe, of Eleutherian Mills, has been an instructive co-worker in the field of women's history. I am indebted as well to the staff of the university archives and manuscript divisions of Stanford University, the Bancroft Library, University of California at Berkeley, the Chester County Historical Society in Westchester, Pennsylvania, the Iowa State Historical Society, the Minnesota Historical Society. And still I have not acknowledged the half of my debt to these keepers of the word.

I have discussed and argued with, and always learned from, so many scholars over this past decade, I scarcely know where to begin in acknowledging their very great contributions to my perceptions and to my growth. I do know that without them, my understanding would not have developed as it has. With the traditional caveats that, while my work has been constantly enriched by them, my errors are my own, let me name only a few of those from whom I have benefited. I begin with the teachers who first drew me to history, Helen Mulvey and Richard Lowett, then of the Connecticut College for Women, David Donald, Robert Cross, and Richard Hofstadter, then of Columbia University. Then let me simply list the names of those who know how much they have given to me: Sacvan Bercovitz, Richard Beeman, Joan Berner, Jesse Bernard, Blanche Weissen Cook, Natalie Davis, Françoise Ducroq, Paola di Cori, Yasmine Ergas, Lucienne Frappier-Mazur, Judith Friedlander, Sandra Gilbert, Susan Gubar, Diana Hall, Myra Jehlen, Esther Newton, Phyllis Rackin, Donald Rackin, Rayna Rapp, Adrienne Rich, Patricia Roemer, Ruth Rosen, Alice Rossi, Dagmar Schultz, Ann Scott, Joan Scott, Gaye Tuckman, Daniel Walkowitz, Judith Walkowitz, Marilyn Young, Lazar Ziff, and Michael Zuckerman. Scholars across disciplines and around the world mourn the premature deaths of Erving Goffman and of Victor Turner. I, like so many, am the less for no longer having their wise comments and insights. The Berkshire Conference of Woman Historians has proved one of the pivotal influences in my professional and personal life. Through both formal and informal comments upon a succession of papers, Berkshire members have contributed to my development as a woman historian and a historian of women.

These scholarly influences could not have affected me had not my parents, Angela Haug Smith and Carroll Abbott Smith, first opened my mind to the magic and the intricacies of the past, and at every point encouraged and aided me. I am deeply indebted to one reader in particular whose sharp mind tolerates no carelessness, no half-steps or short cuts, either of thought or of literary style, who pounces gleefully upon redundancy and who has given endlessly of time and insight. Lastly, I wish to thank that fine scholar and intellectual companion, Leah Reade Rosenberg. When all is said, it is to and for our daughters and their generation that we write. We want to tell them what we know. We wish them to understand what impelled us to fight to learn it—what it, and most especially, they, mean to us.

PART ONE

Hearing Women's Words: A
Feminist Reconstruction of History

Women's history bridges the scholarly and political, weaving their disparate visions into one. The political feminism of the 1960s and 1970s drew scholars and students to the field of women's history, informing the questions women's historians first addressed. Self-conscious feminism strengthened the resolve of those who insisted upon restructuring the scholarly canon to make the study of women's roles and visions, power and oppressions central to historical analysis. If the personal was the political, so too was the historical. Yet at the same time women's historians claimed Clio, muse of history, as their second mother. While a sense of personal oppression and revolt against marginality and invisibility shaped the questions women's historians first addressed, those questions in turn pushed the methodological approaches and conceptual framework of traditional history to new frontiers. They revolutionized historians' understanding of the family, of the processes of economic change, and of the distribution of power within both traditional and industrial societies. A vision of past cultures as multilayered composites of women's and men's experiences, rich in complexity and conflict, emerged from women's historians' merger of the political and the professional.

Revolutionaries are rarely trained for their roles. They come forward to answer unexpected challenges, at times when old paradigms prove obsolete and new visions are required. Certainly those of us who in the early 1970s responded to the feminist call to discover our collective past had been brought up in the assumptions and methods of conventional history. We were not trained to study women, nor had we thought to do so until the women's movement transformed our lives and our consciousness. Then, we struggled to master the skills necessary to reconstruct women's past. The vision and determination that characterized these early years of women's history—the excitement of our discoveries; the sense of a collective enterprise; the long debates as to the place of women's history within traditional scholarship; the ideological and practical need to develop new, cooperative, noncompetitive approaches to research; the dedication of those who founded the first feminist presses and journals, in their living rooms, during hours stolen from work and family—all are now largely lost to history. We have so quickly become part of the professional mainstream that it is easy to forget the spirit of those early years, the camaraderie with which we turned to each other.[1]

Without question, our first inspiration was political. Aroused by feminist charges of economic and political discrimination, angered at the sexualization of women by contemporary society and at the psychological ramifications of that sexualization, we turned to our history to trace the origins of women's second-class status. Perhaps the most revolutionary aspect of contemporary women's history was our refusal to accept gender-role divisions as natural. Gender, we insisted, was man-made, the product of cultural definitions, not of biological forces. No universal femaleness or maleness existed. Rather, economic, demographic, and ideational factors came together within specific societies to determine which rights, powers, privileges, and personalities women and men would possess.

For us the search to determine what concatenation of factors had decreed the particular gender assumptions the Western world imposed on its women and its men was far from academic. These assumptions had shaped our own lives. The intricate relation between the construction of gender and the structure of power became our principal concern.

We began our investigation by examining the impact of industrialization upon the construction of gender roles in both the work force and the family.[2] Certainly the gender division of labor, as Engels argued a hundred years ago, had predated capitalism. But why, feminist historians asked, had not industrialization undercut those distinctions and made new roles and economic opportunities available for women? Mechanization, by minimizing the importance of brawn to production, had opened up a host of new areas to the potential of female employment. Certainly it was to the economic advantage of the entrepreneurial class to expand the labor force. Why, then, did entrepreneurs bar women from most areas of manufacturing? Who profited from such discrimination? Did the fact that entrepreneurs structured the radically new labor force of an industrializing economy around traditional role divisions suggest that, at the very outset of industrialization, male capital and male labor shared a fundamental social and economic vision that cut across class lines and, in the face of violent economic change, reasserted male social cohesion? If this were true, we would have discovered one critical factor that had kept the emerging and uncertain world of nineteenth-century industrial capitalism from fragmenting. A key social function of women's economic oppression would then become clear, a function that presumably continues to play a vital role in its perpetuation. Historians of women began to examine the ramifications of economic discrimination against women, pointing to the ways it spread out in a ripple effect to alter virtually all forms of social relations.[3] Low wages, the absence of upward mobility, depressing and unhealthy working conditions, all made marriage an attractive survival strategy for working-class women. Once married, women found the workplace closed even more firmly against them. A vicious cycle of economic and psychological dependency emerged, with few if any escape routes even for women of talent and ambition.[4] Of course, feminist historians were not the first to uncover the social construction of women's domestic dependency. Theodore Dreiser had described Sister Carrie's horror when brought face to face with the barren drabness which both her married sister and the unmarried "girls" in the sweatshops experienced. Anzia Yezierska's stories detail the blighted hopes and wasted lives of countless married and unmarried immigrant women.[5]

Within the bourgeois world, a confining ideology reinforced these pervasive patterns of economic discrimination. Erecting the nonproductive woman into a symbol of bourgeois class hegemony, the new bourgeois men of the 1820s, 1830s, and 1840s formulated the Cult of True Womanhood, which prescribed a female role bounded by kitchen and nursery, overlaid with piety and purity, and crowned with subservience.[6] The women who rejected these constraints, or who, pushed by poverty, entered the labor force, were viewed as unnatural.[7] Intrigued by the proliferation of bourgeois literature that sought to reinforce these economic dictates, the new women's historians began to pore over advice books to young women and men, to young wives and husbands. We surveyed children's literature, school curricula, religious sermons, popular magazines, fiction, and poetry.

We compared the presentation of gender by women and men writers. In short, we began to dissect the nineteenth century's construction of gender.[8]

The contemporary feminist movement, especially in its earliest years, had focused on the sexual objectivization of women, seeing in it the psychological roots of women's passivity. Choosing abortion as their premier issue, feminists of the 1960s and 1970s demanded that women assert control over their own bodies. Again, the focus of women's historians followed contemporary feminist concerns. We explored the clinical use of women's bodies by the nineteenth century's male-dominated medical profession. We discovered that, as male physicians transformed gynecology and obstetrics—traditional female mysteries—into male surgical specialties barred to women practitioners, they sought clinical subjects to use in expanding their medical and surgical knowledge. European laws regulating prostitution—requiring regular gynecological examination and hospitalization for venereal disease—provided one such group of subjects. In America, early nineteenth-century physicians had turned to Afro-American slaves and to almshouse inhabitants. Later in the century, they encouraged working-class women to frequent the lying-in hospitals and the outpatient clinics medical schools established to provide students with clinical training. In fact, beginning in the 1880s and extending into the twentieth century, the growing centrality of clinical training to medical education, the provision of inexpensive medical care for poor women, and the exclusion of all but the token woman from medical schools went hand in hand. Professionalization and male dominance within medicine became synonymous.[9]

As political feminists and historians we searched history for political "foremothers." We retraced the development of the nineteenth-century suffrage movement. We reconstructed the ties that bound the early feminists to Garrisonian abolitionism and the political realities that severed those ties. We searched for the origins of the feminist movement in earlier British radical and utopian socialist movements—in the writings of Mary Wollstonecraft and the work of Fanny Wright, Robert Dale Owen, and others.[10] We turned to women's religious enthusiasm, tracing the influence of millennial religion on women's reform activities and role expansion. Some women who held back from self-conscious feminism, we discovered, had nevertheless assumed innovative roles as urban philanthropists, public-health advocates, opponents of child labor. They had battled male power under the banner of the Women's Christian Temperance Union and waged a victorious war against the inhumanity of lynching. Women had actively forged a native American brand of socialism, encouraged their sisters to form trade unions, lobbied successfully for social legislation.[11]

A fundamental commitment to women's history, even a common political perspective, did not preclude the development of heated controversies among women's historians. One of the more long-lived of these debates focused on the relation of economic productivity to power and status, and on the relative power of women before and after industrialization. Did women within agrarian and artisan societies have more or less power than the economically unproductive bourgeois matron of Victorian America? One school of women's historians argued that women exercised far more power in a preindustrial than in an industrialized society.[12] As long as the family constituted America's work force and production took place within the home, women contributed in a major way to family productivity. They worked side by side with artisan fathers, brothers, and husbands. As farming wives and daughters they produced a cash income, selling their spinning and weaving along with their eggs and cheese. Colonial widows, these scholars argued, ran their husbands' shops or opened their own businesses. Farm families routinely sought medical assistance from women wise in the ancient skills of herbal medicine and midwifery. All these women moved easily within the agora, for in those innocent days no rigid line demarcated the public from the private. Industrialization, the scholars continued, ended this halcyon era. By removing women from the work force, industrialization produced the dependent, isolated nineteenth-century housewife, a pale reflection of her colonial mother and grandmothers.

Not so, their critics argued. Industrialization and the rise of the bourgeois state actually increased women's power and options. A host of religious, political, and legislative restraints had severely restricted colonial women's sphere, depriving married women of the right to own or inherit property, earn wages, or will goods. Women's status and rights, this second school contended, did not improve until pressure from the Enlightenment for women's education and the general reform enthusiasms of the first half of the nineteenth century gave women roles outside the home. Then, aided by the proliferation of nondomestic institutions, they were able for the first time to distinguish their identity from that of their families—to move into a separate sphere.[13] Bourgeois women, buoyed up by religious enthusiasm, used their newfound autonomy to agitate for the rights of others, and gradually, by mid-century, for their own rights.

A second bitter debate among historians followed, as to the nature of that agitation. Concerned with charges that our own movement was bourgeois, that it lacked a class analysis and ignored the concerns of black and working-class women, we anxiously analyzed the motives and goals of early women activists. Some women's scholars argued that bourgeois class interests and a commitment to social control shaped the extra-domestic roles these women had created for themselves. In the name of a Protestant Christ, nineteenth-century women activists sought to contain the sexuality of working-class women or sought to remove Catholic children from their "undesirable" homes and place them as apprentices on Protestant farms. Encapsulated within the Cult of True Womanhood, they sought influence, not power.[14] Others of us, impressed by the achievements of the reforming women who had reared elaborate institutional structures outside the home and had asserted women's right to a public voice, heard in their rhetoric more than a simple defense of class values and prerogatives. These women, we argued, had proclaimed the solidarity of all women, across race, class, and religious boundaries. They had denounced bourgeois men as the economic and sexual exploiters of all women. Their work to ameliorate the evils of industrialization (urban prostitution, the fragmentation of the slum and immigrant families, slavery fed by the sweated needle trades in England and the North) had transformed them into experts on the process of economic change and of urbanization. In defense of home, Christ, and morality, generation after generation of bourgeois women had molded a public role for women as critics and reformers of a male world. It was this tradition that the women's movement of the 1960s and 1970s had drawn upon.[15]

These varied explorations and disputes raised two significant and as yet unresolved theoretical issues. The first concerns the causal relations of role to status and power. Responding to technological and economic forces, women's roles changed radically between the seventeenth and the nineteenth centuries. Yet no matter what we would argue about the productivity of colonial women or the role expansion of Victorian women reformers, women's status and power relative to men changed little during these two hundred years. In the female experience, power appears to stand removed from role and economic class, status from productive contributions. How could we explain this odd consistency in a world so in flux?

A second, quite distinct theoretical question followed. If women—bourgeois or working-class, agrarian or urban—lacked power, did it follow that women were only actors in a male play? We are used to thinking of women as victims or as co-opted spokespersons for male power relations. This view of women focuses primarily on the impact of male gender definitions and of economic and political power upon women (or, for that matter, upon any low-status or marginal social group—blacks, children, etc.). It fails to look for evidence of women's reaction, of the ways women manipulated men and events to create new fields of power or to assert female autonomy. It is part of a general historical vision that sees individual lives as molded by impersonal economic and institutional forces. Women's historians, for the most part, reject a view of individuals in general and women in particular as puppets. We see history as an ongoing struggle between women and men actors for control of the script, a struggle that ultimately transforms the play, the players—even the theater itself. But if we reject the view of women as passive victims, we face the need to identify the sources of power women used to act within a world determined to limit their power, to ignore their talents, to belittle or condemn their actions.

The daughter of political feminism, women's history played a critical role within the growing sophistication of contemporary social history. The New Social History popularized techniques developed by French historical demographers in the 1950s and 1960s that encouraged social historians to turn from a study of the notable and public to an analysis of the hitherto largely overlooked domestic world of the inarticulate, the black, the working class, the immigrant—and even of women within these groups. Innovative demographic techniques threw open the accumulated census, town, and church records of earlier centuries. Historians could now trace developments in family and household structure, birth and death rates, patterns of geographic or economic mobility. The new social historians borrowed analytic concepts and interpretive models from L'Ecole des Annales in France, from British and American behavioral scientists, and from the New Economists. They began to investigate child-rearing practices and their effect on later personality developments, generational relations within the family, sexual values. Institutions and processes central to women's lives emerged as central to the historical process. Women's historians adopted the new methods and analytic framework.

Women's history's relation to the New History was not one of dependency but of mutual enrichment. The history of women has significantly expanded the horizons of other social historians, broadening the questions they ask about *both* men and women, encouraging a far more complex view of social processes. For despite their focus upon institutions and events of greatest concern to women, the new historians of the family, religion, medicine, education, and the working class tended to ignore women. In doing so they often dealt superficially with a major segment of the population, and underestimated the complexity of institutional arrangements and of social processes. The new male historians expressed little enthusiasm for examining the ways gender informed economic and political decisions and channeled their impact, for the fact that women's and men's interests within the family and the workplace might be not only different but in conflict. Class, religious, and family structures, as seen by historians who looked only at the male experience, took on a more monolithic—at times static—appearance than they possessed.[16] In contrast, women's historians self-consciously searched for that excluded Other. A far more heterogeneous and inharmonious view of the past characterized our analysis. We insisted that women and men experienced, used, and conceived of the family, religion, work, and public and private space differently. The factory imposed distinctive burdens and offered divergent opportunities for women and for men, as did religious piety.

Like male social historians, we borrowed analytical tools from anthropology, sociology, and psychology, but at the same time we remained critical of the insensitivity so many scholars in those disciplines had displayed toward women's experiences and perceptions. We saw rituals of cohesion not as constructive social dramas but as potentially repressive of legitimate female protest and supportive of male hegemony. We did not take as a statement of inevitability Lévi-Strauss's insight that families, and indeed civilization itself, are structured around male traffic in women, rather we transformed it into a fundamental criticism of social structures.[17] We explored the complex ways language, transposed into myth, distorts reality, so that what is too conflicted to be spoken directly can nevertheless be said. In Roland Barthes's terminology, we became myth decipherers, skeptical of all institutions and processes that presented themselves as "natural."[18] In all of these ways we sought to compensate for perceived limitations in the assumptions of both conventional and social-science history. We have been constructive iconoclasts, or, rather, pioneers who helped open to scholarly analysis a new continent of experiences and relations.

In this sense women's history challenges traditional history in a far more basic way than do any of the other new subspecialties in conveniently labeled "minority history." Male historians have customarily linked women's history with black or ethnic history, or with the study of homosexuality. To the extent that women are an oppressed social category, a group whose economic and political exploitation finds parallels within a scholarly canon which discounts their significance, the analogy of women's history and minority history is appropriate. Both minority and women's history, moreover, constitute radically innovative and creative forms of historical analysis. Both challenge historical conventions. Both insist on new approaches and demand new answers. Furthermore, women comprise a central component within all minority history. But, at rock bottom, the essential difference distinguishing them is this: women are not a forgotten minority. Rather, women constitute the forgotten majority in virtually every society and within every social category. To ignore women is not simply to ignore a significant subgroup within the social structure. It is to misunderstand and distort the entire organization of that society. Incorporating women's experiences into our social analysis involves far more than adding another factor to our interpretation and thus correcting an admittedly glaring oversight. It forces us to reconsider our understanding of the most fundamental ordering of social relations, institutions and power arrangements within the society we study.

But how can we effectively integrate women into social analysis? By inverting the questions we customarily ask, Joan Scott argues. Feminist historians, concerned with the ways social arrangements and the distribution of power affected women, Scott continues, have ironically maintained the centrality of male decisions and institutions within their analytic schemas. They thus kept women as but one variable within a larger (male) picture. By asking, instead, what the particular conformation of gender in a society tells us about the society that so constructed gender, we will make women and gender central to social analysis.

Like so many other women historians of my generation, I came to women's history in part by accident, in part as a self-conscious political statement. Women's history had not been a recognized subdiscipline when I was in

graduate school. I had focused then on the problems of urban poverty in
early- and mid-nineteenth-century America.[19] Urban populations proliferated during those years, as did crowded and unsanitary living conditions,
heightened disease incidence, and family fragmentation. I traced the way
the emerging bourgeois elite sought to understand and contain those
problems, by turning first to religion and later to the public-health movement and professionalized philanthropy. Bourgeois men—the new merchants and entrepreneurs, the new professionals—led this movement. But,
at all times, female institutions grew up within its interstices—indeed,
frequently along its cutting edges. As early as the 1810s, women ran schools
for black and slum children, sought out destitute women for relief, and
protested the condition of America's first child laborers. I persistently
ignored these women, even though they were among the most innovative,
the most radical, of America's early urban philanthropists. Their existence
did not lead me to ask what factors took bourgeois women out of their
comfortable homes and drew them into the cities' worst slums. Nor was
I particularly interested in the ways the new urban economy affected
working-class women. In the mid-1960s few historians considered women
a socially significant category—no matter how central they were to the
problems historians studied, no matter how innovative and effective their
efforts. And I was no different. Automatically I subsumed women urban
reformers and the female poor under a male model of economic and
intellectual development.

However, one early-nineteenth-century organization was so self-
consciously female, so militantly antimale that it resisted all my efforts to
subordinate it to a male schema. The rhetoric and programs of the American Female Moral Reform Society forced me to recognize it as a uniquely
female institution, radically different from male philanthropies and reforms. Founded as a separate women's organization, not as the female
auxiliary of a male society, the Female Moral Reform Society launched
a bitter attack upon male sexual and economic greed, which, these women
argued, had led to the economic exploitation of unprotected women, to
urban poverty, and to family fragmentation. Urban prostitution and the
double standard symbolized for these women the helplessness of all women
—both working-class and bourgeois—within the new, male-dominated
cities. They focused their attention on the problems of female poverty; they
agitated to open the new clerical positions in the cities to female employ-

ment; and they steadfastly insisted on hiring only women workers, from typesetters for their bimonthly journal to business agents. Using religious and sexual millennialism, these women openly expressed their deep-seated resentment of women's powerlessness within the emerging world of bourgeois America, and, at the same time, dramatically worked to undo that powerlessness.

The American Female Moral Reform Society's very existence compelled me as a social historian to view the bourgeois revolution of the early nineteenth century in a far more complex light than I had before I admitted the significance of gender to my analysis. The majority of the Society's members were women who had only just moved into the new and bewildering world of urban America. The novelty of their own situation and the fact that as bourgeois women they possessed leisure, money, and social standing went far to explain their involvement in urban philanthropy. But these factors did not explain why they blamed the problems of the cities on the unbridled sexual greed of bourgeois men rather than on the sins of working women. Nor did it explain the striking fact that these women rationalized their experiences of radical economic and institutional change, the emergence of a new class structure, and the rise of cities in the language of female protest against male sexual exploitation.

Why did their vision differ so radically from that of same-class men? Why did sexual conflict between bourgeois women and men surface at this particular moment of economic transformation and urban growth? At the time I only dimly perceived the importance of these questions. Consequently, I focused on the content, not the form of their rhetoric. Their angry words and bitter castigations of lecherous men illustrated the then startling fact that conflict between same-class women and men existed in Jacksonian America. I did not hear in their rhetoric reflections upon massive economic and institutional changes that transformed America. I heard only the anger of women caught between the promises of political power and social equality that Jacksonian society held out to all Americans, and the restrictions the Cult of True Womanhood placed on all women. My analytic perspective, that is, remained that of an intellectual historian. I had yet to develop a social-structural framework into which to place women's (or men's) political rhetoric.

As time progressed, and social-structural analyses grew in sophistication, so did my own reading of the language of social protest. I have recently returned, for a third time, to examine the experiences and rhetoric of the women connected with the Female Moral Reform Society. I have now begun to hear, hidden in their wild disregard for social proprieties, the voice of women in movement between social locations, faced, in that moment, with boundless new opportunities. Their castigations of the new men of business and their simultaneous romanticization of their agrarian past, read in this light, become angry protests against the escalation of male power which the commercial and early industrial revolutions brought—and even more fundamentally, against the uncertainties of change itself. Two essays in Part II of this volume—"Beauty, the Beast, and the Militant Woman" and "The Cross and the Pedestal"—exemplify my altered approach to women's religious protests during the Age of Jackson.

The discovery of this lost world of female militancy had momentous effects upon my historical vision. The strident voices of the female moral reformers, echoing over the nearly one hundred fifty years that separated us, transformed my understanding of women and of society. Converted, I became a historian of women. Intrigued by the Female Moral Reform Society's bold discussions of prostitution and seduction, I began a search for other areas of sexual confrontation between women and men. The contemporary feminist focus on sexual and psychological issues reinforced this decision. I turned to the medical literature of the nineteenth century (a source already familiar to me as a traditional social historian) for information concerning women's sexuality and health—and to trace the history of medical and psychological attitudes toward women. Male physicians had produced a prolific literature discussing women's health, both general and reproductive. Domestic medical books, written for families unable or unwilling to consult physicians regularly, detailed the ills that could befall a woman and her children and prescribed explicit nursing regimens.[20] This literature made it possible to reconstruct certain aspects of women's lives: the fears they expressed concerning childbirth, the difficulties breastfeeding could bring, the traumas of childhood diseases—and of child mortality. A world of endless nursing duties, with little help and much hindrance from the allopathic medical profession, emerged from the pages of these books.

So did physicians' attitudes toward their women patients. Physicians were particularly interested in women's reproductive history. In their eyes, those aspects of woman's physiology that were uniquely female—menstruation, pregnancy, childbirth, lactation, and menopause, as well as a host of gynecological diseases—determined all of a woman's other physical and social experiences.[21] With increasing frequency as the nineteenth century progressed, male physicians pictured women as fragile creatures, dominated by their reproductive processes. From puberty to menopause, these processes established the reason and the rhythm of women's lives. They made women weaker physically than men, more delicate, domestic, nervous. To thwart the requirements of the reproductive organs was to court disease, insanity, and death.

As the ovaries came to dominate women's lives, so they came to dominate women's sexuality—at least within medical orthodoxy. Early-nineteenth-century male physicians had followed the eighteenth century's latitudinarian attitudes toward sex in general and female sexuality in particular. Highly respected medical writers in the 1820s and 1830s had described women as naturally lusty and capable of multiple orgasms. They defined female frigidity as pathological.[22] By the 1860s and 1870s, however, their professional counterparts counseled husbands that frigidity was rooted in women's very nature. Women's only sexual desire, these doctors argued, was reproductive.[23]

The male medical vision of women's physiology and sexuality served to reinforce a conservative view of women's social and domestic roles. The male medical argument was simple: genitals determined gender, gender determined social role to which economic options were ineluctably associated. In other words, as legitimate roles outside the home developed during the mid- and late nineteenth century, male allopathic physicians began systematically to transpose the Cult of True Womanhood (originally phrased in the language of religion) into a medical and scientific dogma. Any violation of the cult—such as demands for education or for employment outside the home, or the practice of fertility control—called forth furious jeremiads from the profession. The nonreproductive woman endangered society—and herself. Education deprived the nation of robust mothers and healthy children by endangering their ovarian functions and robbing young women of health. Married women's selfish practice of birth control and their perverted use of abortion threatened the very survival of Protestant America. God and nature would punish these sinful women with cancer, insanity, and a wasting death.[24]

Medical jeremiads quickly turned into political campaigns. Using abortion, fears of race suicide and of the spread of venereal disease among the youthful male population, the American Medical Association worked with male state legislators to secure legislation that greatly expanded state intervention in the lives of everyday citizens.[25] Between the 1870s and the 1890s, abortion became illegal, birth-control information was banned from the U.S. mails, brothels were closed or prostitutes made to register and submit to gynecological examinations. Courts began to treat female juvenile offenders—as potential fallen women—far more severely than they did male juvenile offenders.[26] Steadily the state increased the areas of its control under the rubric of protecting health and morals. In this process of medical reform, the same legislators passed laws restricting their rights to practice freely to the AMA's traditional professional rivals—health reformers and women physicians. Male allopathic physicians had formed an alliance with state legislators. Women—bourgeois and working-class, married matrons and working prostitutes—all experienced the constraining power of the state as the male-controlled medical profession and increasingly active state legislatures cooperatively expanded their power.[27]

Were these physicians unique among Victorian men in their desire to restrict women's roles? I wondered. If so, their motivation would in all probability be linked primarily to pressures within the profession and to the doctor-patient relationship. If bourgeois rhetoric in general revealed a similar pattern, then one would have to look at broader social-structural issues to explain the bourgeois man's insistence on increasing gender-role rigidity. Searching for common themes, I surveyed two other critical genres: children's literature and general advice books for women and men.

Like the medical literature, late-eighteenth- and early-nineteenth-century children's books demonstrated an unself-conscious acceptance of male and female sexuality. While Victorian spelling books and grammars presented a content devoid of sexuality, their eighteenth-century predecessors blithely used "fornication" as an example of a four-syllable word, and catechisms discussed Solomon's one thousand harlots.[28] One story, published in Boston in the 1790s and, from evidence on the flyleaf, owned and read by a young boy, featured seduction and gang rape as part of its melodramatic plot.[29] The mid-Victorian era brought a purification of children's literature parallel to physicians' growing vision of women as asexual. As the audience for children's books became increasingly bourgeois and urban, all matter-of-fact discussions of sexuality, whether of barnyard animals or of ancient kings, disappeared from the genre, as did any but the most romantic and pietistic discussions of physical punishment and death. The earthy world of the seventeenth and eighteenth centuries disappeared from children's books as it had from medical theories. The child reader of the mid-nineteenth century lived within a thoroughly expurgated world. So did her mother and older sisters. Mid-nineteenth-century advice literature, pressed upon young girls and married women, differed little from medical treatises or children's literature in its message.[30] In fact, the medical reformers who first advanced a view of women as frigid were also those who most actively socialized women to a role of domesticity and powerlessness. The first three chapters of sex and health reformer William Alcott's *The Young Wife,* for example, were entitled "Domesticity," "Obedience," and "Submission." "Cheerfulness" followed them as chapter four.[31] Religious sermons and school curricula echoed Alcott's advice. It thus appeared that the opinion setters of the new bourgeois world—male physicians, publishers, educators, and religious leaders —had indeed united in their efforts to impose a dependent self-image and a restricted social and sexual role on women. The woman who failed to comply courted divine and physiological retribution and social condemnation.[32]

Two fundamental omissions flawed my early approach to women's history. By returning to traditional male historical sources—advice books and children's literature, the writings of prominent male physicians, theologians, and educators—I had begun to see women, not as they had experienced themselves, but as men had depicted them. To my eyes, nineteenth-century women appeared as passive victims, without resources, isolated in a world of powerful men. Women's experiences of their bodies, of their homes and families, women's relations with their daughters and female friends, their responses to the men in their lives, their anger, their own words (present, if somewhat opaquely, in the rhetoric of the Female Moral Reform Society), did not appear in my analysis. Instead, male visions, fears, fantasies, political alliances filled my pages. Although feminist scholarship in sociology and psychology and the concerns of the contemporary feminist movement informed the essays I wrote at this time, I now realize they constituted histories of men's, not women's, experiences.

The second limitation that characterized my work at this time was the omission of a social-structural perspective from which to view male rhetoric. Male medical arguments, as we have seen, became progressively more repressive during the nineteenth century. Good social history, either of men or of women, had to account for this pattern. At the time I sought its roots in the transformation of the medical profession beginning at mid-century. Now I see that my focus, while not inaccurate, was too narrow. Changes in both male medical rhetoric and the medical profession grew out of more fundamental social and economic transformations: the alteration of work and family that characterized the first half of the nineteenth century; the maturation of bourgeois culture beginning in the 1850s and 1860s; the restructuring of that culture during the century's closing decades as a result of the emergence of financial capitalism, mass production, national and international markets; the appearance during the 1870s and 1880s of that innovative social phenomenon, the New Woman. At that time, however, I did not see medical rhetoric as a symbolic language reflective of fundamental social transformations. As in my initial analysis of the Female Moral Reform Society, I focused on the content of the male medical rhetoric and on the psychological tensions between Victorian women and men which that male rhetoric displayed. Still concerned with the origins of contemporary role definitions, I planned an elaborate study of the socialization of female and male roles at key points in the nineteenth century, a project that promised to lead me ever more deeply into male literature and an analysis of dominant social values.

But suddenly, as a result of a series of serendipitous events, I rediscovered women's voices. Traveling in California, I looked around for research material on women that would not duplicate holdings on the East Coast. I decided to examine the manuscript collections of California women. Certainly, I thought, they would not replicate work I could do closer to home. Perhaps they would reveal patterns of gender-role socialization that differed from those suggested by Eastern advice and child-rearing books, differences that might indicate the existence of greater autonomy among Western women.

The manuscript librarian at Stanford University, hearing that I was interested in children's books as examples of role socialization, kindly suggested I examine a collection of letters a children's-book illustrator had written while traveling with her husband, a mining engineer, through a series of Western mining camps. Perhaps her letters would provide some background for her illustrations, the librarian suggested; I might find out as well something about women's lives in the mining camps of the 1870s and 1880s.

The illustrator, Mary Hallock Foote, the librarian added, had written for forty years to a close female friend, Helena DeKay Gilder. My interest was caught, far less by the expected descriptions of mining-camp life than by the thought that two women had written to each other for forty years. What emotions lay behind such devotion? Opening the collection, I found not the typical tale of movement west within a male world, but letters of intimacy and passion between two women artists living together in lower Manhattan in the late 1860s and the 1870s. Molly's letters to Helena began just after the two young women met while attending the Cooper Union Institution of Design for Women. They wrote passionately to each other —of blissful weeks spent together, sealed off from winter storms and the external world; of nights wrapped in each other's arms, the light of a full moon illuminating their pillow; of passionate kisses; of bathing and anointing each other's bodies. After they had lived together for several years, Molly finally acquiesced to family pressure and announced her engagement to Arthur Foote. Helena responded by deciding to marry Molly's editor at *Century* magazine, Richard Gilder. This was a stormy period for both women, marked by violent fights and expressions of deep unhappiness. Molly expressed some of her ambivalence about the future in her letter congratulating Gilder on his engagement to Helena. Molly bitterly regretted his attachment to Helena and openly discussed Helena's and her own passion. "She loved me almost as girls love their lovers," she reported. "Don't you wonder that I can stand the sight of you."[33] Marriage did not end their letters, their affection, their intimacy, all of which continued for nearly half a century, terminated only by death.

This collection of letters radically transformed my approach to women's history. I ceased to search in men's writings for clues to women's experiences. Rather, I retraced the steps that had originally led me to the study of women. I recommended the search for women's own words begun when I first recognized the significance of the Female Moral Reform Society. Intrigued by the richness of this one collection, I searched for others. Suddenly, everywhere I looked, the private papers of ordinary women beckoned. Some consisted of precise diaries, others of letters between mothers and daughters, between cousins or lifelong friends. At times I uncovered a dense web of documents: letters to and from mothers, sisters, cousins, friends, combined with diaries. Or, to give another example: a mother's letters to a distant married daughter, the diary of her unmarried teenage daughter written at the same time, the diary of that daughter's own teenage daughter written some thirty years later.[34]

The complex pattern of women's lives slowly emerged. I felt I was engaged in a dialogue with hundreds of American women—a dialogue that stretched across the continent and spanned two hundred years: with teenage girls in the late colonial cities; with young women on the Ohio frontier of 1800 or in Oregon in the 1850s; with farming women from the wheat belt of the 1880s; debutantes in Civil War Philadelphia; women educators at the turn of the century; urban Quakers and Episcopalians; Mormon women isolated on a distant frontier; Irish Catholic domestics. They spoke simply about their lives. Yet their words revolutionized my vision of women, of the family, and of female-male relations. In an essay I wrote at that time, "The Female World of Love and Ritual," I sought to reveal their experiences as the women themselves described them, not as men attempted to direct them.

The letters and diaries of eighteenth- and nineteenth-century women revealed the existence of a female world of great emotional strength and complexity. It was a world of intimacy, love, and erotic passion. Uniquely female rituals drew women together during every stage of their lives, from adolescence through courtship, marriage, childbirth and child-rearing, death and mourning. Women revealed their deepest feelings to one another, helped one another with the burdens of housewifery and motherhood, nursed one another's sick, and mourned for one another's dead. It was a world in which men made only a shadowy appearance. Living in the same society, nominally part of the same culture (bourgeois, farming, or working-class), certainly members of the same family, women and men experienced their worlds in radically different ways. Female rituals rigorously excluded male kith and kin, rituals so secret that men had little knowledge of them, so pervasive that they patterned women's lives from birth to death. Discovering the existence of this world brought into question all my assumptions about the nature of both bourgeois and working-class families, and about female sexuality. I began to wonder, did it point as well to the existence of separate female and male cultures?

For me, to concentrate on women's private writings meant not only to reveal a long-hidden world of women; it meant experimenting with a radically new form of social history. Of course, social historians had always used diaries and private correspondence to substantiate material found in published sources. Biographers and political historians had sought evidence for hidden connections and deals, for insights into public decisions from similar unpublished sources. Now, through the systematic study of the unpublished private papers of ordinary women—or of men, for that matter —social and cultural historians were provided with an indispensable medium to add an experiential component to the New Social History. Women's discussions of the normal events of every day permitted us to endow census data with the warmth of emotional reality. Now we could test the accuracy of prescriptive materials against the reality of what people actually did. This would permit us to analyze prescription as a cultural form, a symbolic language in its own right, rather than using it only as a distorted window into social realities. We could begin to reconstruct the behavioral and the emotional realities of times past.

The novelty of this approach required the creation of guidelines for further research. My own first resolve was to use only unpublished material. By selecting letters and diaries meant only as a personal record, I might avoid the overt, public presentation of self that characterizes diaries self-consciously written for publication or selectively edited and published posthumously by family members. Second, I sought to create a broad sample of collections by region, class, ethnicity, and age. Of course, the search is difficult. We cannot summon up well-rounded samples as if we were social surveyors in the 1980s. Women's unpublished collections constitute gifts from the Fates, precious for having been preserved despite their very anonymity and supposed insignificance.

Further, I believe we must approach such writings with a dual vision. These letters and diaries provide us with a unique opportunity to hear women's own words directly, not filtered through a male record. Male voices have so often drowned out or denied women's words and perceptions that the rediscovery of women's unique language must be our first priority—and our first defense, as women scholars, against the undue influence of theories formed in ignorance of women's experiences. On one level, therefore, we must let women's experiences and women's words emerge pristine from these ancient letters and diaries, as photographic images do from developing fluids. But as twentieth-century scholars, we know that our approach to this material is informed by contemporary

psychological, anthropological, and economic theories—theories that have
proved generally helpful but whose principles reflect a male rather than
a female perspective. Our own approach, therefore, must delicately balance
our openness to the unique and the unexpected in these women's writings
with our need for an analytic framework. Our goal is, of course, the
construction of new models that weave together the male and female
experience.

Lastly, the quantity of the material available and the slow process of
analyzing it make it impossible for any single scholar to exhaust the
manuscript remains of a world that had been for so long a *terra incognita*
for modern scholars—and for modern women.

By now, of course, unpublished manuscripts have become a central
source for women's history. Historians recognize that women's definition
and experience of the family often differed radically from those of men.
Historians routinely search for evidence of the existence of networks of
female kin and friends and have demonstrated the ways late-nineteenth-
and early-twentieth-century women sought to re-create these systems in
women's colleges, settlement houses, and reform organizations. A complete
re-evaluation of female sexuality is under way. The history of lesbianism
is now a respected area of scholarly investigation. Friendship, a hitherto
ignored aspect of social relations, has become an important area of cultural
and historical analysis.

Once published, the "Female World" essay assumed a life of its own.
Readers found in it implications that had escaped me, drew conclusions
I had left ambiguous, or, using my data, rejected my conclusions. Some
scholars saw in it evidence of a Garden of Eden of mother-daughter
intimacy and trust; others, a female utopia of support and empathy. Still
others saw evidence of a lesbian world, while their critics used this same
essay to deny the existence of lesbianism in nineteenth-century America.
Some scholars even attacked the essay as "seductive," accusing me of
ignoring the repressive reality of women's lives and of failing to put this
world within a larger, social-structural perspective.[35] The issues that were
raised were not the ones I initially sought to address when I conceived the
essay. They were arguments which had taken form gradually, as the
research of many scholars across disciplinary boundaries made us all increasingly aware of the complex nature of the world of nineteenth-century
women. The ensuing discourse has affected my subsequent research, both

directly and obliquely. After years of explorations and debate, we have solved a few of the riddles posed for us by the lives of women in the nineteenth century. Indeed, the longer we have debated these issues, the more innovative our conceptual framework and methodological approaches have become, the more complex the questions have appeared.

The first question we addressed as explorers of an unfamiliar land concerned the nature and the origins of the separate world of nineteenth-century women. What factors brought it into existence and set its form? Conversely, what destroyed it and suppressed the memory of it? Some feminist theoreticians have argued that the female world grew out of factors inherent in women's psychosexual development. Recognizing certain implications in the literature of ego psychology and object relations, they hypothesized that the female world was a product of psychobiological factors rooted in a daughter's earliest experiences of love, dependency, and arousal. Even Freud had described these factors as characteristic of the oral phase of the mother–daughter intimacy. Besides physical intimacies, they continued, mothers and daughters shared a fundamental biological identification as women. As a result, mother–daughter relationships are unusually intense and separation difficult. The relations adult women form with one another differ in nature from the relations they form with men. These writers rejected Freud's essentially Darwinian assumption that the human psyche evolves from the primitive state of polymorphous sexuality into heterosexuality by the age of three. Citing Lévi-Strauss and other anthropologists, they saw heterosexual marriage as a culturally determined artifact imposed, along with incest taboos, in an effort to create social bonds between groups of men. The cultural privileging of heterosexuality provided an institutional framework for social organization. Within this psychological-anthropological perspective, nineteenth-century women's intimacy is seen as natural, its repression by twentieth-century norms and institutions as unnatural. Adrienne Rich has brilliantly elucidated this theme in *Of Woman Born*. [36]

Other scholars and social commentators have dissented vigorously. The female world, they argued, was the artificial product of the unnatural separation of the sexes rooted in Victorian prudery. The industrial revolution, they continued, by separating work from residence, had thrust men out into the world of business and isolated women within a fortified domesticity. Victorian sexual norms completed the isolation of women and men. Female-male relations became problematic. Young women and men, strangers socialized to have different personalities and to live in alien spheres, met during well-chaperoned forays—an artificiality that would continue throughout their married lives. From this perspective, the female world of intimacy, dependency, and eroticism seems unnatural, an aberration developed as a substitute for more wholesome male-female interaction. Once artificial divisions between men's and women's worlds were removed, they concluded, intimacy between women and men returned.[37]

Few issues could be more bitterly controversial. To see heterosexuality as an artificial construct imposed upon humanity is a revolutionary concept, even if advanced under the imprimatur of Lévi-Strauss. On the other hand, female love and intimacy cannot be seen as an exclusively Victorian construction rooted in the separation of work and home. We find it in cultures around the world and across centuries. It exists in our own times, underscoring family life in American ethnic neighborhoods, and in European working-class communities.[38] It has been consciously articulated among bourgeois women as well. To this day we consider it natural among young girls, until interrupted by the pressures of high-school dating.

My own research has suggested that the rich world of nineteenth-century female intimacy in fact resulted from an intricate weaving together of psychosexual and social-structural forces. At the heart of this world lay intense devotion and identification between mothers and daughters. Mothers and daughters took joy and comfort in one anothers' presence. They often slept with one another throughout the daughters' adolescence, wept unashamedly at separation, and rejoiced at reunions. Mother-daughter bonding served as the model for subsequent relations with other women.[39]

Yet while female intimacy grew out of the biological and psychological realities of women's lives, economic and demographic forces that originated outside the purview and the control of women structured the forms it would take, intensified it at certain times, mitigated it at others. First, a relative continuum characterized women's roles from the eighteenth through the first two-thirds of the nineteenth century. Although the world external to the home changed dramatically, and the functions and the size of the family became increasingly circumscribed, women's role within the family remained relatively static. Furthermore, few viable alternatives to marriage developed before the 1870s and the 1880s, even for the most adventuresome. This was equally true for working-class and bourgeois women. Working-class women, while of necessity contributors to their families' income after marriage, would have been sorely pressed to support themselves as single women on the wages women earned during the nineteenth century. Marriage secured them a share in a man's higher wages, and later in their children's wages—as well as the anticipation of support from children in old age. For bourgeois women, life outside of marriage was at least as forbidding, for they faced the same economic hardships and, in addition, the loss of social respectability. Only school-teaching, and possibly the precarious life of a woman writer or a small shopkeeper, offered an alternative to marriage, and all three would bring social isolation and economic hardship.

Thus, daughters walked in their mothers' footsteps and mothers strove to impart their domestic skills and lore. The world of grandmothers, mothers, and daughters formed a relatively harmonious whole, oddly isolated in critical respects from the rapidity of change that lay beyond the home. Not until economic and intellectual change offered bourgeois daughters (and, far more slowly, working-class daughters) viable alternatives to their mothers' domestic roles did generational conflict and criticism mar this unself-conscious intimacy. Then, however, daughters began to experience their mothers' lives as oppressive. Mothers, ignorant of the new world their daughters wished to enter, pressed inappropriate advice and sought to control where earlier they had gently aided. Many mothers experienced as a personal rejection their daughters' repudiation of the domestic role they, the mothers, had so faithfully followed. Harsh generational conflict broke forth as psychological factors compounded institutional change.[40]

The second external factor that I felt helped shape the original female world was demographic. The clean lines that distinguish the generations in twentieth-century families, that set apart members of the nuclear household from first cousins, aunts, uncles, even grandparents, were inconceivable in most eighteenth- and nineteenth-century homes. The ages of biological siblings could span the twenty-odd years of their mother's reproductive life, easily permitting the firstborn daughter to mother the lastborn children, or mothers and daughters to be pregnant and give birth together.[41] Parents frequently brought their own younger siblings into their households, thus again bridging the gap that separated parents from children. Cousins moved in and out of one another's homes. Consequently, a spectrum of alternative maternal figures surrounded the young girl. As the young woman moved toward maturity, aunts, older sisters, and cousins functioned as caretakers, confidantes, playmates, and instructors.[42] This proliferation of maternal figures diffused the intensity of mother–daughter bonding, which has become so psychologically problematic within the isolated nuclear family of the twentieth century. Within the nineteenth-century extended female-kin system, the process of psychological separation developed more gradually and never became as complete as it would in the twentieth century. The overall result was a female adolescence far less fraught with rebellion and crisis.

Biological and psychosexual factors, woven together, constituted the woof and warp of that intricate tapestry. To comprehend the intricacies of the nineteenth-century world of love and ritual among women is not to explain its end. We must analyze the fears that undercut the intimacy of that world and explore women's response to its loss. Only then will we be prepared to examine women's relations in succeeding worlds, especially our own.

We have seen how the demography of smaller, nucleated families with sharp generational distinctions combined with geographic mobility to erode women's networks and throw wives and husbands together for mutual support. We also know that the multiplication of female role alternatives, beginning in the 1880s and 1890s, strained relations between successive generations of women, proving particularly erosive to mother-daughter intimacy and trust. But the overtly political must enter our analysis as well. The years immediately preceding and following the First World War saw women's greatest professional visibility and political activism. The number of women receiving advanced degrees and entering the professions reached a peak not to be equaled again until the late 1970s. Neither before nor since have women been so political—and so politically successful. They battled for peace, suffrage, child-labor and protective labor legislation, for birth control and sexual liberation. They encouraged women's participation and leadership in the trade-union movement. They helped to found the NAACP and fought lynching.[43] Flamboyantly, they not only supported but reported the Bolshevik revolutions in Russia, in Germany, and in Hungary.[44]

During these same years, male politicians, aided by male physicians, sex reformers, and educators, launched a concerted political attack condemning female friendships as lesbian and separate female institutions—whether educational or political—as breeding places for "unnatural" sexual impulses.[45] These attacks constituted an integral part of the 1920s' assault on feminists and radicals. Whatever the psychosexual and social roots of the loving world of women, these men saw women's relationships in highly politicized terms. They transformed women's private emotions into a public issue, placing them at the interface of the sexual, the economic, and the political. It is this transformation that has so radically separated the nineteenth-century women's world from ours. It is at this moment of male invasion and politicization that women's as well as men's languages changed radically. It is here that we focus our analysis.

For the past eight years feminist scholars and theoreticians have debated the qualities and implications of the female friendship. Always these debates have revolved around an interpretation of language. Nineteenth-century women wrote to and about one another using words that we of the twentieth century no longer understand. Feminist scholars have struggled to reconstruct the lost meaning of these words at the same time as we have attempted to trace the forces that caused the radical rift in language. Public words and private meanings weave in and out of our explorations. Why and when did normative—that is, male—definitions of such critical terms as "love" and "sex" change? How did women respond to these alterations? As women began to adopt the new male lexicon, did they accept the new meanings men gave to these words, or, for a while at least, did women and men use identical words but give them radically different meanings? These questions underscore the historians' dependence upon language at the same time that they illustrate the sensitivity of language to social pressures. They graphically demonstrate the ways language simultaneously mirrors and transforms the world in which it is found. Women's historians' increasing awareness of the complexity of language as a cultural artifact coincides with the growth of a parallel awareness among the new literary critics. Women's history thus offers one of the most promising avenues for a comparative historical and literary study of the interaction between words and the world that speaks them.

Nineteenth- and twentieth-century readers concur about one matter: nineteenth-century women wrote love letters to one another. But did the word "love" connote to these women, as it does to us, the recognition of

sexual desire? Did nineteenth-century women refer, rather, to a sublimated
form of sexual love? Or, alternatively, to feelings rooted not in sexual
desire but in experiences of intimacy and affection that grew out of
women's shared physical and psychological realities? Their categories and
ours differ and thus obscure the meaning. Their words, while graphic, do
not illuminate automatically.

To a twentieth-century reader, their words convey erotic, sensual
feelings; they speak of physical pleasures. They wrote of longing to be with
their loved ones, of bittersweet kisses, of passionate embraces, of nights
spent in one another's arms, of dancing together, of burning jealousies.
Nearly thirty years after they first met, Molly could still write to Helena:
"It isn't because you are good that I love you—but for the essence of you
which is like perfume."[46] Had these women been writing to men, their
letters would clearly fall within one of our post-Freudian conceptual
categories—heterosexuality. We would not hesitate to deduce sexual desire, if not sexual relations, from their words. If women had written these
letters to other women and expressed the need for secrecy, guilt, remorse,
a struggle against passion, we could place their passion within a second
socially agreed-upon category: self-conscious lesbian deviance. But these
women wrote unself-consciously of their passion for other women. They
showed their letters to husbands, daughters, and friends. Neither they nor
their families defined their emotions as sexually "unnatural." Their passion
eludes our twentieth-century categories, presenting us with two possible
explanations: either these women used words differently than we do, so
that their erotic declarations were in fact asexual statements, a natural
component of that *rara avis,* the nineteenth-century platonic friendship—
or Victorian society did not find erotic passion between married women
emotionally unnatural or socially disruptive.

Either alternative leads the historian onto increasingly unfamiliar
turf, for each forces us to analyze the interaction between conceptual
categories, behavior, and emotions. Some scholars argue that because Victorian society did not explicitly define loving relations between women
as sexual, these women did not have a conceptual framework into which
to put their erotic feelings and thus did not act upon them.[47] These scholars
have argued, in effect, that individuals cannot experience feelings or engage
in behavior for which there is no concept within their culture. Such an
argument constitutes an extreme form of nominalism. Indeed, much of the

scholarly disagreement that rages at present concerning sexual behavior and sexual norms takes the form of a debate between nominalists and realists. The nominalists, adopting Freudian terms, argue that human sexuality is polymorphously perverse: the actual sexual patterns that occur in particular cultures at particular times take their form from the sexual categories and values that a society imposes on its members. The realists demur: Human sexuality falls "naturally" into a certain number of categories that remain relatively constant across time and space. Although their specific form may change in response to ideational influences, feelings and behavior exist separate from social categories. Categories reflect behavior, not the reverse.

John Boswell, one of the most respected scholars to address the relation between sexual categories and sexual behavior, pleads against the adoption of either a rigid nominalist or realist interpretation. Each, Boswell argues, artificially simplifies the complex interaction that exists between ideas and behavior. Boswell's own work focuses precisely on the interplay between normative sexual categories and actual sexual behavior. Sexual categories, he implies, both shape and reflect actual behavior. If carefully plumbed, they will reveal, consequently, a wealth of information concerning actual sexual behavior.[48]

Boswell's approach is highly suggestive of the complex interaction of norms and behavior.[49] It ignores one critical factor, however—the impact of the larger social structure of which both categories and behavior form a part. Categories, ideology, behavior are all equally social constructs, reactions to, reflections of underlying structures and power relations. Conceptual systems, colloquial usages, formal ideologies, informal sexual norms all grow out of and reflect specific structural arrangements (the distribution of wealth and power, modes of production, institutional structures, demographic patterns, and technological realities). The shape both sexual and nonsexual ideas assume, in their turn, affects our sexual options, feelings, acts. Ideas thus function as a conduit (usually unself-consciously) linking fundamental material and social forces to sexual behavior. But economic, demographic, and institutional factors act directly as well as indirectly upon sexual behavior. They influence the respective age of sexual partners, the frequency of pregnancy and disease—and thus the ways one makes love and how often one does so. They affect one's ability to find a sexual partner and the nature of that partnership. Once formed, sexual norms and sexual behavior each takes on a life of its own, reacting back upon the social and material forces that initially brought it into being. To examine sexual values and categories solely for the information they can reveal concerning sexual behavior narrows our field of vision just at that moment when it should be most broadly focused. Studied in relation to the world that created them, sexual values and categories will tell us as much about the social construction of power as they do about actual sexual behavior.

To explain more graphically what I have in mind, let me use an example that Boswell himself suggests. Boswell presents a schematic description of two radically different societies. One society valued reproductive sexuality to the exclusion of all other forms of sexual behavior. This society also insisted on complementary relations between the genders. It saw women as beautiful, sexually desirable, and sexually passive; men as powerful and sexually active. Neither gender could, with propriety, assume the characteristics of the other. This society condemned male homosexuality. The second society legitimated sexuality as a pursuit of pleasure and beauty. It valued male beauty and perceived men as sexually desirable —as sexual objects, as well as sexual actors. This society accepted male homosexuality as a legitimate form of sexual expression.

Seeing sexual categories as the critical causal factor in sexual attitudes and, ultimately, sexual behavior, Boswell argues that the high value the first society set on sex for reproduction led that society to condemn male homosexuality. Conversely, the society that linked sex, beauty, and pleasure did not condemn male homosexuality, thus permitting it to exist.[50] An elegant analysis—but one that aborts itself mid-argument. Boswell must take the next logical step and ask why each society espoused the particular ideology it did. We see only part of a complex interaction of social, ideological, and psychological factors if we focus exclusively on the impact of ideology on behavior, and on ideology's reflection of behavior.

The more suggestive questions—and the more significant causal patterns—may well concern the interplay between social organization, the distribution of power, and sexual ideology. One could hypothesize, for example, that in the first society, the heterosexual family served as the principal agency in constructing alliances between powerful men; hence the centrality of reproduction and of women to that social organization.[51] Sexual ideology reflected the institutional and political organization of society at the same time that it helped shape sexual behavior. Boswell's second society may well have had other institutional mechanisms for establishing male alliances; hence the marginality of both sexual reproduction and women to the flow of power, to official male ideologies, and to normative sexual behavior. (The analytic approach I suggest would reveal more about the place of women within those societies, and something as well about attitudes toward lesbianism—an issue Boswell ignores.)

In short, if we explore the ways in which sexual words, categories, and ideology mirror the organization of society as a whole, and not focus exclusively on the interaction of sexual ideology and sexual behavior, a far more complex causal pattern will emerge. We will have placed the distribution of power and the nature of social organizations to the center of our analysis of sexual relations. We will have entered into an analysis of language as political discourse.

Until the late nineteenth century, British and American men defined women's relations in platonic and romantic terms. Indeed, for centuries, within Western societies women's love for one another was considered to be one of women's noblest characteristics. Both men and women praised women's lifelong friendships, their passionate declarations of love for other women. Although such loving relationships have existed in every century, the first two-thirds of the nineteenth century enveloped them with the aura of intense romanticism. Victorian women and men alike collected and published stories of women's love for other women. They transformed the ladies of Llangollen in Wales, for example—two wealthy Anglo-Irish women who set up an idyllic retreat that quickly became a center for intellectual women in the early nineteenth century—into Victorian models for ideal love and devotion. In Germany, Goethe insisted on publishing the love letters his fiancée, Bettine Brentano, exchanged with the Canoness Gunderode, and Margaret Fuller published these letters in America. Perhaps the most famous example of the romanticization of women's love for one another as the pinnacle of human emotions was William R. Alger's book, *Friendships of Women*. First published in Boston in 1869, the book had reached its twelfth edition by 1890. It circulated widely among educated women and feminists of the time.[52]

A medical prototype for female homosexuality did predate the late nineteenth century. British and American physicians, however, always presented the homosexual woman as an extreme transvestite who, dressed in armor, had lived long ago and far away. Seventeenth-century French court records discuss female homosexuality, albeit again associating it with cross-dressing. Occasional references to homosexuality among prostitutes appeared in eighteenth-century French and British pornography. Diderot's *La Religieuse* discusses lesbianism. By the mid-nineteenth century, lesbianism had become a minor but recognized theme in male French literature.[53] None of this literature, however, would have been available to the genteel Victorian matrons whose letters still puzzle us. Not even their daughters, newly admitted to college education (the first generation of New Women), would have read them. Neither these women nor the men who surrounded them found passion between women either disturbing or deviant. By the First World War, as we have seen, all that had changed. Beginning in the 1880s and 1890s, male sexologists and psychologists initiated a public attack upon women's love for one another, using a new medico-sexual language.[54] These women's love was sexual, they boldly asserted: the women were unnatural and perverted.

A number of feminist scholars have argued that the late nineteenth century's novel sexual language and categorical systems constituted a central component of social Darwinism and of the eugenics movement.[55] I would expand this argument, seeing social Darwinism, eugenics, sexology, all as parts of a metaphoric discourse in which the physical body symbolized the social body, and physical and sexual disorder stood for social discord and danger. Within this analytic framework, the sexologists, by insisting that conventional sexuality (heterosexual, monogamous, reproductive, quintessentially bourgeois, as Michel Foucault reminds us[56]) constituted the apex of human sexual evolution, made heterosexuality both essential to and symbolic of social order. Within their evolutionary model, all other forms of sexuality (nonreproductive, fetishistic, homosexual) became organically "unnatural," atavistic, degenerate—symbols of social disorder. The New Woman and the New Man of the 1920s, debating the reconstruction of a world fragmented by war, revolution, and economic change, adopted the politico-sexual language developed earlier by the male sexologists. To both women and men, the "intermediate sex" symbolized the New Woman's demand for a role beyond conventional gender restraints; the "Mannish Lesbian" embodied *her* demand to exercise male rights and powers—to act, that is, as if she were a man! To male physicians, politicians, even modernist writers, the New Woman/Mannish Lesbian symbolized disorder in a world gone mad. To feminists she underscored the irrationality and "unnaturalness" of a world ordered around male definitions of gender and sexuality.

Public words reach beyond the political and literary arena into the private sphere of the psyche and the bedroom. They not only permit political protest; they affect a person's self-image, her most private fantasies and acts. How did this highly charged political debate between the New Woman and the New Man (in which women abandoned their time-honored romantic language and discussed their desires in the new male sexual language) in turn affect women's sexual self-image, and their actual behavior? This question, it seemed to me, provided an ideal avenue for studying that old historical problem, the relation between normative values and individual behavior. To answer it we must re-examine women's personal and public writings between the 1890s and the 1930s. Did some women privately protest against the sexologists' vocabulary and its political impact? Did others embrace it as liberating? That is, by providing sexual words for women's feelings, did the new language empower those feelings, permitting them to become acts? What words did those women who chose to accept a male definition of themselves as lesbians use to record their growing internalization of the category "sexual and social deviant"?

Queries follow one upon the other. Did this enigmatic world of nineteenth-century women constitute a separate female culture? But if women possessed a separate culture, did men as well? If so, how are we to understand the normative culture? Is that a shared construction, the composite of women's and men's languages, visions and fears? Or is it only a more public and inclusive version of a hidden male world?

These questions threaten to draw us into the labyrinthine debate among anthropologists as to the nature of culture. Their political implications are explosive. If we assert that nineteenth-century women in particular, and perhaps all women, constitute an autonomous female culture, we assert that women's separate sphere and experiences are the product, not of men's ghettoization of women, but of women's distinctive psychosexual and biological nature. We then unambiguously proclaim women's absolute Otherness. In doing so, we not only reject male assertions of female dependence and complementarity; we reject all male categories and depictions of reality as nothing more than partial.[57]

The complexity of women's experiences underscores the fascination —and the difficulty—of these questions, especially for the historian who cannot think of culture divorced from social structure. Certainly, nine-teenth-century women lived in a world rich with distinctive female rituals, shaped by the needs and tempos of women's bodies. Many of these rituals spanned class lines, unifying women's experiences across religious, ethnic, and economic distinctions, sharply distinguishing women's lives from those of same-class men. Yet the values, experiences, and needs of women differed sharply along class lines. Women thus existed simultaneously as a unique caste within a male world; as active participants in the dominant male class structure; as male-constructed symbols of class distinctions. They confound the social-structural categories we bring to their analysis. We must not conclude, however, that women are an eternal enigma. Rather, we must recognize that our conceptual frameworks oversimplify precisely because they so often ignore the way gender distinctions divide social categories and fragment apparent social unity. Put another way, it is simply that our road maps and compasses are not sufficiently sophisticated to guide us through the *terra incognita* of the world of nineteenth-century women.

Faced with these intellectual dilemmas, I decided not to attempt to work within a conventional model of culture—whether that of an-thropologists or of literary critics—but to focus on the subject of language itself. I began to examine women's and men's images and metaphors, testing for similarities and differences, to explore the ways language changes across time, between cultures and classes, to seek out the complex ways words both reflect and alter the world in which they are spoken. It seemed to me that in this way I could use language to examine the heterogeneity of modern cultures and to explore the emotional components of that heterogeneity. On yet another conceptual level, I felt that the richness and diversity of language (epitomized by the ways women created and altered their words and meanings) underscores the diversity and ambiguity that characterize all human experience, men's as much as women's. The com-plexity of reality will always elude the conceptual systems we construct for its capture. Change proceeds without end—or beginning. Institutions are always in transition. Structure is a fictive and fleeting concept, protean and ever changing. It was created by the human imagination to provide the semblance of order—not the substance. Behavioral and social scientists have long struggled to construct an analytic model that would reflect the diversity and fluidity of social relations. They have searched for a system that would tie feelings and language to a social-structural location and still avoid the pitfalls of economic determination. In short, they desired a system that would recognize women and men as actors within a distinct social setting.

To my mind, the complexity of language makes it an ideal building block for the construction of such a model. Language is by nature open-ended, filled with nuance, in constant flux. It uses metaphor and analogy to bridge the seemingly unconnected and thus succinctly gives voice to layers of disparate feelings and perceptions. Actor and reactor, I believe that language subtly mirrors the social location and relative power of its speakers. At this point, however, a word of explanation is necessary. I use "language" in the broadest possible manner to include grammar and dialect, unconscious symbols and self-conscious metaphors, conceptual systems, folk narratives, and political or sexual discourses. Black English, Cockney or Scots dialects (to select a few obvious examples) deviate from standard American or English in ways that precisely mirror both their speakers' marginality within the American or British political and economic power structure and the social diversity of those societies. For me, language reflects the microcosm of individual feelings as well as the macrocosm of social structure. Specific metaphors, anachronisms, alternative grammars, voice their individual speaker's sense of isolation from power, nostalgia for a past in which she (or he) was not marginal, and her (or his) defiance of the dominant culture.

Language is not limited to words. If by "language" we mean symbolic communication, then a host of nonverbal forms can be adopted. Dress and food codes, religious rituals, theories of disease etiology, the varied forms of sexuality, all function in societies around the world in highly expressive ways. They constitute shared systems of signs or symbolic languages rooted in, and expressive of, social relationships and social experiences.

Since social structure implies diversity—a multiplicity of locations and roles within a system, rather than a monolithic sameness—a variety of symbolic systems will coexist within any heterogeneous society. Ideological diversity will in turn increase the complexity of social relations and psychological processes. As members of such a heterogeneous society, we may—indeed, we frequently must—master a variety of symbolic languages or discourses. But our linguistic skills can be costly. To speak the language of a group not one's own—for the marginal to assume the language of the politically and economically powerful, for women to adopt a male discourse, for blacks to speak the privileged discourse of the white power elite—may entail the denial of an essential aspect of the speaker's own identity or require the careful maintenance of a dual identity.

Words assume different meanings depending upon which symbolic dialect is being spoken. Especially during times of radical social transformation, symbolic languages will proliferate in a way that reflects the formation of new economic and institutional configurations. People embedded in the old social system, people who experience the thrust of change differently, will frequently misunderstand the language of other groups and read their own meanings into others' words, taking literally what is intended metaphorically. Social disorder thus increases semantic disorder. At the same time it encourages greater freedom. During moments of social restructuring, no one group will possess the power to impose its language, values, or behavior upon any other. When economic and cultural hegemony reemerge, however, limits upon both disorder and freedom are reinstituted. Then socially dominant groups will infuse their words with political and economic power and regulate the words and behavior of those they deem deviant. The deviant will, in turn, restructure their own semantic and behavioral responses in ways that both reflect the new power relations and express their own concerns and visions. And so words and the world maintain their intense yet ever-changing interaction.

(A caveat and a defense seem appropriate at this moment. As a historian, I approach the exploration of language with very different questions from those of literary critics, anthropologists, and linguists. A complex discourse on the subject exists within literature, philosophy, linguistics, and anthropology. Feminist scholars from these disparate fields, however, working on common problems, have begun to develop a common analytic discourse. It is this discourse that intrigues me and that I hope to embellish with some of the concerns of the historian.[58])

Historians ordinarily distinguish between "public language," which appears in printed, formal sources (political speeches, religious sermons, prescriptive literature), and "private language," the secret thoughts of individuals found in letters and diaries which the writers never expected strangers to read. Historians assume a radical disjuncture between "public" and "private" languages, the latter expressing "true emotions." Anthropologists and literary critics demur. "Private language" mirrors the "public language" in a thousand ways; conceptual systems reflective of public pressures and formulated in public discourse wash over and shape private experiences. Conversely "public language," no less than "private language," deals with the emotions. "Public language" exists to convey socially shared experiences in an affective but deliberately distorted manner. Driven to discuss what is too painful or too political to be discussed overtly, societies as a whole, or specific groups within them, develop metaphoric or mythic systems that cloak real meanings behind symbolic masks. The most "public language" thus can be decoded to reveal the interplay of social experiences and emotional realities. Sociological realities and political motivations will then emerge, not stripped bare by analysis, but enveloped in the feelings that constitute one of their most central components.[59]

For the past five years, I have experimented with merging an analysis of women's sociological otherness with an investigation of language as a symbolic medium.[60] By tracing differences between nineteenth-century women's and men's mythic constructs, I sought to re-create the way gender channeled the impact of social change and the experience and exercise of power. The dialectic between language as social mirror and language as social agent formed the core of my analysis. To undertake this study, I returned to printed sources—at times to the very medical and philanthropic sources I had used earlier. This time I read them with far different eyes. I no longer focused upon their literal arguments. Rather, I read the divergent physiological alarms of male physicians and female reformers as metaphors and myths which hid within their opaque layers a rich discussion of conflicting social experiences and dreams. Nineteenth-century women were, as Nathaniel Hawthorne reminds us, damned scribblers. They spoke endlessly to one another in private letters and journals. They spoke as well in the public sphere, to one another and to men, about religion, gender roles, their sexuality and men's, about prostitution, seduction, and intemperance, about unwanted pregnancies and desired education, about their relation to the family and the family's to the world. They embraced the radical disorder of religious revivals, of Christian Perfectionism, and of utopian experimentation.[61] These same and other women condemned male disorder and power, which they depicted in sexual terms. Prostitution symbolized that male power to many Jacksonian women. Rich merchants and their clerks easily invaded rural families, and carried off daughters to the new cities and to prostitution. In this way, Jacksonian women transformed commercialized sex into a metaphor for commercialization itself. The friendless prostitute symbolized for women their own powerlessness within the new urban economy.[62]

Later, Victorian matrons shifted their concern from illicit sex outside the family to male sexual abuse within. Lustful husbands, they claimed, forced unwanted pregnancies upon their physically and emotionally crippled wives.[63] Other husbands, women reported in the pamphlets of the WCTU, crazed by drink, brutalized and exploited wives and daughters.[64] Women novelists during the closing years of the nineteenth century depicted bourgeois marriage as a crass system of mutual exploitation, as alienated and sexually meaningless.[65] Some women constructed imaginary worlds of safety and happiness within a female-dominated family and female-controlled sexual practices.[66] But in all these female languages, male power, discussed in sexual terms, continued to threaten vulnerable and innocent women. At best, Jacksonian and, later, Victorian matrons waged a defensive war. By the 1870s and 1880s, however, as we have seen, younger women (the New Women) had begun to forge an alternative self-image around the themes of education, intellectual self-fulfillment, and service to humanity outside the family. The New Women's language was self-assertive, and at times aggressive.

Victorian men also talked endlessly about gender and generations, power and the family. Their words, however, differed radically from women's. Within the male mythic systems, wild young men revolted against their fathers' wise authority, or, conversely, tyrannical fathers sought to destroy autonomous young men. Youthful male masturbation obsessed Jacksonian men with the same intensity that prostitution captured the imagination of Jacksonian women.[67] This disjuncture of women's and men's physiological concerns and sexual images continued throughout the century. While Victorian women used images of marital rape to protest male social power, male physicians and legislators saw bourgeois women's rejection of motherhood as the principal source of familial and social disorder. Wild-eyed aborting matrons, hysterical young women unwisely seeking education, unmarried professional women, all bespoke male social anxieties in an uncertain world.[68]

Fusing biological determinism with traditional gender distinctions, men constructed new models of social order, systems that symbolically, if not literally, would contain the social fragmentation symbolized by female sexual disorder. Women, men assured themselves, were prisoners of their reproductive system, which dictated heterosexual marriage, female domesticity, women's economic and psychological dependence on men. Gender distinctions were rooted in biology, and so, therefore, was the patriarchal world order. For either women or men to question conventional gender distinctions—for women to grasp power, for men to relinquish it—would violate nature. Disease and death, social disarray, all would result within the elaborate physiological systems men had created. The gender violator emerged as "unnatural" and perverted.[69]

The radically inharmonious sexual and medical languages which nineteenth-century women and men constructed constituted an intense sexual discourse. Its immediate object, however, was not sexual reform or regulation. At all times, I am convinced, women's and men's sexual jeremiads, cries for medical reform, rejection of traditional religious liturgies, theories of disease etiology, constituted complex metaphoric codes which mirrored the social relations and power experiences of their speakers. These varied and conflicted words rallied disparate groups to social or political actions or cemented group cohesion. They thus helped alter the very relations and experiences that had given them birth. Words and the world, each reflector, actor, respondent, fused and fell apart in highly complex ways.

Historians usually do not seek the meaning of economic or social conflict in metaphoric discourse. In order to decipher women's and men's languages, and thus gain further insights into the complexity of social relations, I had to learn how to discover the meaning behind the metaphor, the intention that informed the symbol. Three writers in particular influenced this aspect of my education: symbolic anthropologists Mary Douglas and Victor Turner and semiologist Roland Barthes. All three insisted that an intricate relationship existed between words and the world that spoke them. All three, I believe, are particularly useful to the historian.

Words, conceptual categories, rituals, and codes, Mary Douglas argues in *Natural Symbols,* are rooted in and reflect the world that produced and espoused them. Cultural forms mirror social structure. Highly structured languages and formal cosmologies will characterize rigidly hierarchical societies. Elaborate categories will demarcate social and spiritual outcasts; spontaneity will be condemned. More open and competitive societies will denigrate hierarchical systems and rituals.[70] Their cosmology, reflecting movement and detachment, will be flexible and accessible, will reject rituals and structure. As social arrangements inform conceptual systems, Douglas continues, so they affect an individual's perception of her world, and especially of her body. Influenced by Marcel Mauss, Douglas insists that there is no natural way to experience the human body. Our mind, shaped by its social experiences, Douglas argues, interprets the physical body's impulses, requirements, and sensations, shaping them into culturally anticipated categories. What the physical body needs for food, warmth, clothing, cleanliness, what it experiences as physical pain or sexual pleasure—all reflect the influence of conceptual categories we have accepted as socially legitimate and therefore as "natural."[71] Yet the semiotic interplay between the physical and the social body, Douglas argues, grows ever more complex. The biological body, transformed by the human mind into a cultural construct, undergoes a second metamorphosis, emerging as the symbolic representation of the social forces that created it. Theories of sexuality, purification rituals, and pollution fears, all can be read as symbolic languages in which the physical body stands for the social. Bodily parts, functions, boundaries, points of entrance and exit, openings, excretions, are endlessly transposed into metaphors for different social groups for the correct relations between them—for the healthy or diseased operation of society.[72]

Within Douglas's model, the structures of cultural forms and of social relations merge with visions of the body. Hierarchical societies, concerned with the rigid maintenance of order, will act out these concerns upon the physical body. Such societies will categorize physical organs and metabolic processes as elevated or base, respectable or *déclassé*. They will see disease as rooted in the violation of these culturally perceived physiological hierarchies. They will insist upon rigid dress codes and rules of physical decorum. Alternatively, societies or specific social groups that are in the throes of rapid change—in movement toward either less structure or a new and untried structure—will experience physical and sexual disorder as particularly threatening. Trances, sexual orgasms, dirt, will be suspect, associated with witchcraft or insanity. Those who are perceived as marginal to society, outside its regulations or between social categories, will be treated as simultaneously sexually dangerous and physically polluting. Stern efforts will be made to control and contain them. Loosely structured societies—and groups who experience themselves as marginal to or inferior within a social structure, or who are in revolt against that structure—in contrast, will seize upon the body as a vehicle expressive of their revolt against structure. They will see bodily regulations, dress codes, physical formalities, sexual restraints, as symbols of social control and political tyranny. They will embrace bodily disorder and sexual experimentation. The stage is then set for sexual discourse and confrontation as social fears and economic conflicts are writ large upon the physical body and acted out in sexual dramas.[73]

Douglas's model radically altered my understanding of Victorian America's theories of disease etiology and their sexual alarms and diversions. It was Douglas who led me from a concern with literal content to a dissection of metaphor. Writing about pollution taboos, Douglas suggested that the answers to three questions asked of physical symbolism would lay bare the social concerns that the symbols hid. Her questions were: What is the polluting (dangerous) act? Who is the polluter (the dangerous person)? Who is polluted (endangered, the victim)?[74] Carefully distinguishing between different authors and audiences by gender, generations, and social location, I began to apply these questions to the elaborate medical and sexual constructions of Victorian women and men. The emotional realities of that rapidly changing society—the disparate conflicts and fears of women and men—suddenly revealed themselves.

Victor Turner shares Douglas's fascination with the way the imagination, using metaphor and myth, links the physical and the social body, the natural and the cultural, the psychological and the sociological. He argues that symbols are bipolar, a union of the sensory and the sociological. Social groups use the sensory aspects of the body and of sex incorporating the affect of primitive emotions, shaping the carnal and the timeless into a socially shared experiential vocabulary expressive of social values and time-specific concerns. The grossly physical, the sensual, the sexual, so rich and vibrant in themselves, assume their full meaning only when seen as culture-specific constructs used by specific groups at specific times to reinforce or to debate the sociological.[75]

Semiologist Roland Barthes concurs. Symbol and myth, by nature, are historical entities understandable only within a specific political setting. Barthes transposes Turner's concept of the bipolarity of symbols into the language of semiotics. Symbols, Barthes argues, consist of three elements: the signifier or the external form of the metaphor (Turner's "grossly physical" pole, Douglas's physical body), the signified or intention (Turner's "structural normative" pole, Douglas's social body), and the signification, the fusion of form with intent. The signifier, Barthes argues, now transforming a semiotic into a political analysis, is natural, politically innocent, timeless. The signified is historical, political. The signification appears innocent, but is not. Myth deliberately seeks to distort. The form of the myth is opaque. In other words, symbol and myth exist to make the politically or socially contingent appear eternal, ahistorical, natural.[76]

As such, myth is the "natural" language of the bourgeoisie. The bourgeoisie, Barthes argues, desires to deny its existence as a specific economic class and a historico-political phenomenon. It seeks to merge its identity with that of the nation—or with universal man—to depict interests and behavior that are class-specific as "natural" or patriotic. Bourgeois myth masks bourgeois reality. It denies the economic man under the mask at the same time as it disavows all who do not wear the mask. "The flight from the name 'bourgeois' is not . . . an accidental . . . or insignificant phenomenon; it is the bourgeois ideology itself, the process through which the bourgeoisie transforms the reality of the world into an image of the world, History into Nature. And this image has a remarkable feature: it is upside down. The status of the bourgeoisie is particular, historical; man as represented by it is universal, eternal."[77]

The nineteenth century was the Age of the Bourgeoisie. The bourgeoisie emerged as a new class during the commercial and industrial revolutions that initiated the nineteenth century; by the 1860s and 1870s, the bourgeoisie had established its unquestioned hegemony; the late nineteenth century saw significant changes in its composition, and struggles for dominance among its concomitant parts. Under Barthes's tutelage, I sought the political intention hidden within the claims to naturalness and appeals to patriotism that characterized so much of nineteenth-century American rhetoric. A Barthesian perspective transposed the religious, medical, and reform rhetoric of Jacksonian women and men into the origin myths of a far from harmonious bourgeoisie. The dramatic differences between female and male imagery and metaphor underscored the fact that economic upheaval and class formation affected women and men in radically different ways. Later, as the male bourgeoisie encountered new stress and conflict, and as institutional proliferation and affluence made new roles for women possible (and simultaneously eroded male hegemony and the bourgeois family), men and women again resorted to warring bodily metaphors and mythic sexual constructions to dispute the new order.

To read the sexual as political, I merged Barthes's language and class perspective with Douglas's insights concerning physical and sexual imagery. I began to see how both women and men put the psychosexual and biological richness of the physical body at the service of political intention. The Female Moral Reform Society, medical opponents of women's education or of abortion, sexologists, and women modernists alike all had enveloped the body politic within the carnal body, simultaneously distorting and enriching both. Ironically, through its fusion with the physical, the social body became innocent. Seen through the eyes of mythic distortion, its political realities, economic desires, power relations appeared biologically natural. Nothing, indeed, could be more "natural" than to link these twin cultural constructs through symbol and myth, for, as we have seen, the human body, known only through the social body's conceptual categories, has never existed as a "natural" entity. Always experienced as a cultural construct, its carnal realities are easily transformed into a cloak for political and economic forces.

The relation between semiotic models and history is not a one-way street. Anthropological theories grew out of field work among technological and institutionally simple tribal societies. They must be radically expanded when applied to the heterogeneous and conflicted societies of the Western world. This has certainly been the plea of feminist anthropologists, a plea seconded by feminist literary critics. Feminist literary critics were among the first to introduce the concept of diversity and change into literary analytic models and into the formation of a literary canon. Even Barthes, sensitive as he is to class distinctions, in his early work on myth ("Myth Today" in *Mythologies*) failed to see diversity in myth construction. Myth in Barthes's early theory emerges as a bourgeois *monologue*. In fact, he rather rashly asserted that the political (male-dominated) left did not construct myths, but spoke the nonallegorical language of political action and "truth."[78] Feminist literary critics early discovered and criticized such a monolithic and phallocentric vision.

It is far from accurate, however, to characterize the three particular symbolic analysts I call tutors as perpetuators of static or monolithic visions. Victor Turner, especially in his later work, criticizes the conventional structural-functionalist vision within anthropology for imposing an artificial stasis upon an ever-changing social and cultural reality. Structure and order, far from being a positive good, Turner argues in *Dramas, Fields and Metaphors,* do not exist. They are a figment of the imagination called forth by the fear of disorder and of chaos. Social structure is but the accumulation of an endless chain of social interactions. Words and actions not only mirror but transform the world that called them forth.[79] Barthes, in his discussion of "the Text" as the interaction between reader and writer, gives the audience the power to create endlessly. Metaphors and myths are not complete once written or spoken. The imagination and experiences of their audience continue to transform them so they become not static work but living, endlessly alterable text. "Thus is the Text restored to language," Barthes writes, "like language it is structured but off centered without closure . . . the Text is plural."[80]

Let us take Barthes's vision of the Text literally. Douglas, Turner, Barthes all offer us their work. It is for us, their audience, to transpose their works into our Text, to play with concepts, create medleys, modify the semiologists' vision with the historian's need to place cultural forms within an economic setting, to see societies as patterns of conflicting relationships, to respect the unpredictability and openendedness of change. If we do all this we will have come far toward creating an analytic model suggestive of the complex ways of social interaction and of the human imagination.

The Female World of Love and Ritual: Relations Between Women in Nineteenth-Century America[1]

The female friendship of the nineteenth century, the long-lived, intimate, loving friendship between two women, is an excellent example of the type of historical phenomenon that most historians know something about, few have thought much about, and virtually no one has written about.[2] It is one aspect of the female experience which, consciously or unconsciously, we have chosen to ignore. Yet an abundance of manuscript evidence suggests that eighteenth- and nineteenth-century women routinely formed emotional ties with other women. Such deeply felt same-sex friendships were casually accepted in American society. Indeed, from at least the late eighteenth through the mid-nineteenth century, a female world of varied and yet highly structured relationships appears to have been an essential aspect of American society. These relationships ranged from the supportive love of sisters, through the enthusiasms of adolescent girls, to sensual avowals of love by mature women. It was a world in which men made but a shadowy appearance.[3]

Defining and analyzing same-sex relationships involves the historian in deeply problematical questions of method and interpretation. This is especially true since historians, influenced by Freud's libidinal theory, have discussed these relationships almost exclusively within the context of individual psychosexual development or, to be more explicit, psychopathology.[4] Seeing same-sex relationships in terms of a dichotomy between normal and abnormal, they have sought the origins of such apparent deviance in childhood or adolescent trauma and detected the symptoms of "latent" homosexuality in the lives of both those who later became "overtly" homosexual and those who did not. Yet theories concerning the nature and origins of same-sex relationships are frequently contradictory or based on questionable or arbitrary data. In recent years such hypotheses have been subjected to criticism, both from within and without the psychological professions. Historians who seek to work within a psychological framework, therefore, are faced with two hard questions: Do sound psychodynamic theories concerning the nature and origins of same-sex relationships exist? If so, does the historical datum exist which would permit the use of such dynamic models?

I would like to suggest an alternative approach to female friendships —one that would view them within a cultural and social setting rather than from an exclusively individual psychosexual perspective. Only by thus altering our approach will we be in the position to evaluate the appropriateness of particular dynamic interpretations. Intimate friendships between men and men and women and women existed in a larger world of social relations and social values. To interpret such friendships more fully, one must relate them to the structure of the American family and to the nature of sex-role divisions and of male-female relations, both within the family and in society generally. The female friendship must not be seen in isolation; it must be analyzed as one aspect of women's overall relations with one another. The ties between mothers and daughters, sisters, female cousins, and friends, at all stages of the female life cycle, constitute the most suggestive framework the historian can use to begin an analysis of intimacy and affection between women. Such an analysis would not only emphasize general cultural patterns rather than the internal dynamics of a particular family or childhood; it would shift the focus of the study from a concern with deviance to that of defining configurations of legitimate behavioral norms and options.[5]

This analysis will be based upon the correspondence and diaries of women and men in thirty-five families between the 1760s and the 1880s. These families, though limited in number, represented a broad range of the American middle class, from hard-pressed pioneer families and orphaned girls to daughters of the intellectual and social elite. It includes families from most geographic regions, rural and urban, and a spectrum of Protestant denominations ranging from Mormon to orthodox Quaker. Although scarcely a comprehensive sample of America's increasingly heterogeneous population, it does, I believe, reflect accurately the literate middle class to which the historian working with letters and diaries is necessarily bound. It has involved an analysis of many thousands of letters written to women friends, kin, husbands, brothers, and children at every period of life from adolescence to old age. Some collections encompass virtually entire life spans; one contains over a hundred thousand letters as well as diaries and account books. It is my contention that an analysis of women's private letters and diaries which were never intended to be published permits the historian to explore a very private world of emotional realities central both to women's lives and to the middle-class family in nineteenth-century America.[6]

The question of female friendships is peculiarly elusive; we know so little, or perhaps have forgotten so much. An intriguing and almost alien form of human relationship, they flourished in a different social structure and amid different sexual norms. Before I attempt to reconstruct their social setting, therefore, it might be best first to describe two not atypical friendships. These two friendships, intense, loving, and openly avowed, began during the women's adolescence and, despite subsequent marriages and geographic separation, continued throughout their lives. For nearly half a century these women played a central emotional role in one another's lives, writing time and again of their love and of the pain of separation. Paradoxically to twentieth-century minds, their love appears to have been both sensual and platonic.

Sarah Butler Wistar first met Jeannie Field Musgrove while vacationing with her family at Stockbridge, Massachusetts, in the summer of 1849.[7] Jeannie was then sixteen, Sarah fourteen. During two subsequent years spent together in boarding school, they formed a deep and intimate friendship. Sarah began to keep a bouquet of flowers before Jeannie's portrait and wrote complaining of the intensity and anguish of her affection.[8] Both young women assumed noms de plume, Jeannie a female name, Sarah a male one; they would use these secret names into old age.[9] They frequently commented on the nature of their affection: "If the day should come," Sarah wrote Jeannie in the spring of 1861, "when you failed me either through your fault or my own, I would forswear all human friendship, thenceforth." A few months later Jeannie commented: "Gratitude is a word I should never use toward you. It is perhaps a misfortune of such intimacy and love that it makes one regard all kindness as a matter of course, as one has always found it, as natural as the embrace in meeting."[10]

Sarah's marriage altered neither the frequency of their correspondence nor their desire to be together. In 1864, when twenty-nine, married, and a mother, Sarah wrote to Jeannie, "I shall be entirely alone [this coming week]. I can give you no idea how desperately I shall want you. . . ." After one such visit Jeannie, then a spinster in New York, echoed Sarah's longing: "Dear darling Sarah! How I love you & how happy I have been! You are the joy of my life. . . . I cannot tell you how much happiness you gave me, nor how constantly it is all in my thoughts. . . . My darling how I long for the time when I shall see you. . . ." After another visit Jeannie wrote: "I want you to tell me in your next letter, to assure me, that I am your dearest. . . . I do not doubt you, & I am not jealous but I long to hear you say it once more & it seems already a long time since your voice fell on my ear. So just fill a quarter page with caresses & expressions of endearment. Your silly Angelina." Jeannie ended one letter, "Goodbye my dearest, dearest lover—ever your own Angelina." And another, "I will go to bed . . . [though] I could write all night—A thousand kisses—I love you with my whole soul—your Angelina."

When Jeannie finally married in 1870, at the age of thirty-seven, Sarah underwent a period of extreme anxiety. Two days before Jeannie's marriage, Sarah, then in London, wrote desperately: "Dearest darling— How incessantly have I thought of you these eight days—all today—the entire uncertainty, the distance, the long silence—are all new features in my separation from you, grievous to be borne. . . . Oh Jeannie. I have thought & thought & yearned over you these two days. Are you married I wonder? My dearest love to you wherever and *who*ever you are."[11] As was true for many other women in this collection of thirty-five families, marriage brought Sarah and Jeannie physical separation; it did not cause emotional distance. Although at first they may have wondered how marriage would affect their relationship, their affection remained unabated throughout their lives, underscored by their loneliness and their desire to be together.[12]

During the same years that Jeannie and Sarah wrote of their love and need for each other, two slightly younger women began a similar odyssey of love, dependence, and—ultimately—physical, though not emotional, separation. Molly and Helena met in 1868, while both attended the Cooper Union Institution of Design for Women in New York City. For several years these young women studied and explored the city together, visited each other's families, and formed part of a social network of other artistic young women. Gradually, over the years, their initial friendship deepened into an intimacy which continued throughout their lives. The tone in the letters Molly wrote to Helena changed over these years from "My dear Helena," and signed "your attached friend," to "My dearest Helena," "My Dearest," "My Beloved," and signed "Thine always" or "thine Molly."[13]

The letters they wrote to each other during these first five years permit us to reconstruct something of their relationship together. As Molly wrote in one early letter:

> I have not said to you in so many or so few words that I was happy with you during those few so incredibly short weeks but surely you do not need words to tell you what you must know. Those two or three days so dark without, so bright with fire-light and contentment within I shall always remember as proof that, for a time, at least—I fancy for quite a long time—we might be sufficient for each other. We know that we can amuse each other for many idle hours together and now we know that we can also work together. And that means much, don't you think so?

She ended, "I shall return in a few days. Imagine yourself kissed many times by one who loves you so dearly."

The intensity and even physical nature of Molly's love was echoed in many of the letters she wrote during the next few years, as, for instance, in this short thank-you note for a small present:

> Imagine yourself kissed a dozen times my darling. Perhaps it is well for you that we are far apart. You might find my thanks so expressed rather overpowering. I have that delightful feeling that it doesn't matter much what I say or how I say it, since we shall meet so soon and forget in that moment that we were ever separated. . . . I shall see you soon and be content.[14]

At the end of the fifth year, however, several crises occurred. The relationship, at least in its intense form, ended, though Molly and Helena continued an intimate and complex relationship for the next half-century. The exact nature of these crises is not completely clear, but it seems to have involved Molly's decision not to live with Helena, as they had originally planned, but to remain at home because of parental insistence. Molly was now in her late twenties. Helena responded with anger and Molly became frantic at the thought that Helena would break off their relationship. Though she wrote distraught letters and made despairing attempts to see Helena, the relationship never regained its former ardor—possibly because Molly had a male suitor.[15] Within six months Helena had decided to marry a man who was, coincidentally, Molly's friend and editor. Two years later Molly herself finally married. The letters toward the end of this period discuss the transition both women made to having male lovers—Molly spending much time reassuring Helena, who seemed depressed about the end of their relationship and her forthcoming marriage.[16]

It is clearly difficult, from a distance of a hundred years and from a post-Freudian cultural perspective, to decipher the complexities of Molly and Helena's relationship. Certainly Molly and Helena were lovers— emotionally if not physically. The emotional intensity and pathos of their love becomes apparent in several letters Molly wrote Helena during their crisis:

> I wanted so to put my arms round my girl of all the girls in the world and tell her . . . I love her as wives do love their husbands, as *friends* who have taken each other for life—and believe in her as I believe in my God. . . . If I didn't love you do you suppose I'd care about anything or have ridiculous notions and panics and behave like an old fool who ought to know better. I'm going to hang on to your skirts. . . . You can't get away from [my] love.

Or, as she wrote after Helena's decision to marry: "You know dear Helena, I really was in love with you. It was a passion such as I had never known until I saw you. I don't think it was the noblest way to love you." The theme of intense female love was one Molly again expressed in a letter she wrote to the man Helena was to marry: "Do you know sir, that until you came along I believe that she loved me almost as girls love their lovers. *I know I loved her so.* Don't you wonder that I can stand the sight of you." This was in a letter congratulating them on their forthcoming marriage.[17]

The essential question is not whether these women had genital contact and can therefore be defined as homosexual or heterosexual. The twentieth-century tendency to view human love and sexuality within a dichotomized universe of deviance and normality, genitality and platonic love, is alien to the emotions and attitudes of the nineteenth century and fundamentally distorts the nature of these women's emotional interaction. These letters are significant because they force us to place such female love in a particular historical context. There is every indication that these four women, their husbands and families—all eminently respectable and socially conservative —considered such love both socially acceptable and fully compatible with heterosexual marriage. Emotionally and cognitively, their heterosocial and their homosocial worlds were complementary.

One could argue, on the other hand, that these letters were but an example of the romantic rhetoric with which the nineteenth century surrounded the concept of friendship. Yet they possess an emotional intensity and a sensual and physical explicitness that are difficult to dismiss. Jeannie longed to hold Sarah in her arms; Molly mourned her physical isolation from Helena. Molly's love and devotion to Helena, the emotions that bound Jeannie and Sarah together, while perhaps a phenomenon of nineteenth-century society, were not the less real for their Victorian origins. A survey of the correspondence and diaries of eighteenth- and nineteenth-century women indicates that Molly, Jeannie, and Sarah represented one very real behavioral and emotional option socially available to nineteenth-century women.

This is not to argue that individual needs, personalities, and family dynamics did not have a significant role in determining the nature of particular relationships. But the scholar must ask if it is historically possible and, if possible, important to study the intensely individual aspects of psychosexual dynamics. Is it not the historian's first task to explore the social structure and the world view that made intense and sometimes sensual female love both a possible and an acceptable emotional option? From such a social perspective a new and quite different series of questions suggests itself. What emotional function did such female love serve? What was its place within the hetero- and homosocial worlds which women jointly inhabited? Did a spectrum of love-object choices exist in the nineteenth century across which some individuals, at least, were capable of moving? Unless we attempt to answer these questions, it will be difficult to understand either nineteenth-century sexuality or the nineteenth-century family.

Several factors in American society between the mid-eighteenth and the mid-nineteenth centuries may well have permitted women to form a variety of close emotional relationships with other women. American society was characterized in large part by rigid gender-role differentiation within the family and within society as a whole, leading to the emotional segregation of women and men. The roles of daughter and mother shaded imperceptibly and ineluctably into each other, while the biological realities of frequent pregnancies, childbirth, nursing, and menopause bound women together in physical and emotional intimacy. It was within just such a social framework, I would argue, that a specifically female world did indeed develop, a world built around a generic and unself-conscious pattern of single-sex or homosocial networks. These supportive networks were institutionalized in social conventions or rituals that accompanied virtually every important event in a woman's life, from birth to death. Such female relationships were frequently supported and paralleled by severe social restrictions on intimacy between young men and women. Within such a world of emotional richness and complexity, devotion to and love of other women became a plausible and socially accepted form of human interaction.

An abundance of printed and manuscript sources exists to support such a hypothesis. Etiquette books, advice books on child-rearing, religious sermons, guides to young men and young women, medical texts, and school curricula all suggest that late-eighteenth- and most nineteenth-century Americans assumed the existence of a world composed of distinctly male and female spheres, spheres determined by the immutable laws of God and nature.[18] The unpublished letters and diaries of Americans during this same period concur, detailing the existence of sexually segregated worlds inhabited by human beings with different values, expectations, and personalities. Contacts between men and women frequently partook of a formality and stiffness quite alien to twentieth-century America, and which today we tend to define as "Victorian." Women, however, did not form an isolated and oppressed subcategory in male society. Their letters and diaries indicate that women's sphere had an essential integrity and dignity that grew out of women's shared experiences and mutual affection and that, despite the profound changes that affected American social structure and institutions between the 1760s and the 1870s, retained a constancy and predictability. The ways in which women thought of and interacted with one another remained unchanged. Continuity, not discontinuity, characterized this female world. Molly Hallock's and Jeannie Field's words, emotions, and experiences have direct parallels in the 1760s and the 1790s.[19] There are indications in contemporary sociological and psychological literature that female closeness and support networks have continued into the twentieth century—not only among ethnic and working-class groups but even among the middle class.[20]

Most eighteenth- and nineteenth-century women lived within a world bounded by home, church, and the institution of visiting—that endless trooping of women to one another's homes for social purposes. It was a world inhabited by children and by other women.[21] Women helped one another with domestic chores and in times of sickness, sorrow, or trouble. Entire days, even weeks, might be spent almost exclusively with other women.[22] Urban and town women could devote virtually every day to visits, teas, or shopping trips with other women. Rural women developed a pattern of more extended visits that lasted weeks and sometimes months, at times even dislodging husbands from their beds and bedrooms so that dear friends might spend every hour of every day together.[23] When husbands traveled, wives routinely moved in with other women, invited women friends to teas and suppers, sat together sharing and comparing the letters they had received from other close women friends. Secrets were exchanged and cherished, and the husband's return at times was viewed with some ambivalence.[24]

Summer vacations were frequently organized to permit old friends to meet at water spas or share a country home. In 1848, for example, a young matron wrote cheerfully to her husband about the delightful time she was having with five close women friends whom she had invited to spend the summer with her; he remained at home alone to face the heat of Philadelphia and a cholera epidemic.[25] Some ninety years earlier, two young Quaker girls commented upon the vacation their aunt had taken alone with another woman; their remarks were openly envious and tell us something of the emotional quality of these friendships: "I hear Aunt is gone with the Friend and wont be back for two weeks, fine times indeed I think the old friends had, taking their pleasure about the country . . . and have the advantage of that fine woman's conversation and instruction, while we poor young girls must spend all spring at home. . . . What a disappointment that we are not together. . . ."[26]

Friends did not form isolated dyads but were normally part of highly integrated networks. Knowing one another, perhaps related to one another, they played a central role in holding communities and kin systems together. Especially when families became geographically mobile, women's long visits to one another and their frequent letters filled with discussions of marriages and births, illnesses and deaths, descriptions of growing children, and reminiscences of times and people past provided an important sense of continuity in a rapidly changing society.[27] Central to this female world was an inner core of kin. The ties between sisters, first cousins, aunts, and nieces provided the underlying structure upon which groups of friends and their network of female relatives clustered. Although most of the women within this sample would appear to be living within isolated nuclear families, the emotional ties between nonresidential kin were deep and binding and provided one of the fundamental existential realities of women's lives.[28] Twenty years after Parke Lewis Butler moved with her husband to Louisiana, she sent her two daughters back to Virginia to attend school, live with their grandmother and aunt, and be integrated back into Virginia society.[29] The constant letters between Maria Inskeep and Fanny Hampton, sisters separated in their early twenties when Maria moved with her husband from New Jersey to Louisiana, held their families together, making it possible for their daughters to feel a part of their cousins' network of friends and interests.[30] The Ripley daughters, growing up in western Massachusetts in the early 1800s, spent months each year with their mother's sister and her family in distant Boston; these female cousins and their network of friends exchanged gossip-filled letters and gradually formed deeply loving and dependent ties.[31]

Women frequently spent their days within the social confines of such extended families. Sisters-in-law visited one another and, in some families, seemed to spend more time with one another than with their husbands. First cousins cared for one another's babies—for weeks or even months in times of sickness or childbirth. Sisters helped one another with housework, shopped and sewed for one another. Geographic separation was borne with difficulty. A sister's absence for even a week or two could cause loneliness and depression and would be bridged by frequent letters. Sibling rivalry was hardly unknown, but with separation or illness the theme of deep affection and dependency re-emerged.[32]

Sisterly bonds continued across a lifetime. In her old age, a rural Quaker matron, Martha Jefferis, wrote to her daughter Anne concerning her own half-sister, Phoebe: "In sister Phoebe I have a real friend—she studies my comfort and waits on me like a child. . . . She is exceedingly kind and this to all other homes (set aside yours) I would prefer—it is next to being with a daughter." Phoebe's own letters confirmed Martha's evaluation of her feelings. "Thou knowest my dear sister," Phoebe wrote, "there is no one . . . that exactly feels [for] thee as I do, for I think without boasting I can truly say that my desire is for thee."[33]

Such women, whether friends or relatives, assumed an emotional centrality in one another's lives. In their diaries and letters they wrote of the joy and contentment they felt in one another's company, their sense of isolation and despair when apart. The regularity of their correspondence underlines the sincerity of such words. Women named their daughters after one another and sought to integrate dear friends into their lives after marriage.[34] As one young bride wrote to an old friend shortly after her marriage, "I want to see you and talk with you and feel that we are united by the same bonds of sympathy and congeniality as ever."[35] After years of friendship, one aging woman wrote of another, "Time cannot destroy the fascination of her manner . . . her voice is music to the ear. . . ."[36] Women made elaborate presents for one another, ranging from the Quakers' frugal pies and breads to painted velvet bags and phantom bouquets.[37] When a friend died, their grief was deeply felt: Martha Jefferis was unable to write to her daughter for three weeks because of the sorrow she felt at the death of a dear friend, and such distress was not unusual. A generation earlier, a young Massachusetts farm woman filled pages of her diary with her grief at the death of her "dearest friend" and transcribed the letters of condolence other women sent her. She marked the anniversary of Rachel's death each year in her diary, contrasting her faithfulness with that of Rachel's husband, who had soon remarried.[38]

These female friendships served a number of emotional functions. Within this secure and empathetic world women could share sorrows, anxieties, and joys, confident that other women had experienced similar emotions. One mid-nineteenth-century rural matron, in a letter to her daughter, discussed this particular aspect of women's friendships: "To have such a friend as thyself to look to and sympathize with her—and enter into all her little needs and in whose bosom she could with freedom pour forth her joys and sorrows—such a friend would very much relieve the tedium of many a wearisome hour. . . ." A generation later Molly more informally underscored the importance of this same function in a letter to Helena:

"Suppose I come down . . . [and] spend Sunday with you quietly," she wrote Helena, ". . . that means talking all the time until you are relieved of all your latest troubles, and I of mine. . . ."[39] These were frequently troubles that apparently no man could understand. When Anne Jefferis Sheppard was first married, she and her older sister Edith (who then lived with Anne) wrote in detail to their mother of the severe depression and anxiety they experienced. Moses Sheppard, Anne's husband, added cheerful postscripts to the sisters' letters—which he had clearly not read—remarking on Anne's and Edith's contentment. Theirs was an emotional world to which he had little access.[40]

This was, as well, a female world in which hostility and criticism of other women were discouraged, and thus a milieu in which women could develop a sense of inner security and self-esteem. As one young woman wrote to her mother's long-time friend: "I cannot sufficiently thank you for the kind unvaried affection & indulgence you have ever shown and expressed both by words and actions for me. . . . Happy would it be did all the world view me as you do, through the medium of kindness and forbearance."[41] They valued one another. Women, who had little status or power in the larger world of male concerns, possessed status and power in the lives and worlds of other women.[42]

An intimate mother–daughter relationship lay at the heart of this female world. The diaries and letters of both mothers and daughters attest to their closeness and mutual emotional dependency. Daughters routinely discussed their mothers' health and activities with their own friends, expressed anxiety when their mothers were ill and concern for their cares.[43] Expressions of hostility which we would today consider routine on the part of both mothers and daughters seem to have been uncommon indeed. On the contrary, this sample of families indicates that the normal relationship between mother and daughter was one of sympathy and understanding.[44] Only sickness or great geographic distance was allowed to cause extended separation. When marriage did result in such separation, both viewed the distance between them with distress.[45] Something of this sympathy and love between mothers and daughters is evident in a letter Sarah Alden Ripley, at age sixty-nine, wrote her youngest and recently married daughter: "You do not know how much I miss you, not only when I struggle in and out of my mortal envelop and pump my nightly potation and no longer pour into your sympathizing ear my senile gossip, but all the day I muse away, since the sound of your voice no longer rouses me to sympathy with your joys or sorrows. . . . You cannot know how much I miss your affectionate demonstrations."[46] A dozen aging mothers in this sample of over thirty families echoed her sentiments.

Central to these mother–daughter relations is what might be described as an apprenticeship system. In those families where the daughter followed the mother into a life of traditional domesticity, mothers and other older women had carefully trained daughters in the arts of housewifery and motherhood. Such training undoubtedly occurred throughout a girl's childhood but became more systematized, almost ritualistic, in the years following the end of her formal education and before her marriage. At this time a girl either returned home from boarding school or no longer divided her time between home and school. Rather, she devoted her energies to two tasks: mastering new domestic skills and participating in the visiting and social activities necessary to finding a husband. Under the careful supervision of their mothers and of older female relatives, such late-adolescent girls temporarily took over the household management from their mothers, tended their young nieces and nephews, and helped in childbirth, nursing, and weaning. Such experiences tied the generations together in shared skills and emotional interaction.[47]

Daughters were born into a female world. Their mothers' life expectations and sympathetic network of friends and relations were among the first realities in the life of developing children. As long as the mothers' domestic role remained relatively stable and few viable alternatives competed with it, daughters tended to accept their mothers' world and to turn automatically to other women for support and intimacy. It was within this closed and intimate female world that the young girl grew toward womanhood.

One could speculate at length concerning the absence of that mother–daughter hostility today considered almost inevitable to an adolescent's struggle for autonomy and self-identity. It is possible that taboos against female aggression and hostility were sufficiently strong to repress even that between mothers and their adolescent daughters. Yet these letters seem so alive, and the interest of daughters in their mothers' affairs so vital and genuine, that it is difficult to interpret their closeness exclusively in terms of repression and denial. The functional bonds that held mothers and daughters together in a world that permitted few alternatives to domesticity might well have created a source of mutuality and trust absent in societies where greater options were available for daughters than for mothers. Furthermore, the extended female network—a daughter's close ties with her own older sisters, cousins, and aunts—may well have permitted a diffusion and a relaxation of mother-daughter identification and so have aided a daughter in her struggle for identity and autonomy. None of these explanations are mutually exclusive; all may well have interacted to produce the degree of empathy evident in those letters and diaries.

At some point in adolescence, the young girl began to move outside the matrix of her mother's support group to develop a network of her own. Among the middle class, at least, this transition toward what was at the same time both a limited autonomy and a repetition of her mother's life seemed to have most frequently coincided with a girl's going to school. Indeed, education appears to have played a crucial role in the lives of most of the families in this study. Attending school for a few months, for a year, or longer was common even among daughters of relatively poor families, while middle-class girls routinely spent at least a year in boarding school.[48] These school years ordinarily marked a girl's first separation from home. They served to wean the daughter from her home, to train her in the essential social graces, and, ultimately, to help introduce her into the marriage market. It was not infrequently a trying emotional experience for both mother and daughter.[49]

In this process of leaving one home and adjusting to another, the mother's friends and relatives played a key transitional role. Such older women routinely accepted the role of foster mother; they supervised the young girl's deportment, monitored her health, and introduced her to their own network of female friends and kin.[50] Not infrequently, women who had been friends from their own school years arranged to send their daughters to the same school, so that the girls might form bonds paralleling those their mothers had made. For years Molly and Helena wrote of their daughters' meeting and worried over each other's children. When Molly finally brought her daughter east to school, their first act on reaching New York was to meet Helena and her daughters. Elizabeth Bordley Gibson virtually adopted the daughters of her school chum, Eleanor Custis Lewis. The Lewis daughters soon began to write Elizabeth Gibson letters with the salutation "Dearest Mama." Eleuthera DuPont, attending boarding school in Philadelphia at roughly the same time as the Lewis girls, developed a parallel relationship with her mother's friend, Elizabeth McKie Smith.

Eleuthera went to the same school as and became a close friend of the Smith girls, and eventually married their first cousin. During this period she routinely called Mrs. Smith "Mother." Indeed, Eleuthera so internalized the sense of having two mothers that she casually wrote her sisters of her "Mamma's" visits at her "mother's" house—that is, at Mrs. Smith's.[51]

Even more important to this process of maturation than their mother's friends were the female friends young women made at school. Young girls helped one another overcome homesickness and endure the crises of adolescence. They gossiped about beaux, incorporated one another into their own kinship systems, and attended and gave teas and balls together. Older girls in boarding school "adopted" younger ones, who called them "Mother."[52] Dear friends might indeed continue this pattern of adoption and mothering throughout their lives; one woman might routinely assume the nurturing role of pseudo-mother, the other the dependency role of daughter. The pseudo-mother performed for the other woman all the services we normally associate with mothers; she went to absurd lengths to purchase items her "daughter" could have obtained from other sources, gave advice, and functioned as an idealized figure in her "daughter's" imagination. Helena played such a role for Molly, as did Sarah for Jeannie. Elizabeth Bordley Gibson bought almost all Eleanor Parke Custis Lewis's necessities—from shoes and corset covers to bedding and harp strings—and sent them from Philadelphia to Virginia, a procedure that sometimes took months. Eleanor frequently asked Elizabeth to take back her purchases, have them redone, and argue with shopkeepers about prices. These were favors automatically asked and complied with. Anne Jefferis Sheppard made the analogy very explicitly in a letter to her own mother written shortly after Anne's marriage, when she was feeling depressed about their separation: "Mary Paulen is truly kind, almost acts the part of a mother and trys to aid and *comfort me,* and also to *lighten my new cares.*"[53]

A comparison of the references to men and women in these young women's letters is striking. Boys were obviously indispensable to the elaborate courtship ritual girls engaged in. In these teen-age letters and diaries, however, boys appear distant and warded off—an effect produced both by the girls' sense of bonding and by a highly developed and deprecatory whimsy. Girls joked among themselves about the conceit, poor looks, or affectations of suitors. Rarely, especially in the eighteenth and early nineteenth centuries, were favorable remarks exchanged. Indeed, although hostility and criticism of other women were so rare as to seem almost tabooed, young women permitted themselves to express a great deal of hostility toward peer-group men.[54] If unacceptable suitors appeared, girls might even band together to harass them. When one such unfortunate came to court Sophie DuPont, she hid in her room, first sending her sister Eleuthera to entertain him and then dispatching a number of urgent notes to her neighboring sister-in-law, cousins, and a visiting friend, who all came to Sophie's support. A wild female romp ensued, ending only when Sophie banged into a door, lacerated her nose, and retired, with her female cohorts, to bed. Her brother and the presumably disconcerted suitor were left alone. These were not the antics of teen-agers but of women in their early and mid-twenties.[55]

Even if young men were acceptable suitors, girls referred to them formally and obliquely: "The last week I received the unexpected intelligence of the arrival of a friend in Boston," Sarah Ripley wrote in her diary of the young man to whom she had been engaged for years and whom she would shortly marry. Harriet Manigault assiduously kept a lively and gossipy diary during the three years preceding her marriage, yet did not once comment upon her own engagement or, indeed, make any personal references to her fiancé—who was never identified as such but always referred to as Mr. Wilcox.[56] The point is not that these young women were hostile to young men. Far from it: they sought marriage and domesticity. Yet in these letters and diaries men appear as an other or out group, segregated into different schools, supported by their own male network of friends and kin, socialized to different behavior, and coached to a proper formality in courtship behavior. As a consequence, relations between young women and men frequently lacked the spontaneity and emotional intimacy that characterized the young girls' ties to one another.

Indeed, in sharp contrast to their distant relations with boys, young women's relations with one another were close, often frolicsome, and surprisingly long-lasting and devoted. They wrote secret missives to one another, spent long, solitary days with one another, curled up together in bed at night to whisper fantasies and secrets.[57] In 1862 one woman in her early twenties described such a scene to an absent friend:

> I have sat up to midnight listening to the confidences of Constance Kinney, whose heart was opened by that most charming of all situations, a seat on a bedside late at night, when all the

household are asleep & only oneself & one's confidante survive
in wakefulness. So she has told me all her loves and tried to get
some confidences in return but being five or six years older than
she, I know better. . . .[58]

Elizabeth Bordley and Nelly Parke Custis, teen-agers in Philadelphia in
the 1790s, routinely secreted themselves until late every night in Nelly's
attic, where each wrote a novel about the other.[59] Quite a few young
women kept diaries, and it was a sign of special friendship to show their
diaries to one another. The emotional quality of such exchanges emerges
from the comments of one young girl who grew up along the Ohio
frontier:

> Sisters CW and RT keep diaries & allow me the inestimable
> pleasure of reading them and in turn they see mine—but O
> shame covers my face when I think of it; theirs is so much better
> than mine, that every time. Then I think well now I *will* burn
> mine but upon second thought it would deprive me the pleasure
> of reading theirs, for I esteem it a very great privilege indeed,
> as well as very improving, as we lay our hearts open to each
> other, it heightens our love & helps to cherish & keep alive that
> sweet soothing friendship and endears us to each other by that
> soft attraction.[60]

Girls routinely slept together, kissed and hugged one another. Indeed,
while waltzing with young men scandalized the otherwise flighty and
highly fashionable Harriet Manigault, she considered waltzing with other
young women not only acceptable but pleasant.[61]

Marriage followed adolescence. With increasing frequency in the
nineteenth century, marriage involved a girl's traumatic removal from her
mother and her mother's network. It involved, as well, adjustment to a
husband, who, because he was male, came to marriage with both a different
world view and vastly different experiences. Not surprisingly, marriage
was an event surrounded by supportive, almost ritualistic, practices. (Wed-
dings are one of the last female rituals remaining in twentieth-century
America.) Young women routinely spent the months preceding their
marriage almost exclusively with other women—at neighborhood sewing

bees and quilting parties or in a round of visits to geographically distant friends and relatives. Ostensibly they went to receive assistance in the practical preparations for their new homes—sewing and quilting trousseaux and linen—but, of equal importance, they appear to have gained emotional support and reassurance. Sarah Ripley spent over a month with friends and relatives in Boston and Hingham before her wedding; Parke Custis Lewis exchanged visits with her aunts and first cousins throughout Virginia.[62] Anne Jefferis, who married with some hesitation, spent virtually half a year in endless visiting with cousins, aunts, and friends. Despite their reassurance and support, however, she would not marry Moses Sheppard until her sister Edith and her cousin Rebecca moved into the groom's home, met his friends, and explored his personality.[63] The wedding did not take place until Edith wrote to Anne, "I can say in truth I am entirely willing thou shouldst follow him even away in the Jersey sands believing if thou are not happy in thy future home it will not be any fault on his part. . . ."[64]

Sisters, cousins, and friends frequently accompanied newlyweds on their wedding night and wedding trip, which often involved additional family visiting. Such extensive visits presumably served to wean the daughter from her family of origin. As such they often contained a note of ambivalence. Nelly Custis, for example, reported homesickness and loneliness on her wedding trip. "I left my Beloved and revered Grandmamma with sincere regret," she wrote Elizabeth Bordley. "It was some time before I could feel reconciled to traveling without her." Perhaps they also functioned to reassure the young woman herself, and her friends and kin, that though marriage might alter it would not destroy old bonds of intimacy and familiarity.[65]

Married life too was structured about a host of female rituals. Childbirth, especially the birth of the first child, became virtually a *rite de passage,* with a lengthy seclusion of the woman before and after delivery, severe restrictions on her activities, and finally a dramatic re-emergence.[66] This seclusion was supervised by mothers, sisters, and loving friends. Nursing and weaning involved the advice and assistance of female friends and relatives. So did miscarriage.[67] Death, like birth, was structured around elaborate, unisexed rituals. When Nelly Parke Custis Lewis rushed to nurse her daughter who was critically ill while away at school, Nelly received support, not from her husband, who remained on their plantation, but from her old school friend Elizabeth Bordley. Elizabeth aided Nelly in caring for her dying daughter, cared for Nelly's other children, played a major role in making arrangements for the elaborate funeral (which the father did not attend), and frequently visited the girl's grave at the mother's request. For years Elizabeth continued to be the confidante of Nelly's anguished recollections of her lost daughter. These memories, Nelly's letters make clear, were for Elizabeth alone. "Mr. L. knows nothing of this" was a frequent comment.[68] Virtually every collection of letters and diaries in my sample contained evidence of women turning to one another for comfort when facing the frequent and unavoidable deaths of the eighteenth and nineteenth centuries.[69] While mourning for her father's death, Sophie DuPont received eloquent letters and visits of condolence —all from women. No man wrote or visited Sophie to offer sympathy at her father's death.[70] Among rural Pennsylvania Quakers, death and mourning rituals assumed an even more extreme same-sex form, with men or women largely barred from the deathbeds of the other sex. Women relatives and friends slept with the dying woman, nursed her, and prepared her body for burial.[71]

Eighteenth- and nineteenth-century women thus lived in emotional proximity to one another. Friendships and intimacies followed the biological ebb and flow of women's lives. Marriage and pregnancy, childbirth and weaning, sickness and death, involved physical and psychic trauma which comfort and sympathy made easier to bear. Intense bonds of love and intimacy bound together those women who, offering one another aid and sympathy, shared such stressful moments.

These bonds were often physical as well as emotional. An undeniably romantic and even sensual note frequently marked female relationships. This theme, significant throughout the stages of a woman's life, surfaced first during adolescence. As one teen-ager from a struggling pioneer family in the Ohio Valley wrote in her diary in 1808, "I laid with my dear R[ebecca] and a glorious good talk we had until about 4[A.M.]—O how hard I do *love* her. . . ."[72] Only a few years later, Bostonian Eunice Callender carved her initials and Sarah Ripley's into a favorite tree, along with a pledge of eternal love, and then waited breathlessly for Sarah to discover and respond to her declaration of affection. The response appears to have been affirmative.[73] A half-century later, urbane and sophisticated Katherine Wharton commented upon meeting an old school chum: "She was a great pet of mine at school & I thought as I watched her light figure how often I had held her in my arms—how dear she had once been to me." Katie maintained a long, intimate friendship with another girl. When a young man began to court this friend seriously, Katie commented in her diary that she had never realized "how deeply I loved Eng and how fully." She wrote over and over again in that entry, "Indeed I love her!," and only with great reluctance left the city that summer, since it meant also leaving Eng with Eng's new suitor.[74]

Peggy Emlen, a Quaker adolescent in Philadelphia in the 1760s, expressed similar feelings about her first cousin, Sally Logan. The girls sent love poems to each other (not unlike the ones Elizabeth Bordley wrote to Nelly Custis a generation later), took long, solitary walks together, and even haunted the empty house of the other when one was out of town. Indeed, Sally's absences from Philadelphia caused Peggy acute unhappiness. So strong were Peggy's feelings that her brothers began to tease her about her affection for Sally and threatened to steal Sally's letters, much to both girls' alarm. In one letter that Peggy wrote the absent Sally, she elaborately described the depth and nature of her feelings:

> I have not words to express my impatience to see My Dear Cousin, what would I not give just now for an hours sweet conversation with her, it seems as if I had a thousand things to say to thee, yet when I see thee, everything will be forgot thro' joy. . . . I have a very great friendship for several Girls yet it dont give me so much uneasiness at being absent from them as from thee. . . . [Let us] go and spend a day down at our place together and there unmolested enjoy each others company.[75]

Sarah Alden Ripley, a young, highly educated woman, formed a similar intense relationship, in this instance with a woman somewhat older than herself. The immediate bond of friendship rested on their atypically intense scholarly interests, but it soon involved strong emotions, at least on Sarah's part. "Friendship," she wrote Mary Emerson, "is fast twining about her willing captive the silken hands of dependence, a dependence so sweet who would renounce it for the apathy of self-sufficiency?" Subsequent letters became far more emotional, almost conspiratorial. Mary visited Sarah secretly in her room, or the two women crept away from family and friends to meet in a nearby wood. Sarah became jealous of Mary's other young woman friends. Mary's trips away from Boston also thrust Sarah into periods of anguished depression. Interestingly, the letters detailing their love were not destroyed but were preserved and even reprinted in a eulogistic biography of Sarah Alden Ripley.[76]

Tender letters between adolescent women, confessions of loneliness and emotional dependency, were not peculiar to Sarah Alden, Peggy Emlen, or Katie Wharton. They are found throughout the letters of the thirty-five families studied. They have, of course, their parallel today in the musings of many female adolescents. Yet these eighteenth- and nineteenth-century friendships lasted with undiminished, indeed often increased, intensity throughout the women's lives. Sarah Alden Ripley's first child was named after Mary Emerson. Nelly Custis Lewis's love for and dependence on Elizabeth Bordley Gibson only increased after her marriage. Eunice Callender remained enamored of her cousin Sarah Ripley (Stearns) for years and rejected as impossible the suggestion by another woman that their love might someday fade away.[77] Sophie DuPont and her childhood friend Clementina Smith exchanged letters filled with love and dependency for forty years while another dear friend, Mary Black Couper, wrote of dreaming that she, Sophie, and her husband were all united in one marriage. Mary's letters to Sophie are filled with avowals of love and indications of ambivalence toward her own husband. Eliza Schlatter, another of Sophie's intimate friends, wrote to her at a time of crisis: "I wish I could be with you present in the body as well as the mind & heart—I would turn your *good husband out of bed*— and snuggle into you and we would have a long talk like old times in Pine St.—I want to tell you so many things that are not *writable*. . . ."[78]

Such mutual dependency and deep affection are a central existential reality coloring the world of supportive networks and rituals. In the case of Katie, Sophie, or Eunice—as with Molly, Jeannie, and Sarah—their need for closeness and support merged with more intense demands for a love that was at the same time both emotional and sensual. Perhaps the most explicit statement concerning women's lifelong friendships appeared in the letter that abolitionist and reformer Mary Grew wrote at about the same time, referring to her own love for her dear friend and lifelong companion, Margaret Burleigh. Grew wrote, in response to a letter of condolence from another woman on Burleigh's death:

Your words respecting my beloved friend touch me deeply.
Evidently . . . you comprehend and appreciate, as few persons
do . . . the nature of the relation which existed, which exists,
between her and myself. Her only surviving niece . . . also does.
To me it seems to have been a closer union than that of most
marriages. We know there have been other such between two
men and also between two women. And why should there not
be. Love is spiritual, only passion is sexual.[79]

How, then, can we ultimately interpret these long-lived intimate female
relationships and integrate them into our understanding of Victorian sexuality? Their ambivalent and romantic rhetoric presents us with an ultimate
puzzle: the relationship along the spectrum of human emotions between
love, sensuality, and sexuality.

One is tempted, as I have remarked, to compare Molly, Peggy, or
Sophie's relationship with the friendships adolescent girls in the twentieth
century routinely form—close friendships of great emotional intensity.
Helena Deutsch and Clara Thompson have both described these friendships
as emotionally necessary to a girl's psychosexual development. But, they
warn, such friendships might shade into adolescent and postadolescent
homosexuality.[80]

It is possible to speculate that in the twentieth century a number of
cultural taboos evolved to cut short the homosocial ties of girlhood and
to impel the emerging women of thirteen or fourteen toward heterosexual
relationships. In contrast, nineteenth-century American society did not
taboo close female relationships but, rather, recognized them as a socially
viable form of human contact—and, as such, acceptable throughout a
woman's life. Indeed, it was not these homosocial ties that were inhibited
but, rather, heterosexual leanings. While closeness, freedom of emotional
expression, and uninhibited physical contact characterized women's relationships with one another, the opposite was frequently true of male-
female relationships. One could thus argue that within such a world of
female support, intimacy, and ritual it was only to be expected that adult
women would turn trustingly and lovingly to one another. It was a
behavior they had observed and learned since childhood. A different type
of emotional landscape existed in the nineteenth century, one in which
Molly and Helena's love became a natural development.

Of perhaps equal significance are the implications we can garner from this framework for the understanding of heterosexual marriages in the nineteenth century. If men and women grew up, as they did, in relatively homogeneous and segregated sexual groups, then marriage represented a major problem in adjustment. From this perspective we could interpret much of the emotional stiffness and distance that we associate with Victorian marriage as a structural consequence of contemporary sex-role differentiation and gender-role socialization. With marriage both women and men had to adjust to life with a person who was, in essence, a member of an alien group.

I have thus far substituted a cultural or psychosocial for a psychosexual interpretation of women's emotional bonding. But there are psychosexual implications in this model which I think it only fair to make more explicit. Despite Sigmund Freud's insistence on the bisexuality of us all, or the recent American Psychiatric Association decision on homosexuality, many psychiatrists today tend explicitly or implicitly to view homosexuality as a totally alien or pathological behavior—as totally unlike heterosexuality. I suspect that in essence they may have adopted an explanatory model similar to the one used in discussing schizophrenia. As a psychiatrist can speak of schizophrenia and of a borderline schizophrenic personality as both ultimately and fundamentally different from a normal or a neurotic personality, so they also think of both homosexuality and latent homosexuality as states totally different from heterosexuality. With this rapidly dichotomous model of assumption, "latent homosexuality" becomes the indication of a disease in progress—seeds of a pathology which belie the reality of an individual's heterosexuality.

Yet, at the same time, we are well aware that cultural values can affect choices in the gender of a person's sexual partner. We, for instance, do not necessarily consider homosexual-object choice among men in prison, on shipboard, or in boarding schools a necessary indication of pathology. I would urge that we expand this relativistic model and hypothesize that a number of cultures might well tolerate or even encourage diversity in sexual and nonsexual relations. Based on my research into this nineteenth-century world of female intimacy, I would further suggest that, rather than seeing a gulf between the normal and the abnormal, we view sexual and emotional impulses as part of a continuum or spectrum of affect gradations strongly affected by cultural norms and arrangements, a continuum influenced in part by observed and thus learned behavior. At one end of the continuum lies committed heterosexuality, at the other uncompromising homosexuality; between, a wide latitude of emotions and sexual feelings. Certain cultures and environments permit individuals a great deal of freedom in moving across this spectrum. I would like to suggest that the nineteenth century was such a cultural environment. That is, the supposedly repressive and destructive Victorian sexual ethos may have been more flexible and responsive to the needs of particular individuals than those of the mid-twentieth century.

PART TWO

Bourgeois Discourse and the Age
of Jackson: An Introduction

Change is the one human constant. Few societies exemplify this truth with greater clarity than America did between the 1790s and the 1850s. For half a century three massive revolutions—the commercial, transportation, and industrial—swept through American society. As the basic modes of economic production and institutional organization changed, so did the experience of time and space, the functions, structure, and internal dynamics of the family, gender and generational relations. Earlier visions of God, the apt mirrors of earlier experience, shattered.[1] By the 1840s, the world that colonial Americans had carefully crafted lay in fragments. Yet the form the new order would take was not yet clear. Conflicting economic, social, and ideological systems battled for hegemony. The obsolete coexisted with the novel. So much was new that all appeared uncertain.[2]

We can trace the beginnings of these changes to the 1750s and 1760s, perhaps even earlier. Certainly by the end of the Revolutionary War, the pace of change had accelerated. Centered initially in the port towns of the Eastern Seaboard and the densely populated farm lands and villages that surrounded them, the commercial and transportation revolutions began slowly to affect America's agricultural hinterland.[3] Merchants invested profits won from European, West Indian, and Chinese trade in Western land speculation and in transportation systems to make those lands commercially viable. They built toll roads to connect sleepy villages with surrounding farming communities. Canals hesitatingly reached out.[4] Then, suddenly, in one bold stroke, New York State and her innovative mercantile leaders committed themselves to constructing the world's longest canal, the Erie, which would reach 366 miles from the Hudson River to the Great Lakes. The Erie Canal confirmed New York City's already established pre-eminence as the commercial center of America. The city's influence now reached across New York State into the new territories of Illinois, Michigan, Wisconsin, and Minnesota. The canal transformed the isolated lands of western New York State, only recently wrested from the Iroquois, into the most commercially profitable wheat-producing region in the world. Boom towns burgeoned along the canal as farming families and cattle moved west, wheat and flour flowed east.[5]

The revolution in commercial agriculture and transportation that called Greater New England into being destroyed the agricultural base of old New England. Poor and marginal lands, overfarmed for generations, could not compete with the alluvial lands of the Genesee Valley and of the Great Lakes Plains. As early as the 1760s and the 1770s, New England's agricultural villages had begun to stagnate.[6] By the opening decade of the nineteenth century, the stage was set for a massive exodus of the young. Villages, whole regions witnessed an outflowing of the young and the ambitious. The first wave left between the 1810s and the 1830s. The 1850s saw a second stage of outward migration as the railroad boom of those years sealed the demise of New England agriculture.[7]

These emigrés from New England's agricultural communities had responded to a push-pull process. Forced out by land scarcity and declining agricultural prices, lured west by rich lands and new commercial opportunities, young women and men fled their fathers' lands and their quiet ancestral villages. The more affluent moved with family and kin to new Western farms.[8] Those without capital resources more frequently moved alone. Lured on by the excitement and the bustle of the new commercial and industrial towns and cities, they sought jobs as clerks or artisans if men; if women, as mill hands or domestics. Economic forces beyond their control or even their understanding had pushed these youths free of family and village ties and pulled them restlessly along the country's new and complex systems of rivers and canals.[9]

The economic revolution that compelled these young people to take to the roads and canals simultaneously transformed the economy into which they moved. The position of clerk in the booming economy of the 1820s, 1830s, and 1840s differed radically from the position of clerk during the quieter days of the eighteenth century. Then a clerk had been a merchant's apprentice, chosen from among the sons of other merchants.

Familiar with the city and the world of commerce, the eighteenth-century clerk moved easily from his father's establishment to his new master's. He fully expected, as well, to rise from clerk to partner, with the partnership not infrequently sealed by marriage. Sharing economic interests and class assumptions, living under one roof, ties of familiarity and trust bound together merchant and clerk. The great expansion in the scale of markets brought about by the commercialization of Western agriculture and the canal boom shattered these ties. Mercantile houses grew in size. Clerks became low-level bureaucrats, the processors of the reams of paper produced by the commercial revolution. Few if any would be taken into the inner sanctum of trust and upward mobility that had governed the earlier world of commerce. The demographic profile of this new generation of clerks changed as radically as had the positions they filled. Country boys, new to commerce, new to the cities, they brought few skills. It was feared they felt few loyalties. No longer regular members of merchants' households, they found lodgings in the cities' hotels and boardinghouses. They ate in restaurants, drank in saloons, sought sex in irregular alliances. They floated outside conventional social institutions and morality. Transient, marginal, replaceable, they constituted a novel phenomenon in a changing economy. They were at one and the same time frightened and frightening figures.[10]

Their sisters also struggled against economic insecurity and social marginality. Virtually all women had married in eighteenth-century New England—albeit at increasingly older ages.[11] The grand exodus of young men in the 1820s and 1830s, either to the West or to the new urban frontier, altered that pattern. Now, to remain in the village of one's birth frequently meant spinsterhood and economic dependence. Depressed farming communities, moreover, could not afford to maintain large numbers of unmarried women. New England's daughters, like New England's sons, set off upon the roads and canals of the new commercial world. A few sought education and employment in the burgeoning common-school systems of the North.[12] Others flocked to Lowell, to Lawrence, or to the textile towns that, in the 1820s and 1830s, began to dot New Hampshire's rivers.[13] Still others turned to larger cities, where they sought to survive as domestic servants in the new bourgeois households or as needleworkers in the garment industry. In either case, these women experienced the full brunt of the economic changes which swept through urban America. Their fields of work were among the first transformed by the bourgeois and industrial revolutions. Economic hardships and insecurity rewarded their efforts—as did social marginality.[14]

In a number of significant ways, the situation of the new domestic servant paralleled that of the new mercantile clerk. Eighteenth-century servants had occupied a place within the family analogous to that of children. Illness, even illegitimate pregnancies would not break these time-honored bonds of rights and responsibilities.[15] The new bourgeois families of the 1820s and 1830s, themselves so recently moved to the city, did not share in these traditions. Rather, they treated their servants as employees, to be released for the smallest infraction of rules or for minor incompatibilities of personality. Certainly few masters expressed much sense of responsibility to their servants, or to their community for their servants' well-being.[16]

Women in the needle trades, like their sisters in domestic service, were at the cutting edge of new class relations. As early as the 1790s, the garment industry had entered a putting-out phase of merchant capitalism, complete with sweated labor. Producing cheap clothing for men along the frontier, or for Southern slaves, male wholesale merchants advertised for seamstresses to do piecework at home. Characteristically, many more women responded to the ads than could be given work. The fortunate received cut pieces to be made into cheap shirts, pantaloons, or vests, which they would return completed the next week. If their work was accepted as satisfactory they would be given more. Otherwise the wholesale merchant could simply confiscate the pieces. These women constituted one of America's first groups of proletarianized laborers. They possessed no specialized or highly valued skills. (All women, after all, could sew.) They lacked any job security; they had no control over their wages. Harsh exploitation followed. Shirts and pantaloons that took hours to make brought a few pennies in wages. Most often single women or widows, women needleworkers, like their brother clerks, lived outside traditional family arrangements alone in the cities. Unlike the more highly paid clerks, however, seamstresses could not afford rooms in respectable boarding-houses or hotels; they clung together in sordid tenement dwellings. Not infrequently, they turned for survival to that other major form of female wage labor—prostitution.[17]

The same economic forces that so bewildered these country-born seamstresses and clerks, as radically altered the lives of urban youths, who had been raised within an artisan culture. The years between the 1740s and the 1830s had constituted a golden age for American artisans. Production had centered on the family workshop, where family members, aided by a few journeymen and apprentices, had participated in the ancient mysteries of hand production. Apprentice and journeyman had lived under the master's roof, eaten and drunk with him, attended his church. The master not only taught them their trade; he also assumed responsibility for their general education. The long winter evenings might well be spent reading and debating economic, political, and moral tracts. This was a world in which the craft constituted a way of life, skills, the prime source of pride and identity. The slow process of age and learned skill would take the young man from apprenticeship through the stage of journeyman to the mature status of master craftsman. All masters had traveled this path and knew well the fears, frustrations, and expectations of apprentice and journeyman. Cooperation and shared concerns bound apprentice, journeyman, and master within a seamless web. These were the years when the artisan and the yeoman farmer, politicians and ministers agreed, constituted the backbone and the sinew of republican America.[18]

The placing-out system, task differentiation, and the sweated system of labor, beginning in the 1830s, slowly eroded this world, gradually transforming apprentices and journeymen into the employees of an entrepreneur. Skills became obsolete; crafts died. Wage labor replaced apprenticeship. As the average workshop of eight men and women gave way, by the 1850s, to factories employing from fifty to five hundred men, the intimate relations that had characterized the master-apprentice bond disappeared. Uncertainty prevailed. Some master craftsmen, possessing capital and connections, became wholesale merchants, profiting from the sweated labor of former apprentices, journeymen, and fellow master craftsmen. Others entered the new factories as foremen and managers. Neither type, however, experienced much security, for frequent booms and busts, scarcity of credit, the uncertainties of the market, made the early entrepreneur an endangered species. If he failed, he fell, along with the majority of journeymen and poorer master craftsmen, into the ranks of the semiskilled workers. This transition period lasted for more than a generation. Some crafts succumbed quickly to the process of industrialization; others remained untouched until the 1840s; still others saw the new and the old systems battle for dominance for several decades.[19]

The industrial revolution not only transformed the work place; it also radically altered the function, composition, and power dynamics of the working-class family. The artisan family had been patriarchal. Fathers chose their sons' trades; sons most frequently followed in their fathers' footsteps, learning their craft at home or from uncles, older brothers, or other kin. British common law and tradition, still accepted by all American states in the 1840s and 1850s, had deprived married women of the right to own property or earn wages, yet married women contributed in central ways to the family economy. Daughters skilled in the family craft made valuable wives for other artisans. The destruction of the crafts destroyed these patterns. Members of the artisan family, no longer bound together as producers, moved as individuals into the wage market to negotiate their own conditions. Sons, repudiating the old ways, sought to establish themselves in new trades. In 1850, Susan Hirsch reports, 75 percent of Newark working-class fathers did not have sons working in their same trade. By the 1860s, their number had climbed to 86 percent.[20]

Yet the new working-class family did not fragment. While old patterns of familial cohesion and interdependency passed away, new ones emerged. Within the artisan world, the apprentice system had removed adolescents from their parents' homes. Because most industrial employers preferred to hire young adults rather than child and adolescent laborers, industrialization kept working-class adolescents as economic dependents within their parents' homes. Thus, in 1860, while adult sons sought their own careers, 71 percent of teen-age boys in industrialized Newark lived with their parents. The more industrialized the craft, the more likely the boy was to spend his youth at home. Ironically, the urban and economic revolutions that cut rural sons and daughters free from the family farm created new patterns of dependency for urban working-class adolescents.[21] Other dependency patterns emerged as well. The low wages that prevailed in the new factories forced employed family members to pool resources in order to survive as a consumer unit. The wages paid young women, as already noted, made self-sufficiency for working-class women next to impossible. Parents, furthermore, needed the assistance of young adult workers to care for younger, still-dependent children—or to provide for old age. On the other hand, sons and daughters, freed from the need to learn skills through the slow process of apprenticeship, tended to marry at younger ages than their artisan parents had, and to establish their own households quickly. But autonomy for the son, newly established as head of his own household, did not bring autonomy to his wife. Marrying removed the working-class daughter not only from her parents' home but from the work force. She moved from dependence on parents and siblings to dependence on husband and children. Patriarchy remained, albeit in a significantly altered form.[22]

The working-class family resisted the forces of fragmentation. The commercial and industrial city did not. Merchants and artisans no longer lived side by side on shaded streets, or master craftsmen above their shops. The geographic and social cohesion of the new inland towns and of the older port cities along the East Coast splintered as they developed distinctive commercial, manufacturing, and residential districts. Class, ethnic, and religious lines intensified these geographic divisions until America's cities became disjointed pockets of rich and poor, immigrant and native-born, artisans, laborers, and merchants, each group harboring suspicions and hostilities toward all the others. Geographic mobility transformed difference into near chaos. The young, especially those who had recently come from the countryside, moved through American cities with discomfiting speed. Rochester, New York, newspapers reported in the mid-1820s that an average of twenty persons left Rochester every day, while even more arrived; Rochester's wage-earning population experienced an almost complete turnover every six years. New York City's population grew 60 percent per decade between 1820 and 1860, while hundreds of thousands passed through the city without leaving any trace. The nineteenth-century city was, as Stuart Blumin argues, more process than geographic place. Even within cities, transience predominated. Our image of ethnic and working-class communities where neighbors knew and supported one another is largely a bourgeois romance. Blumin traced an escalating rate of movement between neighborhoods among Philadelphians who remained in that city during the pre–Civil War decades—nearly 27 percent in the 1820s, nearly 38 percent in the 1850s.[23]

Our triad of revolutions splintered time as well as space. In artisan and agrarian America, no sharp divisions had marked work and recreation as artisans chattered with well-known customers and nature imposed her own rhythm upon the farming family. The divorce of home and work, task differentiation, and, by the 1840s and the 1850s, the introduction of mechanization altered the easy flow of time. Recreation and work became binary opposites. So did public and private space. Women, of course, experienced this division more intensely than men. Artisan and farming women had played a central role in preindustrial production at a time when home and marketplace were indistinguishable. When work left the home, men freely followed it into the agora, to countinghouses and factories. Women, in contrast, found themselves confined within an increasingly isolated domesticity. The female life cycle became compartmentalized into permitted and forbidden space and acts. Yet many bourgeois matrons fought back. Cloaking themselves in the robes of millennial and philanthropic enthusiasm, they claimed the right to take the values of the Christian home into the world. That world, of course, was none other than the new commercial city complete with slums and brothels, factories, shops, and newspapers, schools and libraries. Territorial conflicts between men and women resulted from these female efforts to domesticate and sanctify men's newfound public space. The issue of the extension of "Home Rule" hid the equally fundamental question of who should rule at home.[24]

The speed and relentlessness of these changes threatened to shatter social cohesion. The newly emerging bourgeoisie had few resources with which to resist disintegration. The beneficiary of the commercial and industrial revolutions, it consisted of an inharmonious grouping of quite disparate economic and social components: an older mercantile elite; new wholesale merchants only just risen from peddler to prince; smaller shopkeepers; the new industrial entrepreneurs; the equally new professionals. So ill-assorted an amalgam could scarcely be considered a solidified class. Certainly its membership demonstrated extreme instability. Specie shortage, bank wars, acts of nature such as fires and shipwrecks, the uncertainty of new markets, all could destroy budding careers, throw families into want and despair. Wealth proved transitory even for the new country's mercantile elite. The aristocratic father-in-law of New York City's social chronologist, George Templeton Strong, failed financially, as did New York's two most famous merchants, Arthur and Lewis Tappan, and, earlier, philanthropist and social commentator James Pintard.[25] The middle ranks proved no more secure. Stuart Blumin found that between the 1820s and the 1850s—in Philadelphia, at least—downward economic mobility far exceeded upward movement. It did likewise in Buffalo in the 1850s and 1860s. Within this unknown and evolving world, few could be certain where they would find either places of power or zones of safety.[26]

The bourgeoisie struggled to impose order on the chaos that surrounded them. Moving into cities that had known few institutions outside the family and the church, the bourgeoisie constructed institutions that would both act to contain disorder and serve their specific economic and emotional needs as an emerging class. Voluntary societies proliferated as the new bourgeois women and men sought to extend religion and literacy to the new urban poor, to draw wild youths into temperance societies or keep them out of brothels, to care for dependent widows, vagrant children, young women seeking jobs in the new urban economy.[27] These societies also served the more personal needs of their founders. Moral reform and temperance societies, lyceums, volunteer fire companies—radically unlike one another—all nevertheless gave their members a sense of belonging in a fragmenting world.[28] Facilitating the creation of social contacts, they helped fight the feelings of isolation that beset new residents in a new city.

Seeking to establish the legitimacy of its new economic hegemony, the bourgeoisie proclaimed that its own class characteristics were the dictates of God, nature, and human reason. Cleanliness, temperance, and frugality became indistinguishable from godliness. Monogamous and reproductive sexuality emerged as the only "natural" form of sexual expression. Women's biology dictated a homebound maternal role for women.[29] Yet bourgeois cultural hegemony was far from secure—or universally acknowledged. A host of religious and ideological revolts against bourgeois ideology characterized the Jacksonian Age. Shakers, Mormons, Oneida Perfectionists (attracting their followers in the hill country of New England and northern New York State) espoused widely disparate social and religious visions. Nevertheless, all united in rejecting the nuclear and isolated bourgeois family and bourgeois sexual norms.[30] Others who resisted incorporation within the new bourgeois structures underscored their structural separateness by advocating utopian socialism, free love, spiritualism, radical dietary and health reform.[31] Thus a new and fragmented social order, competing cosmologies, and ideological conflict all characterized the emergent capitalist class structure of America in the 1830s, 1840s, and 1850s.

These years of momentous social change affected not only the reorganization of economic power but also the emotional experience of the individual men and women involved. Most Americans, not surprisingly, did not know how to relate their individual experiences to the overall changes in their social fabric. They sought to understand such change in terms of what was most immediate and concrete in their lives. Many

Americans conceptualized the social and economic reorganization consequent on the development of, first, commercial and then industrial capitalism in terms of changing family structures and generational relations. And,
as we have seen, the transformation of the family (bourgeois, working-
class, and farming) was perhaps the most striking and immediate institutional change to accompany the emergence of the new urban, commercial,
and industrial society. By the 1850s, for both the bourgeoisie and the
working class, the multifunctional traditional family had shrunk in size.
Nuclear, isolated, it had lost all but its most intimate sexual and emotional
functions. In terms of male-male interaction, the old unity was shattered.
Sons found themselves within a world neither they nor their fathers
understood. The young man stood alone. The men of Jacksonian America
experienced themselves both as sons loosed from the fathers' ways and as
fathers increasingly troubled as to how to provide for, control, or even to
understand the experiences of their sons. For fathers and sons, the male
adolescent became the symbol of both the vitality and the problems inherent in these massive social changes.[32]

Women's experience of these economic and structural changes
equaled the men's in intensity and conflict. In movement between farm and
city, young women experienced much the same uncertainty as their brothers. At the same time, the commercial and industrial revolutions sharply
divided women's and men's experiences. This was especially true for those
on the cutting edge of economic and institutional change—the new bourgeoisie. No longer working side by side with men on the family farm or
in the artisan shop, bourgeois women developed a gender-specific sense of
time and space, of permissible and forbidden behavior. Yet we must be
careful not to exaggerate women's exclusion from the new bourgeois
values and institutions. The very economic and institutional forces that
gave birth to the bourgeoisie and to the new bourgeois family (thus
restricting women's roles) had, as we have seen, led the bourgeoisie to
found a host of extra-domestic institutions. Some had religious aims: Bible
and Tract societies, Sunday schools. Others were openly philanthropic:
societies for the relief of poor widows with young children, schools for
black children, orphan asylums, refuges for "fallen women" or destitute
seamstresses. Some, such as temperance organizations and anti-slavery societies, were political. New bourgeois matrons and their daughters flocked
to these institutions. They founded new, separatist female ones. Through

these institutions they moved from the private home into the public world of reform, education, and philanthropy.[33] They became knowledgeable about childhood vagrancy, infant mortality, and slum housing.[34] They formed national organizations, published newspapers, petitioned municipal, state, and federal governments. Thus, during the very years when bourgeois men began to formulate the Cult of True Womanhood, bourgeois women left the home in droves to purify the world, to elevate themselves, to fight injustice—to create meaningful and fulfilling female roles. Ironically, then, as men increasingly defined women as separate from and unlike men, women's experiences came to parallel those of men. This does not mean, however, that early bourgeois women and men did not experience their lives and their interests as increasingly distinct and conflicted.

Against this backdrop of relentless change and uncertainty, bourgeois women and men sought to express their experiences, resist change, assert order. The three essays that follow explore three different bourgeois voices. The "Davy Crockett" essay examines the male bourgeois voice—of fathers and sons—debating the effect of economic revolution on father-son relations and, beyond that, on the interaction between the individual and his community. "Beauty, the Beast, and the Militant Woman" seeks to decode bourgeois women's concern with prostitution. On one level, their concern represented an early response to the impact of the urban economy on women workers. It constituted as well a metaphoric discourse through which bourgeois women protested their growing powerlessness in the new urban world. The last essay, "The Cross and the Pedestal," examines the revival and reform enthusiasm of the Second Great Awakening as an expression of both geographic and class movement.

Davy Crockett as Trickster: Pornography, Liminality, and Symbolic Inversion in Victorian America[1]

Individuals, experiencing themselves as powerless in the face of massive and unremitting social transformation, respond by attempting to capture and encapsulate such change within a new and ordered symbolic universe. They seek through imagery and myth to mitigate their feelings of helplessness by deflecting and partially distorting change and thus bringing it within the control of the imagination. Especially when the social fabric is rent in fundamental ways, bodily and familial imagery will assume ascendancy. At such times individuals will revert to their most primitive experience of human interaction and social ordering. On an even more instinctive level, when all the world spins out of control, the last intuitive resource of any individual is her or his own body, and especially its sexual impulses. That, at least, one can control and manipulate. Thus sexuality and the family, because of their primitive psychic and social functions, serve as reservoirs of physical imagery through which individuals seek to express and rationalize their experience of social change.[2]

Beginning in the late eighteenth century, the Western world experienced a sexual explosion—not of acts, licit or illicit, but of words, images, fantasies, fears. Thus far we have viewed the growing sexual obsessions of this era as an effort to control behavior, sexual and otherwise, to expand the power of the state, to reach into the minds and hearts of millions.[3] Possibly, but also too simply. To understand the full complexity of this politico-sexual phenomenon, we must begin our analysis at a far earlier state of the process—before the manipulation of others becomes an object. The ocean of sexual words that rhythmically beats against the nineteenth century's awareness initially came into being not so much to control the behavior of others as to control that which was perceived as uncontrollable, the process of change itself.

The nineteenth century's obsession with categorizing the physical, and especially the sexual, with describing the abnormal, and with defining the legitimate must be seen first as an effort to impose order upon the chaos of the nonsexual world. Different social groups sought to do so through the psychological and imaginative technique of constructing fantasied systems of sexual control built upon elaborate and rigid physical and sexual categories. These systems were not real. They existed only within the minds of their believers. Their true object of concern was not people but their formulators' own experience of social disorder. Here lies the root of this era's sexual discourse and of its complexity. For the eighteenth and nineteenth centuries' sexual discourse was just that, a discourse, at times a babel, but never a monologue. Different social and economic groups, experiencing economic and demographic change differently, having different degrees of power with which to respond to the alterations that affected their lives, created disparate fantasies, debated with one another, condemned one another—all in the language of sexuality. Gradually, however, one voice began to dominate the discourse as it came to dominate the social structure —the voice of the bourgeois male. In the end it is his voice that we most remember.

Bourgeois men began to express their ambivalence about both the process of change itself and the emerging new social order by postulating two competing mythic dramas. Father-and-son conflict and the role and character of the male adolescent formed the core of both these plays, which were simultaneously family and sexual dramas.

We can assume that both scripts were available for reading by many of the same men. Certainly both sets of playwrights were aware of each other's plots and dramatic conclusions. I would argue, consequently, that Jacksonian men engaged in a debate about generational relations and social structure, using a symbolic language they all understood only too well.

In one play, a frail and endangered male adolescent emerged as the problematic figure.[4] With puberty, powerful sexual urges tempted him to masturbate, engage in illicit sexual encounters, and marry early. These urges violated a rigid system of physiological laws based on a hierarchy of bodily proprieties and a closed energy system. Energy devoted to the lower, sexual organs robbed the higher organs—brain, heart, nervous system—of vital blood and energy. If the young man violated an elaborate system of dietary laws—if he drank, ate meat, rich sauces, or other food associated with the new commercial centers—his lower organs and instincts would become uncontrollable, destroy the body's hierarchical order, and lead to an irreversible progression of diseases culminating in death.

Fortunately, this dangerous and endangered young man lived within a rural patriarchal family of fathers and grandfathers, or as an apprentice within the home of a patriarchal master. These older men, assisted by a shadowy cast of virtuous and sexual mothers and daughters, would guide the young man past the maelstroms of sexual desire into a safe maturity of self-control and devotion to family. If the young man remained obedient to his father throughout the father's life (as sons within the structured and patriarchal traditional agrarian villages of eighteenth-century New England had frequently been required to do), if he remained faithful to his apprenticeship, married in his early thirties, and limited his sexual activity within marriage to an infrequent procreative act (at a time when the New England and Eastern urban birthrate was dropping precipitously), he would be rewarded by becoming one healthy link in an endless chain of fathers and sons which would stretch unbroken into a physiological and social millennium in which order would reign.

The authors of this play were a group of self-styled male moral reformers, gathering under their banner such diverse enthusiasms as food and health reform, temperance, educational reform, and phrenology. While we have traditionally seen these groups as the lunatic fringe of Jacksonian America, it is important to remember that on an operational level they were fully accepted and functioned within the bourgeois urban world. Though born in small farm villages in western New England or New York State, they early moved to Boston or New York, entering the new middle-class professions as educators, physicians, publicists, or corporate bureaucrats. They built fortunes or national reputations as publishers and writers and adopted the cheap popular press to build regional and national reform movements. Most important, they consistently addressed issues central to the emerging bourgeoisie.

A second, strikingly different—if equally fabulous—young man danced charismatically across the male Jacksonian imagination. Joyfully embracing change and christening it "progress," the autonomous young man of the frontier was the mirror image of the fragile and dependent son of the Eastern reformers. Wild and rough-featured, dressed in animal skins, pitted daily against a wild and relentless nature, Davy Crockett and his cohort of riverboat men, trappers, and backwoods squatters fought with their fathers, broke apprenticeships, rebelled against education, and escaped into a mythical wilderness of forests and rivers. They drank heavily, killed and ate the animals of the forest, fought viciously with one another, masturbated, and whored. Far from suffering a system of orderly laws to be obeyed, nature was a chaotic power that simultaneously enticed and demanded taming. Imagery was rife with phallic and other sexual themes.

The Davy Crockett myths flourished during the same years that fear of youthful masturbation reached its apex—the 1830s through the 1850s. The first Davy Crockett almanacs appeared in 1835. Perhaps the best known of the Davy Crockett series was published in Nashville, Tennessee, between 1835 and 1841.[5] But 1835 also saw the publication of a *Crockett's Yaller Flower Almanac* in New York City.[6] For the next fifteen years, Boston, New York, Philadelphia, and Baltimore publishers all brought out Davy Crockett comic almanacs which were augmented by pseudo-autobiographies and accounts of the Texas campaign.[7] Later, the Crockett myth spread to England, where British comics adapted it to their own interest and symbolic systems.[8]

While adopting the literary persona of the illiterate frontiersman, the authors of the Davy Crockett almanacs, like their counterparts the male moral reformers, were actually members of the urban bourgeoisie—printers and publishers working in the major cities of the Eastern Seaboard. Like the male moral reformers, they used the cheap, popular press to create a national audience, even lampooning the male moral reformers and their causes. Significantly, as well, they addressed the same audience—the new and loose young men of the cities and commercial *entrepôts*. [9]

In the following pages, let me first present the fabled career of Davy Crockett as it appeared in these comic almanacs and then suggest the ways in which this was not simply an idle spoof or entertainment. Indeed, I will argue that behind the scatology and humor lay one of the earliest and most paradigmatic myths of the origins of the American bourgeoisie.

Davy Crockett—autonomous, free-roaming adolescent—ironically functioned as the central figure in a family drama. The very first episode in the first Crockett almanac focused upon the central theme of father-son conflict. Fables concerning Crockett's childhood and youth, like those presenting his adult character and career, inverted absolutely the values and admonitions of the male moral reformers. Crockett's father, far from representing an idealized and temperate rural past, was a bankrupt Irish

farmer who ran a tavern near the Cumberland Gap and eked out a
questionable living selling liquor to wagoners. Crockett thus could not
look back to an orderly patrimony of New England God-fearing fathers.
He came out of disorder; he could claim no heritage.[10]

It followed, of course, that as a child Crockett roamed the wilderness
learning to hunt and driving cattle for passing wagoners. When he was
twelve, however, his father made one serious attempt to assert paternal
control, enrolling Davy within what was clearly one of the first bourgeois,
Eastern-oriented institutions on the Tennessee frontier—a country school.
Within days Crockett had disrupted classroom order by physically beating
another boy and, in an effort to avoid a whipping, by playing hooky.
When Crockett's duplicity was discovered, a violent confrontation between father and son ensued. Crockett's father sided with the schoolmaster
and traditional social order. Crockett determined to submit to neither
parental nor school discipline. In telling the story, the mythic Crockett
depicts his father as a tyrannical and yet, at the same time, ridiculous and
ineffective figure. Unsuccessful the first time he tries to trick his father by
playing hooky, Crockett succeeds in his second and more serious attempt
—his break for autonomy. In discussing his father's response, the mythic
Crockett informed his 1833 audience:

> Said he if you don't instantly go to school I'll whip you an
> eternal sight worse than the master. . . . Finding me rather too
> slow about starting, he gathered about a two year "old hickory"
> and broke after me. I put out with all my might and soon we
> were both up to the top of our speed. We had a tolerable tough
> race for about a mile; but mind me not on the school-house
> road, for I was trying to get as far as possible the other way.
> And I yet believe if my father and the school master could both
> have levied on me at that time, I should never have been sent
> to Congress for they would have used me up.

Hiding in the woods, Crockett eludes his father, whom he describes passing
by his hidingplace in terms of ridicule and denigration: "The old gentleman passed by, puffing and blowing as though his steam was high enough
to burst his boiler." Crockett's escape was ensured. That night Crockett
sought out a friend who was just leaving for the West with a drove of

cattle. After some three years as a driver, Crockett went home—but neither his family nor his old friends recognized him, "I had grown so." Crockett had thus overthrown his father's authority, refused education—the quintessential bourgeois value—and turned his back, quite literally, on his family. He spent his adolescence in revolt and in the wilderness.[11]

None of his ways were the ways of the frail and conforming son of the male moral reformers. Rather than submitting to a lengthy and docile apprenticeship and delaying marriage until thirty—the advice of the male moral reformers—the adolescent Crockett selected and courted his future wife without adult supervision. Interestingly, his future mother-in-law, like Crockett's father an Irish immigrant, both encourages Crockett's pursuit of her daughter and then provides the young couple with cash and livestock to start their own farm.[12] Both of these actions reverse the nineteenth-century's gender-role stereotyping: mothers do not typically encourage poor young men's sexual advances; fathers, not mothers, provide dowries. But Crockett's wife, like Crockett himself, no longer had a father.

Once married, Crockett moves ever farther west, as a hunter and a backwoods farmer, far from kin and former neighbors. His own brothers are never mentioned after the school episode.[13] Crockett's father reappears only once in the later almanacs. Little reference is made to Crockett's children. Only twice over a fifteen-year period are sons even mentioned, and then only in passing, as shadowy and absent figures. For the most part, Crockett is childless; occasionally he appears as the father of daughters.[14] He thus assumes an almost Peter Pan quality—the young man escaping to a magical forest where he remains the perennial adolescent, without father and without sons. In this way Crockett negates simultaneously the male moral reformers' visions of the dutiful son and of the loving patriarchal father. He is loose, liminal, and wild.

Crockett spends the remainder of his life in a boundless wilderness, daily battling with wild animals and wilder nature. We never see Crockett as Cincinnatus at the plow. Indeed, the one time when his farm is mentioned it is described as being so rocky that he must plant his seeds by shooting them with his rifle into crevices between the rocks.[15] The frontier of the Davy Crockett almanacs is not dotted with agrarian villages, pinpointed with church spires or crisscrossed by toll roads, canals, and railroads —all attributes of the commercial East. Like the hero who ruled over it, it is a mythic world without boundaries or limits. "It is so heavy timbered

that a humming bird could not fly through it," one of Davy Crockett's
cohorts, identified only as Wolverene, commented.[16] Only rivers, free-
flowing, unpredictable, and occasionally uncontrollable, intersected this
world. Directions were fluid, boundaries nonexistent. Thus, when Crockett
was asked how one would find where he lived, he responded, "Why sir,
just run down the Mississippi till you come to the Obion river, run a small
streak up that, jump ashore anywhere and inquire for me."[17]

Violence as well as disorder characterized the Crockett frontier.
Crockett's life consisted of daily battles with the ferocious animals of this
wilderness. His hunting prowess—not his agricultural skills—fed his family. Every volume of the Crockett almanacs is filled with descriptions of
predatory animals and of bloody hunting and trapping exploits. One
winter Crockett reported that he had killed 105 bears. The following year
he had headed west to slaughter buffalo. Finding a bear and an alligator
in deadly combat, he killed both, salted and ate them.[18] No laws governed
these animals. Panthers and cougars crouched on tree branches waiting to
spring at the unwary hunter. Logs turned into alligators. Bears burst into
homes to attack the inhabitants. Wolves surrounded travelers, tearing them
to pieces.

Gradually, Crockett and his cohort took on the violent and chaotic
qualities of the animals they fought and consumed. Indeed, by moving into
this wilderness, Crockett had crossed the line between human and animal,
between civilization and chaotic nature. Like the hunters of Kentucky
before him, Crockett himself became, in his own words, half man and half
alligator, a steam engine, a snapping turtle. He slid along the ground like
a snake, became as angry and hungry as a wolf. He crowed, roared, and
screamed.[19] One almanac described a mythic debate between the fictional
Crockett and the erudite and well-mannered Senator Everett of Massachusetts, which Crockett began with barks and animal hoots. In this debate
Crockett proceeded to admit that he was as out of control as his mode of
speech had just demonstrated. "I've had a speech in soak this six month,"
he told his fellow congressmen in imagery suggestive of violent sexual
arousal:

> And it has swelled me like a drowned horse; if I don't deliver
> it I shall burst and smash the windows. . . . In one word I'm
> a screamer. . . . I'm a lettle the savagest creature you ever *did*

see. . . . I can run faster, dive deeper, stay longer under and come out drier, than any *chap* this side of the big *Swamp.* I can outlook a panther and outstare a flash of lightning; tote a steamboat on my back and play at rough and tumble with a lion. . . . To sum up all in one word, *I'm a horse.* . . . I can walk like an ox, run like a fox, swim like an eel, yell like an Indian, fight like a devil, and spout like an earthquake, make love like a mad bull, and swallow a nigger whole without chocking if you butter his head and pin his ears back.[20]

Hunting and fighting exacerbated this blending of worlds and natures. After a ferocious battle with a wildcat, Crockett cut off the animal's head and stuck the still-bleeding member on his own head to challenge the "entire wild puss nation." One hunter, after strangling a whooping crane, gnawed through its neck with his teeth.[21]

Obliterating the line between the human and the animal underlined the lack of restraint and of reason that is the key to these episodic struggles. When Crockett left his family he entered a world of chaos. Indeed, to Jacksonian Americans a predictable universe outside of and without the family was inconceivable. Yet power emanated from the violation of categories and the fusion with chaos. Crockett as half alligator, half man combined the ferocious strength of the reptile and the cunning of the human. By losing part of his humanity, he had become superhuman. But he had also become uncontrollably violent—that is, uncivilized.

Violence, mindless and excessive, characterized interactions between men as well. Like adolescent animals in the wild, the young men of Crockett's frontier engaged in a never-ending process of provoking and accepting challenges. The mythic Crockett reported one such incident that occurred shortly after he left his father's home. A young man along the Mississippi River approached Crockett with the words "Says he, you [Kentuckians] call themselves half-horse and half-alligator but I'll let you know that I'm whole alligator with a cross of wild cat." "I jumped up and snapped my fingers in his face . . . and I spit right in his mouth," Crockett reported. "I snapped at his nose and seized it between my teeth. He roared and struggled but I held on like a pair of pincers until at last off came his nose. 'That's to you' says I, for an alligator—you see I'm crossed with the snapping turtle."[22]

Gradually the stories assumed a more and more macabre and sadistic tone. This was especially true if Indians or blacks were Crockett's antagonists, for Crockett disclosed an ominous foreshadowing in his encounters with nonwhites. In a fight between Crockett and an "Indian half-breed" who Crockett felt was "uppity," a fight recounted in an 1839 almanac published in New York City, Crockett killed the Indian by chewing through his jugular and letting him bleed to death. Dismemberment followed, and Crockett's wife kept the scalp "fastened to a stick to brush the flies off the table when we were at dinner."[23] Some seven years later, Crockett, assisted by his pet bear, Death Hug, killed and scalped four Indians "in the natural way with our teeth." "After that," Crockett reported, underlining the merger that occurred between animal and human and which this type of fighting between white and native American epitomized, "we washed the injun juice from our paws, took a hug and a shake. . . ."[24]

By 1849, Crockett, when fighting with native Americans, had become a cannibal. With the assistance of his dog, he killed two Indians; then, he reported, "I smashed number one into injun gravy with my foot, and spread it over number two, and made a dinner for me and my dog. It was superlicious."[25] Crockett had killed the Indians. In the process he and his dog had become one.

How can we explain these bizarre adventures, this mythic universe beyond boundaries and civilization?

On one level the two mythic adolescents are real. The discourse literally addressed the ways societies seek to socialize and contain adolescence—that intensely problematic stage of life. The adolescent—neither child nor adult—stands between social categories and roles. Most societies perceive this as a time of danger for the individual, for his family, and for society as a whole. The person between categories is perceived as outside of categories, institutions, and values. As such he embodies all the chaotic power of formlessness and disorder. The stage of being between categories and the power inherent in that process have been designated by anthropologists as liminality. Male moral reformers and the writers of comic almanacs were engaged in an intense debate over the dangers of adolescent liminality and the appropriate ways of containing it.

The male moral reformers' drama idealized the institutions and ideologies through which preindustrial New England had organized and structured adolescence. Theirs was a regressive drama. The writers of the comic almanacs, conversely, attacked those traditional methods, praising instead the adolescent's freedom from institutional restraints. The chaos of the Crockett frontier—the unrestrained movement of young hunters along its liminal waterways, the episodic frame of the myth—symbolized and glorified the innate liminality of adolescence in a society with few institutions to mold or control it.

But on another level this was not simply a debate about containing the liminality of actual adolescents. It was a debate about the liminality of Jacksonian society, poised between the traditional agrarian and mercantile social order and the new ways of commercial and industrial capitalism. The nationalistic orators were right. American society was itself the adolescent. The mythic male adolescents functioned as condensed symbols for two contrasting stages of social-structural development. In this sense the myths transcended the actual Jacksonian adolescent, or, rather, captured him, drained him of his historical reality, and transformed him into the signifier of the process of massive social-structural change.

The male moral reformers' patriarchal stem family, within its orderly and predictable universe, symbolized the rigid social hierarchies, delineated social boundaries, ascribed roles, and ritualized morality of late-seventeenth- and early-eighteenth-century New England village life. The idealized son symbolized the passive self within that social system. In point of fact, however, early-eighteenth-century New Englanders had not created the male moral reform myth: nineteenth-century Bostonians and New Yorkers had. The myth thus reflected not so much an idealized past as the stress and fears of the present. Written by men caught in the eye of social change, it mirrored a world of conflicting values. The nation extolled ambition, change, and individualism at the same time that it continued to praise the family and traditional social order. For men raised in the value systems of eighteenth-century New England, Jacksonian America promised contradictory rewards and held out impossible goals. The myth fought to contain change and contradiction through pollution taboos and magically reiterated categories of social rejects. But even within the myth the authors recognized the reality of youthful autonomy. Their mythic adolescent, seemingly held within the vise of rigid physiological laws, was, in fact, not passive. On the contrary, he was sorely tempted to act upon an autonomy all too real. Even within the myth he could drink, masturbate, and disobey his father. And though he might suffer inordinately for his assertion of self, nevertheless the patriarchal family and the traditional social order would be destroyed. The myth in fact affirmed the power of youth. It replicated a society in transition. It voiced the fears of men impotent to avert change.

The Crockett myth glorified the very change the moral reformers feared. The unstructured and violent natural universe of the Crockett myth reflected, on a dramatic and oversized scale, the institutional fragmentation of pre- and early industrial America. Within this institutionally undifferentiated world, personal forms of control replaced communal consensus. The individual was valued above the family or community. Within this uncharted and unbounded mythic world, three figures emerge as signifiers or symbols. The first is the father who, outwitted and eluded by his son, embodied traditional patriarchal institutions and hierarchical value systems, by now outmoded and ineffective. Crockett himself symbolized simultaneously both the loose young man and the new economic and demographic forces of change that had destroyed the old ways of the fathers. The impotent schoolmaster symbolized the new bourgeois institutions—especially the school—which were not yet sufficiently developed to establish a secure social order. At that point in time, Davy Crockett could still escape. Within Jacksonian America at the very outset of the industrial revolution, form had yet to contain formlessness.

Yet why did the Crockett mythmakers choose a slaughterer and a cannibal to symbolize economic and institutional transition? This is a Victorian, not a Brechtian, play.

The Crockett myth deals explicitly with the process of change—with the explosive power of formlessness at war with structure at a time when antistructure was still victorious and form in disarray. All society, Mary Douglas argues, is built upon an assertion of order and the containment of disorder. Order and disorder, Douglas argues, are pitted against each other in all cultures: "Order implies restriction; from all possible materials, a limited selection has been made and from all possible relations a limited set has been used. . . . Disorder by implication is unlimited. . . ."[26] Disorder possesses its own wild power. The comic writers, in glorifying change, necessarily had to incorporate within their myth the power and fury of the disorder inherent in the process of massive social-structural change. Crockett's orgy of violence epitomized this formless fury.

Another way of attempting to conceptualize and analyze violence within the Crockett myth is to return to our paradigm of liminality—that quality of being between categories. Crockett epitomizes the liminal. He is the man turned beast, the white man who scalps Indians, the uncultured civilizer. He lives beyond boundaries, on rivers, literally between states. Anthropologist Victor Turner has delineated three different types of liminality.[27] The first is a form of structured liminality—liminality that is recognized and contained within a culture's ritualized processes. This liminality does not really threaten social order—it only appears, momentarily, to do so. Adolescence itself, and the revival-conversion experience, are examples. In these cases liminality is limited, terminating with the re-entry of the individual into society—the revival convert becomes a church member, the adolescent an adult.

To the structured liminality of adolescence, Crockett fused a second, less contained liminality—that of the socially and economically marginal, of the individual or group existing outside institutional frameworks. Crockett symbolized the marginality of Jacksonian men poised between economic classes and socially acknowledged institutional niches: the sons of artisans, suspended between the hope of emerging as successful entrepreneurs and the fear of sinking into the industrialized and unskilled work force, farmers' sons seeking to chisel out new bourgeois professions, clerks caught between the hope of rising into partnerships and the fear of ending their days as bureaucratic ciphers.

Lastly, the mythic Crockett epitomized the liminality of the social and economic inferior. He is presented in the garb of poverty and in the traditional trappings of the lower orders. He is unwashed, uneducated, ungrammatical. He lives in a hovel. He and his family wear animal skins, are illiterate, drink, and curse. His father is Irish, ostensibly the Scots Irish of the frontier, but the word also raises the aura of later Catholic immigrants to Boston and New York. Crockett, as signifier, absorbs the personnel of the literal backwoodsmen of Appalachia never to be fully integrated by canals and railroads into a capitalist world market; the boatmen of the Western rivers, furiously autonomous yet ultimately to be submerged by Eastern transportation corporations—even the newly emergent and much-feared young men of the urban working classes, without skills, often organized in gangs.

Thus Crockett fuses the antistructural and chaotic power of three liminalities; his unnatural violence gives voice to this confluence of the unstructured forces that prevailed in American society at this point in the process of social and economic change and which appeared to violate all of society's traditional restraints and categories.

But at all times we must remember that this is only a joke, a tall tale, Southwestern humor. The Crockett myth is a play on credulity. Its frame is the comic almanac; its fabled hero, the Trickster and the Fool. As Crockett announces in the introduction to the first Crockett almanac: "As a plain matter-of-fact, I will convince them [the readers] that I can run faster,—jump higher,—squat lower,—dive deeper,—stay longer under,— and come out drier than any other man in the whole country."[28] In other words, Davy Crockett has set out to present as "possible" what author and audience both know is impossible. Both author and audience, that is, choose to enter, for the sake of humor, a world of illusion and distortion. Interestingly, Roland Barthes argues that the object of the author and the audience of a bourgeois myth is similar—to play with language with the object of making what is unnatural (that is, political or contrived) seem natural and inevitable.[29] The joke and the myth are both concerned with illusion and distortion. The one assumes a heroic, the other a comic form.

Why did Jacksonian men choose the joke as the mythic form through which to glorify change and individualism? To answer that question we must explore the meaning and the function of the joke. For Mary Douglas the essence of humor is the confrontation between a system of social control and those who are controlled, in which the controlled overthrow order. The object of the joke is to challenge or undermine hierarchy. "All jokes," Douglas claims, "have . . . [a] subversive effect on the dominant structure of ideas." Douglas counterposes the joke and the ritual. Both must be seen as culture-specific artifacts. The ritual, she argues, "is enacted to express what ought to happen. . . . [It] imposes order and harmony while jokes disorganize. . . . The message of a standard rite is that the ordained patterns of social life are inescapable. The message of the joke is that they are escapable."[30]

Scatology forms an essential part of comic inversion. Dirt, like humor, is an "expression of undifferentiated, unorganized, uncontrollable relations." Dirt, obscenity, and humor epitomize disorder. Dirt and obscenity thus become the ideal affective components of the joke. All three are, as well, cultural constructs, meaningful only within specific social-structural contexts. Something is experienced as dirty, obscene, or funny because it challenges or reverses a particular cultural conformation.[31]

As both scatology and joke the Crockett myth symbolically inverts not only the fantasies of the male moral reformers but the early-nineteenth-century bourgeois social norms as well. The Crockett myth flourished during the very years when the bourgeoisie was struggling to legitimize itself as the country's dominant class and to establish itself as socially, as well as economically, distinct from and superior to the new working class. To do so it created a mythic system built around a multitude of rigid social rules that regulated every aspect of life, from speech through clothes, food, and etiquette to sexual behavior. The myth praised cleanliness, order, and sexual repression; it condemned dirt, disorder, and uncontrolled sexuality. Crockett—dirty, drunken, and sexual—humorously challenged this myth. Outside class boundaries and the proprieties of dressing and dining, elaborately violating the grammatical proprieties so dear to the bourgeois heart, Crockett denied the naturalness, the desirability, and the inevitability of bourgeois values and class distinctions.

The almanacs constantly and overtly lampooned Eastern affectation and New England commercial astuteness and ambition. The New England peddler always appeared as a ludicrous character who is tricked and finally banished by resourceful frontier women and men. Eastern reformers, especially Quakers and male moral reformers, were even more harshly depicted. Evangelical ministers are afraid of Western women, chased by bears, frightened by owls. Temperance advocates and schoolteachers are the butt of countless jokes, as are a number of the other emerging bourgeois professions. All are depicted as fleeing a West too wild and frightening for them.[32]

The women of Crockett's frontier parody the gentility of their Eastern sisters. Certainly the almanacs lampoon the bourgeois woman's growing obsession with the etiquette of dress. Colonel Coon's wife, Judy, for example, "wore a bearskin petticoat, an alligator's hide for an overcoat, an eagle's nest for a hat with a wild cat's tail for a feather. . . . [She] sucked forty rattlesnake's eggs . . . to give her sweet breath the night she was married."[33] Davy Crockett's wife kept a pet bear in her dressing room to scratch her back, and, as we have seen, an Indian scalp on a stick to chase flies from the dining table.[34]

Significantly, the bourgeois family emerged as the institution most frequently lampooned in the Crockett almanacs. We have seen the ways in which young Western men and women violated generational and sexual proprieties in courtship and marriage.[35] Their refusal to adhere to gender-role stereotypes also undercut values and arrangements central to the maintenance of the bourgeois family. The wild women of the West systematically violated the system of rigid proprieties which the Cult of True Womanhood imposed upon bourgeois women. They drank, toted guns, wielded knives, killed or tamed animals, and defended their beaux and husbands when the men were attacked by wild animals or other wild men. The women were ugly, boisterous, and autonomous. They were not sexually repressed.[36]

Indeed, they freely agreed to bundle with men they met in the woods, and assumed in their own right mythic sexual qualities that far exceeded those of the loose young men. In one such episode, Davy Crockett, after a vigorous day hunting and killing wild animals, fell asleep in the woods, his head against a tree. While he slept his head became wedged in the crotch of the tree he leaned against. He woke up to find his head held as in a vise and eagles pulling out his hair to build their nests with. His pain, he reported, was excruciating. Then, suddenly, a beautiful young woman walked into the clearing and asked if he needed help. Crockett described her as a powerful woman. "She was a strapper. She was as tall as a sapling and had an arm like a keel boat's tiller." Crockett explained his predicament and the young woman took charge. First she screamed so loud she frightened the eagles away. Then she climbed the tree to release the captive Crockett. "She . . . spanned her legs over my head like a rainbow," Crockett reported, "she put one foot against one side of the crotch and the other foot against the other, and pushed as hard as she could. I was always as modest as an unweaned calf, but I could not help looking up as my head was held in one position. But I soon felt the limbs begin to loosen, and then I jerked out my head." Upon being released, Crockett asked the young woman, who remains nameless throughout the episode, to bundle with him. She informed him that although she could never consider marrying him while her father lived, she would bundle with him—at her father's house. On the way home, her garter snaps. A modern frontier virgin, she picked up a rattlesnake from his nest, knocked out his brains with a stone, and tied him around her leg as a garter. "She said," Crockett continued, "she could not play on the piano nor sing like a nightingale, but she could outscream a catamount and jump over her own shadow."

When they reached her father's home, the young woman took off all her clothing except her petticoat. The petticoat, however, in classic fairy-tale style, was made of "brier bushes woven together." "I could not come near her without getting stung most ridiculous." Crockett confessed, "I would as soon have embraced a hedgehog." He fled, leaving his raccoon cap behind.[37]

Central to this mythic buffoonery was Crockett's obsession with sexuality, especially sexuality that was oral, exhibitionistic, violent, and nonreproductive—sexuality that avoided fathers or became impotent in their presence. He challenged not only bourgeois morality in general, but, more specifically within our mythic dialogue, the elaborate purity classification system of the male moral reformers, for whom liquor, meat, and sex, especially masturbation, symbolized the destructive aspects of social change, and who tied sexuality to reproduction and fatherhood. Crockett, in his classic role as ritual Joker and Trickster, violated each taboo. For Crockett, hunting and drinking were intricately related; masturbation, the anathema of the male moral reformers, was frequently if covertly referred to. Rather than being polluted and weakened by each violation, as we have already seen, Crockett only gained in power. One night, for instance, Crockett, alone in the forest after slaughtering a vicious bear, feared he might freeze to death. "I thought I would do the best I could do to save my life," he reported, "so I went to a tree about two feet threw and not a limb on it for thirty feet, and would climb up to the limbs and then locking my arms and legs together around it, and slide down to the bottom again. This would make the inside of my legs and arms feel mighty warm and good."[38]

The scenario is repeated in several other episodes, as when a freezing Crockett "commenced flapping an old oak tree . . . with my arms til the fire flew and bark began to smoke an crack again. . . ."[39]

Sex and violence are intertwined. Such veiled masturbation scenes always preceded or followed violent fights with animals. A strong link also existed between physical and sexual violence. Indeed, sadism emerged as a powerful theme in the Crockett almanacs. A battle with two wildcats, for example, revolved around dismemberment and brutality. "I scalped an old he wild cat . . . clear down to his neck," Crockett reported,

and made a nice cap which I put on my head, as a sign of victory and defiance o' the hull wild puss nation. . . . Well, . . . the arnel

Wild Puss Chief . . . seeing the head and scalp of one of his relatives stuck fresh and bloody on the top of my oak knot, he pointed at it unhowled . . . while I patted the pusses top knot and grinned all sorts of tantilization at him. At me he came; and into him I went; and the way we hugged and gouged, made the old tree smoke and shake again; . . . I grabbed him by the neck like any other puss, and squeezed it into dislocation, kicked his back bone of o' jint and . . . split his brains out. . . .[40]

The animals in these episodes are almost always male and raise the issue of thinly veiled male homosexuality. In an 1846 almanac, for example, Crockett described taming a beautiful wild stallion.

I grabbed him by the scuff of the mane, jerked him down instantly and mounted him slick as a cow bird on the back of a brindle bull. I then locked my feet under him, tight as a belly band, and off we put . . . a little bit faster than express lightening. So jest as we cum to Mad Creek, boilen an hissen hot, the tarnal critter tried to . . . brush me off, but I pull his head . . . give him a kick in the flank and made him jump clear over it. . . . After that he laid right down, and grunted the perfect cart-horse submission an tameness.[41]

Some of these incidents involved not simply male animals but actual men, as when Crockett engaged in a bitter struggle with a stagecoach driver.

Says I, take care how I lite on you, upon that I jumped right down upon the driver and he tore my trowsers right off me. I was driven almost distracted and should have been used up, but luckily there was a poker in the fire which I thrust down his throat, and by that means mastered him. Says he, stranger you are the yellow flower of the forest. If you are ever up for Congress I'll come all the way to Duck river . . . for you. . . .[42]

Along the Crockett frontier, male sexuality was violent, nonreproductive, usually nongenital, and frequently homosexual. Most significantly, it was emphatically not related to the family. On one level, it symbolized the loose young man and young woman, at the height of their liminality. On another level, it inverted repressive bourgeois heterosexuality, the bourgeois family, and bourgeois social order.[43]

But in the end Crockett is a Trickster, the Crockett myth a joke. A joke is not serious. The function of humor is to challenge order but not to overthrow it. Humor is possible only because author and audience are secure in the knowledge that the social order is not endangered. As Mary Douglas points out: "The joke merely affords the opportunity for realizing that an accepted pattern has no necessity. Its excitement lies in the suggestion that any particular ordering of experience may be arbitrary and subjective. It is frivolous in that it produces *no real alternative,* only an exhilarating sense of freedom from form in general."[44] The frontier will not replace bourgeois propriety, except within the covers of the Crockett almanacs. Crockett's smoking logs, his wild horses and wrestling matches are humorous. And in that sense they are not really obscene. Obscenity offends as well as challenges propriety. Obscenity is serious because it attacks social arrangements perceived as too sacred or fragile to sustain a challenge.[45] But bourgeois sexual proprieties, heterosexual marriage, and the family—while relatively new institutions—were not fragile or in danger in the 1830s and 1840s. Too many economic and political forces sustained them. With each year these institutions steadily gained in power as agents of social control. Crockett, the stage driver, Judy Coon, could lampoon them but not endanger them. In the end Crockett's violence and sexual encounters were only good clean fun.

But here lies the final irony and the real meaning of the Crockett myth. This paean to the free individual, to American society loosed from the restraints of traditional mercantilism and the hierarchical values of the eighteenth century did indeed offer only "an exhilarating sense of freedom from form in general." It was formulated at the very time when institutions in the service of commercial and industrial capitalism and, often, with the specific purpose of socializing and controlling the youthful population, first proliferated. At the very time that the Crockett myth praised the young man beyond institutional boundaries, formal institutions, indeed state institutions, had increasingly begun to replace the informal and domestic modes of social control which had characterized traditional eighteenth-century society. America had never been so mythically free and so actually institutionalized.

The Crockett myth offered the young men of Jacksonian America a fabled frontier, not economic power. Davy Crockett mythologized the death of the old patriarchal social order. He did not describe it. Within the myth, angry adolescents revolted against the father. In reality impersonal economic forces eroded father-son unity and sent young men off alone into a frightening world. The Crockett myth distorted the actual disappearance of the old order just as it denied the reality of the new institutionally differentiated industrial world. This, it has been argued, is the precise purpose of bourgeois myth—to deny the existence of the bourgeoisie as a distinct economic and political class—to depict what is class-specific as timeless and universal.[46] Nationalism is brought to overlay the bourgeoisie like a mythic mask—denying the economic man under the mask at the same time as it disavows all who do not wear the mask.

At its most basic level of meaning, then, Crockett presents the mythic origins of the American bourgeoisie. The Crockett myth, by asserting that youthful autonomy toppled the old order, denied both the economic and political factors that gave birth to the bourgeoisie and the economic and political realities of the social order the bourgeoisie established to perpetuate its hegemony. By glorifying anti-structure and youth, the Crockett myth succeeds in obscuring the reality of social class. It substitutes nationalism for economic and historical reality. At its very moment of birth, that is, the American bourgeoisie sought to distort and obscure its nature—to drain from its name all economic significance.

What emerges from the Crockett myth as natural, timeless, and inescapable is not capitalism and the bourgeoisie but young male violence —violence directed toward women but more overtly toward the inhabitants of the wilderness—toward Indians, Mexicans, and escaped slaves. Racism is central to the Crockett myth—a racism whose objective is to justify barbarism and cannibalism against nonwhites. The Crockett myth offered young Jacksonian men neither real institutional or economic autonomy nor an understanding of the economic events that shaped their lives. Rather, it offered them an outlet for hostility and frustration in the violence of jingoism and racism, which it defined as the natural characteristic of the young white American male.

Beauty, the Beast, and the Militant Woman: A Case Study in Sex Roles and Social Stress in Jacksonian America

On an evening in May 1834, a small group of women met at the revivalistic Third Presbyterian Church in New York City to found the New York Female Moral Reform Society. The Society's goals were ambitious indeed; it hoped to convert New York's prostitutes to evangelical Protestantism and close forever the city's numerous brothels. This bold attack on prostitution was only one part of the Society's program. These self-assertive women hoped as well to confront that larger and more fundamental abuse, the double standard, and the male sexual license it condoned. Too many men, the Society defiantly asserted in its statement of goals, were aggressive destroyers of female innocence and happiness. No man was above suspicion. Women's only safety lay in a militant effort to reform American sexual mores—and, as we shall see, to reform sexual mores meant in practice to control men's sexual values and autonomy. The rhetoric of the Society's spokesmen consistently betrayed an unmistakable and deeply felt resentment toward a male-dominated society.[1]

Few if any members of the Society were reformed prostitutes or the victims of rape or seduction. Most came from middle-class native-born American backgrounds and lived quietly respectable lives as pious wives and mothers. What needs explaining is the emotional logic which underlay the Society's militant and controversial program of sexual reform.

I would like to suggest that some nineteenth-century women channeled their frustration with women's restricted roles combined with a sense of superior righteousness legitimized by the Cult of True Womanhood into the reform movements of the first half of the nineteenth century; and in the controversial moral-reform crusade such motivations seem particularly apparent. While unassailable within the absolute categories of a pervasive evangelical world view, the Female Moral Reform Society's crusade against illicit sexuality permitted an expression of antimale sentiments. And the Society's "final solution"—the right to control the mores of men—provided a logical emotional redress for the feelings of passivity the Cult of True Womanhood enjoined on Victorian matrons. It should not be surprising that between 1830 and 1860 a significant number of militant women joined a crusade to establish their right to define—and limit—men's sexual behavior.

Yet adultery and prostitution were unaccustomed objects of reform, even in the enthusiastic and millennial America of the 1830s. The mere discussion of these taboo subjects shocked most Americans; to undertake such a crusade implied no ordinary degree of commitment. The founders of the Female Moral Reform Society, however, were able to find both legitimization for the expression of grievance that normally went unspoken, and an impulse to activism in the moral categories of evangelical piety. Both pious activism and sex-role anxieties shaped the early years of the Female Moral Reform Society. This conjunction of motives was hardly accidental.

The lady founders of the Moral Reform Society and their new organization represented an extreme wing of that movement within American Protestantism known as the Second Great Awakening. These women were intensely pious Christians, convinced that an era of millennial perfection awaited human effort. In this fervent generation, such deeply felt millennial possibilities made social action a moral imperative. Like many of the abolitionists, Jacksonian crusaders against sexual transgression were dedicated activists, compelled to attack sin wherever it existed and in whatever form it assumed—even the unmentionable sin of illicit sexuality.

New Yorkers' first awareness of the moral-reform crusade came in the spring of 1832, when the New York Magdalen Society (an organization that sought to reform prostitutes) issued its first annual report. Written by John McDowall, their missionary and agent, the report stated unhesitatingly that ten thousand prostitutes lived and worked in New York City. Not only sailors and other transients, but men from the city's most respected families were regular brothel patrons. Lewdness and impurity tainted all sectors of New York society. True Christians, the report concluded, must wage a thoroughgoing crusade against violators of the Seventh Commandment.[2]

The report shocked and irritated respectable New Yorkers—not only by its tone of righteous indignation and implied criticism of the city's old and established families. The report, it seemed clear to many New Yorkers, was obscene, its author a mere seeker after notoriety.[3] Hostility quickly spread from McDowall to the Society itself; its members were verbally abused and threatened with ostracism. The Society disbanded.

A few of the women, however, would not retreat. Working quietly, they began to found church-affiliated female moral-reform societies. Within a year, they had created a number of such groups, connected for the most part with the city's more evangelical congregations. These pious women hoped to reform prostitutes, but more immediately to warn other God-fearing Christians of the pervasiveness of sexual sin and the need to oppose it. Prostitution was, after all, only one of many offenses against the Seventh Commandment; adultery, lewd thoughts and language, and bawdy literature were equally sinful in the eyes of God. These women, at the same time, continued unofficially to support their former missionary, John McDowall, using his newly established moral-reform newspaper to advance their cause, not only in the city but throughout New York State.[4]

After more than a year of such discreet crusading, the women active in the moral-reform cause felt sufficiently numerous and confident to organize a second citywide moral-reform society, and renew their efforts to reform the city's prostitutes. Thus it was that, on the evening of May 12, 1834, they met to found the New York Female Moral Reform Society.[5]

Nearly four years of opposition and controversy had hardened the women's ardor into a militant determination. They proposed through their organization to extirpate sexual license and the double standard from American society. A forthright list of resolves announced their organization:

> Resolved, That immediate and vigorous efforts should be made to create a public sentiment in respect to this sin; and also in respect to the duty of parents, church members and ministers on the subject, which shall be in stricter accordance with . . . the word of God. . . .
> Resolved, That the licentious man is no less guilty than his

victim, and ought, therefore, to be excluded from all virtuous female society.

Resolved, That it is the imperious duty of ladies everywhere, and of every religious denomination, to co-operate in the great work of moral reform.

A sense of urgency and spiritual absolutism marked this organizational meeting, and, indeed, all of the Society's official statements for years to come. "It is the duty of the virtuous to use every consistent moral means to save our country from utter destruction," the women warned. "The sin of licentiousness has made fearful havoc . . . drowning souls in perdition and exposing us to the vengeance of a holy God." Americans hopeful of witnessing the promised millennium could delay no longer.[6]

The motivating zeal which allowed the rejection of age-old proprieties and defied the criticism of pulpit and press was no casual and fashionable enthusiasm. Only an extraordinary set of legitimizing values could have justified such commitment. And this was indeed the case. The women moral reformers acted in the conscious conviction that God imperiously commanded their work. As they explained soon after organizing their Society: "As Christians we must view it in the light of God's word—we must enter into His feelings on the subject—engage in its overthrow just in the manner he would have us. . . . We must look away from all worldly opinions or influences, for they are perverted and wrong; and individually act only as in the presence of God."[7]

Though the Society's pious activism had deep roots in the evangelicalism of the Second Great Awakening, the immediate impetus for the founding of the Moral Reform Society came from the revivals Charles G. Finney conducted in New York City between the summer of 1829 and the spring of 1834.[8]

Charles Finney, reformer, revivalist, and Perfectionist theologian from western New York State, remains a pivotal figure in the history of American Protestantism. The four years Finney spent in New York had a profound influence on the city's churches and reform movements, and upon the consciences generally of the thousands of New Yorkers who crowded his revival meetings and flocked to his churches. Finney insisted that his disciples end any compromise with sin or human injustice. Souls were lost and sin prevailed, Finney urged, because men chose to sin—

because they chose not to work in God's vineyard, converting souls and reforming sinners.[9] Inspired by Finney's sermons, thousands of New Yorkers turned to missionary work; they distributed Bibles and tracts to the irreligious, established Sunday schools, and sent ministers to the frontier.[10] A smaller, more zealous number espoused abolition as well, determined, like Garrison, never to be silent and to be heard. An even smaller number of the most zealous and determined turned—as we have seen—to moral reform.[11]

The program adopted by the Female Moral Reform Society in the spring of 1834 embraced two quite different, though to the Society's founders quite consistent, modes of attack. One was absolutist and millennial, an attempt to convert all of America to perfect moral purity. Concretely, the New York women hoped to create a militant nationwide women's organization to fight the double standard and, indeed, any form of licentiousness —beginning, of course, in their own homes and neighborhoods. Only an organization of women, they contended, could be trusted with so sensitive and yet monumental a task. At the same time, the Society sponsored a parallel and somewhat more pragmatic attempt to convert and reform New York City's prostitutes. Though strikingly dissimilar in method and geographic scope, both efforts were unified by an uncompromising millennial zeal and by a strident hostility to the licentious and predatory male.

The Society began its renewed drive against prostitution in the fall of 1834, when the executive committee appointed John McDowall their missionary to New York's prostitutes and hired two young men to assist him.[12] The Society's three missionaries visited the female wards of the almshouse, the city hospital and jails, leading prayer meetings, distributing Bibles and tracts. A greater proportion of their time, however, was spent in a more controversial manner, systematically visiting—or, to be more accurate, descending upon—brothels, praying with and exhorting both the inmates and their patrons. The missionaries were especially fond of arriving early Sunday morning—catching women and customers as they awoke on the traditionally sacred day. The missionaries would announce their arrival by a vigorous reading of Bible passages, followed by prayer and hymns. At other times they would station themselves across the street from known brothels to observe and note the identity of customers. They soon found their simple presence had an important deterring effect, many men, with doggedly innocent expressions, pausing momentarily and then hastily walking past. Closed coaches, they also reported, were observed to circle suspiciously for upward of an hour until, the missionary remaining, they drove away.[13]

The Female Moral Reform Society did not depend completely on paid missionaries for the success of such pious harassment. The Society's executive committee, accompanied by like-thinking male volunteers, regularly visited the city's hapless brothels. (The executive-committee minutes for January 1835, for example, contain a lengthy discussion of the properly discreet makeup of groups for such "active visiting."[14]) The members went primarily to pray and to exert moral influence. They were not unaware, however, of the financially disruptive effect that frequent visits of large groups of praying Christians would have.[15] The executive committee also aided the concerned parents (usually rural) of runaway daughters who, they feared, might have drifted to the city and been forced into prostitution. Members visited brothels asking for information about such girls; one pious volunteer even pretended to be delivering laundry in order to gain admittance to a brothel suspected of hiding a runaway.[16]

In conjunction with their visiting, the Moral Reform Society opened a House of Reception, a would-be refuge for prostitutes seeking to reform. The Society's managers and missionaries felt that if the prostitute could be convinced of her sin, and then offered both a place of retreat and an economic alternative to prostitution, reform would surely follow. Thus they envisioned their home as a "house of industry" where the errant ones would be taught new trades and prepared for useful jobs—while being instructed in morality and religion. When the managers felt their repentant charges were prepared to return to society, they attempted to find them jobs with Christian families—and, so far as possible, away from the city's temptations.[17]

Despite their efforts, however, few prostitutes reformed; fewer still appeared, to their benefactresses, to have experienced the saving grace of conversion. Indeed, the number of inmates at the Society's House of Reception was always small. In March 1835, for instance, the executive committee reported only fourteen women at the house. A year later, total admissions had reached but thirty—only four of whom were considered saved.[18] The final debacle came that summer, when the regular manager of the house left the city because of poor health. In his absence, the executive committee reported unhappily, the inmates seized control, and discipline and morality deteriorated precipitously. The managers reassembled in the fall to find their home in chaos. Bitterly discouraged, they dismissed the few remaining unruly inmates and closed the building.[19]

The moral rehabilitation of New York's streetwalkers was but one aspect of the Society's attack upon immorality. The founders of the Female Moral Reform Society saw as their principal objective the creation of a woman's crusade to combat sexual license generally and the double standard particularly. American women would no longer willingly tolerate that traditional —and role-defining—masculine ethos which allotted respect to the hearty drinker and the sexual athlete. This age-old code of masculinity was as obviously related to man's social pre-eminence as it was contrary to society's explicitly avowed norms of purity and domesticity. The subterranean mores of the American male must be confronted, exposed, and rooted out.

The principal weapon of the Society in this crusade was its weekly, *The Advocate of Moral Reform.* In the fall of 1834, when the Society hired John McDowall as its agent, it voted as well to purchase his journal and transform it into a national women's paper with an exclusively female staff. Within three years, *The Advocate* grew into one of the nation's most widely read evangelical papers, boasting 16,500 subscribers. By the late 1830s the Society's managers pointed to this publication as their most important activity.[20]

Two themes dominated virtually every issue of *The Advocate* from its founding in January 1835 until the early 1850s. The first was an angry and emphatic insistence upon the lascivious and predatory nature of the American male. Men were the initiators in virtually every case of adultery or fornication—and the source, therefore, of that widespread immorality which endangered America's spiritual life and delayed the promised millennium. A second major theme in *The Advocate*'s editorials and letters was a call for the creation of a national union of women. Through their collective action such a united group of women might ultimately control the behavior of adult males and of the members' own children, particularly their sons.

The founders and supporters of the Female Moral Reform Society entertained several primary assumptions concerning the nature of human sexuality. Perhaps most central was the conviction that women felt little sexual desire; they were in almost every instance induced to violate the Seventh Commandment by lascivious men who craftily manipulated not their sensuality but, rather, the female's trusting and affectionate nature. A woman acted out of romantic love, not carnal desire; she was innocent and defenseless, gentle and passive.[21] "The worst crime alleged against [the fallen woman] in the outset," *The Advocate*'s editors explained, "is . . . 'She is without discretion.' She is open-hearted, sincere, and affectionate. . . . She trusts the vows of the faithless. She commits her all into the hands of the deceiver."[22]

The male lecher, on the other hand, was a creature controlled by base sexual drives which he neither could nor would control. He was, *The Advocate*'s editors bitterly complained, powerful and decisive; unwilling (possibly unable) to curb his own willfulness, he callously used it to coerce the more passive and submissive female. This was an age of rhetorical expansiveness, and *The Advocate*'s editors and correspondents felt little constraint in their delineation of the dominant and aggressive male. "Reckless," "bold," "mad," "drenched in sin" were terms used commonly to describe erring males; they "robbed," "ruined," and "rioted." But one term above all others seemed most fit to describe the lecher—"The Destroyer."[23]

A deep sense of anger and frustration characterized *The Advocate*'s discussion of such all-conquering males, a theme reiterated again and again in the letters sent to the paper by rural sympathizers. Women saw themselves as having few defenses against the determined male; his will was far stronger than that of woman.[24] Such letters often expressed a bitterness that seems directed not only against the specific seducer, but against all American men. One representative rural subscriber complained, for example: "Honorable men; they would not plunder; . . . an imputation on their honour might cost a man his life's blood. And yet they are so passingly mean, so utterly contemptible, as basely and treacherously to contrive . . . the destruction of happiness, peace, morality, and all that is endearing in social life; they plunge into degradation, misery, and ruin, those whom they profess to love. O let them not be trusted. Their 'tender mercies are cruel.' "[25]

The double standard seemed thus particularly unjust; it came to symbolize and embody for the Society and its rural sympathizers the callous indifference—indeed, at times almost sadistic pleasure—a male-dominated society took in the misfortune of a passive and defenseless woman. The respectable harshly denied her their friendship; even parents might reject her. Often only the brothel offered food and shelter. But what of her seducer? Conventional wisdom found it easy to condone his greater sin: men will be men, and right-thinking women must not inquire into such matters.[26]

But it was just such matters, the Society contended, to which women must address themselves. They must enforce God's commandments, despite hostility and censure. "Public opinion must be operated upon," the executive committee decided in the winter of 1835, "by endeavoring to bring the virtuous to treat the guilty of both sexes alike, and exercise toward them the same feeling." "Why should a female be trodden under foot," the executive committee's minutes questioned plaintively, "and spurned from society and driven from a parent's roof, if she but fall into sin—while common consent allows the male to habituate himself to this vice, and treats him as not guilty. Has God made a distinction in regard to the two sexes in this respect?"[27] The guilty woman too should be condemned, the Moral Reform Society's quarterly meeting resolved in 1838: "But let not the most guilty of the two—the deliberate destroyer of female innocence —be afforded even an 'apron of fig leaves' to conceal the blackness of his crimes."[28]

Women must unite in a holy crusade against such sinners. The Society called upon pious women throughout the country to shun all social contact with men suspected of improper behavior—even if that behavior consisted only of reading improper books or singing indelicate songs. Churchgoing women of every village and town must organize local campaigns to outlaw such men from society and hold them up to public judgment.[29] "Admit him not to your house," the executive committee urged, "hold no converse with him, warn others of him, permit not your friends to have fellowship with him, mark him as an evildoer, stamp him as a villain and exclaim, 'Behold the Seducer.' "[30] The power of ostracism could become an effective weapon in the defense of morality.

A key tactic in this campaign of public exposure was the Society's willingness to publish the names of men suspected of sexual immorality. *The Advocate*'s editors announced in their first issue that they intended to pursue this policy, first begun by John McDowall in his *Journal.*[31] "We think it proper," they stated defiantly, "even to expose names, for the same reason that the names of thieves and robbers are published, that the public may know them and govern themselves accordingly. We mean to let the licentious know, that if they are not ashamed of their debasing vice, we will not be ashamed to expose them. . . . It is a justice which we owe each other."[32] Their readers responded enthusiastically to this invitation. Letters from rural subscribers poured in to *The Advocate,* recounting specific instances of seduction in their towns and warning readers to avoid the men described. The editors dutifully set them in type and printed them.[33]

Within New York City itself the executive committee of the Society actively investigated charges of seduction and immorality. A particular target of their watchfulness was the city's employment agencies—or information offices, as they were then called; these were frequently fronts for the white-slave trade. *The Advocate* printed the names and addresses of suspicious agencies, warning women seeking employment to avoid them at all costs.[34] Prostitutes whom the Society's missionaries visited in brothels, in prison, or in the city hospital were urged to report the names of the men who had first seduced them and also of their later customers; they could then be published in *The Advocate.* [35] The executive committee undertook as well a lobbying campaign in Albany to secure the passage of a statute making seduction a crime for the male participant.[36] While awaiting the passage of this measure, the executive committee encouraged and aided victims of seduction (or, where appropriate, their parents or employers) to sue their seducers, on the grounds of loss of services.[37]

Ostracism, exposure, and statutory enactment offered immediate, if unfortunately partial, solutions to the problem of male licentiousness. But for the seduced and ruined victim such vengeance came too late. The tactic of preference, women moral reformers agreed, was to educate children, especially young male children, to a literal adherence to the Seventh Commandment. This was a mother's task. American mothers, *The Advocate*'s editors repeated endlessly, must educate their sons to reject the double standard. No child was too young, no efforts were too diligent in this crucial aspect of socialization.[38] The true foundations of such a successful effort lay in an early and highly pietistic religious education, and in the inculcation of a related imperative—the son's absolute and unquestioned obedience to his mother's will. "Obedience, entire and unquestioned, must be secured, or all is lost." The mother must devote herself wholeheartedly to this task, for self-will in a child was an ever-recurring evil.[39] "Let us watch over them continually. . . . Let us . . . teach them when they go out and when they come in—when they lie down, and when they rise up. . . ."[40] A son must learn to confide in his mother instinctively; no thought should be hidden from her.

Explicit education in the Seventh Commandment itself should begin quite early, for bitter experience had shown that no child was too young for sensual temptation.[41] As her son grew older, his mother was urged to instill in him a love for the quiet of domesticity, a repugnance for the unnatural excitements of the theater and tavern. He should be taught to prefer home and the companionship of pious women to the temptations of bachelor life.[42] The final step in a young man's moral education would come one evening shortly before he was to leave home for the first time. That night, *The Advocate* advised its readers, the mother must spend a long, earnest time at his bedside (ordinarily in the dark, to hide her natural blushes) discussing the importance of maintaining his sexual purity and the temptations he would inevitably face in attempting to remain true to his mother's religious principles.[43]

Mothers, not fathers, were urged to supervise the sexual education of sons. Mothers, the Society argued, spent most time with their children; fathers were usually occupied with business concerns and found little time for their children. Sons were naturally close to their mothers and devoted maternal supervision would cement these natural ties. A mother devoted to the moral-reform cause could be trusted to teach her son to reject the traditional ethos of masculinity and accept the higher—more feminine—code of Christianity. A son thus educated would be inevitably a recruit in the women's crusade against sexual license.[44]

The Society's general program of exposure and ostracism, lobbying and education depended for effectiveness upon the creation of a national association of militant and pious women. In the fall of 1834, but a few months after they had organized their Society, its New York officers began to create such a women's organization. At first they worked through *The Advocate* and the small network of sympathizers John McDowall's efforts had created. By the spring of 1835, however, they were able to hire a minister to travel through western New York State "in behalf of Moral Reform causes."[45] The following year the committee sent two female missionaries, the editor of the Society's newspaper, and a paid female agent on a thousand-mile tour of the New England states. Visiting women's groups and churches in Brattleboro, Deerfield, Northampton, Pittsfield, the Stockbridges, and many other towns, the ladies rallied their sisters to the moral-reform cause and helped organize some forty-one new auxiliaries. Succeeding summers saw similar trips by paid agents and managers of the Society throughout New York State and New England.[46] By 1839, the New York Female Moral Reform Society boasted some 445 female auxiliaries, principally in Greater New England.[47] So successful were these efforts that within a few years the bulk of the Society's membership and financial support came from its auxiliaries. In February 1838, the executive committee voted to invite representatives of these auxiliaries to attend the Society's annual meeting. The following year the New York Society voted at its annual convention to reorganize as a national society—the American Female Moral Reform Society; the New York group would be simply one of its many constituent societies.[48]

This rural support was an indispensable part of the moral-reform movement. The local auxiliaries held regular meetings in churches, persuaded hesitant ministers to preach on the Seventh Commandment, urged Sunday-school teachers to confront this embarrassing but vital question. They raised money for the executive committee's ambitious projects, convinced at least some men to form male moral-reform societies, and did their utmost to ostracize suspected lechers. When the American Female Moral Reform Society decided to mount a campaign to induce the New York State legislature to pass a law making seduction a criminal offense, the Society's hundreds of rural auxiliaries wrote regularly to their legislators, circulated petitions, and joined their New York City sisters in Albany to lobby for the bill (which was finally passed in 1848).[49]

In addition to such financial and practical aid, members of the moral-reform society's rural branches contributed another crucial, if less tangible, element to the reform movement. This was their commitment to the creation of a feeling of sisterhood among all morally dedicated women. Letters from individuals to *The Advocate* and reports from auxiliaries make clear, sometimes even in the most explicit terms, that many American women experienced a depressing sense of isolation. In part, this feeling merely reflected a physical reality for women living in rural communities. But since city- and town-dwelling women voiced similar complaints, I would like to suggest that this consciousness of isolation also reflected a sense of status inferiority. Confined by their nonmaleness, antebellum American women lived within the concentric structure of a family organized around the needs and status of husbands or fathers. And such social isolation within the family—or, perhaps more accurately, a lack of autonomy both embodied in and symbolized by such isolation—not only dramatized, but partially constituted, a differentiation in status.[50] The fact that social values and attitudes were established by men and oriented to male experiences only exacerbated women's feelings of inferiority and irrelevance. Again and again the Society's members were to express their desire for a feminine-sororial community which might help break down this isolation, lighten the monotony and harshness of life, and establish a countersystem of female values and priorities.

The New York Female Moral Reform Society quite consciously sought to inspire in its members a sense of solidarity in a cause peculiar to their sex, and demanding total commitment, to give them a sense of worthiness and autonomy outside woman's traditionally confining role. Its members, their officers forcefully declared, formed a united phalanx twenty thousand strong, "A UNION OF SENTIMENT AND EFFORT AMONG ... VIRTUOUS FEMALES FROM MAINE TO ALABAMA."[51] The officers of the New York Society were particularly conscious of the emotional importance of female solidarity within their movement—and the significant role that they as leaders played in the lives of their rural supporters. "Thousands are looking to us," the executive committee recorded in their minutes with mingled pride and responsibility, "with the expectation that the principles we have adopted, and the example we have set before the world will continue to be held up & they reasonably expect to witness our *united onward* movements till the conflict shall end in Victory."[52]

For many of the Society's scattered members, the moral-reform cause was their only contact with the world outside farm or village—*The Advocate* perhaps the only newspaper received by the family.[53] A sense of solidarity and of emotional affiliation permeated the correspondence between rural members and the executive committee. Letters and even official reports inevitably began with the salutation "Sisters," "Dear Sisters," or "Beloved Sisters." Almost every letter and report expressed the deep affection Society members felt for their like-thinking sisters in the cause of moral reform—even if their contact came only through letters and *The*

Advocate. "I now pray and will not cease to pray," a woman in Syracuse, New York, wrote, "that your hearts may be encouraged and your hands strengthened."[54] Letters to the Society's executive committee often promised unfailing loyalty and friendship; members and leaders pledged themselves ever ready to aid either local societies or an individual sister in need.[55] Many letters from geographically isolated women reported that the Society made it possible for them for the first time to communicate with like-minded women. A few, in agitated terms, wrote about painful experiences with the double standard which only their correspondence with *The Advocate* allowed them to discuss and share.[56]

Most significantly, the letters expressed a new consciousness of power. The Moral Reform Society was based on the assertion of female moral superiority and the right and ability of women to reshape male behavior.[57] No longer did women have to remain passive and isolated within the structuring presence of husband or father. The moral-reform movement was, perhaps for the first time, a movement within which women could forge a sense of their own identity.

And its founders had no intention of relinquishing their newfound feeling of solidarity and autonomy. A few years after the Society was founded, for example, a group of male evangelicals established a Seventh Commandment Society. They promptly wrote to the Female Moral Reform Society suggesting helpfully that since men had organized, the ladies could now disband; moral reform was clearly an area of questionable propriety. The New York executive committee responded quickly, firmly —and negatively. Women throughout America, they wrote, had placed their trust in a female moral-reform society and in female officers. Women, they informed the men, believed in both their own right and their own ability to combat the problem; it was decidedly a woman's issue, not a man's.[58] "The paper is now in the right hands," one rural subscriber wrote. "This is the appropriate work for *women.* . . . Go on Ladies, go on, in the strength of the Lord."[59]

In some ways, indeed, the New York Female Moral Reform Society could be considered a militant women's organization. Although it was not overtly part of the women's-rights movement, it did concern itself with a number of feminist issues, especially those relating to women's economic role. Society, *The Advocate*'s editors argued, had unjustly confined women to domestic tasks. There were many jobs in society that women could and should be trained to fill. They could perform any light indoor work as well as men. In such positions—as clerks and artisans—they would receive decent wages and consequent self-respect.[60] And this economic emphasis was no arbitrary or inappropriate one, the Society contended. Thousands of women simply had to work; widows, orphaned young women, wives and mothers whose husbands could not work because of illness or intemperance had to support themselves and their children. Unfortunately, they had now to exercise these responsibilities on the pathetically inadequate salaries they received as domestics, washerwomen, or seamstresses—crowded, underpaid, and physically unpleasant occupations.[61] By the end of the 1840s, the Society had adopted the cause of the workingwoman and made it one of their principal concerns—in the 1850s even urging women to join unions, and, when mechanization came to the garment industry, helping underpaid seamstresses rent sewing machines at low rates.[62]

The Society sought consciously, moreover, to demonstrate women's ability to perform successfully in fields traditionally reserved for men. Quite early in their history they adopted the policy of hiring only women employees. From the first, of course, only women had been officers and managers of the Society. And after a few years, these officers began to hire women in preference to men as agents and to urge other charitable societies and government agencies to do likewise. (They did this although the only salaried charitable positions held by women in this period tended to be those of teachers in girls' schools or supervisors of women's wings in hospitals and homes for juvenile delinquents.) In February 1835, for instance, the executive committee hired a woman agent to solicit subscriptions to *The Advocate.* That summer, as we have seen, she joined two female missionaries on a tour of New England and New York State organizing auxiliaries and giving speeches to women on moral reform. In October 1836, the executive officers appointed two women as editors of their journal—undoubtedly among the first of their sex in this country to hold such positions.[63] In 1841, the executive committee decided to replace their male financial agent with a woman bookkeeper. By 1843, women even set type and did the folding for the Society's journal. All these jobs, the ladies proudly, even aggressively stressed, were appropriate tasks for women.[64]

The broad feminist implications of such statements and actions must have been apparent to the officers of the New York Society. And, indeed, the Society's executive committee maintained discreet but active ties with the broader women's-rights movement of the 1830s, 1840s, and 1850s; at one point, at least, they flirted with official endorsement of a bold women's-rights position. Evidence of this flirtation can be seen in the minutes of the executive committee and occasionally came to light in articles and editorials appearing in *The Advocate*. As early as the mid-1830s, for instance, the executive committee began to correspond with a number of women who were then or were later to become active in the women's-rights movement. Lucretia Mott, abolitionist and pioneer feminist, was a founder and secretary of the Philadelphia Female Moral Reform Society; as such she was in frequent communication with the New York executive committee.[65] Emma Willard, a militant advocate of women's education and founder of the Troy Female Seminary, was another of the executive committee's regular correspondents. Significantly, when Elizabeth Blackwell, the first woman doctor in either the United States or Great Britain, received her medical degree, Emma Willard wrote to the New York executive committee asking its members to use their influence to find her a job.[66] The Society did more than that. *The Advocate* featured a story dramatizing Dr. Blackwell's struggles. The door was now open for other women, the editors urged; medicine was a peculiarly appropriate profession for sensitive and sympathetic womankind. The Society offered to help interested women in securing admission to medical school.[67]

One of the most controversial aspects of the early women's-rights movement was its criticism of the subservient role of women within the American family, and of the American man's imperious and domineering behavior toward women. Much of the Society's rhetorical onslaught upon the male's lack of sexual accountability served as a screen for a more general —and less socially acceptable—resentment of masculine social pre-eminence. Occasionally, however, *The Advocate* expressed such resentment overtly. An editorial in 1838, for example, revealed a deeply felt antagonism toward the power asserted by husbands over their wives and children. "A portion of the inhabitants of this favored land," the Society admonished, "are groaning under a despotism, which seems to be modeled precisely after that of the Autocrat of Russia. . . . We allude to the tyranny exercised in the HOME department, where lordly man, 'clothed with a little brief authority,' rules his trembling subjects with a rod of iron, conscious of entire impunity, and exalting in his fancied superiority." The Society's editorialist continued, perhaps even more bitterly: "Instead of regarding his wife as a help-mate for him, an equal sharer in his joys and sorrows, he looks upon her as a useful article of furniture, which is valuable only for the benefit derived from it, but which may be thrown aside at pleasure."[68] Such behavior, the editorial carefully emphasized, was not only common-place, experienced by many of the Society's own members—even the wives of "Christians" and of ministers—but was accepted and even jus-tified by society; was it not sanctioned by the Bible?

At about the same time, indeed, the editors of *The Advocate* went so far as to print an attack upon "masculine" translations and interpretations of the Bible, and especially of Paul's epistles. This appeared in a lengthy article written by Sarah Grimké, a "notorious" feminist and abolitionist.[69] The executive committee clearly sought to associate their organization more closely with the nascent women's-rights movement. Calling upon American women to read and interpret the Bible for themselves, Sarah Grimké asserted that God had created woman the absolute equal of man. But throughout history, man, being stronger, had usurped woman's natural rights. He had subjected wives and daughters to his physical control and had evolved religious and scientific rationalizations to justify this domi-nation. "Men have endeavored to entice, or to drive women from almost every sphere of moral action." Miss Grimké charged: " 'Go home and spin' is the . . . advice of the domestic tyrant. . . . The first duty, I believe, which devolves on our sex now is to think for themselves. . . . Until we take our stand side by side with our brother; until we read all the precepts of the Bible as addressed to woman as well as to man, and lose . . . the conscious-ness of sex, we shall never fulfil the end of our existence." "Those who do undertake to labor," Miss Grimké wrote from her own and her sister's bitter experiences, "are the scorn and ridicule of their own and the other sex." "We are so little accustomed *to think for ourselves,*" she continued,

> that we submit to the dictum of prejudice, and of usurped authority, almost without an effort to redeem ourselves from the unhallowed shackles which have so long bound us; almost without a desire to rise from that degradation and bondage to which we have been consigned by man, and by which the faculties of our minds, and the powers of our spiritual nature, have been prevented from expanding to their full growth, and are sometimes wholly crushed.

Each woman must re-evaluate her role in society; no longer could she depend on husband or father to assume her responsibilities as a free individual. No longer, Sarah Grimké argued, could she be satisfied with simply caring for her family or setting a handsome table.[70] The officers of the Society, in an editorial comment following this article, admitted that she had written a radical critique of woman's traditional role. But they urged their members, "It is of immense importance to our sex to possess clear and *correct* ideas of our rights and duties."[71]

Sarah Grimké's overt criticism of woman's traditional role, containing as it did an attack upon the Protestant ministry and orthodox interpretations of the Bible, went far beyond the consensus of *The Advocate*'s rural subscribers. The following issue contained several letters sharply critical of her—and of the managers, for printing her editorial.[72] And, indeed, *The Advocate* never again published the work of an overt feminist. Their membership, the officers concluded, would not tolerate explicit attacks upon traditional family structure and orthodox Christianity. Antimale resentment and anger had to be expressed covertly. It was perhaps too threatening or—realistically—too dangerous for respectable matrons in relatively close-knit semi-rural communities in New York, New England, Ohio, or Wisconsin so openly to question the traditional relations of the sexes and demand a new and ominously forceful role for women.

The compromise the membership and the officers of the Society seemed to find most comfortable was one that kept the American woman in the home—but which greatly expanded her powers as pious wife and mother. In rejecting Sarah Grimké's feminist manifesto, the Society's members implicitly agreed to accept the role traditionally assigned woman: the self-sacrificing, supportive, determinedly chaste wife and mother who limited her "sphere" to domesticity and religion. But in these areas her power should be paramount. The mother, not the father, should have final control of the home and family—especially of the religious and moral education of her children. If the world of economics and public affairs was his, the home must be hers.[73]

And even outside the home, woman's peculiar moral endowment and responsibilities justified her playing an increasingly expansive role, one that might well ultimately impair aspects of man's traditional autonomy. When man transgressed God's commandments, through licentiousness, religious apathy, the defense of slavery, or the sin of intemperance—woman had both the right and the duty of leaving the confines of the home and working to purify the male world.

The membership of the New York Female Moral Reform Society chose not to espouse openly the women's-rights movement. Yet many interesting emotional parallels remain to link the moral-reform crusade and the suffrage movement of Elizabeth Cady Stanton, the Grimké sisters, and Susan B. Anthony. In its own way, indeed, the war for purification of sexual mores was far more fundamental in its implications for women's traditional role than the demand for women's education—or even the vote.

Many of the needs and attitudes, moreover, expressed by suffragette leaders at the Seneca Falls Convention, and in their efforts during the generation following, are found decades earlier in the letters of rural women in *The Advocate of Moral Reform*. Both groups found women's traditionally passive role intolerable. Both wished to assert female worth and values in a heretofore entirely male world. Both welcomed the creation of a sense of feminine loyalty and sisterhood that could give emotional strength and comfort to women isolated within their homes—whether in a remote farmstead or a Gramercy Park mansion. And it can hardly be assumed that the demand for votes for women was appreciably more radical than a moral absolutism which encouraged women to invade bordellos, befriend harlots, and publicly discuss rape, seduction, and prostitution.

It is important as well to re-emphasize a more general historical perspective. When the pious women founders of the Moral Reform Society gathered at the Third Free Presbyterian Church, it was fourteen years before the Seneca Falls Convention—which has traditionally been accepted as the beginning of the women's-rights movement in the United States. There simply was no women's movement in the 1830s. The future leaders were either still adolescents or just becoming dissatisfied with aspects of their role. Women advocates of moral reform were among the very first American women to challenge their completely passive, home-oriented image. They were among the first to travel throughout the country without male chaperons. They published, financed, even set type for their own paper, and defied a bitter and longstanding male opposition to their cause. They began, in short, to create a broader, less constricted sense of female identity. Naturally enough, they were dependent upon the activist impulse and legitimizing imperatives of evangelical religion. This was indeed a complex symbiosis, the energies of pietism and the grievances of role discontent creating the new and activist female consciousness which characterized the history of the American Female Moral Reform Society in antebellum America. Their experience, moreover, was probably shared, though less overtly, by the thousands of women who devoted time and money to the great number of reform causes that multiplied in Jacksonian America. Women in the abolition and the temperance movements (and to a lesser extent in more narrowly evangelical and religious causes) also developed a sense of their ability to judge for themselves and of their right to criticize publicly the values of the larger society. The lives and self-image of all these women had changed—if only so little—because of their new reforming interests.

The Cross and the Pedestal:
Women, Anti-Ritualism, and the
Emergence of the American Bourgeoisie[1]

During the first half of the nineteenth century, the Second Great Awakening's violent upheavals, its theological and liturgical disputes transformed American Protestantism—and, temporarily at least, the religious experiences of American women. New sects emerged. Utopian and millennial communes embodied futuristic visions of idealized domestic, sexual, and racial relations. Individualism reigned. The immediate experience of the Holy Spirit, not the moral and orderly progress of the fathers, signified piety. Youth criticized age. Perfectionism beckoned to a boundless and unknowable future. Individual mystical experiences broke through the boundaries between the divine and the human, female and male. Within the regular churches, "New Men and New Measures" struggled for dominance. Clerical radicals criticized an educated, tradition-bound ministry. Time-honored liturgies no longer seemed relevant.[2]

Male clerics and reformers led this movement. Yet women were their most zealous adherents. Through sheer numbers, women dominated the Second Great Awakening's revivals and spiraling church membership.[3] Silenced in Christian churches since the days of Paul, women now seized sacred space. They interrupted services to pray aloud for their own souls, and for other women—but they prayed as well for husbands, sons, and male community leaders. Some women cried out, spun around, or danced. Others spoke in tongues. Possessed by the Holy Spirit, still other women felt called upon by God to preach and prophesy. Male religious rebels actively encouraged these enthusiastic women. They called on them to organize prayer meetings, to criticize ministers opposed to revivals, to leave their homes and go forth into the byways of the cities to perfect the world.[4] In fact, Free Will Baptists and some Presbyterian congregations, at the height of revival enthusiasm, permitted women to ascend the pulpit during church services. Male theological rebels had transformed this new female elect into the voice and symbol of their theological revolt.[5]

Women's religious activities multiplied. Female revival converts formed Holy Bands to assist the evangelist in his revival efforts. They gathered with him at dawn to help plan the day's revival strategies. They posted bills in public places urging attendance at revival meetings, pressured merchants to close their shops and hold prayer services, buttonholed sinful men and prayed with them. Although "merely women," they led prayer vigils in their homes that extended far into the night.[6] These women for the most part were married, respected members of respectable communities. Yet, transformed by millennial zeal, they disregarded virtually every restraint upon women's behavior. They self-righteously commanded sacred space as their own. They boldly carried Christ's message to the streets, even into the new urban slums.[7] They threatened to revolutionize women's secular as well as sacred roles.

Ironically, during the very years when the new bourgeois men began to proselytize for the confining Cult of True Womanhood, wild, religious women created a public and powerful role for themselves as a female conscience and moral voice crying in a wilderness of male corruption. No matter how modified over time, this image would always offer an alternative to the male, Christian construct of pious submission and isolated domesticity.

To implement their newfound sacred and social responsibilities more effectively, many respectable women moved beyond individually inspired behavior to form a score of untraditional—indeed, iconoclastic—organizations. Some women, new to American cities, the wives of recently established merchants and professionals, invaded brothels to plead with prostitutes and admonish men. Other radical women sought active roles as temperance orators.[8] Still others, espousing William Lloyd Garrison's anarchistic message, assumed controversial roles within the American Anti-Slavery Society. Temperance and abolitionist women asserted their right to speak publicly, to hold office in male organizations, to petition state and federal legislators, all in the name of a higher inner light.[9] Other religiously inspired white women crossed the sharply drawn lines of race to found schools for black children and adolescents, at times inciting community violence against themselves and their schools.[10] It is significant that most of these women remained rooted within a bourgeois world of marriage and motherhood.

However, some women did not. Apocalyptic visions and wild voices pulled significant numbers of women away from their families and communities, leading a few of them to see themselves as the New Incarnation, encouraging others to follow the new, female messiahs. Social and sexual proprieties no longer bound these women. They saw themselves as messengers of the Lord, harbingers of a new world, beyond the restraints of moral codes and community norms. As early as the 1780s, two charismatic women foreshadowed the coming religious enthusiasms and disorder, leading women and men into revolutionary religious movements. These were Jemima Wilkinson, leader of the Universal Friends, and Ann Lee, founder of Shakerism. Devotion to a charismatic female leader, believed to be the new Christ, expectation of an immediate millennium, and insistence upon the equality of women and men characterized both movements. These common features suggest the appeal that radically disruptive religion held for women, and the way in which women could use such religion to express criticism of the old, male-dominated ways, as well as to restructure their own lives.

One of the first voices to announce the return of religious enthusiasm and the Second Great Awakening, Jemima Wilkinson established her new religious sect in the years immediately following the Revolutionary War. Wilkinson, daughter of a well-to-do Rhode Island commercial farmer, believed that she had died and God, resurrecting her, had sent her back to earth as His Second Incarnation. The name she chose for her reincarnation, the Public Universal Friend, emphasized the values of universality and *communitas* which dominated the movement. Repudiating the material world, relying upon the direct inspiration of the Holy Spirit, Wilkinson led her followers to the New York State frontier to form a New Jerusalem in the wilderness. Merging Quakerism with more mystical beliefs, her movement broke through denominational categories, did away with formal theology and an educated ministry.[11] She urged the renunciation of sin, condemned war and slavery, advocated celibacy and simple communal living, plain language and plain dress. As the reincarnation of Christ, she embodied the new powers religious enthusiasm gave women. In short, she turned the religious assumptions of the eighteenth century upside down.[12]

Only a few years after Wilkinson established her New Jerusalem,

Mother Ann Lee, proclaiming a similar, equally radical message, led a band of British artisans, calling themselves Shakers, to the New World. Like the Public Universal Friend, Mother Ann believed herself to be God's reincarnation. Recruiting followers from the economically marginal agricultural villages that dotted the Berkshire hills, the Mother preached a gospel that violated virtually every social, economic, and theological convention. Appealing to the poor and the marginal, she built her church upon a faith in the equality of all believers (including blacks) and her communities upon the principle of absolute celibacy and economic collectivity. Her religious iconoclasm reflected her social message. Ann Lee explicitly rejected the paternalism inherent in traditional Christianity. At once the Father of Power and the Mother of Wisdom, the Shaker God was equally female and male. As God's second incarnation and Christ's equal, the Mother embodied God's female persona.

Liturgical disorder paralleled the Shakers' radical reconstruction of traditional Christian theology. Throwing traditional liturgy to the winds, early Shaker meetings followed no order. Each Shaker sang, danced, spoke in tongues, prophesied, sat silently, or spun in circles for hours, as the Spirit directed. Shaker anti-ritualism ebbed and flowed during the nineteenth century. The 1830s to 1850s, however, a period the Shakers called "Mother Ann's Days," saw a burgeoning of spiritual enthusiasm and disorder. Spiritualism, spirit writings, frequent messages from the Woman Clothed in the Sun (a central figure in Revelation, prefiguring the end of the earth and the beginning of the millennium) characterized Shaker belief and practices, especially those of Shaker women. Spirit wine intoxicated, spirit clothing charmed, and Shakers reported watching the Father of Power, the Mother of Wisdom, Christ, and Mother Ann dancing joyfully on Shaker graves. The anti-ritualism that permeated Shaker theology and liturgy thus paralleled Shaker rejection of normative familial and capitalist structures. Institutionally and ideologically, these struggling British artisans and the equally marginal American enthusiasts rejected all established boundaries and categories—those between the individual and the community, between public and private, women and men, time and eternity, spirit and matter.[13]

Yet another source of enthusiastic disorder loomed upon the spiritual horizon, drawing women out of their traditional homes and away from religious and sexual respectability. Evangelical Perfectionists believed that, once saved by Christ, they lived beyond the limitations of the Law. No sin or routinized morality, no traditional demands of community or familial conformity, could again bind those whom Christ had freed. Some Perfectionist women followed John Humphrey Noyes into his experimental community at Oneida, New York, where, sexually united to all other community members, they lived beyond the restraints of traditional Christianity and of monogamous marriage. Other women sought a more individualistic Perfectionist vision, outside of all communal regulations.[14] Still other women opened their minds and hearts to the spirit world, repudiating not only the Trinity and an educated ministry, but all boundaries between male and female, corporeal and spiritual, time past and time future.[15]

Male religious rebels had initially encouraged women's religious enthusiasms—both within evangelical denominations and among the less restrained utopians. At a certain point, however, the revolutionary thrust of religion ebbed for male spiritual leaders. While antistructural religious experimentation maintained its appeal for some women and men through the 1840s and 1850s, by then spiritual order had returned to the established churches. "New Men and New Measures" emerged as a new norm. Ministers once again urged their congregations to seek spiritual solace in traditional rituals and symbols. A public morality, increasingly in harmony with the economic individualism and self-reliance preached in more secular texts, took priority over private religious inspiration. Horace Bushnell's *Christian Nurture,* not revival disorder, pointed the direction American Protestantism would take.[16]

At this point, male religious rebels began to dissociate themselves from iconoclastic and socially rebellious women. Repudiating their female prophets, such men glorified a novel Victorian figure, the patient and homebound mother, and a new institution, the bourgeois family, isolated and nuclear. De-emphasizing the intense piety of revivalistic conversions, clergymen now argued that salvation blossomed within the Christian nursery as a result of loving, maternal discipline. Reinstating the time-honored boundaries of women's sphere, evangelical ministers shepherded their female adherents back toward the contained family and traditional femininity. They insisted that the Cult of True Womanhood constituted female piety, not religious ecstasy and militancy. The woman who had imbibed activism at a religious font had either to renounce her expectations for radical new social and religious roles or re-examine her adherence to evangelical Protestantism.[17]

Women did both. Many followed their ministers back into respectability. They accepted the dictum preached by the General Association of Congregational Ministers, and by the newly appointed president of Oberlin College, Charles Finney, that women should abhor the public arena.[18] Their revival fervor ebbing, these women eschewed public demonstrations of religious devotion, adhered to the old liturgies, resumed their silence within sacred confines. They renounced their earlier reform enthusiasm and moved into hierarchically structured and socially acceptable philanthropic organizations. Women's auxiliaries, which at the height of the revivals had assumed innovative and autonomous roles, relinquished leadership to male societies. Formerly iconoclastic and radical women's organizations now began to glorify the home and act in ways that recognized and ultimately reinforced new class patterns. Female societies raised money to send poor young men to divinity schools that barred women as a matter of course.[19]

But other religiously inspired women clung to their revolutionary religious and social visions. Poor farm women continued to join Shaker communities or, rejecting both traditional Christianity and the new bourgeois family, followed the Mormon exodus to Utah. Some radical reformers found they could relinquish neither their intense, individualistic religious commitment nor their experience of a new, unrestricted female role. Through the 1840s and 1850s, these women continued their assault upon ritual order, both within and without religious confines. Especially for those women who had followed Garrison into the abolitionist movement, a decade of religious and reform millennialism had led them to fuse religious anti-ritualism and feminism. Indeed, the 1840s and 1850s saw them engaged in an intense religious hegira. As Evangelical Protestantism reasserted the necessity of hierarchical organization and of ritual, and as orthodox Friends maintained their quietist tone, those women sought intellectual and spiritual purity in an increasingly antistructural religious and reform posture. Quaker feminists such as the Grimkés, Susan B. Anthony, and Lucretia Mott repudiated orthodox Quakerism. Anthony, along with former Congregational minister Antoinette Brown Blackwell, embraced Universalism. Congregationalist Sally Holley denounced Trinitarianism to become a Unitarian. Others, seeking religious affiliations that stressed personal revelation, loose democratic structures, and individual activism, moved first to the Hicksite meetings and then to the unorthodox and unstructured Progressive Friends. Elizabeth Cady Stanton, aided by Mary Livermore, constructed her own feminist Bible, which rejected both traditional Christianity and gender assumptions. The Grimké sisters, Abby Kelley Foster, and many other feminists turned their backs upon traditional Christianity completely, espousing spiritualism.[20] The more assertive the feminist, the less easily she remained within the confines of traditional Christianity or of hierarchically structured and socially accept-able reform organizations.

The religious protests of the persistently radical cadre and, at the height of their enthusiastic commitment, of their less constant sisters repre-sented a broad spectrum of denominational and political alternatives. Yet they shared a number of basic characteristics: the repudiation both of ritual and of formal organizational structures; a preference for intuitive or in-stinctive forms of knowledge and religious experience; a glorification of the individual; a rejection of communal norms and of harsh systems of punishment for their violation; a weakening—even the denial—of bound-aries between this world and the next. Wild bodily behavior and physical disorder frequently characterized women's religious enthusiasm. Their reli-gious experiences thus fell within the category of what anthropologists have defined as religious anti-ritualism.[21]

As we have seen, their anti-ritualism presents a complex pattern: an initial conflation of female and male religious iconoclasm followed by the reassertion of ritual and order by male religious radicals, and its acceptance by some, though not all, women. Overarching all, we find that through-out the Second Great Awakening anti-ritualism appealed with far greater intensity to women than to men—as measured in numbers of revival converts and church members, and in forms of iconoclastic behavior. This pattern is not unique to Jacksonian America or to Evangelical Protestant-ism. Variations on it existed within Albigensianism and other popular medieval religious movements; within Reform Protestantism in France and Germany in the sixteenth century; in New England during the antinomian controversy; and in England during the Civil War.[22]

A series of questions suggest themselves: Why does anti-ritualism hold a greater appeal for women than for men? Why does this appeal wax and wane for some women but not for others? Women are a sociological category. Questions concerning the greater appeal that enthusiastic, disor-derly religion holds for them raise the broader issue of the interaction between social experiences and the espousal of particular religious forms and behavior. Can we relate the persistent espousal of anti-ritualism to one type of social experience, its embrace but ultimate rejection to another? What factors linked women's religious iconoclasm to women's demand for role expansion and political rights?

Women's anti-ritualism occurs most frequently at times of rapid social upheaval, yet its complexity confounds a simple economic explanation. We cannot, for instance, see anti-ritualism solely as the voice of social marginality. Female exponents of anti-ritualism come from a variety of social divisions as well as formal theologies. It is true that they include the economically oppressed and the socially marginal (displaced artisan women from the north of England during the Civil War, British Shakers from Manchester a century later, enthusiastic women from New England's marginal agrarian communities in the opening decades of the nineteenth century). But they number as well aristocratic and most especially bourgeois women: we find Anne Hutchinson and Jemima Wilkinson as well as Mary Dyer and Ann Lee.

At the same time that women's religious responses span class distinctions, their diverse and changing nature within class (not all bourgeois or marginal women espouse anti-ritualism, some who do soon renounce it) defeats any effort to generalize from similarities across class to the existence of women as a monolithic social or cultural group. In terms of unraveling the relation that exists between the espousal of religious anti-ritualism, social location, and gender experiences, our two constants (that anti-ritualism most frequently accompanies violent and unpredictable social change, and that anti-ritualism holds a far greater appeal for women than for men) complicate our puzzle even as they offer clues to a solution. To solve our historical conundrum we must explore the relation between two analytic variables—the experience of social-structural change and uncertainty, the espousal of shifting and diverse forms of religious anti-ritualism. While apparently only a further complication, a consideration of gender will ultimately illuminate their interaction.

A minor caveat is perhaps in order. Hypotheses suggest new questions, new approaches to the study of old puzzles. They bring existing theories together in novel ways, substantiating their innovative suggestions with reference to existing data. They offer models, which new empirical research must test.[23] This essay does not announce new empirical data. Rather, it suggests alternative approaches to the study of American revivalism, and perhaps adds new insights into the appeal anti-ritualism holds for women and men during periods of radical social change.

Methodologically, I have built my hypothesis around the behavior of differing groups of women and men: groups who first espoused and then rejected religious enthusiasm, groups of the structurally marginal who moved restlessly in the direction of greater religious and political anti-ritualism. These constitute analytic rather than empirical clusters. I have artificially constructed them out of their central social characteristics: geographic movement along the new canals and toll roads of Jacksonian America, movement into the emerging bourgeois urban structures, prolonged marginality within the new commercial and industrial structures. They never constituted self-defined social groups who self-consciously commented upon their commonality.[24] Indeed, their very transience and marginality frequently rendered them unusually inarticulate—that is, in terms of historically retrievable sources. Existing historical studies of communities torn by economic and institutional change and by religious enthusiasm (Utica and Rochester, New York, for example, New York City during Charles Finney's two great revivals, Philadelphia during these same years) suggest the legitimacy of these artificial groupings, as do the biographies of leading women reform activists.[25] But much new research must be done before we can unreservedly assert that anti-ritualism voices the experience of structural movement or marginality. It is especially necessary if we are to understand the complexity and changeability of anti-ritualism as a symbolic or metaphoric language, for, I will argue, anti-ritualism conveyed differing social meaning depending upon the social group that espoused it. The women of America's Second Great Awakening, with their varied expressions of religious enthusiasm, existing as they did at the vortex of economic and institutional change, offer an ideal opportunity for exploring the complexity of religious anti-ritualism as a social "language."

Historians of women are not alone in exploring these issues. Other historians of American religion are examining the interaction between religious and social disorder. These studies, while ignoring women for the most part, do touch tangentially on the questions we have raised.[26]

William McLoughlin, in *Revivals, Awakenings, and Reforms,* proffers one of the most sophisticated of the new analyses.[27] Influenced by anthropologist Anthony Wallace's study of religious revitalization among the Seneca,[28] McLoughlin argues that America's major religious revivals, from the eighteenth century to the present, coincided with and helped moderate "periods of fundamental social intellectual reorientation." Intel-

lectual and social fragmentation, McLoughlin and Wallace argue, follow
hard upon economic and institutional transformations. Old beliefs and
relations collapse; chaos threatens. Unless a new ideology or leader can
appear at such a moment, offering a world view that harmonizes new
realities with old values, the "culture will disintegrate: their birth rate will
decline, psychic disorder will increase and some wild ghost-dance of religion will mark the final sputtering out."[29] America's major religious
revival movements, McLoughlin argues, assumed just such a cohesive and
mediating role. They provided Americans with a sense of national unity
and a collective emotional experience which counterbalanced the centrifu-
gal forces of economic revolution and institutional restructuring. Connect-
ing past and future, revival theologies accommodated social change while
reaffirming America's most fundamental beliefs. At the same time, the
revival experience itself permitted hundreds of thousands of Americans,
across class, denominational, and geographic divisions, to reaffirm their
connectedness as Christian Americans by participating in a nationwide
religious ritual. In this way, revivals provided rituals of cohesion just at
the moment that economic forces threatened to tear society asunder.[30]

A fascinating thesis, one that may well explain the experiences and
careers of male religious rebels from the eighteenth through the twentieth
century. Most frequently New Men (as McLoughlin has argued persuasively elsewhere), male rebels opened the church to change at the same time
that they preserved its most critical and universal tenets and reaffirmed
social order.[31] They spoke to and for countless other men caught in the
vortex of social transformation. But did they speak for women? Women,
like men, in the throes of radical change need to reaffirm beliefs held up
as "eternal verities"; they need a sense of continuity. But the changes
women embrace, as we have already seen, frequently strike male rebels as
a prelude to social and theological disorder and ultimate cultural death.
The "eternal verities" which women and men uphold as beacons in a world
of confusion also differ dramatically.

The McLoughlin-Wallace thesis does not explore the positive social
contributions of disorder and anti-ritualism or their legitimate appeal to
discontented groups.[32] Change, dislocation, and fragmentation within the
McLoughlin-Wallace model are dangerous moments threatening social
disintegration. They are points of crisis, like the dramatic fevers that occur
in the 1930s Hollywood melodramas. Will the fever break and the patient-

culture return to a "normal" sense of order and identity (will "the eternal verities" be reaffirmed and distortion end)? the McLoughlin-Wallace thesis seems to ask. Or will the patient-culture die? McLoughlin fails to explore the way individuals and groups, repressed by dominant synthetic structures —white women, black women and men, the young of both genders—see these moments as times when they may force a redistribution of power and a redefinition of roles.

McLoughlin and Wallace struggle against a static structural-functionalist approach. Yet their model remains mechanistic, suspicious of change (they retain an organic, indeed a psychological, approach that identifies social change with psychological disorientation), and impervious to the diversity of responses present within a single revival. We must continue our search for a model of how religious disorder mirrors social disorder —a model that will use differences between women's and men's experiences to underscore the diversity present in all revivals and to point to the positive aspects of social disorder and fragmentation.

I have embarked on this search by first altering the approach historians traditionally have taken to the study of religion. Historians have focused primarily on the content or the substance of religious beliefs and theological disputes. I have elected to focus on their form. Religious enthusiasm and religious rituals as liturgical forms constitute one of the symbolic languages individuals use to express social experiences. Complex culture-specific creations, they are simultaneously a reflective and an expressive medium. Religious practices and beliefs take forms that mirror the structure of the society in which they are found (especially the marginality or the centrality of their believers) and provide an eloquent metaphoric language. Using this language groups and individuals speak about the impact on their lives of social change, of economic and political power, about gender conflict and family tensions. Once spoken, these words acquire the potential for altering both the speakers and the world that produced them.[33] Speech is action, especially for women, whose millennia of silence has symbolized male hegemony. Reading nineteenth-century women's religious responses—women's espousal of anti-ritualism or, conversely, their renunciation of discord and reaffirmation of structure—as a symbolic discourse, we will begin to hear ancient voices of women reflecting upon the social changes that transformed their lives, demanding new roles, resisting or acquiescing in the restoration of social order, talking without stop through fifty years of religious enthusiasm about their emotional, economic, and institutional experiences.

This vision may be new to history; it is not to other disciplines. Anthropologists have long seen ritual and its repudiation as symbolic systems expressive of social arrangements or conflicts. Mary Douglas, for instance, insists that an intrinsic harmony exists between sociological structures and cultural forms. The degree of formality or spontaneity that characterizes a society's religious and political practices, aesthetic forms, dress or food codes, values and beliefs, mirrors that society's underlying economic and institutional organization.[34] Anti-ritualism, Douglas maintains, does not constitute a revolt against excessive structure. Rather, we must see it as an expressive medium possible only within societies or among social groups where institutional structure, hierarchical arrangements, and social control exert minimal pressure. We will find the espousal of anti-ritualism in heterogeneous or highly mobile, loosely structured societies; where family and political institutions are informal and flexible; where economic or political centralization is weak or exercised in highly impersonal ways; in societies characterized by economic and political competitiveness or by a loose sense of social affiliation. Such societies will espouse political and religious ideologies that value the individual over the community and family, youth over age, inner experience rather than conformity to social norms. They will praise intuitive and instinctive forms of knowledge. They will use language to challenge revealed ideas, to encourage autonomy, to question or deny boundaries, to reject authoritarian control and symbols of hierarchical power. In such cultures, Douglas tells us, "God has turned against ritual." It is here, she predicts, that we will find both enthusiastic religion and the "literature of revolt."[35]

While loosely organized societies espouse religious anti-ritualism, so do societies caught in the process of radical social and economic transformation. The experience of social change itself, Douglas argues, leads to the denunciation of ritual, the praise of disorder, and the affirmation of individualism. Radical or prolonged social change destroys old institutional and hierarchical arrangements. Definitions no longer elicit cultural consensus or reinforcement. Boundaries are no longer clearly defined. Members of societies in the process of change face contradictory demands and rewards. Subgroups in those societies experiment with altering categories of the social outcast. In doing so they redefine social spheres, boundaries, and divisions of power. The individual, detached from a complex web of social interactions and agreed-upon values, is outside known order, loose, unconnected. Cosmology, reflecting movement and detachment, will be flexible, open, will reject rituals and structure.[36]

The destruction of one form of social organization, however, leads not to permanent disorder but ultimately to the reconstitution of order. As economic and demographic change progresses, a new social equilibrium evolves, satisfactory to some of the protesters. Form, pattern, ritual, classification return, reflecting, reinforcing, embellishing new economic and institutional arrangements. But for those still dissatisfied with the new order, or marginal to it, disorder and fluidity may maintain their attraction; these groups may continue to use religious anti-ritualism to resist the new social structure and power dynamic, or simply to give voice to their marginality. Their cosmology may prove anachronistic, pointing only to the promise of change already belied. Or it may be a harbinger of further discontinuities. Much revolves around the nature of the social change, the socioeconomic location of the social dissidents, and the amount of actual power they can mobilize.[37]

Douglas's conceptual framework provides a remarkably accurate overview of the essential congruence between the massive economic and institutional upheavals of the first half of the nineteenth century, and the religious anti-ritualism of the Second Great Awakening. Predictably, Americans in the throes of social change questioned traditional authority and denigrated religious rituals. The Shakers offer an ideal example. Their wild religious beliefs and practices first emerged among British artisans struggling unsuccessfully against the incursions of the putting-out system and early industrialization, and among their equally marginal agrarian counterparts in the depressed farming communities of the Berkshire hills. Excluded from the new structures and ways of power, these women and men transfigured the epitome of marginality and powerlessness—a poor woman, Ann Lee—into God's Second Incarnation. The social and economic content of their religion did not stop with this one radical statement. The women and men who worshiped the Father of Power and the Mother of Wisdom, and who received spirit messages from the Woman Clothed in the Sun, repudiated the new laissez-faire capitalism and the new nuclear and isolated bourgeois family. The Shaker family was coterminous with the Shaker village; Shakers owned and worked their land communally.

Nor were the Shakers alone in expressing their rejection of the nuclear and increasingly isolated families that proliferated in America's burgeoning *entrepôts*. Other "refugees" from the declining farming communities of the Berkshires, Vermont, and northern New York State helped John Humphrey Noyes construct his new Oneida "Family" and Joseph Smith and Brigham Young to re-form both Christianity and the nuclear family.

Douglas's analytic framework holds true not only for the economically and ideologically marginal. These years of radical social change saw the radical transformation of mainstream Protestantism. The last vestiges of orthodox eighteenth-century Congregationalism—an insistence on an all-powerful Father-God, upon the passivity and powerlessness of man, upon an eternity patterned after agrarian patriarchy, and upon a spiritual economy of scarcity represented theologically by predestination—all were challenged and ultimately abandoned.[38] God became a loving brother—indeed, a living and concerned mother.[39] Man was responsible for his own salvation.

Millennialism opened the window of speculation onto an unstructured world of *communitas* and Perfectionist euphoria. Within this millennialist vision, religious and reform enthusiasm fused, occasionally assuming the form of religiously rooted political anarchism.[40] Within the untried social setting of Jacksonian America, reflecting its growing social and cultural heterogeneity, conflicting categories of good and evil proliferated. Secular and political values paralleled the sacred as Americans generally embraced individualism, christened change "progress," and engaged in bitter electoral conflicts. This was called the Era of the Common Man. It was the Age of Finney—and of Garrison.

And it was just at this moment in time that male religious rebels turned to women as a receptive population and as a group whose activism symbolized a more general rejection of traditional rituals and boundaries. As we have seen, women responded to the male invitation with enthusiasm. Using religion to develop extra-domestic roles, they created powerful local and nationwide single-sex organizations expressive of women's particular angers, anxieties, and demands. Momentarily, the needs of male religious spokesmen and of women coincided.

They coincided; they did not merge. Rooted in different social experiences, women's and men's anti-ritualism constituted two quite distinct metaphoric languages. If we are to understand either the bourgeois revolution or the reform enthusiasm that characterized the Jacksonian Age, we must learn to distinguish between these two symbolic systems. Of course, women's religious enthusiasm reflected the general social fragmentation and movement, which women and men experienced together. Like their fathers, brothers, and husbands, women went through the painful process of geographic, institutional, and class relocation. But, as we have seen, these changes affected women in far more complex and ultimately more ambiguous ways then they did men.

The eighteenth century's agrarian-artisanal institutions and values had imposed a far greater passivity upon women than they had upon any white man. Despite their economic productivity, seventeenth- and eighteenth-century women moved in an orbit of economic and legal dependency, dropping the role of dependent daughter only to assume that of dependent wife. Marriage deprived a woman of all legal and economic rights, at a time when few women could support themselves except through marriage. Even widowhood held few benefits. Most New England women died the dependents of their sons, boarders in a home that had never legally been theirs.[41] Women's enforced silence in religious space ritually underscored a pervasive pattern of institutional, legal, and economic inferiority.

America's emergence as a commercial and early industrial state seemed, momentarily, to open the possibility of new roles and power for women. It increased the number of single women and delayed marriage for many others. It reduced the birthrate.[42] Multiplying the number of nondomestic institutions, especially in the new urban centers (schools, publishing houses and journals, orphanages, homes for the homeless), the commercial, industrial, and urban revolutions created novel employment opportunities for women. They made it possible for the new bourgeois woman to aspire to economic autonomy.[43] By proletarianizing the artisan family and destroying the economic base of the New England farming family, they forced growing numbers of working-class women to assume that autonomy.[44] At the same time, these economic and demographic evolutions transformed women's roles in the family. Old sureties evaporated along with the old restraints. New roles brought new responsibilities and options—but also new, even more rigorous constraints. In the balance, no one knew if women's autonomy would increase or diminish. Uncertainty reigned within the new world of women—even more than it did within the new world of men.

In the midst of these confusions—indeed, mirroring them—changes in church governance and ritual began to benefit women directly. From having been ritually and repeatedly silenced within sacred confines, women were now offered a central role in the religious revolution—a centrality that also promised increasing secular visibility and power. Psychological as well as sociological gains accrued to the religiously enthusiastic woman. The denigration of hierarchical structures, the assertion of individual autonomy against the primacy of community and familial norms resonated to their particularly female experience of suppression under the patriarchy. Thus, at the height of what was both the bourgeois revolution and the Second Great Awakening, women across class, married and unmarried, briefly experienced revolutionary, even frightening changes. A vision of new power and autonomy danced before them, held out and authorized, if only momentarily, by their male spiritual leaders.

But in the end both social disorder, and an open social structure which offered new freedoms to women and to youth, proved to be temporary. Impersonal modes of economic organization and social control developed to deal more efficiently with problems of scale and with rapid population turnover. Economic hegemony only narrowed and intensified.[45] A new theology and new religious institutions developed to enforce that hegemony—as did new values and rituals.[46] Nor did many of the beneficiaries of disorder resist order's return. The unattached youth of this transitional period were not social protesters but, rather, loose young women and men cast off by a declining agrarian economy, at sea in a new commercial and urban environment. Their own desire was to establish themselves securely within the new bourgeois hierarchy.

In an era of such rapid economic and institutional change and uncertainties, ideological and political alliances are at best short-lived. The self-interest of divergent groups will coincide momentarily and then part disruptively. Not surprisingly, the interests and vision of male revival leaders and of enthusiastic women did not remain wedded for long. The revolutionary thrust of Evangelical Protestantism ebbed before women were able to use religion to restructure female-male power relations permanently. As male religious leaders had used women's activism and public presence to symbolize their male revolt against an older, Congregational world order, and the experience of a new and changing social order, women's silence became equally symbolic to male religious leaders who sought to restore order and ritual to the social and religious world. By the

1840s, the Victorian woman, economically impotent and religiously de-
mure, had emerged as the symbol and personification of male bourgeois
hegemony. Clearly, some women, sensitive to the loss of their new power
and centrality, fought male clerics' desire to silence them once again.
Religious and social antistructuralism expressed their continued social
discontent, which surfaced finally as feminism.

But while the congruence of social and cosmological structures seems
clear, as do basic dissimilarities between women's and men's social and
religious experiences, critical questions remain. Why did the vast majority
of evangelical women shed their recently acquired autonomy so promptly
to follow male ministers back into respectability and order? Which
women, resisting the pressures of religion and society, persisted in their
new deviance? While Douglas's macrocosmic approach offers the historian
a dazzling new breadth of vision, these questions underscore certain weaknesses inherent in such a broad sweep. A macromodel does not permit us
to focus narrowly upon cultural diversity and conflict. It does little to
explain why bourgeois women adopted such varied religious voices. Yet
it is just this issue of diversity and conflict within social structures and even
specific groups that we must address. The babel of women's discordant
religious voices not only tells us about women; it underscores the uncertain
and conflicted nature of social order in Jacksonian America itself. If we are
to explore more fully the interface between social-structural relations and
cultural forms, we must shift our focus from the macrocosm of grand
trends and overall characteristics to a microcosmic study of women's social
experiences and religious voices.

Utica and Rochester, situated deep within the agricultural heartland
of New York State, emerged as two of America's most rapidly growing
commercial and industrial centers. They provide a critical social setting for
our exploration of the interaction between the sociological and the cultural. Utica was one of the first boom towns to arise during America's
westward migration, a harbinger of the commercial development that
would quickly transform one of our first frontiers. By the 1830s, Rochester
had become the foremost wheat-processing city in the world. Between the
1810s and 1840s the full force of economic revolution radically altered these
two cities. Both played a critical role in the economic development of
early-nineteenth-century America. During these same years, religious enthusiasm kept steady pace with the process of economic change. At the

center of the Burned-Over District, both welcomed evangelical revival enthusiasm. Both fostered the newborn feminist movement of the 1850s. Each is the subject of a fine historical study.[47]

Blending a class and a gender analysis, let us seek to determine which groups of women within these two communities persisted in the language of revolt and which internalized the language of acquiescence. For the purpose of such a precise analysis, let us focus, for the moment, only on religious revivalism, holding in abeyance the less structured options that stretched beyond evangelical enthusiasm into a utopian or formless world. When we have accounted for the waxing and waning of women's response to revival enthusiasm, we can then proceed to an explanation of discordant female voices.

Between 1810 and the 1840s, the transportation and industrial revolutions dramatically altered Utica's class and family structures. As wealthy families and landless farming youth both moved into Utica, the former as a new bourgeois elite, the latter as a newly proletarianized working class, the amorphous social and economic categories of farmer and artisan, which had structured eighteenth-century Utica, became obsolete. A stratified bourgeoisie, consisting of merchants, industrial entrepreneurs, professionals, shopkeepers, and clerks, emerged ever so slowly, as did the new working class. Household size and structure changed as the family lost most of its production functions and work and residence were separated. These transformations, beginning with a pre–Erie Canal boom in 1810 and essentially completed by the late 1830s, paralleled Utica's revival enthusiasm, which began in 1813–14 and continued through the late 1830s.[48]

Having at our disposal Mary Ryan's prize-winning study of Utica, rich in economic, institutional, and religious details, sensitive to gender distinctions, we are in a position to explore who within Utica's increasingly diversified society espoused religious anti-ritualism—and for how long. Certain characteristics remained constant for participants in Utica's revival: youth, transience, and being female. Though their percentage of revival conversions did vary by church and by revival, women always constituted a majority of revival converts during each of Utica's revivals. The lowest percentage of female converts occurred during Utica's first revival in 1813–14, when women constituted 52 percent of converts (a figure nevertheless well above their representation in the general population of this frontier village). In Utica's last major revival, 1838, they comprised 72 percent of the converts. Geographic rootlessness was the second major characteristic of the revival convert. Most converts, both men and women, could not be found in any of Utica's censuses or city directories. Of male converts, for instance, more easily traced by historical demographers than women, Ryan could trace only one-fourth from any given revival in any of the city directories. Among those male converts who could be located in subsequent church records, 30 percent requested letters of dismissal within five years of their conversion so that they could leave Utica and join churches in other communities. Presumably many others left with far less formality—especially women. Again, of those who remained in Utica long enough for Ryan to trace them, youth was a significant characteristic. Sixty-five percent of the traceable male converts (presumably the most stable and oldest of those converts) listed themselves as boarders. In terms of the social structure of early industrial America, this meant young men, divorced from their family of origin, not yet married, recently moved to the city, men who most likely had found employment as clerks in Utica's growing mercantile houses, or as semiskilled laborers for wholesale merchants or in Utica's new factories. Sixty percent of Utica's female revival converts appear to have been neither mothers nor married and thus formed a group comparable to the youthful male boarder.[49] "It is safe to make this single conclusion about this silent majority of converts," Ryan tells us. "They were largely young and, in the short term at least, a peripatetic lot with fragile roots in church and community. Thus far it would seem that the Second Great Awakening expressed the waxing religious enthusiasm of a second generation, recently uprooted from their frontier families."[50]

"Thus far," the Douglas hypothesis, when tested against a close demographic study of revival converts, holds true. The rejection of orthodox dogmas and the repudiation of traditional rituals appealed primarily to the uprooted and potentially dispossessed of the new economic order, to those, momentarily at least, cast out from the traditional family and agrarian village, outside of structure—and, among these, especially to young women. The comments of contemporaries underscore the relationship between youth, rootlessness, and anti-ritual. In a pastoral letter, the ministers of the Oneida Association, one of the Presbyterian pillars of communal propriety, complained in 1827 that revival enthusiasm "allow[ed] anybody to speak and pray . . . as they pleased." Young men, the letter reported, had harshly criticized established ministers and church elders, saying, " 'You old grey headed sinner, you deserve to have been in hell long ago,' 'This old hypocrite,' 'That old apostate' . . . 'That old veteran servant of the devil' . . ."[51] Clearly revivals permitted those marginal to Utica's social structure to express tension and discontent. As we saw earlier, revivalists also encouraged women to criticize antirevival ministers and church elders.

But while these overall characteristics remained constant over our twenty-five-year period, significant changes also marked the pattern of Utica's revival conversions, changes crucial to our understanding of the precise functions of anti-ritualism within a rapidly changing society, and thus to our understanding of women's diverse pattern. The percentage of male revival conversions was greatest during Utica's 1813–14 revival—the revival coincided with the first major impact of commercial and transportation revolutions on Utica's traditional, agrarian social structure. Women, as 52 percent of the converts of this revival, though in excess of their percentage of the population, were significantly below their percentage of prerevival church membership—which had been 72 percent.[52] Thus, for this one period when the full force of the commercial revolution hit Utica for the first time, male religious enthusiasm peaked and came as close to paralleling women's as it would ever do. A second significant factor characterized this first revival. A cadre of Utica's economic elite renounced orthodoxy and embraced revivalism. This elite contained an unusually high percentage of men. Though outnumbered by marginal and transient men, merchants and lawyers (and their wives) were, Ryan tells us, "conspicuously present" among the converts, as were Utica's leading landholders and industrialists. The Van Rensselaers, for example, converted en masse.

During Utica's second revival, in 1819, when the first touches of the canal boom had begun to spread through agrarian Oneida County, a significant change in the social and economic composition of the convert group occurred. During this revival, men from the lower rather than the upper echelon of Utica's emerging bourgeoisie—artisans and small shopkeepers—joined in the enthusiasm and embraced the new ways. Utica's upper-middle class, on the other hand, no longer responded to the appeal of antistructuralism; their enthusiasm had already been restructured.[53] We must remember, however, that in discussing male merchants and petty shopkeepers we are analyzing only a small, albeit significant, minority of all converts. Both of these economic groups were more often represented by their female than by their male members. A class analysis without a simultaneous gender analysis is deceiving. But let us hold that level of analysis in abeyance for the moment.

The Utica revivals suggest that the interaction between cultural expressions and sociological experience is more varied than Douglas's model suggests. Revival enthusiasm reflected not one but two distinct forms of economic and institutional structurelessness. It appealed to the socially marginal, to those who existed outside of traditional structures. The adolescents who passed through this early boom town epitomized this marginality. As refugees from New England's declining agricultural communities, they were literally "on the move," between childhood and adulthood, between the traditional and the indeterminate. Far from finding a secure niche within a settled community, they would only continue their wanderings. A novel social and economic phenomenon, they signaled the end of one way of life and the necessity for another. Second, and of equal significance, revival anti-ritualism expressed the experiences of those, often older, women and men who were in movement from older forms of social organizations into the emergent bourgeois class structure. Thus, within the same society—indeed, the same community—at the same moment in time, we see that at least two quite distinct kinds of structurelessness coexisted. We must conclude, therefore, that in Utica during the 1810s and 1820s, religious anti-ritualism spoke of the experiences of antistructure, with at least two quite divergent voices. A far more complex pattern of the ways cultural diversity reflects social-structural heterogeneity has thus begun to emerge. Let us examine this second voice in greater detail.

The evidence from Utica suggests that as change flows through the social structure, different groups will embrace anti-ritualism as they themselves are embraced by structural transformation. As different social groups or families were swept up by the commercial and industrial revolutions, that is, and literally moved from the traditional agrarian world into Utica's new class structure (for example, when the Van Rensselaers shifted their economic base within Oneida County from agriculture to commerce, or when less affluent families left their farms and moved into Utica as shopkeepers and artisans), anti-ritualism and revival enthusiasm became a language through which they gave voice to their experience of social-structural relocation, their fears of upheaval, their anticipations of a new life. Those closest to social and economic power responded first (we find them involved in the 1813–14 revival); smaller shopkeepers and artisans, recruited into the bourgeoisie at later stages of commercial and industrial development (themselves more responders than shapers), converted as they moved into the new economic structures (we find them converting during the 1819 revival or during the revivals of the 1820s). Once a group had been successfully incorporated into the bourgeoisie, its response to revivalism slackened significantly: this is especially true of the men within that group. Individuals within the group would maintain their allegiance to key evangelical doctrines, but gradually renounced anti-ritualism and antistructural enthusiasm.

The changing Utica revival profile points out the dynamic interaction between forces of social and ideological change and forces of stabilization. Anti-ritualism, Utica's revivals demonstrate, will appeal to powerful socioeconomic groups—groups clearly committed to the perpetuation of social cohesion—at the moment those groups actively participate in the formation of a new economic and institutional order. Once the new system has become operative and the elite has established its centrality within it, such groups will resume their customary role as spokesmen for cohesion and status. Significantly, from the point of view of changing cosmologies, such elites will continue their opposition to the old ideology which supported the old social order (as orthodox Congregationalism supported the old mercantile-agrarian structures), while espousing the newly evolved counterstructure. And this counterstructure will gradually accumulate an increasingly restrictive cultural overlay in keeping with its function to affirm and reinforce the new class order. As more and more groups become incorporated within the new structure, the acceptance and elaboration of the new restrictive cultural forms and rituals will grow.

It is important, however, not to compress and simplify this process artificially. Social change is never sudden. The birth pangs of the American bourgeoisie encompassed half a century or longer. Economic and technological change affected different groups at different times and with differing intensity. Transients uprooted by the economic revolutions but marginal to the new seats of power, the emerging bourgeoisie, all experienced change in distinctive ways. During these years (roughly, the 1790s to the 1850s), no clear-cut cultural hegemony emerged. Rather, the

A REAL BUCK-EYE.

A cargo of gals, bound for the far West, in care of a Salt River Roarer! (See page 32)

Behind the humor of the comic almanacs lay the ominous suggestion of male violence against women. BELOW: *"Fishing—Catching a Smell-t" appeared in the* American Comic Almanac, 1838. *(Both courtesy of Library Company of Philadelphia)*

FISHING---Catching a *Smell-t.*

The comic almanacs depicted women as both powerful and sexual. Neither of these cartoons conforms to our stereotype of the Victorian's view of women. BELOW: The Judy Finx cartoon appeared in the Crockett Almanac 1839. (Both courtesy of American Antiquarian Society)

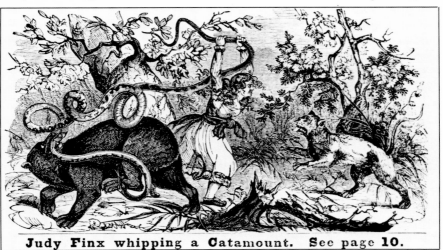

Judy Finx whipping a Catamount. See page 10.

ABOVE: *M. Carey Thomas (seated) and her cousin Elizabeth King, during the time (c. 1873) that Thomas kept her turbulent adolescent diary, in which she first expressed her desire for education and her rage against restrictions on women's roles. She later became president of Bryn Mawr College. (Courtesy of Bryn Mawr College Archives)* RIGHT: *Mid-nineteenth-century men did not find women who cross-dressed either sexually perverted or threatening. (Courtesy of Library Company of Philadelphia)*

THE

AFFLICTED AND DESERTED WIFE:

OR,

SINGULAR AND SURPRISING

ADVENTURES

OF

MRS. ELLEN STEPHENS,

Who, after having experienced much cruel treatment, was deserted by her husband, and in pursuit of whom, (and her infant child,) dressed in MALE attire, and obtaining a birth on board of one of the Steamers on the Mississippi River, as CABIN BOY, in that capacity made several passages up and down the Mississippi River, in 1841 and '42, without her sex being known or suspected.

Annexed is the still more surprising exploits of ALMIRA PAUL, who, garbed as a male in the capacity of Cook, &c., served on board several English and American vessels for the space of ten years, without betraying her sex.

NEW-YORK:
PRINTED FOR C. E. DANIELS, PUBLISHER.

THE MASCULINE WOMAN

She is mannish from shoes to her hat,
Coat, collars, stiff shirt and cravat.
She'd wear pants in the street
To make her complete,
But she knows the law won't stand for that.

LEFT: . . . *But twentieth-century men did.*
(Courtesy of Marshall Weeks. Originally
reproduced in Jonathan Ned Katz's
Gay/Lesbian Almanac, *New York: Harper*
& Row, 1983.) BELOW: *Sarah Butler Wister*
preserved this sensual card, sent to Jeannie
Field Musgrove in 1889. Theirs was a
lifelong correspondence noted for its
passionate expressions. The card reads: "My
darling I must end & how I linger. How &
where will this find you? My heart is too
full whenever I let myself think of you."
(The Wister Family Papers, courtesy of
Historical Society of Philadelphia)

Vol.1 1847 No.14

ELTON'S COMIC ALL-M-NACK

ELTON, Publisher and Engraver,
13 Division-street, New-York.

LEFT: *Illustration of male fear of female sexuality was rampant in the comic almanacs, directed toward a youthful male audience. (Courtesy of Library Company of Philadelphia)* BELOW: *Typical of the sensationalist press's growing exploitation of lesbianism as a sign of social and sexual pathology. (Courtesy of Jonathan Ned Katz. Originally reproduced in* Gay/Lesbian Almanac*)*

Bryn Mawr's 1896 basketball team. Intimacy and informality among women flourished in the new women's colleges. (Courtesy of Bryn Mawr College Archives)

Djuna Barnes. (Courtesy of Parasol Press, Ltd./Berenice Abbott)

The New Woman of the 1920s. Berenice Abbott's portrait of Edna St. Vincent Millay, Paris. (Courtesy of Parasol Press, Ltd./Berenice Abbott)

babel of contentious voices underscored the complexity of these economic and institutional transformations. The cultural forms the varied groups chose to express their new fears and visions consequently varied from one another and changed over time. Only with mid-century, perhaps only after the Civil War, did a Victorian consensus emerge. But by then, of course, new dissidents and new heresies were gathering in the wings.

Yet, if we are now certain that anti-ritualism accompanies movement between social positions, a second question arises: Why? In what ways— conceptual, structural, psychological—does the wild assertion of disorder serve individuals in the throes of social relocation as a language with which to express the emotional qualities of their experience? An analogy suggests itself—the rite of passage. Let us, for the moment, conceive of the successive waves of evangelical revivals—metaphorically—as a massive rite of passage marking the emergence of the American bourgeoisie. Such a frame will help us to examine the various psychological and sociological components of revival anti-ritualism and will thus suggest a different perspective from which to explore our still-unanswered question: Why did certain women pass through the revivals to be reintegrated into the contained social position of the Victorian lady while others did not?

Rites of passage accompany major changes in social position, status, or role; they are the process by which an individual leaves one set of known and recognized rights and responsibilities and adapts to a new social position and public persona. Traditionally, cultures have elaborated rituals that articulate a sense of personal upheaval, of being outside of form, and that simultaneously seek to contain the threat of social disarray. The rituals are particularly charged when the society itself, as well as key groups within the society, are in movement.

Rites of passage, as delineated by anthropologists such as Arnold Van Gennep and Victor Turner, contain three specific states.[54] The first, *separation,* involves "symbolic behavior signifying the detachment of the individual group . . . from an earlier fixed point in the social structure. . . ." The individual then passes through a second phase, *liminality,* when she lies "betwixt and between the positions assigned and arrayed by law, custom, convention and ceremonial." Liminal persons are felt to be outside of social restraints and norms, to embody the limitless power of disorder. In the final state of rite of passage—*aggregation*—society attempts to integrate the liminal person into a new role or social position.

While recognizing—indeed, giving expression to—the power of disorder involved in the process of social change, the rite of passage functions essentially as a conservative or restorative social instrument. Through the rite, social movement and change—and the elation and fear that accompany such movement—by being ritualized, become formalized and controlled. In fact, societies use liminal rituals not only to contain the fragmenting and explosive emotions involved, but also to socialize the unformed individual, to train her to accept her new roles and responsibilities. "Neophytes in many rites of passage," Victor Turner argues, "have to submit to an authority that is nothing less than that of the total community."[55]

Specific parallels exist between the rituals and imagery that Turner associates with the liminal passage and those that historians describe as forming part of the revival conversion. Liminal rites blend characteristics of lowliness and sacredness. The liminal person, during traditional tribal rites, experiences the process as one of death and rebirth, feeling that she has been "reduced or ground down . . . to be fashioned anew." The liminal person is often removed from ordinary communal space, stripped of her normal clothing, left naked or in rags. At the same time she is frequently encouraged or allowed to engage in unrestrained behavior, and to experience new and heady spiritual powers. It is a time when all the old restraints are dead and new ones as yet unforged. Disorder rules, momentarily unchallenged.[56]

This description epitomizes early-nineteenth-century evangelical revivals. Revivals violated the normative confines of sacred space. They could be held in fields and forest clearings. In cities, profane theaters were transformed into new churches as religious enthusiasm spilled out, destroying the distinction between sacred and secular.[57] Revivals disregarded conventional allocations of sacred time as well: they converted working days into God's time, laid claim on the night, continued for weeks. No liturgical traditions constrained the new enthusiasm as form was cast to the winds and souls cried out in fear or joy. The individual sinner, in the throes of conversion, assumed many of the qualities characteristic of the liminal phase. She felt herself cast down, the lowest of the lowly. No social or economic attributes from the secular world seemed relevant or offered consolation. Her naked soul engaged in a promethean struggle with God. Overthrown at last, renouncing the world and its temptations, the saved

Christian emerged a new person, invested with inner light, an agent of the Lord. During the liminal phase of the revival process, she cried out, spoke in tongues, criticized ministers and male political leaders. She renounced time-honored social proprieties, invaded brothels, founded separatist female organizations or new religions.[58]

However, just as the socialization of new roles accompanied and gradually overcame the ritualized disorder of the liminal phase in a rite of passage, so the revivals of the Second Great Awakening, while tolerating temporary liturgical disorder and female role expansion, also functioned as resocializing or reaggregating devices. They proved especially effective mechanisms for containing the protests of women and young men, and for inculcating the new roles of Victorian lady and corporate bureaucrat.

Much in the message disseminated by Finney, Lyman Beecher, and other evangelical revivalists was directly supportive of a new capitalist mentality. Though Charles Finney was overtly critical of an unrestrained drive for material advancement, suspicious of banks and opposed to credit and to debt financing, the two pillars of his revivalistic message would become the pillars of a new commercial order: optimism and self-help. Renouncing a spiritual economy of scarcity, Finney preached a loving God who rewarded with limitless grace those who sought salvation. Anyone, rich or poor, who with her free will would assert her belief in God and her determination to do good could now achieve salvation. The greatest spiritual rewards would go to those who worked the hardest. Salvation, no longer the gift of an arbitrary God, had become the "business" of men.[59] Finney's new saint was the self-reliant individual, not the "helpless brand" plucked up by an omnipotent father-god. To this doctrine of optimism, goal orientation, and self-reliance, Finney added a psychology of delayed satisfaction and control. Frugality lay at the heart of Finney's creed. These beliefs, combined with his insistence upon personal loyalty, honesty, and his acceptance of economic stratification—made an ideal belief system for the emerging bourgeoisie. No wonder that Finney's staunchest supporters included the mercantile elite of revival towns like Utica and Rochester, that the new merchants of New York City, Philadelphia, and Boston flocked to Finney's revivals, or that the Tappan brothers required their clerks to attend church services regularly at Finney's Broadway Tabernacle.[60]

Women, of course, heard and internalized the religious doctrines that so closely dovetailed with the economic world into which their brothers, husbands, and sons had moved. Since these women, as employers of domestic servants and as urban residents, participated along with their male kin in the new bourgeois social and economic order, the spiritual economy preached by Finney and other evangelists helped rationalize the novel capitalist structures in which these women unexpectedly found themselves.

Evangelists thus preached a double message: the saint as the self-reliant, optimistic individual; the soul perceiving herself as the lowest of the low. Men and women heard this message. It may be, however, that women heard and internalized the contradictions inherent in this aspect of evangelical revivalism with greater intensity than men did. Certainly Christian submission was a message their mothers and grandmothers had heard and internalized under orthodox preachers. Furthermore, sociologists of religion have found that women, far more than men, tend to glorify the service and sacrificial aspects of Christian imagery—frequently with the encouragement of male ministers. Indeed, evidence suggests that Jacksonian revival ministers, despite their religious iconoclasm, tended to stress self-sacrifice in their sermons to women. Nancy Hewitt, in her study of revival enthusiasm in Rochester, found that this was the experience of a number of evangelical women, members of Rochester's emerging bourgeoisie. Rochester revival convert Mary Mathews, for example, prayed publicly, denounced nonrevival ministers, and served as an officer of one of the women's volunteer reform associations. Her religious experiences, however, gradually led her "to see more and more [my] utter weakness" and "utter dependence on Christ."[61] Humility, submissiveness, devotion to others, in theory ideal goals for all evangelical elect, in reality constituted the role-defining characteristics of that new creature, the bourgeois housewife. Thus, while revivalism had freed the new bourgeois woman from eighteenth-century forms of religious subordination and promised her new powers and access to the public sphere, the new theology contained a highly restrictive message. Though sanctioning individual women's acts of religious self-assertion (in themselves incidents of liturgical disruption), revivals instilled in these women a heightened sense of spiritual inferiority, which could then, as their liminal enthusiasm abated, and as they were integrated into new social roles, be translated into subordination to same-class men and to the new bourgeois family structure.

Women's religious enthusiasm thus assumed a convoluted, often contradictory pattern. On one level, the intensity of women's liminal disorderliness, their bitter confrontations with conservative male spiritual and social leaders, bespoke the attraction that spiritual autonomy, powerful new roles, the very right to speak after years of silence, held for her; for Jacksonian women, liminal disorder carried its own reward. On a second level, the extreme characteristics of each of the three stages of her rite of passage, marked as they all were by radical liturgical inversions (the denial of social and spiritual hierarchies during the phases of separation and liminality; pious submission to family and community norms that marked her entrance into the new bourgeois world) symbolized the contradictory social processes that took her from the legal death of the eighteenth-century wife, through the momentary role expansion of the Jacksonian reform period, to the new constraints placed upon the bourgeois house-wife. The disorderliness of her religious enthusiasm seemed so freighted with anger and demands for real autonomy and power that her reaggrega-tion appeared at all times problematic. It is not surprising, then, that society enveloped that reaggregation with the elaborate rituals of the Victorian era —especially since the new male establishment had chosen her silence, so hard to secure, as the symbol of their hegemony.

A word of caution. We deny the complexity of this process—and of these women's responses—if we see women at the end of the revivals returned to society, shorn of power, passive spokespersons for class and husbands. Of equal importance, we fall into a deterministic interpretive trap if we see enthusiastic women simply as responding to social-structural pressures. Jacksonian women were also social actors. The experience of class and geographic movement drew them to religious enthusiasm as a conge-nial mode of expression. Male religious leaders encouraged their enthusi-asm. But, once carried away by revivalistic disorder, once swept up by millennialist efforts to remake their world and their neighbors, these women changed in ways neither they nor their male religious mentors had anticipated. By the time they had returned to bourgeois society, they had changed, and by changing they transformed the world around them.

Their experiences constitute a perfect example of Turner's thesis that radical actions, though rooted initially in social paradigms, can break those paradigms, restructuring both the actor and the actor's world.[62] In the process of the play, that is, the actor becomes playwright. Jacksonian women emerged from the revivals cloaked with new skills that they had

acquired as participators in their own right in the commercial and communication revolutions. On leaving the home, they had organized and admin-
istered regional and national women's organizations (which could not have
existed half a century earlier) and held such male-sounding public titles as
President, Treasurer, or Trustee. They lobbied city councils and state
legislatures for women's causes, drew up constitutions, raised and spent
money. Their publications and their calls for financial support all followed
the lines laid down by the commercial and transportation revolutions,
which had first transformed these women into bourgeois urban dwellers.
Though these women's organizations in the end came to support, rather
than to undermine, the new economic order, they nevertheless altered the
power balance within the bourgeois home. Through reform organizations,
bourgeois women escaped the home and familiarized themselves with
urban and commercial realities. A new woman had emerged from the
economic changes and religious revivals of the 1820s, 1830s, and 1840s. She
had created extra-domestic roles and organizations. She had made herself
familiar with the external world of politics and economics. She had, in
short, knowledge and power that exceeded the wildest imagination of her
grandmothers and great-grandmothers, or, indeed, of the male religious
rebels who had orchestrated her first efforts at religious self-expression. The
world of women—as well as of men—had altered in ways never anticipated in the late eighteenth and early nineteenth centuries. Women had
not only served but had used and benefited from evangelical revivalism and
the new bourgeois order.

   But it is crucial to underscore an earlier point. The danger of distortion through oversimplification lurks within a literal insistence upon revivals as a rite of passage marking the emergence of the bourgeois woman as
a new social category. The rite of passage can serve the historian only as
an analogy, as a metaphor. Turner saw the rite of passage as a ritual of
mediation. It encapsulated within ritual forms the violence and disorder
of actual conflict and change. The rite of passage functioned to harmonize
diversity, to foster bonds of cohesion, to prevent change. This process,
Turner argued, existed in all societies, not only those defined as cyclical.
For Turner, a dialectic of structure and antistructure lay at the heart of all
social systems. Socially orchestrated and thus socially acceptable rituals of
liminality and *communitas* offered moments of freedom from restraint and
permitted the injection of creativity and innovation into societies other-

wise increasingly weighted down with structural overlays. Quickly, however, these moments of antistructure became counterstructure, and ultimately merged with structure itself. No society, Turner argued, can tolerate prolonged disorder and survive. Structure and cohesion must reassert themselves. Turner's vision is Hegelian in its insistence on balance and, by implication, upon ultimate harmony. And always it is "society" —neuter, monolithic, inclusive—that reasserts order.[63]

But no such orderly, harmonious, and inclusive world exists for the historian, least of all for the historian of Jacksonian America. Formlessness and form did not alternate in Hegelian succession. Dominant groups no longer controlled rituals of consensus and of mediation. There all was in flux. Nothing was predictable, neither the form that rituals and anti-rituals would take nor, as we have seen in the case of women's roles, the resolution of the social conflicts they marked. The conflict and iconoclasm that characterized this period were not contained within a carefully orchestrated rite. They occurred because American society itself stood between forms of economic and institutional organization, powerless to restrain those whom economic forces had thrust from their accustomed positions. A structureless chasm had opened through which whole segments of society moved, unrestrained by a powerful establishment (farm boys in the process of becoming clerks, farming daughters on their way to Lowell or domestic labor in the new cities, master craftsmen in hopes of becoming entrepreneurs, journeymen entering wage labor, farming and artisan wives suddenly transformed into bourgeois matrons, their unmarried sisters seeking jobs as spinster schoolmarms). Tens of thousands of Americans had suddenly been thrown out of a familiar family and village setting into a world of novel institutions and power relations—into a structure that had yet to assume its final form. The violent anti-ritualism of the revivals, the communal and religious experimentation that we have seen commencing as early as the 1780s and flourishing until the 1860s, expressed the uncertainty of this flotsam and jetsam at a time when no single group was numerous or powerful enough to impose a consensus. Disorder was not a ritually orchestrated moment of psychic release lying between firmly established structures. Rooted in economic and institutional realities, it lay beyond the power of ritual to contain or guide it.

At last, however, as Ryan has demonstrated in Utica, a white male bourgeoisie did emerge, as some of these transients were able to establish

themselves within the emerging capitalist structure as merchants, professionals, Victorian matrons and daughters, evangelical ministers. This barely
formed class chiseled out a consensus, embellishing it with rituals. As others
re-entered society or became susceptible to the power of the white male
bourgeoisie (wives and daughters, for instance, or clerks and domestics),
they accepted the proposed consensus, often expressing their acceptance
through newly established rituals of submission to communal and family
norms. But until that consensus was reached and enforced, all was problematic. For years those outside the emerging power structure refused to
acknowledge the victory of the bourgeoisie. Rather, they experimented
with alternative structures or continued to repudiate all structure.

The existence of individuals and groups outside of structure and
resistant to consensus points to one last difference between the revival and
reform enthusiasm of Jacksonian America and Turner's early conceptualization of a rite of passage. Rituals can mediate diversity and conflict only
among those who constitute a part of the social and power structure.
Rituals cannot contain those outside structure. Within any Western society
many groups will remain marginal to the established structure. They thus
escape the impact of rituals of mediation and consensus. As long as the
location of power remains uncertain, they will maintain their assault on
all structure.

This last offers the final clue to answering our question: Why did
some women cling to disorder and war against form? Victor Turner, while
conceptualizing liminality as an encapsulated part of ritual, does nevertheless suggest two other sources of liminality—which take us beyond a
consideration of ritual and into an analysis of economic and social structures. They are the liminality of the socially inferior and the liminality of
the socially marginal.[64] Outside of the dominant structure, they existed
beyond the influence of ritual. It is among these groups—clearly distinct
from the bourgeois women in the throes of class realignment, and in
all probability from our first groups of geographically mobile young
women—that we must look for our perennial radicals, our prophets and
protesters.

Ironically, as the Jacksonian Age progressed and the new bourgeoisie
became ever more economically and institutionally entrenched, the insistence on female inferiority became an unquestioned cultural assumption.
Eighteenth-century women had, of course, been seen as inferior to the men

in their lives. The wills of America's yeoman farmers, the contracts drawn up for indentured servants, the refusal to provide public education for women, all demonstrate women's inferior status. But in the hierarchically structured eighteenth century, this female inferiority was always relative to same-class men. Within such a hierarchically structured society, merchants' wives and daughters, farming and artisan women, sharing in the ascribed status of their family, stood superior to many men—journeymen and apprentices, landless agricultural and urban laborers, farmers poorer than their husbands. As egalitarian rhetoric came increasingly to characterize the political world and educational principles of this Era of the Common Man, women were transformed into the inferiors not only of same-class men but of all white men.

Moreover, whereas the traditional world of the eighteenth century assumed inequality as man's natural lot, the nineteenth century condemned and denigrated it—for all white men. Definitions of female inferiority thus became all-encompassing and carried a more negative social connotation. They became another sign of women's difference from men. Men, intent on resisting women's efforts to seize for themselves the rights that the Enlightenment and nineteenth-century republicanism had extended to men, developed elaborate justifications for women's separateness and inferiority, clothed in the new language of science and biology. Pietism and ecstatic religion offered women one escape from this new definition of female inferiority, especially since religion posited a cosmological system that could still challenge the authority of science. So did political and reformist attacks upon the new economic hegemony, and specifically upon its exclusion of women from the new promise of equality. Presumably, these aspects of religious and secular reforms were particularly attractive to women.

But, again, to which women? Since men defined all women as inferior, the argument of intellectual and social inferiority within the new bourgeois structures may help to explain why or how women were able to resist their second-class status but does not help us understand which women resisted and which acquiesced. Let us look at Turner's third source of liminality—social marginality. The commercial and industrial revolutions and the accompanying urbanization had transformed the economically productive farming and artisan women of the eighteenth century into economically and institutionally marginal figures. Business and politics—

the world of men and of power—occupied space now forbidden to bourgeois women and, indeed, to all married women. Hence the added appeal
religion held, since the sacred, newly opened to women, was also the only
public space in which they could assert their right to be present and, at
times, to be heard. Millennial enthusiasm also offered a way of transforming secular space into sacred space by commanding women to take Christ's
Word into the streets and byways, and thus to purify the world for His
coming.

To the new and universal female experience of economic and institutional marginality, certain bourgeois women added other forms of marginality. This was especially true of single women, who were institutionally
marginal to the increasingly nuclear family of the bourgeoisie, and ideologically marginal to Victorian social beliefs, which stressed the biologically determined female role of marriage and motherhood. Yet the very
economic and demographic forces that had created the bourgeois class
structure and the bourgeois family had caused, as well, a steady increase
in the number of single women, those who never married as well as those
who married quite late in their lives.

Women experienced another form of social marginality through,
rather than outside, their families. The commercial and industrial revolutions, while irresistible, swept unevenly across the American landscape. As
late as the 1850s, pockets of traditional communities remained. Furthermore individual families might still cling to a preindustrial economic and
institutional order, maintain extended households where apprentices and
journeymen lived with master craftsmen or farmers, and continue to honor
the old values. These families, structurally and economically, were marginal to the bourgeois revolution. At times they remained geographically
or residentially marginal as well. Their social-structural marginality often
had an ideational component—such as membership in a Quaker meeting
in an area where the Presbyterian Church dominated the social and political
spheres. The aggregating force of the new bourgeois economic institutions
thus flowed past these families, leaving their household structures un-
affected. Victorian social and intellectual proprieties did not reshape their
attitudes, behavior, or domestic power dynamics. These families stood aside
from the emerging order, refused to join its political parties, its respectable
churches, its philanthropies, which increasingly acted to shore up the
establishment. It was as if they observed the new ways from afar and judged
them—often quite harshly.

Nancy Hewitt's study of the social mobilization of women in Rochester pinpoints such a group of structurally marginal families who, in the 1840s and early 1850s, maintained an extended household structure. They lived outside the center of Rochester's economic and political power base and also, significantly, on the residential fringes of the city. They were frequently Quakers or had reform connections with Rochester's Quaker families. They joined with Quakers in abolitionist and pacifist efforts. Women from these families espoused extreme anti-ritualistic positions, in terms of both religion and reform. These were the women who engaged in a restless spiritual hegira, moving ever in the direction of religious anti-ritualism. They shocked society by publicly espousing the anarchism inherent in Garrisonian abolitionism. They advocated women's rights. Their reform organizations were loosely structured. Their vision was not tied to parochial roots but was universalist, with strong regional, national, and international religious and reform connections.[65]

Outside of structure, these women fused the experiences of social-structural marginality with that of intellectual and political inferiority. So armed, they vigorously resisted social reincorporation, turned the power of women marginal to the new order against the structure that would suppress them. That structure, as yet tentative—indeed, still in the process of formation—lacked the power to restrain their assaults. For decades these women and their counterparts in other towns and villages were able to assert their ideological autonomy. These were the female prophets who refused to be silenced, the disorderly women who persistently rejected structure, the angry women who repudiated the new capitalist modes and demanded social justice and equality for all of society's outcasts—especially for women.

A quest to understand women's attraction to religious anti-ritualism has covered a difficult and shifting terrain, but it has led me to the formulation of a new hypothesis concerning the relation of cultural forms and social experience, a formulation that draws equally upon anthropology's sensitivity to ritual and anti-ritual as symbolic languages, and history's awareness of heterogeneity, change, and conflict. Central to this hypothesis is the insistence that anti-ritualism constitutes a complex and at times warring medley of symbolic languages, each reflecting a different aspect of social change or marginality. During times of massive social transformation and of religious enthusiasm, divergent social groups may appear to speak identical symbolic languages. Observed over time, however, their languages will begin to alter, growing increasingly distinct as social differences divide the speakers and at times bring them into bitter conflict.

We have seen that a number of anti-ritualistic symbolic systems coexisted during the economic and institutional transformations that characterized America during the first half of the nineteenth century. In its simplest form, religious anti-ritualism bespoke the immediate experience of social upheaval and disorder. Those suddenly released from old forms of social control, those momentarily cast outside of institutional and economic structures, embraced religious enthusiasm as a language expressive of their social-structural situation. One thinks of the daughters and sons of New England's static agrarian communities who, between the 1790s and the late 1840s, in flight from their fathers' farms, moved into the economically and institutionally unformed commercial cities. These young people accounted both for the phenomenal rate of transience that America's new cities reported, and for the majority of those cities' revival converts. We can find the rural counterparts of the urban transients in the frontier communities that proliferated north and south of the Mason-Dixon line during these same years. In the throes of creating new settlements, far removed from familiar sights, the new Western farming women and men at times espoused extreme forms of revival and camp-meeting enthusiasm. Geographic transience and institutional novelty led both urban and rural youth to embrace religious disorder.

At the same time, anti-ritualism expressed the experiences of a quite different social group—those in movement between an older, agrarian-artisan-mercantile world and the new, commercial economy. The founders of mercantile houses in Utica and Rochester, in New York and Philadelphia, new industrial entrepreneurs and professionals, their wives and daughters, made up this second group. The Van Rensselaers, just moved to Utica from Oneida County, Arthur and Lewis Tappan, and a number of Finney's other New York City supporters, especially the husbands of the founders of the New York Female Moral Reform Society, are representative of this group. Geographic movement, fused with the novelty and financial instability of the new urban economy, exacerbated their sense of uncertainty and transition, and so intensified their revival enthusiasm. But once select members of this group established a secure foothold within the new world of commerce and industry, they and their wives drew back from their earlier espousal of religious disarray.

The experience of massive social transformations, the uncertainty that a position at the cutting edge of the new economy brought with it, affected not only the bourgeoisie. Rather these changes crossed the new lines that demarcated the bourgeoisie and the working class. Bruce Laurie found that a small and discrete group within Philadelphia's working class also espoused revival enthusiasm (albeit, again this was more true of wives and daughters than of husbands). This group exhibited many of the same characteristics that the more upwardly mobile merchants and professionals did: movement to Philadelphia from a rural background, employment at the cutting edge of industrial development, youth, the expectation of upward mobility. The young women and men from farming communities who attended the new academies and post-Revolutionary colleges that came to dot rural New England and Greater New England had also deliberately left an older, outmoded form of social organization. Like the young merchants and Philadelphia's new factory workers, they had yet to find a secure niche in the new world. Predictably, they also participated in the frequent and impassioned religious revivals that swept through these institutions.[66]

The final component of our hypothesis refers to the prolonged anti-ritualism of those who remained marginal to or excluded from the new power structures. Nancy Hewitt's group of Rochester women activists epitomizes this group. Marginality rather than geographic transience or social-structural movement characterized these women's families, and frequently the women themselves. Their religious and reform radicalism stood in stark contrast to the growing religious and reform conservatism of Rochester's more established and affluent evangelical women. They would embrace increasingly radical forms of antistructure as the new social forms coalesced around them, excluding them.

But why is anti-ritualism's appeal for women so much more intense and widespread than it is for men? In all cultures and at all times women constitute THE OTHER, THE MARGINAL. Thus they seize upon the language of anti-ritualism, making it their own. With its words they can condemn not only patriarchal structure but structure *per se.* They can demand their right to individual fulfillment, unrestrained by consideration of community and family or by male definitions of female biology. In this extreme form, anti-ritualism appeals to most women only fleetingly, only during those rare times when society itself pauses briefly, hesitatingly, between structures, and political and cultural hegemony is momentarily suspended.

At such times, the powerless and marginal will speak. Anti-ritualism's appeal disappears the moment a new structure is asserted and women assume socially acceptable niches within that world. Indeed, women's renunciation of anti-ritualism and their acceptance of the new rituals become the symbol of stability within the new order. Only those who simultaneously experience structural marginality and social inferiority will be able to resist the pressures—and attractions—of reaggregation and of ritual which accompany the reinstitution of order and a hierarchy of power. For them, anti-ritualism remains a vehicle of protest and resistance. In Western societies, such extreme marginality is far more commonly the experience of women than of men.

Finally, however, the new order will establish its hegemony. The new wielders of power will move to suppress symbolic as well as literal disorder. The language of diversity will be muffled. We will be left with the sounds of silence. Until, that is, the ongoing and irresistible forces of change again disrupt structure, permitting the marginal and the inferior—and, among them, women in particular—to break free.

PART THREE

Bourgeois Discourse and the
Progressive Era: An Introduction

Crisis and uncertainty had marked the gradual emergence of the American bourgeoisie. Throughout the slow and at times stumbling process of formulation and elaboration, the bourgeoisie reached back systematically into America's past for collective memories into which to place its experiences, and a familiar language through which to express them. In this way it attempted to transform the formless and uncertain into the structured and familiar. Its efforts succeeded. By the 1860s and 1870s, America's most revolutionary class had convinced itself and others that its values, its life style, its institutional creations, represented simultaneously the epitome of progress and the oldest of America's traditions.

America's first bourgeoisie established itself most successfully in the small towns that dotted the agrarian hinterland. Here, in the 1850s, 1860s, and 1870s, momentarily isolated from larger economic processes, the bourgeoisie constructed small-town America in its own image. "Their truths," Robert Wiebe tells us, "derived from what they knew: the economics of a family budget, the returns that come to the industrious . . . the advantages of a wife who stayed home and kept a good house."[1] Wealth and social status, they endlessly assured one another, rewarded self-reliance, honesty, and frugality. This trinity, fused with the drive for personal success, constituted the ethical code of the American bourgeoisie. If social problems arose, small-town bourgeois Americans analyzed them in terms of these unquestioned moral truths and sought personal, informal solutions that would reinforce existing relationships and assumptions.[2]

In the 1870s, the heyday of this early bourgeoisie, the American economy was still predominantly agrarian. America's small towns moved according to the rhythms of the agrarian world in which they nestled and which they served. Their ruling elite consisted of small-scale bankers, merchants, and manufacturers who served the commercial needs of the surrounding farming community. Their horizon rarely extended farther than the neighboring farming community. Small-town shopkeepers, of course, bought much of their stock from wholesalers in Chicago, St. Louis, or the more distant and awesome New York. But salesmen from these urban houses visited each individual shopkeeper, contributing to a sense of mutual respect and understanding. Personally choosing what he would buy from whom, guided solely by his own preferences and those of his local customers, the shopkeeper reigned supreme within his shop—and his world. As did the small-town banker, advancing credit to his neighbors, and the manufacturing entrepreneur, who also produced for people he knew and understood.[3]

An odd medley of personal intimacy and hierarchical structure characterized small-town America. This was not a world of simple democracies but of distinct inequalities in wealth and patterns of social deference. Still, such gradations did not cause alienation, or underscore lines of economic conflict. Protestant and homogeneous, sure that their way was God's way, these communities subjected individual townswomen and -men to strong community pressures. Their mode of social organization and control was highly personal. Everyone knew everyone else, heard similar sermons every Sunday, sent children to the same school. Social restraints and directions flowed along the informal channels of family and church— augmented by small-town gossip. Thinking of themselves as neighbors, they all assumed their allotted places within a commonly agreed upon and precise hierarchy of power and influence based on wealth and Christian gentility. A harmony of outlook and shared expectations marked this world. Such small towns, Robert Wiebe continues, constituted "island communities," autonomous societies, isolated by a weak communications system from other, comparable communities, insulated and relatively self-contained. For these few decades, the bourgeois elite that dominated them felt confident that they both understood and controlled the world in which they lived.[4]

They deceived themselves. They lived in a world both new and in flux. Their social and business leaders had not, for the most part, been born in the towns they governed, but had migrated from other towns or farming communities. John Addams, Jane Addams's father, is a case in point. The pillar of Cedarville, Illinois, society, a prosperous miller and banker, eight times a state senator, one of the founders of the Republican Party in Illinois and a friend of Lincoln, Addams had grown up in Pennsylvania; he moved to Cedarville and entered upon his successful career when already an adult, in the mid-1840s. The world his daughter grew up believing had always existed, John Addams had self-consciously molded during her childhood in the 1860s and 1870s.[5]

Indeed, during the years that marked this first bourgeois hegemony, Americans continued the pattern of geographic transience that their Jacksonian parents had initiated. Small towns and large cities were equally affected. In Buffalo, for instance, founded in the late 1820s and the 1830s, the average length of residence during the 1850s remained only 6.2 years. Even established male heads of households, the most stable population cohort, remained only 8.8 years. Youths, of course, were the most mobile. Between the 1850s and the 1870s, only 37 percent of men in their twenties remained in Buffalo for ten years. Only 44 percent of women in their twenties remained that long. A prosperous small city, Buffalo presented a picture of greater residential stability than the majority of America's commercial and industrial centers. Hamilton, Ontario, more closely approximated the American average. Between 1851 and 1871, the years when the American bourgeoisie sought to establish its roots, two-thirds of Hamilton's population and one-half of its householders moved away each decade.[6] Newburyport, Massachusetts, a rapidly growing manufacturing center, experienced a 65-percent transient rate between 1860 and 1870; over half of Newburyport's population moved again between 1870 and 1880.[7] Geographic mobility characterized all classes. No link existed between persistence and occupation, Michael Katz reports. Merchants and professionals moved as frequently as laborers. "Population movement was ubiquitous."[8]

Insecurities far more unsettling than geographic transience and the newness of neighbors lay under the placid waters of small-town America. By the 1860s, economic survival and bourgeois status had become, if anything, less certain. Prosperous Buffalo, which experienced a 27-percent rate of downward mobility in the 1850s, during the 1860s saw that rate escalate to 43 percent. "The calm, solid façade of power conveyed by a static group portrait masks the turmoil, striving and disaster that frequently characterized the experience of the individual members of the business class during the 1850s and early 1860s," Katz reports. "Neither staying wealthy nor falling, many men struggled from year to year, their economic state marginal and fluctuating."⁹ Individuals moved between cities and across class. Individual families frightened by increasing inequalities in wealth and growing class solidification feared for their future.

Yet while personal insecurity may have escalated, by the 1860s and 1870s the bourgeois class structure had stabilized. The percentages of the male population in business and in manual labor had become relatively constant. The relation of class, occupation, and wealth was set. In big cities, as in small-town America, this structure was hierarchical, based on inequality in the distribution of wealth.¹⁰ Patterns of deference marked class relations and distinctions of wealth within class. Those who had persisted and survived in this new world felt, indeed, that they were the fittest, chosen by God and natural evolution.¹¹

The sharp lines that would come to distinguish small-town and cosmopolitan America only a few years hence had not taken their clear-cut form in the 1860s and 1870s. Not only did inequalities of wealth characterize both, but the larger seaport and manufacturing centers maintained many of the institutional arrangements and ways of doing business familiar in the smaller towns. After all, the white bourgeois population of the large cities had almost all been born in small towns or rural counties and had only recently moved to the denser and more complex centers. The scale of most businesses in urban as in small-town America remained small; the large factory was still an anomaly. Urban America had yet to establish elaborate impersonal means of social control, or a bureaucratic and institutional framework on either a corporate or a governmental scale. The isolation of one large city from another, the relatively small scale of the cities' operations, the newness of each separate ruling class—the newness of many of the cities themselves—gave America's larger cities much the feel of a small town—but increasingly of a small town grown out of control.¹²

Into this barely coalesced social and economic structure, the industrial revolution sent a series of shock waves. By the 1880s and 1890s, the structure of American industry had changed dramatically. Centralized, large-scale manufacturing, national markets, giant corporations, finance capitalism, had concentrated economic power in a few cities. Small-town bankers and merchants became the agents of the distant and awesome determiners of America's fate. The railroads—with no sense of responsibility for the small towns they serviced, oblivious of the merchants, bankers, and lawyers whose lives they shaped—epitomized this shift in the national power balance. Small-town Americans had become flotsam and jetsam in the ongoing maturation of American capitalism.[13]

As America's small towns shrank in political and economic significance, the complexity and density of America's industrial and seaport cities increased. Their populations spiraled, fed by massive immigration from Southern and Eastern Europe and by the migration of ambitious refugees from small-town America. Think, for a moment, of the bright-eyed, breathless Sister Carrie taking the train for the first time to Chicago![14] Yet few set down roots more permanent than Sister Carrie's. Though one and a half million persons passed through Boston during the 1880s, in 1890 fewer than half a million remained.[15] Communications between neighborhoods within the city and between cities, communications between classes and among ethnic and religious groups within a class all had collapsed in face of the growing size and transience of the population. Or possibly, they had never existed. Yet the women and the men of these cities had to grapple with complex and ever-present dilemmas. They needed to transport efficiently raw materials and workers to factories and food and goods to consumers, to educate a polyglot population, to form functioning political coalitions, to provide medical services, lighting and gas, police and fire protection, sewage disposal and pure water. Urban realities impressed the immediacy of these problems upon an urban population and leadership ill-equipped to respond.[16] Communication and transportation systems that were essential to the efficient functioning of the new factories and corporations threatened to collapse. Labor rioted. Child mortality rates among the urban poor escalated. Tuberculosis became endemic among young working-women. Venereal disease ran rampant across class lines. "Once roused the sense of emergency was self-generating," Robert Wiebe points out. "Matters that previously would have been considered separate incidents, or even ignored, were seized and fit into the framework of jeopardy, each reinforcing the others as a further proof of imminent danger."[17]

Not even the oldest of America's cities could turn to a tradition of community cooperation or institutional sophistication in its efforts to deal with these problems. No time-honored ruling class or ancient urban institutions existed to lead the way.[18] Rather, America's male bourgeoisie warred against itself. Small-town merchants and manufacturers felt awed and excluded from the councils of power. The older mercantile and professional core bitterly resented and castigated the new men of corporate and fiscal wealth. Political and philanthropic cooperation proceeded with difficulty. "America in the late nineteenth century," Wiebe asserts, "was a society without a core. It lacked those national centers of authority and information which might have given order to such swift changes. . . . Established wealth and power fought one battle after another against the great new fortunes and political kingdoms carved out of urban-industrial America. The more they struggled, the more they scrambled the criteria of prestige. The concept of the middle class crumbled at the touch."[19] Each lower step on the social ladder echoed the sense of alienation and confusion found at the top. The army of clerks, salesmen, and secretaries that staffed the lower echelons of the business world saw in their jobs and their neighborhoods not a way of life, merely a way to survive. They drifted in an impersonal and threatening world.[20]

The world of large cities, threatening to its own inhabitants, assumed monstrous proportions when viewed from afar by small-town Americans. The giant cities seemed to violate every small-town value. Sodoms and Gomorrahs of sexual excess and sybaritic indulgence, Babels of conflicting languages, religions, and customs, chaotic, ungovernable, the great cities epitomized the foreign, the unknown, and the dangerous. Plutocracy and anarchy became, in the imagination of rural and small-town America, the warring deities of a new world.[21]

Ironically, the very economic and technological forces that demolished the composure and autonomy of small-town America and pressed urban institutions to the breaking point raised up a new generation of managers and professionals as its problem solvers. At home within the new cities, national and professional in their orientation, the new managerial bourgeoisie developed within the new corporate bureaucracies, or came from the professions that serviced those corporations. Alternatively, they emerged from the ranks of corporate America's peer-enemies—the AFL and the national craft unions. They were lawyers, economists, engineers, physicians, labor organizers. Increasingly, the cities themselves called forth even more innovative professionals: social workers, public-school teachers, educational reformers, public-health experts, architects and early city planners, photographers and journalists. Seeing the world in terms of complex patterns of structural interactions, these professionals assumed a pluralistic world and worked through compromise. They did not tap local community loyalties but turned automatically to state and national governments for assistance. They saw themselves as the problem solvers and the facilitators of the new urban industrial world. They were the antithesis of small-town America's bourgeois elite, and they quickly replaced small-town businessmen and professionals as the formulators and spokespersons for the bourgeois way of life. The older bourgeoisie viewed this new bourgeoisie with open hostility. They realized that the leaders of the new generation spoke a language they could not understand, lived by alien values, and fought for goals they rejected. The new bourgeoisie joined the new city in small-town America's opinion as a symbol of danger and alienation.[22]

Women played a major role in both the new city and the new bourgeoisie. They assumed this place at first almost by accident—indeed, by default. The Civil War, in the name of patriotism and humanitarianism, had called hundreds of thousands of women out of their homes. Through the agency of the Sanitary Commissions that sprang up in every Northern city, bourgeois matrons raised money for the war effort, cared for wounded soldiers, and prepared bandages and food for field hospitals. The needs of soldiers' families led these patriotic matrons into city slums, bringing them face to face with urban poverty. These were not, for the most part, the women who had battled urban prostitution and poverty as members of the Female Moral Reform Society, or who had fought for racial justice under Garrison's banner. During the 1850s, having entered the new bourgeoisie, most of these women had self-consciously rejected radicalism and feminism. Drawn from their homes by male patriotic rhetoric, however, they did not return. With grown children or with few children and sizable domestic staffs, a significant number of the new bourgeois matrons turned from the needs of the war to the needs of the new cities.[23]

In doing so they transposed the Cult of True Womanhood to suit their needs. Few of these newly active bourgeois matrons, Mari Jo Buhle argues, questioned the cultural presumptions of women's innate piety, purity, and domesticity. They moved into America's corrupt and unjust cities not as self-conscious feminists but as "True Women." They were, they told husbands, politicians, and industrialists, the conscience and the housekeepers of America. Their virtue constituted a national resource. Selfish and corrupt men had created a chaotic and fragmenting world; the women would set it right.[24] They did more than create extra-domestic roles for bourgeois women. In the face of growing class-consciousness among bourgeois and working-class men, they asserted what Mari Jo Buhle has called "a gender consciousness." Invoking a "universal sisterhood," they asserted women's shared experiences and vision. Constructing institutions that crossed male-created economic divisions, they worked to ameliorate the harsh effects of industrialization.[25] No sooner did the Civil War end than the New England Women's Club conducted a study of working conditions among New England's needleworkers, a report that formed the core for Carroll Wright's pathbreaking study, *The Working Girls of Boston*.[26] In 1877, the Boston Women's Educational and Industrial Union, an outgrowth of the New England Women's Club, continued to survey conditions among workingwomen, operated an employment agency, and opened clubrooms to workingwomen. A score of Western cities emulated the Boston women. Through the YWCA, other women also worked to ease the burden of poverty and work on their less fortunate sisters.[27]

We must not see these women as ineffective ladies bountiful in flight from genteel boredom. Through the 1880s, they maintained a meaningful dialogue with poor workingwomen and, at least in part, addressed their social and economic needs. They did so, that is—Mari Jo Buhle argues—as long as the female labor force remained predominantly native-born and Protestant, composed of single and widowed women from poor farming backgrounds. Women in the needle trades epitomized this group of workingwomen, and dominated the female urban labor force through the 1870s and into the 1880s. Bourgeois women's insistence that all women had the right to labor in dignity, and their belief in self-help through education (and even unionization), struck a note of accord in the minds of such workingwomen. They were indeed sisters separated only by misfortune. When the female labor force became increasingly foreign-born, consisting more and more of married women who worked at sweated home industry with their husbands and children (this occurred in the 1880s and 1890s), the bourgeois women's demand for equal pay for equal work ceased to resonate with working-class women's experiences. These newer working-class women focused, rather, on their families' need to survive. Progress, immigrant wives insisted, lay in decent wages for their husbands and sons. At this point, Buhle argues, communication between women across class began to collapse.[28]

Building new institutions within the new cities, bourgeois women addressed many of their own needs. The women's clubs, Buhle suggests, had two goals. Not only did they reach out to working-class women; they also sought to provide intellectual and social services for their bourgeois members. These were many and varied, for even in the 1860s and 1870s bourgeois women did not constitute a monolithic group. They included the affluent, married, and socially prominent; women whose husbands struggled to remain within the bourgeoisie; women who had not married. Frequently employed in a world that barred genteel women from the work force, the single professional woman occupied a social position midway between the working-class woman and the socially and economically secure matron. Outside of traditional categories, she had novel needs and an ambiguous social standing.[29]

To serve this varied constituency, the women's club developed a variety of services. Look, for example, at the broad range of bourgeois causes and programs the New England Women's Club embraced in addition to their work with women in Boston's needle trades. Concerned with broadening employment options for bourgeois women, they fought to open Massachusetts's state horticultural school to women. With the needs of bourgeois daughters in mind, the club founded the Girls' Latin School. It sponsored the New England Hospital for Women and Children, an alternative medical facility which provided training and positions for women physicians at the same time as it offered medical care for poor women. The Boston Women's Educational and Industrial Union not only operated a club for working-class women; it also ran a downtown club, with a lunchroom, library, and reading room, that attracted more affluent sisters. The union sponsored lecture series on virtually every issue of interest to bourgeois women, from household efficiency through literary, religious, and political controversies. In this way it provided an autonomous space both for the respectable matron who needed a place for herself outside the bourgeois home and for the professional woman who wished to socialize with her female peers.[30]

Thus by the 1870s the new bourgeois woman had emerged. Confident and independent, a self-created urban expert, she spearheaded bourgeois efforts to respond creatively to the new city and the new economy. In the process of working for herself and other women, she had begun to demand equality in education, in employment, and in wages. Certain of her own abilities, she began again to demand the vote, so as to implement her new social visions more effectively.[31] In short, she had politicized gender. Husbands began to view their wives' hard-won expertise, administrative skills, and new demands with alarm. Could respectable bourgeois matrons and their spinster sisters be so talented, so politically aware, so clear about their own separate needs and remain True Women?

If the urban bourgeois matron of the 1860s and 1870s alarmed, her daughter frightened. The 1880s and the 1890s saw the emergence of a novel social and political phenomenon—the New Woman. The New Woman originated as a literary phrase popularized by Henry James. Transposed into a sociological and historical context, it needs some further explanation. James used it to refer to American women of affluence and sensitivity (he usually placed them in a European setting). Young and unmarried, they rejected social conventions, especially those imposed on women. These women fought stagnation. They acted on their own. They were the unique product of American society, James argued, inconceivable in Europe. Within James's novels, they suffered the consequences of their autonomy. Daisy Miller is one example, Isabel Archer another.[32] I have transposed James's term while maintaining James's focus on the New Woman's rejection of convention, her desire to act on her own, her roots in American society. I use the term to refer to a specific sociological and educational cohort of women born between the late 1850s and 1900. They represented the new demographic trends of later marriages for bourgeois women. Benefiting from bourgeois affluence, which endowed colleges for women, they were college-educated and professionally trained at a time when few men were. Few New Women married. By the early twentieth century, many had won a place within the new professions or carved career niches for themselves within the governmental and other nondomestic institutions that proliferated in the late-nineteenth-century city. In short, the New Women, rejecting conventional female roles and asserting their right to a career, to a public voice, to visible power, laid claim to the rights and privileges customarily accorded bourgeois men. They were, at the same time, the daughters of the new bourgeois matrons. Attending lyceum talks on feminism and on the problems of the city, made possible by the women's clubs that their literal and fictive mothers had founded, they grew up in a world already filled with separate women's urban institutions. They inherited a consciousness of women's new role possibilities almost as their birthright.[33]

Who, specifically, were the New Women? Women associated with the settlement-house movement, women educational reformers, physicians, and public-health experts, women writers and artists were the most visible. Jane Addams, Lillian Wald, Alice and Edith Hamilton, Florence Kelley, M. Carey Thomas, Vida Scudder, Mary Woolley leap instantly to mind, as do Sarah Orne Jewett and Willa Cather.[34] The term should incorporate, as well, a host of less visible women who worked as teachers, social workers, physicians, nurses, business women—provided these women lived economically and socially autonomous lives. The New Woman did not have to be a star.

Successive generations of New Women followed one another, differing from each other in significant ways, frequently critical of each other.[35] Those whom I designate as the first generation of New Women attended the new women's colleges in the 1870s and 1880s. They flourished professionally between the 1880s and the First World War. Many were outspoken feminists, addressing issues of industrial, racial, and sexual justice at home and peace in the world. But while they rejected traditional gender definitions, their roots went deep into small-town America. They continued to accept many of the bourgeois values and genteel habits of that world, such as honesty, morality, and service to others. Jane Addams's Victorian parlor in Hull House and her adoration of her father's friend Abraham Lincoln epitomized this world view.[36]

A second generation of New Women followed the first. Educated in the 1890s, often by the first generation of New Women, they came into their own in the years immediately preceding and succeeding the First World War. As political as the first generation, they placed more emphasis on self-fulfillment, a bit less on social service, and a great deal more on the flamboyant presentation of self. We see this as they moved into creative and artistic fields, and in their rejection of bourgeois sexual conventions. More at home in America's larger cities, they moved easily within the bohemian world of New York, Paris, and Berlin. (I refer to Eastman, Stein, Anderson, St. Vincent Millay, Duncan, Barney.)[37]

The second generation of New Women fused their challenge of gender conventions with a repudiation of bourgeois sexual norms. They fought not in the name of a higher female virtue (as women had from the 1860s through the founding of the settlement houses), but for absolute equality. They wished to be as successful, as political, as sexual as men. Their mannish bob, cigarette smoking, boyish figures symbolized their rejection of gender distinctions. Not one shred of the Cult of True Womanhood remained to cloak their life style in the symbols of respectability. They alarmed the first generation of New Women almost as much as they alarmed the respectable and the conventional. They, more than any other phenomenon of the 1910s and 1920s, signaled the birth of another new era.

For half a century, economic and social change had relentlessly formed and re-formed the institutions, values, and behavior of bourgeois America. True to Mary Douglas's prediction, women and men repeatedly transformed the physical body into metaphors and images expressive of their social bewilderment. The languages of science and medicine became dense with double meanings. Formed to function within the ever more exacting realm of clinical and theoretical investigation, these languages suddenly became metaphoric vehicles through which scientists and laity alike responded to social changes and projected visions of an ideal future.

The essays in the last part of this volume trace the gradual evolution of a pivotal set of Victorian physiological metaphors—concerning the bourgeois family and man's pre-eminence in the public sphere. The Victorians asserted gender complementarity and male dominance as "eternal verities" rooted in human biology. They defended them as the last bastions of social order.

Of course, neither "eternal verity" had originated in the nineteenth century. As the urban industrial revolution transformed American society, however, both assumed novel, at times more extreme forms. Certainly their ideological justification grew ever more elaborate. Americans had initially expressed this ideology—what Barbara Welter christened the Cult of True Womanhood—in religious metaphors and in the new language of Romanticism. By the 1840s and 1850s, as medicine and science came to rival religion for ideological supremacy, men affirmed bourgeois gender ideology in the new languages of science and medicine. They made sure, however, that their novel scientific vocabulary in no way challenged the old religious values. As medicine continued its ascendancy, and as bourgeois women began to challenge the pre-eminence of female domesticity within the pantheon of bourgeois values, the male bourgeoisie elaborated, in an increasingly deterministic language, the original medico-scientific insistence that women's biology was women's destiny.

Examining the citations in the "Puberty to Menopause" essay, we find that the original medical reformulation of the Cult of True Woman-hood occurred during the 1840–60 period. It thus coincided with the solidification of the early bourgeoisie and with early efforts to improve standards and to encourage scientific experimentation within the medical profession. It assumed a far more deterministic form during the 1880s and 1890s. By then, of course, deterministic science was in its ascendancy; the new cities, the new economy, and the new managerial bourgeoisie had replaced small-town America in the seats of power; and women had relentlessly and successfully challenged the cult's restrictions on their public roles and political power.

The second essay, "The Hysterical Woman," examines the escalating gender conflicts that characterized mid- and late-nineteenth-century bour-geois society. Men fulminated against the hysterical woman: selfish and demanding, she violated all that was natural in women. Some women, feeling powerless within the new family, used hysteria as an effective means of passive aggression and protest. The conflicting language of hysteria tells us a great deal about gender and power relations within the bourgeois family—the original focus of my inquiry. But, like the medical transposi-tion of the Cult of True Womanhood, it also reflects the impact of external economic and structural forces upon that family. Thus, like the general male medical discussion of women's biological destiny, medical attacks upon the female hysteric (clustering within an 1840s–50s and 1880s–90s chronology) demonstrate the complex ways in which social change and gender conflict come together to create a metaphoric language in which the social becomes the sexual.

I will not pretend that I originally approached the male medical discourse within this conceptual framework. As the quickest reading of the "Puberty to Menopause" essay will make clear, I had focused, rather, on Victorian Americans' responses to the twin psychobiological crises of puberty and aging. I sought, in the hysteria essay, to explore the interaction between role socialization and personality formation. Psychoanalytic con-cerns informed my research. Significantly, I did not even attempt to find letters or diaries in which women discussed their own reproductive experi-ences, attitudes toward sexuality, or angers and depressions. But though I now realize that men's public and symbolic languages shed little light on women's private experiences, I insist all the more strongly that these languages reveal a great deal about men's public experiences. And so, ten years after I wrote these two essays, I ask us to reread them, looking now in the male rhetoric for new clues to men's emotional responses to the massive social-structural forces that reshaped their world.

The last essays in this volume far more self-consciously examine the metaphoric aspects of the male medical discourse. Focusing on the late nineteenth century and the early twentieth, I have traced the transformation of expressive medical metaphors into agencies for social control—a process I have denominated "the politicization of the body." This transformation began in America during the 1870s and 1880s. Until then, of course, physical and sexual metaphors had proliferated. We have watched Jacksonian women and men translate their social anxieties into sexual alarms and their political visions into sexual utopias. Abolitionists transformed the sexual exploitation of female slaves into a symbol of all that was vicious and exploitative in slavery. Nativists attacked the Roman Church as the "Whore of Babylon" and whispered of murdered babies within Boston convents. But as long as the bourgeois hegemony remained uncertain, words remained merely expressive vehicles—innocent of the ability to control, constrain, or punish. By the 1880s, this had changed. The new bourgeois order, supported by its professional cohorts, could now endow its expressive vocabulary with political and bureaucratic power. The issue of abortion exemplifies this wedding of words and power. It exemplifies as well the critical role the new professions, and especially medicine, played in this process.

Whereas the troubled men of Jacksonian America chose a variety of sexual images to express their social concerns, mid-nineteenth-century men turned increasingly to the sexually autonomous and gender-deviant woman. At first bourgeois men focused upon the bourgeois matron's declining birthrate. They molded the twin themes of birth control and abortion (always defining them as women's decisions) into condensed symbols of national danger and decay. Whether they appeared in race-suicide jeremiads or in anti-abortion propaganda, the women who practiced birth control and the aborting mother became metaphors for all that appeared "unnatural" in small-town America. But by the opening decades of the twentieth century, in the wake of a successful anti-abortion campaign, the woman who simply restrained her motherhood no longer threatened male dominance and male order. She ceased to express male social and psychological anxieties. Bourgeois men turned, instead, to her metaphoric daughter—the New Woman. They seized upon the later generation of New Women's overt sexuality and rejection of gender distinctions to construct the ultimate symbol of social disorder and of the "unnatural"— the mannish lesbian. If her sexuality could be constrained and remolded, some men, at least, felt they would have demonstrated man's power to restrain disorder, to control change, to preserve male dominance. The 1920s witnessed a bitter political struggle between women and men, radicals and conservatives, in which women's sexuality played a critical metaphoric role.

But no matter how her mythic representations changed, from the mid-nineteenth century on woman had become the quintessential symbol of social danger and disorder. It is not surprising, therefore, that Victorian men generally and the male medical profession in particular focused some of their earliest legislative efforts at sexually regulating and socially controlling these seditious female figures. Medical arguments, of course, underwrote all bourgeois power relations. Scientific racism had legitimated native-born WASP hegemony, first over blacks and then over the new immigrants. Social Darwinism glorified the rich as the fittest. Ultimately the scientific community and white male politicians sought to regulate the bodies of the poor, of blacks, and of immigrants. But before they attempted to control other men, male physicians and politicians had first experimented with regulating women—and, most significantly, the women of their own class. The medico-political campaign against abortion constituted the first effort at an alliance between the male medical leadership and bourgeois politicians. Having defeated and regulated their own women, bourgeois men then sought to control working-class women through state campaigns against the female prostitute. Only after both campaigns had succeeded did bourgeois men seek to control the bodies and the sexuality of other men.

Puberty to Menopause:
The Cycle of Femininity in
Nineteenth-Century America

Adolescence and the coming of old age are pivotal processes in human experience. On one level, they are socially defined crises, points of entrance into new social roles and responsibilities. More primitively, they are physiological processes that each individual and each culture must incorporate into basic patterns of social structure and ideology. They are marked by hormonal and emotional flux, maladjustment and depression—in the case of old age, by disease and fears of disease. The coming and fading of sexual maturity, moreover, force cultures and individuals to deal with the question of human sexuality. The menstrual blood and wet dreams of puberty, the hot flashes of menopause are physical signposts that even the most sexually repressed and denying culture must acknowledge and rationalize in terms consistent with its social values generally (as must each individual within that culture, in terms appropriate to his or her particular psychic needs). Few values are more central to this process than those relating to women and women's role.

This essay proposes to examine Victorian American attitudes toward puberty and menopause in women. It will do so from one specific perspective—the perspective of the medical profession as expressed in both its professional and its popular writings. Since puberty and menopause are both physiological processes and possible triggers of disease, every nineteenth-century gynecology textbook and the most popular medical guides devoted sections to them, as, of course, did the professional journals. In non-medical Victorian literature, on the other hand, these subjects remained veiled.[1]

Puberty, menstruation, and menopause could be specifically medical problems as well. The depressions and irritability of adolescence, the breast and uterine cancer of the aging woman were conditions physicians had to face—and if not cure, at least explain, and in explaining hope to mitigate. The physician's hypothetical explanation of these disorders thus served to express and rationalize the often intractable realities of puberty and menopause—and, at the same time, helped the physician act out his own role as healer. Inevitably, as well, the physician's would-be scientific views reflected and helped shape social definitions of the appropriate bounds of woman's role and identity. In exploring these medical arguments, then, I want to stress not their internal consistency and even less their scientific significance, but, rather, the ways in which they represent a particular nineteenth-century attempt to resolve the perplexing interplay of socially defined sex roles and the ambivalence surrounding puberty and menopause.

Woman, Victorian society dictated, was to be chaste, delicate, and loving. Yet her Victorian contemporaries assumed that behind this modest exterior lay a complex network of reproductive organs that controlled her physiology, determined her emotions, and dictated her social role. She was seen, that is, as being both higher and lower, both innocent and animal, pure yet quintessentially sexual. The central metaphor in these formulations, central both emotionally and in content, pictures the female as driven by the tidal currents of her cyclical reproductive system, a cycle bounded by the pivotal crises of puberty and menopause and reinforced each month by her recurrent menstrual flow.[2]

The extent to which the reproductive organs held sway over woman's body had no parallel in the male. Male sexual impulses, nineteenth-century physicians and laymen alike maintained, were subject to a man's will; they were impulses that particular men could at particular times choose to indulge or to repress.[3] Not so with woman's sexuality. Woman's sexual and generative organs were hidden within her body, subject not to her will but to a biological clock of which women were only dimly aware and which they were clearly unable to control. Each month, for over thirty years, these organs caused cyclical periods of pain, weakness, embarrassment, irritability, and, in some cases, even insanity. "Woman's reproductive organs are pre-eminent," one mid-century physician explained in typical phrases. "They exercise a controlling influence upon her entire system, and entail upon her many painful and dangerous diseases. They are the source of her peculiarities, the centre of her sympathies, and the seat

of her diseases. Everything that is peculiar to her, springs from her sexual
organization."[4]

Such views had been familiar since classical antiquity. Between 1840
and 1890, however, physicians, reflecting a growing physiological sophistication generally, and, more specifically, increasingly circumstantial knowledge of the female reproductive system, were able to present a far more
elaborate explanation of woman's peculiar femininity—and hence a rationale for her role as wife and mother.[5] Woman became a prisoner not
only of her reproductive functions but quite explicitly of two tiny and
hitherto ignored parts of that system—the ovaries. "Ovulation fixes
woman's place in the animal economy," one doctor explained in 1880.
"With the act of menstruation is wound up the whole essential character
of her system." "A woman's system is affected," health reformer J. H.
Kellogg commented as late as 1895, "we may almost say dominated, by
the influence of these two little glands. . . . Either an excess or a deficiency
of the proper influence of these organs over the other parts of the system
may be productive of disease."[6]

The ovaries began their dictatorship of woman's life at puberty. They
released her, often exhausted and debilitated, at menopause. Puberty and
menopause were thus seen as peculiarly sensitive physiological turning
points in a woman's life—stages at which new physical and emotional
equilibria had to be established.[7] Both men and women, of course, experienced such crises of developmental readjustment. For women, however, such periods of crisis and resolution occurred more frequently, and
seemed both more dangerous and more sexual. Puberty was, for example,
more precipitate and difficult for women—and was followed immediately
by the monthly crisis of menstruation, by pregnancy, childbirth, lactation,
and finally menopause. As late as 1900, a physician could picture the
dangers in these melodramatic terms:

> Many a young life is battered and forever crippled in the
> breakers of puberty; if it crosses these unharmed and is not
> dashed to pieces on the rock of childbirth, it may still ground
> on the ever-recurring shadows of menstruation, and lastly, upon
> the final bar of the menopause ere protection is found in the
> unruffled waters of the harbor beyond the reach of sexual
> storms.[8]

Another physician, perhaps influenced by the moral and religious strivings pictured in *Pilgrim's Progress,* entitled his guide to woman's health *Woman and Her Thirty Year Pilgrimage.* [9]

Puberty and menopause were, moreover, inseparably linked in nineteenth-century medical thought. The way in which a woman negotiated the physiological dangers of puberty was believed to determine her health not only during her child-bearing years but at menopause as well. A painful, unhealthy, or depressed puberty sowed the seeds for disease and trauma at menopause. Indeed, so intertwined were these events that physicians used the age of puberty to predict the age when menopause would occur. Puberty and menopause were, as one nineteenth-century physician revealingly expressed it, "the two termini of a woman's sexual activity." [10] One woman physician even went so far as to liken the menopausal woman to a preadolescent; menopause, she wrote, was "the transition of the (sexual) system from an active ovarian state to the quiet condition of a non-ovulating girl." [11]

Such medical and biological arguments helped, of course, to rationalize woman's traditional role. But they served other social purposes as well. They expressed, that is, the age-old empirical understanding that puberty and menopause were indeed periods of stress—crises of both emotional and social identification and physical health. And they served as well to provide the physician—armed with still-primitive gynecological skills and an equally primitive body of physiological knowledge—with a system with which to explain such biological and emotional realities. The nineteenth century was a time when pregnancies and obstetrical trauma were far more common than today. It was crucial to the physician's professional role, and thus to the psychic comfort of his female patients as well, that he be provided with explanations with which to counsel and to comfort.

At puberty a girl became a woman. Physicians remarked that the change was often startlingly dramatic. Many doctors indulged in romantic eulogies to the young woman's physical and anatomical attributes. They admired her newly rounded limbs, her "swelling breasts," her broadened hips, the transparent nature of her skin, which reflected every blush. Her unfolding beauty was charming indeed. "How sensitive—how tremulous is now her nervous system!" one such physician remarked. "It is as if," another doctor wrote, "a new being, almost, is created." [12]

Yet this beauty, like the opening blossom to which the pubescent girl was so frequently compared, was at the same time weak, dependent, and fragile. Puberty, the nineteenth century never doubted, brought strength, vigor, and muscular development to boys; to women it brought increased bodily weakness, a newfound and biologically rooted timidity and modesty, and the "illness" of menstruation. With puberty, English clinician Michael Ryan explained to his medical audience, "all parts of [a man's] . . . body became developed . . . the principles of life superabound in his constitution, and he vigorously performs all the noble pursuits assigned him by nature. Woman, on the contrary, delicate and tender, always preserves some of the infantile constitution."[13]

Yet the creation of this fragile and ethereal creature was frequently traumatic; female adolescence was often a stormy period. (The emotional difficulties of adolescence were hardly a discovery of the late nineteenth century; they were well known to physicians throughout the century.) Girls would suddenly become moody, depressed, petulant, capricious, even sexually promiscuous. Adolescence, explained a late-nineteenth-century advice book for mothers, "is naturally a time of restlessness and of nerve irritability. Her mind is confused with vague dissatisfaction with all about her, and vaguer desires which she vainly endeavors to define even to herself. . . . Her feelings are especially sensitive and easily hurt." It was a "period of storm and stress," of "brooding, depression and morbid introspection."[14]

Victorian physicians drew upon their "ovarian" model of female behavior both to explain such erratic behavior and to contain it within traditional social bounds. The onset of puberty, they explained, marked perhaps the greatest crisis in a woman's life—a crisis during which a new physiological and emotional equilibrium was being created, an equilibrium that would control a woman's life for the next thirty years. If a girl, especially at the very outset of puberty, violated the laws of her body, a dire chain of pain and disease, of dysmenorrhea, miscarriage, even sterility would surely follow. As one physician explained in his domestic medical text,

> It is now that every hidden germ of disease is ready to spring up; and there is scarcely a disorder to which the young and growing female is subjected, which is not at this time occasionally to be seen, and very often in a fatal form. . . . Coughs

become consumptive and scrofula exerts its utmost influence in the constitution and deforms the figure of the body. . . . The dimensions of that bony outlet of the female frame is also altered and diminished on which so much of safety and comparative ease depends in childbirth. This, indeed, is the cause of almost every distressing and fatal labor that occurs and it is at this period of life . . . that such an unspeakable misfortune may be prevented.

If a woman was to fulfill her ordained role as mother of numerous and healthy offspring, her own mother must carefully oversee her puberty— and be aware of even the slightest evidence of ill-health.[15]

Woman's body, doctors contended, contained only a limited amount of energy—energy needed for the full development of her uterus and ovaries. At the commencement of puberty, then, a girl should curtail all activity. One doctor advised the young woman to take to her bed from the first signs of a discharge until menstruation was firmly established, months or perhaps years later. Not all doctors took so extreme a position, but most did warn that a girl should not engage in any absorbing project at this time. Indeed physicians routinely used this energy theory to sanction attacks upon any behavior they considered unfeminine; education, factory work, religious or charitable activities, virtually any interests outside the home during puberty were deplored, as was any kind of sexual forwardness such as flirtations, dances, and party-going.[16]

There was only one right way for a young woman to behave at puberty. From the onset of menstruation until marriage, she must concentrate on the healthy development of her reproductive organs and the regulation of her menses. Physicians prescribed an elaborate regimen to maintain sexual and general health, a regimen that remained remarkably consistent throughout the nineteenth century. Young women were told to avoid the display of any strong emotions, especially anger, at puberty. They should spend much of their time in the fresh air, enjoy moderate exercise, avoid down beds, corsets, or liquor and other stimulating beverages. Ample rest and a simple diet of unstimulating food were equally necessary. The life style most frequently advocated for the young woman consisted of a routine of domestic tasks, such as bed-making, cooking, cleaning, and child-tending. These would appropriately serve, physicians argued, to provide the best regimen for the full and proper development of her maternal organs.[17]

Medical theories of puberty thus served a number of functions. Such concepts functioned as a way in which physicians—and society generally—could recognize the development and centrality of woman's sexual nature—while at the same time controlling and limiting that sexuality within a reproductive framework. The theories conceded the existence of sexuality and emotionality as normal aspects of adolescence, but served to warn women that they must control these emotions and limit their activities to the home; otherwise, disease, insanity, and even death would surely follow.

Still more subtly, these hypothetical physiological arguments suggest, by implication, a good deal about the social and psychic realities of female adolescence—and their latent function for the physicians who intoned them. Let me be a bit more specific. Nineteenth-century medical discussions of puberty suggested that mother–daughter relations may often have broken down at puberty, thus leaving the young girl isolated from an important emotional support system during a critical and stormy period. Physicians wrote repeatedly of girls left in culpable ignorance by their prudish mothers, terrified at what they could only construe as vaginal hemorrhaging. Many such girls, physicians reported, tried fearfully to stop the flow, immersing their bodies in icy water or wrapping wet clothes around their abdomens. Others, seized with shame and terror, ran away from home, exposed themselves to inclement weather, or wandered the streets at night not wanting to return home. One woman reported that it had taken her "a life time" to forgive her mother for the fear and loneliness she had felt when she was first menstruating.[18] Indeed, so common in medical writings are versions of this traumatic first menstruation that it becomes a kind of primal feminine scene, one encompassing in a single exemplary situation a universe of veiled emotion—emotions that nineteenth-century doctors recognized and attempted to mitigate by castigating those mothers who failed to support their daughters at so critical a period.[19]

Though warnings about rest, diet, and the need for maternal supervision that mark the medical discussions of puberty may seem quaint, perhaps repressive, they tell us a good deal about the female experience of puberty; they tell us that adolescence was traumatic, that it implied an often painful restructuring of intra-familial and social identities—in short, the hypothetical pathology of the critical period and its possibly irreversible damage expressed a consciousness of the real crisis a young girl faced at this time. The emotionally charged picture of first menstruation, its isolation, fears, and dangers, served, that is, to express and rationalize a rather complex insight into the several dimensions of puberty.

Insecurity and a sense of isolation and unworthiness are, of course, not peculiar to adolescent girls in Victorian America. These feelings reflect a multitude of anxieties: fear that menstrual blood might indeed be the result of injury due to masturbation; a fear—probably unconscious and perhaps dating to infancy, of a growing social autonomy and sexual maturity, the reactivation of a fundamental struggle between mother and daughter for both love and independence—a struggle that psychiatrists now suggest predates any Oedipal conflict. Puberty and menstruation do, after all, force every woman to ask and attempt to answer that fundamental question: What is the nature and meaning of my femaleness?

Part of this stress surrounding female puberty was due to the ambivalent and unresolved attitudes that surrounded menstruation itself. The history of attitudes toward menstruation is age-old, varied, yet surprisingly consistent; it was a period of danger, of shame, of punishment. Judeo-Christian folklore attributed menstruation to God's curse on the daughters of a sinning Eve. Because of Eve's transgression, woman needed more forgiveness and regeneration than man, one physician argued, and thus "this special secretion was given them." "Many girls," another reported, "consider [menstruation] as a humiliating badge of their inferiority to the stronger sex." Not surprisingly, many women believed that menstrual blood was peculiarly contaminated; if retained within the body it would corrupt the blood generally and lead to disease.[20]

Physicians, or many of them, tried to counter these feelings of shame and resentment. The tactic normally chosen, of course, was to wash the menstrual blood white in the rhetorical spirituality of marriage and motherhood. "Menstruation is allied to Maternity," one doctor wrote, "leading us to regard this function with reverence." "How strange," another wrote reassuringly, "that woman should regard with shame and distaste this function to which she owed health and life itself."[21] Yet, not surprisingly, such words of paternalistic reassurance were often mixed with expressions of distaste and doubt. One of America's leading gynecologists, for instance, prefaced a medical school lecture on the female reproductive system by "begging" his students "to accompany me in this disagreeable task," while another physician commented in passing that menstrual blood had a rank smell which any man could detect. Others argued that it was not in fact blood but some strange and unclassifiable discharge.[22]

There are other indications in the medical literature that many physicians were ambivalent toward the menstruating woman. Doctors, for instance, frequently began discussions of puberty and menstruation by elaborately recounting ancient myths that granted menstrual blood distinctive and magical powers. Forcefully denying the truth of these myths, the doctors then argued that, quite the contrary, menstruation made women weak, diseased, and dependent.[23] The recurrence of this particular formulation suggests that it may well have proved psychically functional to those male physicians who so tirelessly intoned it; certain physicians may well have felt ambivalent about menstruation or female genitalia—and, by implication, about their own masculinity. Their elaborate and stylized exposition and then destruction of such myths might thus have served the dual psychological purpose of permitting physicians first to displace their own fears of menstruating women onto classical writers or primitive peoples—an effective distancing technique—and then consciously to ridicule and deny the validity of such displaced fears. Their coupling this denial of feminine powers with the theory that menstruating women were indeed weak and fragile supports this hypothesis.

The other patterns found in nineteenth-century medical discussions of menstruation tend to reinforce such a psychological interpretation. A significant number of physicians drew a suggestive nexus between women's sexual appetite and menstruation—seeing menstruation as either the monthly apex of women's sexual desires or as a system to aid women in controlling such impulses. George Rowe wrote in 1844: "In God's infinite wisdom . . . might not this monthly discharge be ordained for the purpose of controlling woman's violent sexual passions . . . by unloading the uterine vessels . . . so as to prevent the promiscuous intercourse which would prove destructive to the purest . . . interests of civil life. . . ."[24]

The insatiate and promiscuous woman is one of man's most primitive and fearful fantasies, a fantasy that in individual men was clearly productive of anxiety such as that evident in Rowe's pious praise of menstruation. Closely paralleling the image of the sexually powerful woman is that of the maniacal and destructive woman. Menstruation, nineteenth-century physicians warned, could drive some women temporarily insane; menstruating women might go berserk, destroying furniture, attacking family and strangers alike, and even killing their infants. Those "unfortunate women," subject to such excessive menstrual influence, Edward Tilt wrote, should, for their own good and that of society, be incarcerated for the length of their menstruating years.[25]

Like puberty, menopause was seen as a physiological crisis, its course shaped by a woman's preceding sexual experiences, its resolution determining her future health.[26] If a woman had followed a sound regimen throughout life and had no predisposition to malignant disease, menopause could bring with it a golden age of health and freedom from the periodic inconvenience, pain, and depression of menstruation. The menopausal period could thus become the "Indian summer" of a woman's life—a period of increased vigor, optimism, and even of physical beauty.[27]

Far more frequently, however, menopause marked the beginning of a period of depression, of heightened disease incidence, and of early death. "There is a predisposition to many diseases, and these are often of a melancholy character," one physician noted in the 1830s. The host of diseases that might develop as a result of the cessation of menstruation included, as one doctor lamented, "almost all the ills the flesh is heir to."[28] They ranged from the classic flushes of menopause, through dyspepsia, diarrhea, severe vaginitis, vaginal inflammation, prolapsed uterus, rheumatic pains, paralysis, apoplexy, and erysipelas to uterine hemorrhaging, tumors, uterine and breast cancer, tuberculosis, scrofula, and diabetes.[29] Emotional or psychological symptoms characterized menopause as well. Irritability, depression, hysteria, melancholy, episodes of severe emotional withdrawal and insanity, seemed particularly common.[30] Clearly, nineteenth-century physicians used menopause as an all-purpose explanation for the heightened disease incidence of the older female; all of her ills were directly or indirectly diseases of the uterus and ovaries.

Physicians postulated a number of mechanisms to explain this pattern of ill health. The diseases of menopause, one theory argued, were rooted in a "plethora," which resulted after the cessation of the menses from the retention of the monthly menstrual blood. It was to such a plethora, or suffusion of the body with fluids, that physicians attributed the hot flashes, circulatory diseases, palpitations, and vaginal hemorrhaging of menopause. "The stoppage of any customary evacuations, however small, is sufficient

to disorder the whole frame and often to destroy life itself," William
Buchan explained in his extraordinarily influential *Domestic Medicine*. [31] By
mid-century, physicians evolved additional explanations of such diseases in
older women. Each month, some contended, the menstrual blood had
carried off the seeds of illness and in this way repressed a host of contagious
and constitutional ailments that then flourished with the repression of
menstruation. Still others argued that the diseases of menopause, especially
cancer of the uterus and breast, were rooted in systemic exhaustion consequent upon the unceasing cycle of menstruation, pregnancy, and lactation. [32]

But the most significant cause of a woman's menopausal disease,
virtually every doctor believed, lay in her violation of the physiological
and social laws dictated by her ovarian system. Education, attempts at birth
control or abortion, undue sexual indulgence, a too fashionable life style,
failure to devote herself fully to the needs of husband and children—even
the advocacy of woman's suffrage—all might guarantee a disease-ridden
menopause. [33]

One of the common causes of hemorrhaging, ovarian tumor, or
insanity at menopause was not, however, a life filled with hygienic mis-
deeds, but, rather, a momentary lack of judgment in old age—that is,
engaging in sexual intercourse during or after menopause. "My experience
teaches me that a marked increase of sexual impulse at the change of life
is a morbid impulse," Edward Tilt wrote in his widely read study of
menopause. "Whenever sexual impulse is first felt at the change of life,
some morbid ovario-uterine condition will be found to explain it. . . . It,
therefore, is most imprudent for women to marry at this epoch without
having obtained the sanction of a medical man." Female sexuality and
reproduction thus formed a comforting nexus, the destruction of which
clearly threatened certain Victorian physicians. [34]

Doctors warned that women must treat menopause as the beginning
of old age. Women should alter their style of life and retire from the world
into the bosom of their family. "We insist," wrote Walter Taylor in 1872,
"that every woman who hopes for a healthy old age ought to commence
her prudent cares as early as the 40th year or sooner. . . . She should cease
to endeavor to appear young when she is no longer so, and withdraw from
the excitements and fatigues of the gay world even in the midst of her
legitimate successes, to enter upon that more tranquil era of her existence

now at hand. . . . Most American mothers," he added with unintentional irony, "can find at hand enough to do for their own families . . . to absorb all their energies."[35] The regimen almost universally prescribed for menopausal women closely paralleled that recommended for their pubescent daughters and granddaughters, a regimen of quiet, avoidance of mental activities, the shunning of new activities and a commitment to domesticity.[36]

Such ideas seem obviously formal and defensive. Male physicians displayed a revealing disquietude and even hostility when discussing their menopausal patients. In the medical literature, the menopausal woman often appeared as ludicrous or physically repulsive. Edward Tilt, for instance, claimed that she characteristically had a "dull stupid look," was "pale or sallow," and tended to grow a beard on her chin and upper lip. Doctors scoffed at women who, long sterile or just married at menopause, believed themselves pregnant. These women, doctors commented heartily, suffered from a little flatulence, somewhat more hysteria, and, most of all, obesity. Such a woman's fantasied fetus, another doctor joked, was just her belly's double chin. More critical were doctors' comments about women who deliberately attempted to appear young after they had reached menopause. Menopausal depression—other physicians remarked—grew out of pique at no longer being considered young and attractive.[37]

Indeed, such hostility and even contempt marked male medical discussions of menopausal women that one woman physician, in a valedictory address to the 1864 class at Woman's Medical College in Philadelphia, cited such animosity as an important reason for women's becoming physicians. Referring specifically to male physicians' treatment of menopausal women, she exhorted: "You will also vindicate the right, scarcely yet conceded to women, to grow *old* without reproach. . . ."[38]

But how did women view this stage of life? From what I can detect thus far from diaries, letters, and the medical literature, I would answer that women viewed menopause with utter ambivalence. Doctors routinely noted that women faced menopause with dread and depression. "Suffering at the later period of life is accepted by many women as unavoidable and proper," one doctor remarked. Another physician commented upon a woman's "fear[s] as her age warns her that she is approaching that mysterious change. Every morbid impulse of her life is discussed with her friends. . . . She anxiously dwells on every little disorder, so charged is her mind with vague fears. . . ." "Indeed," wrote a third some seventy years earlier, "so replete is this time with horrors to some that we may very justly suspect apprehension to be the cause of some of the distressing symptoms. . . ."[39]

There is much, however, to indicate that many women looked forward to menopause as a release from the bondage of menstruation and pregnancy. Doctors, as already mentioned, did report that despite a general pattern of disease and depression, the health of some women improved dramatically with menopause. Indeed, menopause was seen as a specific for long-term depression, lassitude, and hysteria. Other doctors remarked how fresh and lovely some menopausal women looked—with a lightness to their step and a countenance free from anxiety.

The comments of a conservative and socially prominent Philadelphia Quaker matron, Elizabeth Drinker, may throw some light on this sense of freedom. Drinker recorded in her diary a conversation she had with her daughter Sally, who was about to give birth. Each of Sally's births had been protracted and painful; her youngest sister had, just the day before, almost died in childbirth, surviving only to be permanently crippled. Sally was filled with foreboding at the beginning of this labor. "My poor dear Sally was taken unwell last night, . . ." Drinker wrote in October 1799.

> She is in pain at times, forerunning pains of a lingering labour, a little low spirited, poor dear Child. This day is 38 years since I was in agonies bringing her into this world of troubles; she told me with tears that this was her birth day. I endeavour'd to talk her into better spirits, told her that the time of her birth was over by some hours, she was now in her 39th year, and that this might possibly be the last trial of this sort, if she could suckle her baby for two years to come, as she had several times done heretofore.[40]

Elizabeth and Sally Drinker were not the only women who viewed menopause as a release from "a world of troubles." Menopause was indeed an ultimate birth-control technique, and many women welcomed it for that reason. Their feelings were well captured by a woman physician when she described the obstetrical history and feelings of a representative patient at the coming of menopause. As a young woman and newly in love, the patient had believed marriage the summit of human happiness. Within a year, however, she became pregnant "and such pains as accompanied this [birth] she had never before believed that woman could endure." Many pregnancies followed this first, "until ten, twelve or even fifteen children have been born, with an accumulation of troubles to correspond. . . . Then her remarks assume a different tone. . . . She wrings her hands . . . and weeps as she begs her young friends to pause and consider before they leave home at so early an age; for marriage and maternity are not a romance. . . ." It is against a background of such experience that the nineteenth-century woman approached menopause. "She is no longer exposed to the direful risks and pain of child bearing," a male physician remarked some fifty years earlier. "She thanks God for that and takes comfort in the thought."[41]

Perhaps the most forceful mid-nineteenth-century expression of a positive view of menopause was articulated by social reformer and suffrage advocate Eliza Farnham. "My acquaintance with women of the nobler sort," Farnham wrote, "has convinced me that many a woman has experienced, at times, a secret joy in her advancing age." Indeed, Farnham continued, menopause could become woman's golden age; when she was freed from the physical and emotional demands of childbirth and child-rearing, her spiritual nature could develop to its fullest. She found the postmenopausal years the period of woman's "super-exaltation" and condemned those men who had taught women to dread menopause as "an absolutely uncompensated loss of power." "That day is long since past for enlightened women," she continued, "and will be soon for their less understanding sisters. . . . For women developed enough to have opinions and take any ground, teach each other very rapidly. Their presence in the field of masculine errors is like sunlight to the mists of early dawn."[42]

Borrowing Eliza Farnham's imagery, let us examine the forms shrouded by the mists of these Victorian metaphors. On the very simplest level these ideas served as an absolute biological justification for woman's restricted role. They served as well to express and explain traditional empirical observations and folk wisdom concerning the real biological, emotional, and social significance—and stress—of puberty, menstruation, and menopause. They created, moreover, an ideal metaphor in which the Victorian physician could express a characteristic and revealingly inconsistent ambiguity toward woman's sexual and social nature. Within this system, woman was seen at the same time as a higher, more sensitive, more spiritual

creature—and as a prisoner of tidal currents of an animal and uncontrollable nature (and in this way denied the two cardinal Victorian virtues of
control and rationality). At the same time this formula also permitted
Victorians to recognize the sometimes ominous force of female sexuality
and to render such sexuality safe by subordinating it to the limited ends
of child-bearing and nursing.

It is tempting, indeed, to elaborate a psychological interpretation of
these nineteenth-century gynecological metaphors and formulations concerning puberty and menopause. They are suggestively consistent, for
example, with a theory developed some years later by Karen Horney.
Horney argued that male fear of a woman is a basic human emotion that
predates the Oedipal dread of castration. In developing this hypothesis,
Horney suggested that those men fearful of woman's sexuality attempt to
defend against their anxiety in two ways. First, they denigrate women,
especially those aspects of woman's body most closely associated with her
genitals. Second, they overcompensate for their fears and hostility by
romanticizing women, especially those parts of a woman's body and
behavior not immediately associated with genital sexuality.[43]

The conventional formulas of nineteenth-century medical writers
are remarkably compatible with Horney's hypothetical male "dread of
women." Woman's "disagreeable," diseased—and hidden—sexual organs
contrasted unfavorably in the medical literature, that is, with her "blush-
ing" cheeks, her parted lips, her graceful bearing, her luminous eyes. In
addition to defending against primal fears, as suggested by Horney, these
particular rhetorical formulas may have also served as a means through
which "respectable" males could cope with sexuality in the specifically
repressive moral and religious climate of mid-nineteenth-century England
and the United States.[44]

But such interpretations raise serious methodological problems for
the historian. I have attempted in some ways to paint a group psychological
portrait of individuals at a distance of one hundred years, individuals of
whom we know little more than their formal writings. These writings are
suggestive, but to assert more would clearly be gratuitous. Whole segments
of past societies cannot be placed upon a couch that, at best, accommodates
a single individual. And contemporary psychoanalytic theory can hardly
be said to have provided final statements in regard to the development of
human personality. Specifically, for example, though Horney's hypothesis
may indeed be plausible, it is a theory unproved and unprovable.

The Hysterical Woman:
Sex Roles and Role Conflict
in Nineteenth-Century America[1]

Hysteria was one of the classic diseases of the nineteenth century. It was a protean ailment characterized by such varied symptoms as paraplegia, aphonia, hemianesthesia, and violent epileptoid seizures. Under the broad rubric of hysteria, nineteenth-century physicians gathered cases that might today be diagnosed as neurasthenia, hypochondriasis, depression, conversion reaction, and ambulatory schizophrenia. It fascinated and frustrated some of the century's most eminent clinicians; through its redefinition Freud rose to international fame, while the towering reputation of Charcot suffered a comparative eclipse. Psychoanalysis can historically be called the child of the hysterical woman. It was defined as an entity that was peculiarly female and has almost always carried with it a pejorative implication.

For the past half century and longer, American culture has defined hysteria in terms of individual psychodynamics. Physicians and psychologists have seen hysteria as a "neurosis" or character disorder, the product of an unresolved Oedipal complex. Hysterical women, fearful of their own sexual impulses—so the argument went—channeled that energy into psychosomatic illness. Characteristically, they proved unable to form satisfying and stable relationships.[2] More recently, psychoanalysts such as Elizabeth Zetzel have refined this Freudian hypothesis, tracing the roots of hysteria to a woman's excessively ambivalent pre-Oedipal relation with her mother and to the resulting complications of Oedipal development and resolution.[3] Psychologist David Shapiro has emphasized the hysterical woman's impressionistic thought pattern.[4] All such interpretations focus exclusively on individual psychodynamics and relations within particular families. All define the disease as peculiarly female and as, in some ways, indicating an immature personality.

Yet hysteria is also a socially recognized behavior pattern and as such exists within the larger world of cultural values and role relationships. For centuries hysteria has been seen as characteristically female—the hysterical woman the embodiment of a perverse or hyper-femininity.[5] Why has this been so? Why did large numbers of women "choose" the character traits of hysteria as their particular mode of expressing malaise, discontent, anger, or pain?[6] To begin to answer this question, we must explore the female role and role socialization. Clearly not all women were hysterics; yet the parallel between the hysteric's behavior and stereotypic femininity is too close to be explained as mere coincidence. To examine hysteria from this social perspective means necessarily to explore the complex relationships that exist between cultural norms and individual behavior, between behavior defined as disease and behavior considered normal.

Using nineteenth-century America as a case study,[7] I suggest that we explore hysteria on at least two levels of social interaction. The first involves an examination of hysteria as a social role within the nineteenth-century family. By analyzing the function of hysteria within the family and the interaction of the hysteric, her family, and the interceding—yet interacting—physician, we can throw light upon the role of women and female-male relationships within the larger world of nineteenth-century American society. Second, we must examine the relation between female role socialization, female personality options, and the nature of hysterical behavior.

I

Hysteria did not emerge as an endemic disease among bourgeois American women until the mid-nineteenth century. We must see it, therefore, as a disease peculiar to the Victorian bourgeois family and as a disease related, as well, to the role changes and conflicts bourgeois matrons experienced between the 1840s and the 1890s.

Significant inconsistencies characterized the bourgeois ideal of proper womanhood. Painful discontinuities existed between that ideal and the real world in which the bourgeois matron lived.[8] The tensions that existed between the two central roles the bourgeois matron was expected to assume —that of the True Woman and that of the Ideal Mother—exemplify these disjointures, which were simultaneously social and psychological.

The True Woman was emotional, dependent, and gentle—a born follower. The Ideal Mother, then and now, was expected to be strong, self-reliant, protective, an efficient caretaker in relation to children and home. She was to manage the family's day-to-day finances, prepare foods, make clothes, compound drugs, serve as family nurse—and, in rural areas, as physician as well.[9] Especially in the nineteenth century, with its still-primitive obstetrical practices and its high child-mortality rates, she was expected to face severe bodily pain, disease, and death—and still serve as the emotional support and strength of her family.[10] As the eminent Philadelphia neurologist S. Weir Mitchell wrote in the 1880s, "We may be sure that our daughters will be more likely to have to face at some time the grim question of pain than the lads who grow up beside them. . . . To most women . . . there comes a time when pain is a grim presence in their lives." Yet, as Mitchell pointed out, it was boys whom society taught from early childhood to bear pain stoically, while girls were encouraged to respond to pain and stress with tears and the expectation of elaborate sympathy.[11]

Contemporaries noted routinely in the 1870s, 1880s, and 1890s that middle-class American girls seemed ill-prepared to assume the responsibilities and trials of marriage, motherhood, and maturation. Frequently women, especially married women with children, complained of isolation, loneliness, and depression. Physicians reported a high incidence of nervous disease and hysteria among women who felt overwhelmed by the burdens of frequent pregnancies, the demands of children, the daily exertions of housekeeping and family management.[12] The realities of adult life no longer permitted them to elaborate and exploit the role of fragile, sensitive, and dependent child.

Not only was the Victorian woman increasingly ill-prepared for the trials of childbirth and child-rearing, but changes were also at work within the larger society that were to make her particular socialization increasingly inappropriate. Reduced birth and mortality rates, growing population concentration in towns, cities, and even in rural areas, a new, highly mobile economy, as well as new patterns of middle-class aspiration—all reached into the family, altering that institution, affecting domestic relations, and increasing the normal quantity of intra-familial stress.[13] Women lived longer; they married later and less often. They spent less and less time in the primary processing of food, cloth, and clothing.

Despite such basic social, economic, and demographic changes, how-

ever, the family and gender-role socialization remained relatively inflexi-
ble. It is quite possible that many women experienced a significant level
of anxiety when forced to confront or adapt in one way or another to these
changes. Thus hysteria may have served as one option or tactic offering
particular women, otherwise unable to respond to these changes, a chance
to redefine or restructure their place within the family.

So far this discussion of role socialization and stress has emphasized
primarily the malaise and dissatisfaction of the middle-class woman. It is
only a covert romanticism, however, that permits us to assume that lower-
class and farm women, because their economic functions within the family
were more vital than those of their decorative and economically secure
urban sisters, escaped their sense of frustration, conflict, or confusion.
Normative prescriptions of proper womanly behavior were certainly internalized by many poorer women. The desire to marry and the belief that
a woman's social status came not from the exercise of her own talents and
efforts but from her ability to attract a competent male protector were as
universal among lower-class and farm women as among middle- and
upper-class urban women. For some of these women—as for their urban
middle-class sisters—the traditional female role proved functional, bringing material and psychic rewards. But for some it did not. The discontinuity between the child and adult female roles, along with the failure to
develop substantial ego strengths, crossed class and geographic barriers—
as did hysteria itself. Physicians connected with almshouses, and, later in
the century, with urban hospitals and dispensaries, often reported hysteria
among immigrant and tenement-house women.[14]

Against a background of role conflict and psychic discontinuity, what
were the presenting symptoms of the female hysteric in nineteenth-century
America? While physicians agreed that hysteria could afflict persons of
both sexes and of all ages and economic classes (the male hysteric was an
accepted clinical entity by the late nineteenth century), they reported that
hysteria was most frequent among women between the ages of fifteen and
forty and of the urban middle and upper-middle classes. Symptoms were
highly varied. As early as the seventeenth century, indeed, Sydenham had
remarked that "the frequency of hysteria is no less remarkable than the
multiformity of the shapes it puts on. Few maladies are not imitated by
it; whatever part of the body it attacks, it will create the proper symptom
of that part."[15] The nineteenth-century physician could only concur. There

were complaints of nervousness, depression, the tendency to tears and chronic fatigue, or of disabling pain. Not a few women thus afflicted showed a remarkable willingness to submit to long-term, painful therapy —to electric-shock treatment, to blistering, to multiple operations, even to amputations.[16]

The most characteristic and dramatic symptom, however, was the hysterical "fit." Mimicking an epileptic seizure, these fits often occurred with shocking suddenness. At other times they "came on" gradually, announcing their approach with a general feeling of depression, nervousness, crying, or lassitude. Such seizures, physicians generally agreed, were precipitated by a sudden or deeply felt emotion—fear, shock, a sudden death, marital disappointment—or by physical trauma. They began with pain and tension, most frequently in the "uterine area." The sufferer alternately sobbed and laughed violently, complained of palpitations of the heart, clawed her throat as if strangling, and at times abruptly lost the power of hearing and speech. A deathlike trance might follow, lasting hours, even days. At other times violent convulsions—sometimes accompanied by hallucinations—seized her body.[17] "Let the reader imagine," New York physician E. H. Dixon wrote in the 1840s, "the patient writhing like a serpent upon the floor, rending her garments to tatters, plucking out handsful of hair, and striking her person with violence—with contorted and swollen countenance and fixed eyes resisting every effort of bystanders to control her. . . ."[18] Finally the fit subsided; the patient, exhausted and sore, fell into a restful sleep.

During the first half of the nineteenth century, physicians described hysteria principally, though not exclusively, in terms of such episodes. Symptoms such as paralysis and contracture were believed to be caused by seizures and categorized as infraseizure symptoms. Beginning in mid-century, however, physicians became increasingly flexible in their diagnosis of hysteria and gradually the fit declined in significance as a pathognomonic symptom.[19] Dr. Robert Carter, a widely read British authority on hysteria, insisted in 1852 that at least one hysterical seizure must have occurred to justify a diagnosis of hysteria. But, he admitted, this seizure might be so minor as to have escaped the notice even of the patient herself; no subsequent seizures were necessary.[20] This was clearly a transitional position. By the last third of the nineteenth century, the seizure was no longer the central phenomenon defining hysteria; physicians had categorized hysterical symptoms that included virtually every known human ill. They ranged from loss of sensation in part, half, or all of the body, loss of taste, smell, hearing, or vision, numbness of the skin, inability to swallow, nausea, headaches, pain in the breast, knees, hip, spine, or neck, as well as contracture or paralysis of virtually any extremity.[21]

Hysterical symptoms were not limited to the physical. A hysterical female character gradually began to emerge in the nineteenth-century medical literature, one based on interpretations of mood and personality rather than on discrete physical symptoms—one that grew closely to resemble twentieth-century definitions of the "hysterical personality." Doctors commonly described hysterical women as highly impressionable, suggestible, and narcissistic. They were highly labile, their moods changing suddenly, dramatically, and for seemingly inconsequential reasons. Doctors complained that the hysterical woman was egocentric in the extreme, her involvement with others consistently superficial and tangential. Though the hysterical woman might appear to physicians and relatives as quite sexually stimulated or attractive, she was, doctors cautioned, essentially asexual and not uncommonly frigid.[22]

Depression also appears as a common theme. Hysterical symptoms not infrequently followed a death in the family, a miscarriage, some financial setback which forced the patient to become self-supporting; or they were seen by the patient as related to some long-term, unsatisfying life situation —a tired schoolteacher, a mother unable to cope with the demands of a large family.[23] Most of these women took to their beds because of pain, paralysis, or general weakness. Some remained there for years.

The medical profession's response to the hysterical woman was at best ambivalent. Many doctors—and, indeed, a significant proportion of society at large—tended to be caustic, if not punitive, toward the hysterical woman. This resentment seems rooted in two factors: first, the baffling and elusive nature of hysteria itself, and, second, the relation that existed in the physicians' minds between their categorizing of hysteria as a disease and the role women were expected to play in society. These patients did not function as women were expected to function, and, as we shall see, the physician who treated them felt threatened both as a professional and as a rejected male. He was the therapist thwarted, the child untended, the husband denied nurturance and sex.

During the second half of the nineteenth century, the newly established germ theory and discoveries by neurologists and anatomists for the first time made an insistence on disease specificity a *sine qua non* for scientific respectability. Neurology was just becoming accepted as a specialty, and in its search for acceptance it was particularly dependent on the establishment of firm, somatically based disease entities.[24] If hysteria *was* a disease, and not the imposition of self-pitying women striving to avoid their traditional roles and responsibilities—as was frequently charged—it must be a disease with a specific etiology and a predictable course. In the period 1870 to 1900, especially, it was felt to be a disease rooted in some specific organic malfunction.

Hysteria, of course, lacked all such disease characteristics. Contracture or paralysis could occur without muscular atrophy or change in skin temperature. The hysteric might mimic tuberculosis, heart attacks, blindness, or hip disease, while lungs, heart, eyes, and hips remained in perfect health.[25] The physician had only his patient's statement that she could not move or was racked with pain. If concerned and sympathetic, he faced a puzzling dilemma. As George Preston wrote in his 1897 monograph on hysteria:

> In studying the . . . disturbances of hysteria, a very formidable difficulty presents itself in the fact that the symptoms are purely subjective. . . . There is only the bald statement of the patient. . . . No confirming symptoms present themselves . . . and the appearance of the affected parts stands as contradictory evidence against the patient's word.[26]

Equally frustrating and medically inexplicable were the sudden changes in the hysteric's symptoms. Paralysis or anesthesia could shift from one side of the body to the other, from one limb to another. Headaches would replace contracture of a limb, loss of voice, the inability to taste. How could a physician prescribe for such ephemeral symptoms? "Few practitioners desire the management of hysterics," one eminent gynecologist, Samuel Ashwell, wrote in 1833. "Its symptoms are so varied and obscure, so contradictory and changeable, and if by chance several of them, or even a single one be relieved, numerous others almost immediately spring into existence."[27] Half a century later, neurologist Charles K. Mills echoed Ashwell's discouraging evaluation. "Hysteria is pre-eminently a chronic disease," he warned. "Deceptive remissions in hysterical symptoms often mislead the unwary practitioner. Cures are sometimes claimed where simply a change in the character of the phenomena has taken place. It is a disease in which it is unsafe to claim a conquest."[28]

Yet physicians, especially newly established neurologists with urban practices, were besieged by patients who appeared to be sincere, respectable women sorely afflicted with pain, paralysis, or uncontrollable "nervous fits." "Looking at the pain evoked by ideas and beliefs," S. Weir Mitchell, America's leading expert on hysteria, wrote in 1885, "we are hardly wise to stamp these pains as non-existent."[29] Despite the tendency of many physicians to dismiss the hysterical patient contemptuously when no organic lesions could be found, neurologists such as Mitchell, George M. Beard, or Charles L. Dana sympathized with these patients and sought to alleviate their symptoms.

Such pioneer specialists were therefore in the position of having defined hysteria as a legitimate disease entity, and the hysterical woman as sick, when they were painfully aware that no organic etiology had yet been found. Cautiously, they sought to define hysteria formally in terms appropriately mechanistic. Some late-nineteenth-century physicians, for example, still placing a traditional emphasis on hysteria's uterine origins, argued that hysteria resulted from "the reflex effects of utero-ovarian irritation."[30] Others, reflecting George M. Beard's work on neurasthenia, defined hysteria as a functional disease caused either by "metabolic or nutritional changes in the cellular elements of the central nervous system." Still others wrote in terms of a malfunction of the cerebral cortex.[31] All such explanations were but hypothetical gropings for an organic explanation—still a necessity if they were to legitimize hysteria as a disease.[32]

The fear that hysteria might after all be only a functional or an "ideational" disease—to use a nineteenth-century term—and therefore not really a disease at all, underlies much of the writing on hysteria, as well as the physicians' own attitudes toward their patients. These hysterical women might, after all, be only clever frauds and sensation seekers— morally delinquent and, for the physician, professionally embarrassing.

Not surprisingly, a compensatory sense of superiority and hostility permeated many physicians' discussions of the nature and etiology of hysteria. Except when called upon to provide a hypothetical organic etiology, physicians saw hysteria as caused either by the indolent, vapid, and unconstructive life of the fashionable middle- and upper-class woman, or by the ignorant, exhausting, and sensual life of the lower- or working-class woman. Neither was a flattering etiology. Both denied the hysteric the sympathy granted to sufferers from unquestionably organic ailments.

Any general description of the personal characteristics of the well-to-do hysteric emphasized her idleness, self-indulgence, deceitfulness, and "craving for sympathy." Petted and spoiled by her parents, waited upon hand and foot by servants, she had never been taught to exercise self-control or to curb her emotions and desires.[33] Certainly she had not been trained to undertake the arduous and necessary duties of wife and mother. As one late-nineteenth-century physician lectured:

> Young persons who have been raised in luxury and too often in idleness, who have never been called upon to face the hardships of life, who have never accustomed themselves to self-denial, who have abundant time and opportunity to cultivate the emotional and sensuous, to indulge the sentimental side of life, whose life purpose is too often an indefinite and self-indulgent idea of pleasure, these are the most frequent victims of hysteria.[34]

Sound education, outside interests such as charity and good works, moral training, systematic outdoor exercise, and removal from an overly sympathetic family were among the most frequent forms of treatment recommended. Mothers, consistently enough, were urged to bring up daughters with a strong sense of self-discipline, devotion to family needs, and dread of uncontrolled emotionality.[35]

Emotional indulgence, moral weakness, and lack of willpower characterized the hysteric in both lay and medical thought. Hysteria, S. Weir Mitchell warned, occurred in women who had never developed habitual restraint and "rational endurance"—who had early lost their power of "self rule."[36] "The mind and body are deteriorated by the force of evil habit," Charles Lockwood wrote in 1895; "morbid thought and morbid impulse run through the poor, weak, unresisting brain, until all mental control is lost, and the poor sufferer is . . . at the mercy of . . . evil and unrestrained passions, appetites and morbid thoughts and impulses."[37]

In an age when will, control, and hard work were fundamental social values, this hypothetical etiology necessarily implied a negative evaluation of those who succumbed to hysteria. Such women were described as weak, capricious, and, perhaps most important, morbidly suggestible.[38] Their intellectual abilities were meager, their powers of concentration eroded by years of self-indulgence and narcissistic introspection.[39] Hysterical women were, in effect, children, and ill-behaved, difficult children at that. "They have in fact," Robert Carter wrote, "all the instability of childhood, joined to the vices and passions of adult age. . . ."[40]

Many nineteenth-century critics felt that this emotional regression and instability were rooted in woman's very nature. The female nervous system, doctors argued, was physiologically more sensitive and thus more difficult to subject to the will. Some physicians assumed as well that woman's blood was "thinner" than man's, causing nutritional inadequacies in the central nervous system and an inability to store nervous energy—a weakness, Mary Putnam Jacobi stressed, women shared with children. Most commonly, a woman's emotional states generally, and hysteria in particular, were believed to have the closest ties to her reproductive cycle.[41] Hysteria commenced with puberty and ended with menopause, while ailments as varied as menstrual pain and irregularity, prolapsed or tipped uterus, uterine tumor, vaginal infections and discharges, sterility, could all—doctors were certain—cause hysteria. Indeed, the first question routinely asked hysterical women was "Are your courses regular?"[42] Thus a woman's very physiology and anatomy predisposed her to hysteria; it was, as Thomas Laycock put it, "the natural state" in a female, a "morbid state" in the male.[43] In an era when a sexual perspective implied conflict and ambivalence, hysteria was perceived by physician and patient as a disease both peculiarly female and peculiarly sexual.

Hysteria could also result from a secret and less forgivable form of sexuality. Throughout the nineteenth century, physicians believed that masturbation was widespread among America's females and a frequent cause of hysteria and insanity. As early as 1846, E. H. Dixon reported that masturbation caused hysteria "among females even in society where physical and intellectual culture would seem to present the strongest barriers against its incursions. . . ." Other physicians concurred, reporting that harsh public and medical reactions to hysterical women were often based on the belief that masturbation was the cause of their behavior.[44]

Masturbation was only one form of sexual indulgence. A number of doctors saw hysteria among lower-class women as originating in the sensuality believed to characterize their class. Such tenement-dwelling females, doctors reported, "gave free reign to . . . 'passions of the baser sort,' not feeling the necessity of self-control because they have to a pitiably small degree any sense of propriety or decency." Hysteria, another physician reported, was found commonly among prostitutes, while virtually all physicians agreed that even within marriage, sexual excess could easily lead to hysteria.[45]

As might be expected, conscious anger and hostility marked the response of a good many doctors to their hysterical patients. One New York neurologist called the female hysteric a willful, self-indulgent, and narcissistic person who cynically manipulated her symptoms. "To her distorted vision," he complained, "there is but one commanding personage in the universe—herself—in comparison with whom the rest of mankind are nothing." Doctors admitted that they were frequently tempted to use such terms as "willful" and "evil," "angry" and "impatient" when describing the hysteric and her symptoms.[46] Even the concerned and genteel S. Weir Mitchell, confident of his remarkable record in curing hysteria, described hysterical women as "the pests of many households, who constitute the despair of physicians, and who furnish those annoying examples of despotic selfishness, which wreck the constitutions of nurses and devoted relatives, and in unconscious or half-conscious self-indulgence destroy the comfort of everyone about them." He concluded by quoting Oliver Wendell Holmes's acid judgment that "a hysterical girl is a vampire who sucks the blood of the healthy people about her."[47]

Hysteria as a chronic, dramatic, and socially accepted sick role could thus provide some alleviation of conflict and tension, but the hysteric purchased her escape from the emotional and—frequently—from the sexual demands of her life only at the cost of pain, disability, and an intensification of woman's traditional passivity and dependence. Indeed, a complex interplay existed between the character traits assigned women in Victorian society and the characteristic symptoms of the nineteenth-century hysteric: dependency, fragility, emotionality, narcissism. (Hysteria has, after all, been called in that century and this a stark caricature of femininity.) Not surprisingly, the hysteric's peculiar passive aggression and her exploitative dependency often functioned to cue a corresponding hostility in the men who cared for her or lived with her. Whether fathers, husbands, or physicians, they reacted with ambivalence and in many cases with hostility to her aggressive and never-ending demands.

II

What inferences concerning woman's role and female-male relationships can be drawn from this description of nineteenth-century hysteria and of medical attitudes toward the female patient? What insights does it allow into patterns of stress and resolution within the nuclear family?

Because medical wisdom had defined hysteria as a disease, its victims could expect to be treated as sick and thus to elicit a particular set of responses—the right to be seen and treated by a physician, to stay in bed and thus be relieved of their normal day-to-day responsibilities, to enjoy the special prerogatives, indulgences, and sympathy the sick role entailed. Hysteria thus became one way in which conventional women could express—in most cases unconsciously—dissatisfaction with one or several aspects of their lives.

The effect of hysteria upon the family and traditional sex-role differentiation was disruptive in the extreme. The hysterical woman virtually ceased to function within the family. No longer did she devote herself to the needs of others, acting as self-sacrificing wife, mother, or daughter: through her hysteria she could and in fact did force others to assume those functions. Household activities were reoriented to answer the hysterical woman's importunate needs. Children were hushed, rooms darkened, entertaining suspended, a devoted nurse recruited. Fortunes might be spent on medical bills or for drugs and operations. Worry and concern bowed the husband's shoulders; his home had suddenly become a hospital and he a nurse. Through her illness, the bedridden woman came to dominate her family to an extent that would have been considered inappropriate—indeed, shrewish—in a healthy woman. Taking to one's bed, especially when suffering from dramatic and ever-visible symptoms, might also have functioned as a mode of passive aggression, especially in a milieu in which weakness was rewarded and in which women had since childhood been taught not to express overt aggression. Consciously or unconsciously, they had thus opted out of their traditional role.

Women did not accomplish this redefinition of domestic roles without the aid of the men in their family. Doctors commented that the hysteric's husband and family often, and unfortunately, rewarded her symptoms with elaborate sympathy. "The hysterics' credit is usually first established," as one astute mid-century clinician pointed out, "by those who have, at least, the wish to believe them."[48] Husbands and fathers were not alone in their cooperation; the physician often played a complex and in a sense emotionally compromising role in legitimizing the female hysteric's behavior. As an impartial and professionally skilled observer, he was empowered to judge whether or not a particular woman had the right to withdraw from her socially allotted duties. At the same time, such a physician accepted as correct—indeed, as biologically inevitable—the structure of the Victorian family and the division of sex roles within it. He excused the woman only in the belief that she was ill and that she would make every effort to get well and resume her accustomed role. It was the transitory and unavoidable nature of the sick role that made it acceptable to family and physician as an alternate mode of female behavior.[49]

The doctor's ambivalence toward the hysterical woman, already rooted in professional and sexual uncertainties, may well have been reinforced by his complicitous role within the family. It was for this reason that the disease's erratic pattern, its chronic nature, its lack of a determinable organic etiology, and the patient's seeming failure of will, so angered him. Even if she were not a conscious malingerer, she might well be guilty of self-indulgence and moral delinquency. By diagnosing her as ill, he had in effect created or permitted the hysterical woman to create a bond between himself and her. Within the family configuration, he had sided with her against her husband or other male family members—men with whom he would normally have identified.[50]

The quintessentially sexual nature of hysteria further complicated the doctor's professional stance. The hysterical patient in her role as woman may well have mobilized whatever ambivalence toward sex a particular physician felt. In a number of cases, the physician could have played the role of Oedipal father figure to the patient's child-woman role, and in such instances his complicity was not only moral and intellectual but sexual as well. These doctors had become part of a domestic triangle—a husband's rival, the fatherly attendant of a daughter. This intrafamily role may therefore go far to explain the particularly strident and suspicious tone which characterized much of the clinical discussion of hysteria. The physician had, by his alertness to deception and self-indulgence and by his therapeutic skills, to prevent the hysterical woman from using her disease to avoid her feminine duties—and from making him an unwitting accomplice in her deviant role. While tied to her as physician and thus legitimizer of her sick role, he had also to preserve his independence. This unusual power balance may help explain the ways in which physicians were concerned with—and condemned—the power that chronic illness such as hysteria gave a woman over her family. Doctors noted with annoyance that many women enjoyed this power and showed no inclination to get well: it is hardly coincidental that most late-nineteenth-century authorities agreed that removal from her family was a necessary first step in attempting to cure the hysterical patient.[51]

Not only did the physician condemn the hysteric's power within her family; he was clearly sensitive to her as a threat to his own prestige and authority. Many doctors felt themselves to be locked in a power struggle with their hysterical patients. Doctors claimed that such women used their symptoms as weapons in asserting autonomy in relation to their physician; their continued illness was a victory. Physicians perceived hysterical women as unusually intractable and self-assertive. Although patients and women, they reserved the right to judge and approve their male physicians' every action. Indeed, much of the medical literature on hysteria is devoted to providing doctors with the means of winning this war of wills. Physicians felt that they must dominate the hysteric's will; only in this way, they wrote, could they bring about her permanent cure. "Do not flatter yourselves . . . that you will gain an easy victory," Dr. L. C. Grey told a medical-school class in 1888:

> On the contrary, you must expect to have your temper, your ingenuity, your nerves tested to a degree that cannot be surpassed even by the greatest surgical operations. I maintain that the man who has the nerve and the tact to conquer some of these grave cases of hysteria has the nerve and the tact that will make him equal to the great emergencies of life. Your patient must be taught day by day . . . by steady resolute, iron-willed determination and tact—that combination which the French . . . call "the iron hand beneath the velvet glove."[52]

"Assume a tone of authority which will of itself almost compel submission," Robert Carter directed. "If a patient . . . interrupts the speaker, she must be told to keep silent and to listen; and must be told, moreover, not only in a voice that betrays no impatience and no anger, but in such a manner as to convey the speaker's full conviction that the command will be immediately obeyed."[53]

Much of the treatment prescribed by physicians for hysteria reflects, in its draconic severity, their need to exert control—and, when thwarted, their impulse to punish. Doctors frequently recommended suffocating hysterical women until their fits stopped, beating them across the face and body with wet towels, ridiculing and exposing them in front of family and friends, showering them with icy water. "The mode adopted to arrest this curious malady," one physician connected with a large mental hospital wrote, "consists in making some strong and sudden impression on the mind through . . . the most potent of all impressions, fear. . . . Ridicule to a woman of sensitive mind, is a powerful weapon . . . but there is no emotion equal to fear and the threat of personal chastisement. . . . They will listen to the voice of authority."[54]

When, on the other hand, the hysterical patient proved tractable, gave up her fits or paralyses, and accepted the physician as savior and moral guide, he no longer had to appear in the posture of chastising father. He could respond to his hysterical patient with fondness, sympathy, and praise. No longer was she thwarting him with "trials, tears, tricks and tantrums" —as one doctor chose to subtitle a study of hysteria.[55] Her cure demonstrated that he had mastered her will and body. The successful fatherlike practitioner had restored another wayward woman to her familial duties. Thomas Addis Emmett, pioneer gynecological specialist, recalled with ingenuous candor his mode of treating hysterics:

> the patient . . . was a child in my hands. In some respects the power gained was not unlike that obtained over a wild beast except that in one case the domination would be due to fear, while with my patient as a rule, it would be the desire to please me and to merit my approval from the effort she would make to gain her self-control. I have at times been depressed with the responsibility attending the blind influence I have often been able to gain over the nervous women under my influence.[56]

Not surprisingly, S. Weir Mitchell ended one of his treatises on hysteria with the comment that doctors, who knew and understood all women's petty weaknesses, who could govern and forgive them, made the best husbands.[57] Clearly the male physician who treated the hysterical woman was unable to escape the sex-role relations that existed within nineteenth-century society generally.

The hysterical female thus emerges from the essentially male medical literature of the nineteenth century as a "child-woman." Physicians described her as highly impressionable, labile, superficially sexual and exhibitionistic. She was given, they insisted, to dramatic body language and grand gestures. She had strong dependency needs, a masochistic or self-punishing behavior pattern, and decided ego weaknesses. This nineteenth-century vision in many ways resembles the hysterical personality described in the 1968 *Diagnostic and Statistical Manual of Mental Disorders* of the American Psychiatric Association. Modern psychiatrists still describe a personality characterized by "excitability, emotional instability, over-reactivity, self-dramatization, attention seeking, immaturity, vanity and unusual dependence." Her symptoms correspond closely to those described by Kernberg as an infantile personality or by Guze as a hysterical personality.[58] In both centuries we find the hysteric a child-woman, filled with self-doubt, constantly in need of reassurance and attention from others. Yet these characteristics are merely hypertrophied versions of traits and behavior routinely reinforced throughout the nineteenth century in female children, adolescents, and adults.

To understand hysteria's place within the broader social experience of America's women, we must not only look at stress and dysfunction within the hysteric's own psychic background, but at the relation between hysterical character formation and female role socialization. To do so, I propose that we examine the roles male society sought to impose on America's daughters (and on their mothers) in the elaborate child-rearing literature that began to appear during the first third of the nineteenth century.

There is evidence in children's books, child-rearing manuals, marriage guides, and books of etiquette that women were sharply discouraged from expressing competitive inclinations or asserting mastery in such "masculine" areas as physical skill, strength, and courage, or in academic, scientific, or commercial pursuits. Rather they were encouraged to be coquettish, entertaining, nonthreatening, and nurturing. Male religious writers and educators forbade overt anger and violence as unfeminine and vulgar and they did not reward curiosity, intrusiveness, exploratory behavior, in

women. Indeed, when such characteristics conflicted with the higher feminine values of cleanliness, deportment, unobtrusiveness, or obedience, they
were criticized or punished. Yet these same habits of mind are now deemed
essential to the development of autonomy in children and are thought to
be a key to learning, especially in the areas of science and mathematics.
While most children's literature asserted that boys were "brave, active and
lively, Strength swelleth in their bones and labor is their delight all day
long . . . ," girls were taught that their greatest happiness lay in an unending
routine of caring for the needs of others.[59]

Nineteenth-century American society provided but one socially respectable, nondeviant role for women—that of loving wife and mother.
Thus women, who presumably came in assorted psychological and intellectual shapes and sizes, had to find adjustment in one prescribed social
role, one that demanded continual self-abnegation and a desire to please
others. Literature on child rearing, genteel women's magazines, children's
books, all required of women an altruistic denial of their own ambition
and a displacement of their wishes and abilities onto the men in their lives.
We may assume that, for a certain percentage of women, this led to
a form of what Anna Freud and Edward Bibring defined as "altruistic
surrender."[60]

In other cases, training to fit a narrowly defined role must have
resulted in significant ego restriction—the ego choosing not to develop in
certain directions because the pain of punishment or of being defined as
deviant was too great. "When the ego is young and plastic," Anna Freud
wrote, "its withdrawal from one field of activity is sometimes compensated
for by excellence in another, upon which it concentrates. But, when it has
become rigid or has already acquired an intolerance of 'pain' and so is
obsessionally fixated to the method of flight, such withdrawal is punished
by impaired development. By abandoning one position after another it
becomes one-sided, loses too many interests and can show a meager
achievement."[61]

Significant differences appear to lie, as well, in the ways in which boys
and girls were punished in both the nineteenth and the twentieth centuries.
It is true that disciplinary patterns changed during the nineteenth century.
Corporal punishment seems to have decreased in frequency, for boys as
well as girls. Nevertheless, sociological studies indicate that until fairly
recently boys still received far more corporal punishment than girls did.

Girls were punished through the inculcation of guilt and by threats of withdrawal of love or of actual separation from parents. Social psychologists and sociologists like, for instance, Urie Bronfenbrenner have argued that such "love oriented punishment," while producing obedient and docile children, also made children timid, anxious, dependent, and sensitive to rejection. Other psychologists have recently argued that love-oriented punishment and a girl's more socialized behavior in early childhood tend to delay the formation of an independent identity in girls until late adolescence—if then—and lead them to be overly dependent upon the approval of significant others in their lives.[62]

The effect of this socialization may well have been to teach many women to have a low evaluation of themselves, to significantly restrict their ego functions to low-prestige areas, to depend on others, and, altruistically, to wish not for their own worldly success but for that of their male supporters.

There is, I believe, a suggestive parallel between the hysterical woman of the nineteenth century and a masochistic female personality as described by Karen Horney in 1934.[63] The masochistic female personality, Horney argued, suffered from "free floating anxiety," a deep-rooted sense of inferiority, and an absence of adequate aggression. By "aggression" Horney meant the ability to take initiative, to make efforts, to carry things through to completion, and to form and express autonomous views. All of these constitute important ego functions. Insecure, afflicted with anxieties, the masochistic woman demanded constant attention and expressions of affection, which she sought to secure by appealing to pity. She displayed inferiority feelings, weakness, and suffering. Such a self-image and pattern of object relations necessarily "generated hostile feelings [in the masochistic woman], but feelings which the masochistic woman was unable to express directly because they would have jeopardized her dependency relationships." "Weakness and suffering, therefore," Horney observed, "already serving many functions, now also act as a vehicle for the indirect expression of hostility."

Though both men and women develop masochistic personalities, Horney hypothesized that far larger numbers of women than men would do so in cultures in which women more than men (1) "Manifest[ed] . . . inhibitions in the direct expression of demands and aggressions; (2) regard[ed] . . . [themselves] as weak, helpless, or inferior and implicitly or explicitly demand[ed] considerations and advantages on this basis;

(3) [became] emotionally dependent on the other sex; (4) show[ed] . . . tendencies to be self-sacrificing, to be submissive, to feel used or to be exploited, to put responsibilities on the other sex; (5) use[d] . . . weakness and helplessness as a means of wooing and subduing the other sex."[64]

In essence, then, many nineteenth-century women reached maturity with major ego weaknesses and with narrowly limited compensatory ego strengths, all of which implies a relationship between this pattern of socialization and the adoption of hysterical behavior by particular individuals. It seems plausible to suggest that a certain percentage of nineteenth-century women, faced with stress developing out of their own peculiar personality needs or because of situational anxieties, might well have defended themselves against such stress by regressing toward the childish hyper-femininity of the hysteric. The discontinuity between the roles of courted woman and pain-bearing, self-sacrificing wife and mother, the realities of an unhappy marriage, the loneliness and chagrin of spinsterhood may all have made the petulant infantilism and narcissistic self-assertion of the hysteric a necessary alternative to women who felt unfairly deprived of their promised social role and who had few strengths with which to adapt to a more trying one. Indeed, society had structured this regression by consistently reinforcing those very emotional traits characterized in the stereotype of the female and caricatured in the symptomatology of the hysteric. At the same time, the nineteenth-century female hysteric also exhibited a significant level of hostility and aggression—rage—which may have led in turn to her depression and to her self-punishing psychosomatic illnesses. In all these ways, then, the hysterical woman can be seen as both product and indictment of her culture.

I must conclude with a caution. The reasons why individuals displayed that pattern of behavior called by nineteenth-century physicians "hysteria" must in individual cases remain moot. What this essay has sought to do is to suggest why certain symptoms were available and why women, in particular, tended to resort to them. It has sought as well to use the reactions of contemporaries to illuminate female-male and intrafamilial role realities. As such it has dealt with hysteria as a social role produced by and functional within a specific set of social circumstances.

By way of conclusion, there is a methodological point which I believe it is important to make. Nothing is more tempting for the woman historian than to treat male Victorian physicians as the spokesmen and hence the scapegoats of their age. Their frequent chauvinistic comments provoke the militant in us all. But we have no evidence to indicate that physicians were more arrogant in their attitude toward women than any other husbands or fathers. In part, it is simply that male physicians belonged to a group that commented formally and in depth upon women, and whose comments are readily available to the historian.

But perhaps it is more important to see the doctor not just as a man but as a practitioner—one who needed a framework of rationale and hypothesis within which to explain the health and disease of his patients, as well as his interpersonal relations with them. The interaction of a male physician and a female patient can thus be seen—and used by the historian—as a cultural artifact: the physician shaped by his culture's definitions of femininity and masculinity, having to deal on a daily, one-to-one basis with the behavior and needs of his individual female patient.

The Abortion Movement and
the AMA, 1850–1880[1]

Abortion is a loaded word. It evokes feelings about fetal life, violence to a woman's reproductive organs, the retention or expulsion of a foreign body suddenly found within one's own. It compels women and men to face their feelings about man's power to impregnate and woman's power to retain or reject the man's impregnation. On the broader level of demographic patterns and social policy, abortion involves issues of national commitment to population control or expansion, the acceptability of woman's participation in the economy, and, more broadly, woman's appropriate role within the home and society. It exemplifies political control of the personal and the physiological. It thus bridges the intensely individual and the broadly political. On every level, to talk of abortion is to speak of power.

Abortion is a socio-sexual constant. No time, no culture, has been a stranger to it. Yet social responses to women's and men's desires to terminate specific pregnancies have differed sharply between and within cultures. At times the issue of abortion lies quiescent. In these periods certain women and couples may seek out successful abortions; others may accept pregnancy as a *fait accompli.* In either case, their choice or rejection of abortion remains a private, perhaps a moral decision, not an overtly political one. But at other times, forces within a society catapult the issue of abortion to a position of political and moral centrality, transferring the acts of the bedroom and the doctor's office to the most public political arena. At such times decisions surrounding abortion become the central drama of a culture, a play dealing with basic fissures in the social structure, one that raises fundamental issues concerning the distribution of power and the nature of social order. These plays take the form of family dramas. Sexual themes and gender conflict dominate their plots, reflecting the concerns of their audiences. Societies perform these plays during periods when economic change has transformed personal and class relations, and when the distribution of power has been altered, and when these processes coincide (and they almost inevitably will) with significant alterations in the balance of power between women and men, and of male heads of household over their traditional dependents.

Both in our own time and during the second half of the nineteenth century, abortion has emerged as just such a dramatic political and ideological issue, transcending the immediate medical act. The endangered fetus, the physically and politically constrained woman have become condensed, emotionally charged symbols of social change, autonomy, and power— legitimate and illegitimate. Viewed against a backdrop of economic, demographic, and technological factors, the abortion issue can be seen as a political code. It functions as a sexual language through which divergent gender, economic, regional, and religious groups discuss issues of social change and social conflict far broader than the fate of fetuses or even the sexual rights of adult women. If we carefully observe the great abortion drama of the nineteenth century, perhaps we can gain a new perspective from which to understand the one that so grips our own society.

The years 1850 to 1880 saw abortion emerge as a mass political issue in America for the first time. During these years the legality of abortion became the focus of a nationwide lobbying effort, of legislative debate, and of a spate of new legislation. Although its dates coincided with the first feminist movement, this struggle did not mark the beginning of a century-long effort by feminists and social critics to liberalize America's abortion legislation. Quite the contrary: the period 1860 to 1880 saw the first successful lobbying effort by the newly formed American Medical Association, with the cooperation of the Roman Catholic Church and many of the Protestant clergy, to make abortion illegal for the first time in the United States.[2]

Between the early 1860s and 1881, when New York State passed a severe anti-abortion law, individual physicians and state medical societies lobbied and petitioned their state legislation to make "the giving or prescription of a poison or noxious drug or the use of mechanical means to cause an abortion in a pregnant woman" a felony whether the mother died or not. States also passed laws making the women who solicited abortions criminally liable.[3]

Until these laws, abortion during the first four months of pregnancy (before "quickening," to use the nineteenth century's term) that did not involve the mother's death was not an indictable offense in the United States. As always, language is a crucial telltale. Until the AMA campaign, physicians and public alike used the term "abortion" as we today use the term "miscarriage"—to refer to the natural termination of a pregnancy. To abort meant to miscarry. They used the term "criminal abortion" to refer to the artificial termination of a pregnancy after the first trimester —after quickening. This chronology is critical. Laity, lawyers, and doctors alike never used the term "criminal abortion" to indicate artificial termination of a pregnancy that occurred before quickening. Until that point it was believed that pregnancy could not be assumed. Until then, women and their medical advisers believed, the cessation of menses could as easily have resulted from an "unnatural blockage" in the menstrual cycle as from pregnancy. Women and their physicians, therefore, felt justified in using drugs and other means to bring about the "natural" return of menses. Popular folk beliefs reinforced this practice, since most people believed that fetal life began at quickening. The accidental elimination of an unquickened fetus seemed a relatively insignificant matter—until, that is, the AMA systematically sought to alter popular opinion and practice.[4]

United States court rulings and legislation reflected these early permissive attitudes. Until amended in the opening years of Queen Victoria's reign, English common law did not consider abortion before quickening to be a crime, and it treated abortion after quickening as a misdemeanor. Blackstone's commentaries state, "Life begins in the contemplation of law as soon as the infant is able to stir in the mother's womb."[5] Under British common-law rulings, the criminality of abortion lay not in its attack upon fetal life, but in the danger it posed to the mother's life.[6] Early-nineteenth-century United States court decisions followed the British precedent. Two Massachusetts court decisions, in 1812 and 1845, established the legality of abortion before quickening, with the mother's consent. By 1860, there had been nine state-supreme-court decisions concerning abortion; seven held that abortion before quickening did not constitute a criminal offense. In 1879, a Kentucky court ruled that "it never was a punishable offense at common law to produce, with the consent of the mother, an abortion prior to the time when the mother became quick with child." In 1872, a New York State court decision drew a similar conclusion, as did a Wisconsin court decision as late as 1923.[7]

In the 1840s the situation began to change. Several states passed laws making abortion before quickening a misdemeanor. The purpose of this legislation, however, a New Jersey court declared in 1858, "was not to prevent the procuring of abortions so much as to guard the health and life of the mother against the consequences of such attempts." In other words, state legislators sought to control medical malpractice, not to protect the fetus. Penalties imposed by these laws were mild, ranging from three months' to a maximum of three years' imprisonment.[8] Even more significantly, anti-abortion advocates complained, these early laws were simply not enforceable. Unless the mother died, juries and judges alike were loath to convict.[9] These moderate regulatory efforts, moreover, were limited to the Northeast. Southern legislators remained content with common-law precedents.[10] As one Delaware jurist remarked as late as the 1860s, abortion and pederasty were two subjects that should not be addressed in a criminal code.[11] Until the 1860s and 1870s, Southern statute books remained innocent of any effort to regulate abortion.

Public opinion, a number of critics complained, actively condoned abortion. "The frightful frequency of intentional abortion in this country has long been notorious," one physician wrote in a private letter, "no less than the extraordinary ignorance as to its criminality, even among well-educated persons." Thomas W. Blatchford, an elderly physician from Troy, New York, complained to another physician, in a private letter: "But alas, alas, hardly a week passes but I am made cognizant of facts which prove the prevalence of the crime, not only, but the calmness, I had almost said, the approbation in which the public seem to look upon it." Another doctor reported that married women felt that if they "must submit to sexual intercourse, they are justifiable before God and good men to prevent conception."[12]

Another physician took a less empathetic attitude toward women's desire to have abortions: "Ladies boast to each other of the impunity with which they have aborted, as they do of their expenditures, of their dress, of their success in society. There is a fashion in this." Legislators and judges supported women, his lament continued: "The destruction of an unborn child is not at the present day murder at the common law.

. . . In the several states, as Maine, Massachusetts, and New Jersey . . . to cause or to attempt abortion before quickening . . . has been ruled by the Supreme Court not to be indictable even as an assault, if done with consent of the woman. . . ."[13] In the 1870s women could procure an abortion in Boston or New York for as little as ten dollars. Physicians complained that bourgeois women routinely aborted pregnancies that occurred during the first few years of marriage, pleading that polite society considered early pregnancies *déclassé*. Nor did abortion flourish only among the bourgeoisie of the larger cities. The practice occurred as well among small-town bourgeois matrons. The Michigan Board of Health estimated in 1898 that one-third of all the state's pregnancies ended in abortion. From 70 to 80 percent of these were secured, the board contended, by prosperous and otherwise respectable married women who could not offer even the unmarried mother's "excuse of shame."[14]

After a decade of escalating agitation, however, the AMA campaign began to affect state legislators. By the early 1880s, most states had enacted harsh anti-abortion laws.[15] This flurry of legislative activity was the direct result of the lobbying efforts and organizing skills of the Boston gynecologist H. R. Storer. In 1857, Storer succeeded in persuading the national AMA to establish a special committee to ascertain the number of abortions performed throughout the United States. As chairman of this committee, Storer wrote to physicians throughout the country, ostensibly inquiring about the legal status of abortion in their particular states. In these same letters, however, Storer preached the moral and social dangers of abortion. Abortion was an ever-increasing crime, he argued, the equivalent of infanticide and murder. Ignored by judges and legislators, abortion was condoned and practiced by the lay public. The worst offenders were not young unmarried women who loved and trusted unwisely, or struggling, impoverished working women, but, rather, married women of the middle and upper classes. These women sought to avoid marital responsibilities so as to live a life of endless pleasure without responsibility or pain. They "prefer to devastate with poison and with steel their wombs," Storer wrote, "rather than . . . forego the gaities of a winter's balls, parties and plays, or the pleasures of a summer's trips and amusements."[16]

Storer included proposed model legislation in his letters and urged his correspondents to arouse their medical societies to the danger of abortion and the need to lobby among their state legislators. Doctor after doctor wrote Storer thanking him for alerting him to the need for action. Some reported lobbying successes.[17] Many supported Storer in his efforts to get the AMA to adopt a strong anti-abortion resolution at its 1859 national convention.[18] Storer did not rest with the passage of these resolutions. In 1863, he succeeded in getting the AMA to announce a prize for the best popular essay written by a doctor on the subject of abortion, its object being to convince women of the sin of abortion. In 1864, an AMA prize committee chaired by Storer's father, David Humphrey Storer, awarded H. R. Storer the prize for his essay, *Why Not?*[19] Storer followed this essay with a number of books arguing that abortion was but a form of infanticide, that it was dangerously prevalent in the United States, and that doctors, lawyers, and clergymen must unite to eradicate it. As a result of Storer's efforts, articles and books on criminal abortion proliferated in both the popular and the medical press. The clergy added their voices, helping to create a broad, popular movement. States began to revise their legislation, making felonies of abortion without medical grounds and the certification of physicians; judges and jurors meted out increasingly stiff penalties.[20]

The Comstock Law, passed by Congress in 1873, was central to the anti-abortion structure. This law is infamous for forbidding the mailing of art, literature, and other materials deemed obscene by the United States postal agent, Anthony Comstock. Equally important, it banned from the mails any drug, medicine, or article for abortion or contraceptive purposes, forbade the advertisement of such items through the United States mails, and outlawed their manufacture or sale in the District of Columbia and the federal territories. In New York State alone, Anthony Comstock destroyed fifty tons of "obscene" books, four million pictures, twenty-eight tons of plates for their printing. His war against the advocates of birth control and abortion was equally successful. His first notable victory was the suicide of Madame Restell, perhaps Victorian America's most famous abortionist. His last victory came nearly half a century later when he forced Margaret Sanger to flee to England to avoid arrest for advocating the practice of birth control in a journal mailed through the United States mails.[21]

These two termini of Comstock's career are but the highlights of his efforts to make birth control and abortion illegal in the United States. These efforts, in conjunction with those of H. R. Storer, the Harvard Medical School, the AMA, and both the Protestant clergy and the Roman Catholic Church, effectively created the deadly underground of illegal abortions that thrived between the 1870s and the 1970s—an underground that took the lives of thousands of women annually. In one year alone, 1964, ten thousand women suffering from severe complications due to criminal abortions were admitted to New York City's public hospitals. Not all were fortunate enough to reach these hospitals. On December 25, 1955, for instance, Jacqueline Smith, a twenty-two-year-old fashion designer from rural Pennsylvania, went to the home of a Brooklyn hospital orderly. He operated on her, lacerating her uterus. Following her death, he dismembered her body and disposed of the wrapped pieces in trash cans along Broadway.[22] In 1859, virtually one hundred years before Jacqueline Smith died in Brooklyn, Jennie Shaw, a Vermont farm girl, pregnant by the St. Johnsbury farmer who had employed her the previous summer, went with her twin sister to an Irishman purporting to be a trained English surgeon. He contracted to abort her for one hundred dollars. Howard performed four D-and-C's in three days. After six days of delirium and hemorrhaging, Jennie Shaw died. When she was found, the area between her legs was packed with cotton saturated with blood.[23]

Why did American society forbid abortions during the hundred years between the 1870s and 1970s? What factors led the medical profession in the 1850s and 1860s to begin a systematic attack upon America's time-honored permissive attitudes toward abortion? Why did bourgeois men, in politics and the clergy, respond so positively and so promptly to the new medical arguments? The answers lie in the complex interaction between long-term social and economic change and the wide-ranging effects such change had on the bourgeois birthrate, on relations between bourgeois women and men, on abortion practices, and last, but certainly not least, on the needs of the medical profession. The rhetoric of the anti-abortion movement reflects the emotional impact this chain of interactive changes had on bourgeois men in general, and especially on America's new and uneasy men of science—her physicians.

Political rhetoric is an active as well as a reflective vehicle. The anti-abortion arguments did not simply mirror the social and professional experiences of male physicians. They reshaped legal and medical practice and transformed the balance of power within the medical profession. They altered the behavior and attitudes of a century of American women. The anti-abortion campaign offers a clear example of the way an emotive and metaphoric language is politicized, collective fears are transformed into collective actions, and the sexuality of others is regulated.

H. R. Storer began his anti-abortion campaign in the late 1850s, a time when bourgeois domestic relations remained novel and bourgeois sexuality problematic. The birthrate had dropped more precipitously during the 1840s than during any other decade in the nineteenth century.[24] Bourgeois women and men carefully delayed marriage until their mid- or late twenties. Once married, they quite self-consciously continued to reverse the sexual behavior of generations. Until the commercial production of the condom, which awaited the mass production of vulcanized rubber in the 1860s and 1870s, most couples depended upon *coitus interruptus* or continence. Historians have hypothesized about the effects these changes might have had upon bedroom politics, focusing largely on the growing self-conscious and self-controlled aspects of the sexual act itself.[25] Yet the wife's older age and less frequent pregnancies constituted an equally significant aspect of altered sexual relations, for these factors had the potential for sharply altering the power balance between wife and husband.

The bourgeois man's desire to transform his wife into a symbol of his own economic security and social standing further augmented her power within the new bourgeois family and class structure. The bourgeois husband lavished the accoutrements of his wealth upon his wife and upon *her* home. In the process of publicly affirming his own class status, he thus bestowed on a woman, supposed to be docile and dependent, his society's most respected symbols of power. Social-structural changes further heightened the ironic tensions that developed between the dictates of the Cult of True Womanhood and the realities of the bourgeois matron's life. The elaboration of nondomestic institutions, the growing importance of education within a literate society (even for women), Civil War patriotism, and later the need to meliorate the harsh impact of economic revolution, as we have seen, had called the bourgeois matron out of her orbit of domestic subordination. Socially respected, educated, affluent women began to acquire nondomestic organizational skills and a knowledge of the world outside their homes.[26] Such sophisticated and active women constituted at all times a minority of the new bourgeois women. Their existence, however, pointed to the possibility that more women might follow in their footsteps.

As violently conflicting demands were made of them, Victorian matrons entered a Catch-22 situation. The True Woman was domestic, docile, and reproductive. The good bourgeois wife was to limit her fertility, symbolize her husband's affluence, and do good within the world. Society's mandates came into conflict. The True Woman/bourgeois matron balanced them with difficulty. As a bourgeois matron, educated, polished, resplendent in the finery of her class, she was invested with economic resources that were not hers. At the same time, she possessed skills and knowledge far beyond her socially ordained sphere. When bourgeois matrons began to defend their newly honed social roles in the language of religion and social service, the conflict between ascribed status and real skills became increasingly alarming. The good wife had become a potentially dangerous social phenomenon. The medico-scientific insistence that women's biology was women's destiny must be seen in this light. Through the chimera of biological determinism, Victorian male physicians and Victorian men in general sought to hem in changes they had helped initiate.

Surprisingly, perhaps, the mass-circulation urban newspaper constituted a second major factor in the jigsaw puzzle of changes that led to the anti-abortion movement. Made possible by the escalation of an urban population, the industrialization of printing, and the emergence of commercial advertising, the penny press proliferated in the 1840s and the 1850s. In search of ever more advertising, ruthlessly competitive with one another, they used sensationalist stories to capture the ever-growing urban market. In this way mass-circulation newspapers became a catalytic force within the labile new cities and the new economy. Unpredictable and frequently irresponsible, they played a key role both in the commercialization of abortion and in the drive to make abortion illegal.[27]

Abortion-related ads proved a lucrative source of income for the new urban newspapers. By the 1840s and the 1850s, ads for abortifacients filled their pages. This marked a new trend, reflecting not only the bourgeoisie's determination to limit its birthrate, but also the commercialization of the drug industry. Physicians advertised their ability to secure the return of menstrual regularity. Physicians, midwives, and many others who specialized in gynecological ailments, whatever their formal training, set up special clinics, advertised their fee scales, solicited customers, printed cards, even sent business agents out into agrarian areas and smaller towns to solicit business. Madame Restell, one of the most efficiently organized of the new abortionists, aggressively established her dominance in the field through widespread advertising and innovative marketing techniques. By mid-century, abortion had become a big business. The urban and industrial revolutions had precipitated a practice that had once existed quite unself-consciously within the private female world of wives and midwives into the public and commercial world of men. In this process, induced abortion forced itself upon the consciousness of urban Americans.[28]

The role played by mass-circulation newspapers only grew in complexity. Not only did abortion advertisements dot their pages; newspaper editors, in their battle for increased circulations, transformed abortion into sensationalist news. The *New York Police Gazette,* in particular, turned abortion into a scare issue.[29] Women, its headlines cried, had begun to disappear from respectable homes. What had happened to them? Why did their husbands not lead in the search for their whereabouts? Abortionists, the *Gazette* claimed, sold the bodies of aborted babies to medical schools for experimentation. Would the affronts to Christian decency never cease? The discovery of the bodies of two women who had died in Boston from abortions heightened the tone of hysteria. The *Gazette* always focused on urban examples, usually involving well-to-do women. One front-page illustration showed a fashionably dressed and attractive woman whose arms were transformed into devil's wings. From her pelvis emerged a devil's head with fang teeth gnawing on a plump baby.[30]

This illustration is critical for understanding the early manifestation of anti-abortion rhetoric and imagery. On their cover, the editors of the *Police Gazette* had created a dense composite symbol. First, their illustration had invested the image of the new and affluent bourgeois woman with psychologically primitive male fears of the aborting mother and with the even more primitive male dread of *vagina dentata*. It had then merged this sexually cathected and dangerous female figure with the problematic issue of commercialized abortion and hence with the urban economy itself. The result was a new male metaphoric language. Commercialized abortion symbolized commercialization, the unnatural woman, an unnatural world.

Let us carefully examine the construction of this mythic discourse. Their picture first associated abortion exclusively with women, and, most significantly, with the bourgeois matron, portraying her not as an oppressed and abandoned victim (the female vision, as, for example, in the rhetoric of the Female Moral Reform Society[31]) but as an unnatural and monstrous woman, lethal to men and babies alike. The aborting woman, not the complicitous husband or the deceiving male lover, became, in the male-controlled mass-circulation literature of the 1840s and 1850s, the dangerous and destructive figure. The papers then refined the well-dressed and unnatural female aborter into a metaphor for the commercialized city itself. She was urbane, she was affluent. She rejected God's and nature's command that she bear and multiply. She, not the men in her life, threatened social order and the future well-being of the race.

The editors of the *Police Gazette* and of other sensationalist newspapers had created a metaphoric language that expressed in a psychologically covert and distorted manner the many alarms that beset the new men of the new cities: their uncertainty concerning the new bourgeois matron herself; the sexual demands and restraints birth-control practices had suddenly placed upon them; the fears abortion may always induce in men; and, far more generally, the fears of the uncontrollable and irrational new world. All these concerns constituted but fragments of a disturbing whole. Furthermore, by making the bourgeois wife, not the bourgeois husband, responsible for the evils of spiraling abortion, they displaced responsibility for everything the abortion symbol represented—family limitation, the industrial cities, the bourgeois revolution itself—from themselves onto the women in their lives.

The social and psychological intentions that lay behind the male metaphor become clearer when we contrast women's and men's response to the abortion deaths of the two women in Boston. Male "regular" physicians in Massachusetts used the two women's deaths to underscore the dangerous nature of abortion. They made them a central part of their lobbying efforts to debar "irregular" physicians (read: irresponsible abortionists) in Massachusetts. The Female Moral Reform Society also made the abandonment and death of these two young women (in this case they *were* unwed mothers) central to a political drive. The restriction legislation they sought, however, was aimed at seduction and prostitution, not against abortion. Five thousand women, aroused by the Society's campaign, petitioned the Massachusetts state legislature to make seduction a criminal offense. (The petition said not a word about abortion.[32]) Unregulated male sexuality, in the eyes of the supporters of the Female Moral Reform Society, not aborting women, threatened American society. Women and men, their lives transformed in strikingly different ways by the bourgeois revolution, developed antithetical metaphoric languages. Viewing each other with rising suspicion, they constructed elaborate sexual myths of the dangerous and disorderly Other as one way to discuss their fears of an alien and changing world.

The *Police Gazette* metaphors bespoke the anxieties of many of the new bourgeois men. It was, on the other hand, a scandal sheet that few genteel people read. What happened between the 1850s and the 1870s to transform its sensationalist headlines into a political campaign headed by the AMA and many of America's most prestigious physicians? To answer this question we must examine the impact of economic and demographic change on the medical profession, and especially on its Eastern, urban elite. Between the 1840s and the 1870s, a number of external forces severely challenged the self-esteem, economic security, and social standing of the medical profession's governing elite. All these factors would ultimately inform the profession's elaboration of an anti-abortion argument.

Medicine, as practiced in eighteenth-century America, had followed a two-track system. In the cities, the sons of established families, trained in Edinburgh or by leaders of the profession in America, practiced medicine for the well-to-do and for a few carefully selected charity patients. (The urban poor tended to heal themselves or to trust in midwives.) Rural America presented a far different picture. Farming and artisan families turned randomly to women or men believed to be skilled in practical physic: the self-taught, those knowledgeable in herbal lore, ministers because they read Greek, barbers because they could bleed—and most especially women.[33] Women as midwives and as family nurses, women wise in the ancient herbal pharmacopoeia, had always cared for their own and neighboring families. A survey of cook books and women's diaries for the eighteenth and early nineteenth centuries shows that women collected and exchanged recipes for medicines as routinely as they did for pies and cookies.[34]

The commercial and transportation revolutions that disrupted East Coast agriculture and village life broke upon this eclectic and harmonious medical world. Young men from New England and other Eastern farms pushed into the commercial world, sought new skills and secure locations. They turned to medicine as a profession familiar to them, a profession that their rural experience assured them required little special training. Farming parents seeking to aid sons they could no longer endow with land apprenticed those sons to country doctors. Other young men (William Alcott, Bronson Alcott's first cousin and close companion, for example, a man who later became a leading medical reformer) taught in country schools for a few years until they had saved enough money to attend medical school (in Alcott's case, Yale).[35] There they remained for one, at most two years, graduating with medical degrees after such brief training. The number of physicians increased astronomically during the opening decades of the nineteenth century as such minimally equipped young men flooded the market with their medical services.[36]

Another critical factor complicated this already fluid situation. These same years saw a host of medical-reform movements challenge medical orthodoxy. Homeopaths, hydropaths, botanical physicians, eclectics, all highly critical of the European-trained urban and aristocratic physician, launched an attack upon the professional dominance of the allopathic elite (or, as the allopathic physicians preferred to call themselves, the "regulars"). By mid-century, the reformers had established a number of alternative medical schools and hospitals. They focused their criticisms on the allopathic pharmacopoeia and therapeutics. "Regulars," the reformers charged, drugged and bled their patients until they died. Lacking respect for the human body and its recuperative forces, they relied upon unnatural drugs, mercurial compounds, and opiates. In an era before the germ theory, when "regular" physicians did in fact rely heavily on mercury-based drugs, opium, and cupping, the medical reformers offered a plausible alternative to traditional medicine.[37]

Not only did the medical reformers threaten the "regulars" economically; they also questioned their political and social assumptions. Embracing the romantic enthusiasms of their day, they urged men to observe and learn from their own bodies and from nature. Democrats, they sold homeopathic medical texts and simple homeopathic drugs to the common woman and man and charged their patients to cure themselves. Feminists, they trained women as physicians. In the eyes of the hard-pressed "regulars," the reformers' democratic and feminist inclinations made them appear the irresponsible advocates of social and intellectual disorder.

If this host of country-trained and reforming new doctors had remained on the frontier or in isolated rural areas, the establishment might have chosen to ignore them. But, carried along the toll roads and canals of the commercial revolution, using the cheap press which the industrialization of printing had made available, ardent medical reformers and traditionally trained country doctors invaded the new cities. There they found an urban population as recently come from the country as they themselves. These new urban dwellers treated the new country doctors with a respect the urban medical establishment found socially outrageous and economically threatening. The allopathic medical profession was poorly equipped to deal with this rural avalanche. The physician throughout much of the nineteenth century was in reality a small businessman. Dependent for income upon a private practice, he had few institutional resources. Unlike the law, medicine had no longstanding or intimate relation with state legislators and no strong tradition of licensing regulations.[38]

The "regulars" claimed one powerful ally—the mercantile elite in the major seaports. During the late eighteenth and early nineteenth centuries, Peter Dobkin Hall tells us, the mercantile elite took several steps that resulted in an alliance with the medical elite. Quite self-consciously, merchant families decided to shift from a family-company form of business organization to a corporate form, in order to increase capital resources to meet the demands of ever-larger markets. Having done so, however, they had to find careers for sons outside the family business. The new professions offered a likely avenue to financial security and social status. Among them, medicine proved particularly popular. During the opening decades of the nineteenth century, these old families began to endow medical schools and hospitals, which their sons would then direct and staff. These older and powerful families thus had a vested interest in maintaining the status and control of the Eastern urban medical establishment.[39] If the new men were to enter the profession, these wealthy families insisted they must do so on the allopaths' terms.

By the 1850s, well-connected physicians had begun the long struggle to upgrade standards within the medical profession and simultaneously to defend their practices against rural and "irregular" physicians. They founded state and local medical societies. They placed great emphasis on specialization and specialty associations. They began actively to lobby state legislatures, seeking laws that would make medical-school attendance and clinical training prerequisites for licensing. The state, the allopaths argued, had the obligation to protect the lives of innocent citizens from ill-trained, irresponsible "irregulars" and hysterical midwives. The "regulars" acted, they insisted, not out of economic self-interest, but from professional disinterest.[40] And so, by the mid-nineteenth century, the AMA had begun to politicize the human body.

No group of physicians was more insecure than the gynecology/obstetrics specialists. Until the early nineteenth century, few men had challenged the exclusively female domain of midwifery. William Shippen, the first American male physician to lecture on midwifery (in the 1760s), addressed his lectures to women midwives. The first American text of midwifery written by a man appeared in 1807; again, its audience was women midwives. The University of Pennsylvania established the first medical-school chair of midwifery in 1810. Although this initiated obstetrical training for male physicians, the status of obstetrics remained questionable, its position in medical education tangential. The guidelines of the medical school read: "It shall not be necessary in order to obtain the degree of Doctor of Medicine that the student shall attend the professor of midwifery."[41]

Throughout much of the nineteenth century, the legitimacy of obstetrics as medical specialty and the masculinity of the male obstetrician remained in question. During the 1840s and 1850s, physicians and laymen heatedly debated the morality of male physicians' conducting vaginal examinations.[42] As late as the 1860s, H. R. Storer's decision to specialize exclusively in gynecological cases caused widespread criticism and was partly responsible for his removal from the Harvard Medical School faculty.[43] Elizabeth Blackwell defended her decision to seek a medical education on the grounds that women should not be forced to submit to genital examinations by male physicians.[44]

Male obstetricians offered few specialized skills with which to justify their invasion of the female body or female birth mysteries. Physicians had little understanding of gynecological diseases—and less ability to cure them. Knowledge of human embryology remained primitive. Male physicians did not decipher the female ovulation cycle until the 1920s. Far into the nineteenth century, male obstetricians continued to resort to crude force, not surgical skills, in difficult labors, and Cesareans brought pain and almost certain death. Male obstetricians were troubled by their low status, especially once women began to acquire medical training and assert their right to compete with men for obstetrical specialties. Obstetricians wrote privately to one another seeking ways to raise their status. "Our profession here are making no advances [*sic*]," William Henry Brisbane, a Wisconsin gynecologist, wrote to H. R. Storer in 1859. "Our State Society seems to be worthless and those of us who have tried to do something have had everything to discourage us."[45] The mid-nineteenth-century medical literature is filled with similar laments. "It is difficult in the present state of our knowledge . . ." clinical articles typically began. "Much time and labour has been employed in theorizing and speculating on the subject of generation," another admitted, "but after all the experiments of physiologists . . . we must concur with Mr. Abernethy . . . that we know nothing of the phenomenon of conception."[46]

Nowhere is this sense of low status and fear of professional impotence more clearly expressed than in the physicians' attack upon the power of women patients to pick and choose their own physicians. Women freely moved from physician to physician, doctors complained, changing practice whenever the manner of the doctor displeased them. Nor was their choice limited to regular male doctors. For relatively insecure small businessmen, the exercise of such freedom of choice by women patients was both vexing and threatening. S. Weir Mitchell, toward the end of the century, engaged in a bitter diatribe against fashionable matrons who had it within their power to favor or ruin the career of a promising young physician. To Mitchell this power, especially when exerted in a concerted manner, seemed a violation of women's subservient status in society.[47] It is no accident that Mitchell specialized in the treatment of hysterical women. Strong parallels exist between the male physicians' hostility toward the independent, aborting woman and the obstinate hysteric.[48]

Abortion played a key role in the war between the allopaths and the "irregulars" for patients and for power. James Mohr claims that physicians through the first half of the nineteenth century found abortions a sure way of building up a private practice: the couple that came for an abortion tended to keep their abortionist as their regular family physician.[49] (The wording of this sentence in itself demonstrates the world of rhetorical change that lies between the easy days of the 1840s and 1850s and our own.) For complex professional reasons, the "irregulars" had the advantage over the "regulars" in this lucrative area of medical practice. The "regulars" had made the Hippocratic oath central to their struggle both to elevate the

quality of American medical practice and to establish their own professional and ethical pre-eminence. The Hippocratic oath was hostile alike to
birth control and abortion.[50] Conscientious allopaths could not, therefore,
perform abortions. Homeopaths, hydropaths, eclectics, the large number of
rural-born physicians who remained marginal to the world of urban
medical schools and medical societies, in contrast, remained free to do so.
The commercialization of abortion consequently placed the "regulars" at
a distinct disadvantage in competing with the "irregulars" for patients and
for large practices. If, on the other hand, the "regulars" could effectively
identify "irregular" physicians in the popular and political mind with
abortion, and abortion with the murder of innocent children and the
disruption of the happy family, then the allopaths would have forged an
effective tool in their war against the "irregulars." At the very least,
stringent anti-abortion legislation would deprive the "irregulars" of their
competitive edge in the struggle for patients. The anti-abortion campaign
came to assume a central role in the allopaths' struggle for professional
hegemony.[51] The "irregular" physician and the "irregular" wife, the
"regulars" insisted, conspired together against public order and the national
well-being.

Obstetricians and gynecologists assumed leadership of the anti-abortion campaign with a certain ambivalence and, in the public's eyes, irony.
A *double-entendre* was built into the nineteenth century's use of the term
"women's doctor." Not only did this term declare the low status of the
obstetrician's patients and the sexual nature of his practice, but it was also
a common nineteenth-century euphemism for "abortionist." Clearly many
allopathic obstetricians failed to maintain the requisite standards and political unity demanded by the Hippocratic oath and the AMA's campaign.
"Men who have for years been systematically engaged in this abominable
business are recognized in the profession and the community," a physician
complained in the 1870s. "It is but a short time since that a noted abortionist
. . . had the impudence to say it was the custom of the profession to do
so."[52] "It is the painful acknowledgement that our profession is not entirely
clear of complicity in the crime of feticide," a California doctor added in
1878. "Tempted by thirty pieces of silver and more or less assured by the
secrecy which is commonly attainable, individuals may be found in whom
the honorable instincts and teachings of the guild are lost in the influence
of unprincipled cupidity."[53]

Public deprecation of the "regulars'" gynecological skills compounded public doubt as to the sincerity of their ethical espousals. Lay men and women frequently asserted that "regular" gynecologists lacked the experienced abortionists' surgical skills and practical knowledge. A physician writing to one of the medical journals and signing his letter "The Honest Physician" complained: "I verily believe that the masses think that the 'common kind' of doctor, as they call him, has not the knowledge of how to produce an abortion, nor the courage to do it if he knew, and that there is more knowledge and skill in the little finger of one of these destroyers than could be packed into the craniums of a carload of M.D.'s of the honorable stamp."[54]

Obstetricians' and gynecologists' deep concern over their low professional status and public reputation colored their responses to the abortion issue. They desperately needed some reassurance that their claims to be men of science were legitimate. Some, such as J. Marion Sims, sought through the development of virtuoso surgical skills to raise the status of gynecology as a surgical specialty. Others turned to politics, bolstering their own self-esteem through frequent contacts with state and national political figures. It became of critical importance to these physicians to establish the right of gynecologists to set public opinion, sway votes in state legislatures, determine legislative policies—and, ultimately, be invested by law with the power to control their patients' life-and-death decisions. Physicians "alone can rectify public opinion," Hugh Hodge, a leading Philadelphia obstetrician and one of the founders of the anti-abortion movement, wrote as early as the 1830s: "they alone can present the subject in such a manner that legislators can exercise their powers aright. . . ." "The opinions of medical men, on these subjects," Hodge had already argued, "regulate public sentiment, govern the tribunals of justice, and influence even the minds of the mental philosopher and the scrutinizing theologian."[55] Some thirty years later, H. R. Storer wrote in a similar vein: "If [people] . . . were taught by the speech and daily practice of their medical attendants, that a value attaches to the unborn child, they would be persuaded or compelled to a . . . belief in its sanctity and to commensurate respect."[56] A. Lopez, a Mobile, Alabama, physician, wrote bitterly about the resistance that state legislators displayed to his efforts to dictate the state's anti-abortion statute. The legislators, he complained, "usurped the power which belongs to those concerned with the guardianship of human life and moral law." Other physicians, more successful than Lopez, bragged of their abilities to mold legislators and write legislation. Levin Smith Joynes of Richmond, Virginia, claimed exclusive credit for making Virginia "one of the few states in the Union in which the law of abortion has been at length placed on the right basis." He went on to detail his successful lobbying efforts, clearly one of the highlights of his professional career.[57]

Stringent anti-abortion legislation would also increase the allopathic obstetrician's power to assert clear authority over his female patients. Backed by state laws and judicial decisions, he could now spurn his female patients' requests for abortions. Professional security arising out of power over his patients is quite evident in the question and answer one Springfield, Ohio, physician asked concerning abortion: "What then is the duty of the honorable physician when approached upon this subject? . . . In the first place he should explain the enormity of the crime and the penalty which will follow it both physically and mentally. And then he should make known the illegality of the proceeding, and refuse to become a party in its commission. Taking this stand, he will retain his own self-respect and command the respect and confidence of his patients. . . ."[58] The surety that his patients could not turn to more compliant "irregulars" to circumvent his dictates of course greatly augmented the allopath's "self-respect" and self-confidence.

The chronology and much of the intensity of the nineteenth-century anti-abortion movement grew out of the professional needs of the AMA and of "regular" gynecologists and obstetricians. Purely professional concerns, however, do not explain the movement's imagery and rhetoric—or how a small professional association amassed national political power within a relatively brief period. To understand these aspects of the movement, we must unravel the psychological and semantic exchanges that occurred between the medical profession and the general male public. The AMA's campaign succeeded because physicians convinced the male bourgeois public and male politicians that abortion constituted a threat to social order and to male authority. They did so by adopting and elaborating the symbolism that the sensationalist press of the 1840s had originally developed around the image of the willfully aborting bourgeois woman.

Here was a figure the male public mind already identified with the disorders of the new city and the new economy—with the new bourgeois matron's "unnatural" power and autonomy. It was a metaphor that resonated with the gynecologists' bitter resentment of affluent and autonomous matrons who chose their own physicians, lightly discarding those that no longer pleased them. It bespoke, as well, their hostility toward ambitious women physicians who, having been refused admission by the "regulars" to "establishment" medical schools, had forged a professional alliance with homeopathic reformers. To beset "regular" physicians, the financial power bourgeois matrons exercised over male physicians, combined with female physicians' ability to secure medical training, epitomized a medical and social hierarchy turned upside down. Not surprisingly, therefore, the medical profession seized upon those aspects of the abortion metaphor that stressed women's "unnatural" autonomy and elaborated them into a powerful political rhetoric which spoke with equal intensity to "regular" physicians and to bourgeois men generally.

Like the popular press, Storer and the AMA focused responsibility and blame for abortion almost exclusively upon the affluent bourgeois matron. Medical opponents of abortion argued that the chief procurers of abortion were not deceived young women (for whom, they argued, they of course felt great sympathy), but well-to-do matrons motivated solely by the desire to avoid family responsibilities or to assume new nondomestic roles. Although bourgeois husbands undoubtedly participated actively in family-planning decisions, male physicians, like the *Gazette*'s editors, exonerated them completely and sought, rather, to forge a male alliance. The autonomous bourgeois wife, by rejecting the domestic and maternal role bourgeois men had constructed for her, the physicians argued, deceived and threatened them both. The AMA linked doctor and husband as the equally wronged and innocent parties. The aborting wife, in contrast, was unnaturally selfish and ruthless. The rhetorical devices the American Medical Association's Committee on Criminal Abortion resorted to shortly before they secured the passage of the Comstock Law underscores this point— as well as conjuring up fantasies of violence and punishment.

> She becomes unmindful of the course marked out for her by Providence, she overlooks the duties imposed on her by the marriage contract. She yields to the pleasures—but shrinks from the pains and responsibilities of maternity; and, destitute of all delicacy and refinement, resigns herself, body and soul, into the hands of unscrupulous and wicked men. Let not the husband of

such a wife flatter himself that he possesses her affection. Nor can she in turn ever merit even the respect of a virtuous husband. She sinks into old age like a withered tree, stripped of its foliage; with the stain of blood upon her soul, she dies without the hand of affection to smooth her pillow.[59]

These women acted without justification. By their acts they did violence to all that was natural to women: traditional domesticity, nurturing, self-sacrifice, devotion to the needs of others, and especially the biological drive for impregnation. "By some women, abortion is demanded and paid a large price for merely because of the annoyance of pregnancy and the duties involved by the new born helpless child," Boston physician Walter Channing wrote in 1859. "Her self-indulgence in most disgusting forms shows itself." He proceeded to give the example of "Mrs. ———, between eighteen and twenty, who found herself pregnant soon after marriage. This was an unlooked for consequence of that rite. She had no idea of being in the family way unless it was perfectly agreeable to her. She was vexed at what had occurred. She could not and would not have it, and looked around for relief."[60] A few years later, another physician, engaging in a mock debate with a woman seeking to abort, expressed similar hostility and disdain.

> In other words, you do not wish to have your personal indulgences interfered with by children and so you propose to escape by *killing* them in the first mode of existence. . . . Are you not ignoring the demands of *duty,* and pleading the most intense and unmitigated selfishness as a justification for destroying life? Is *self-indulgence* the only thing to be sought in this life? Is there no such thing as duty?

Women, he concluded, sought abortions "simply and solely to give a larger license to selfishness and personal indulgence." And a minister complained, "Women have become altogether immersed in pursuit of mere pleasure and fashion. Nothing must stand in the way of those objects."[61]

She was willful, Storer and other physicians complained. Ignoring doctor, lawyer, and clergyman, she cast caution to the winds; facing pain and the possibility of death, she insisted on having her own way—and that

was not traditional domesticity. The desire to control female behavior was
a central motif within the anti-abortion literature, which was marked as
well by a bitter misogynous tone. "You may talk yourself dumb and
accomplish nothing," Walter Channing complained.

> Why medical men, medical societies, medical writers have writ-
> ten and "resolved" and talked about abortion—producing in
> vain. Instances occur every day. . . . Women for whom this
> office of foeticide, unborn-child-killing, is committed, are
> strong-minded, and the natural is strengthened by the recently-
> established uterine function. It becomes irritable, morbidly sen-
> sitive and what is resolved upon is done.[62]

Other physicians attempted to place the aborting woman within an explicit
political context. They accused the women's-rights movement, popular
health-reform movements, the free-love movement of encouraging an
increase in the number of abortions. They saw all these reform efforts as
part of a concerted atheistic attack upon the sanctity of the home, of
Christian morality, and of the traditional role of woman as nurturing and
subservient.[63] Equally political race-suicide arguments, which, beginning
in the 1870s and 1880s, put the birth-control and abortion issue in a racist
and xenophobic context, also singled out bourgeois matrons as the "unnatural" perpetrators of "unnatural" acts. In a widely circulated anti-abortion
pamphlet, Storer, using a rather obvious image, argued that the fertile
Great Plains were just opening up to settlement: "Shall they be filled with
our children or by those of aliens?" he asked. "This is the question that
our own women must answer, upon their loins depends the future destiny
of the nation."[64]

The fears and hostilities which the new bourgeois matron inspired in
the bourgeois husband came home to roost in the medical as they had in
the popular literature. Bourgeois women, by selfishly curtailing the birthrate, doctors and sensationalist journalists alike argued, had precipitated a
national crisis and a national scandal. The male state must intervene,
regulate women's bodies, and thus save the future race. In this way the male
bourgeois elite—physicians and legislators, editors and their new urban
audience—projected the problematic aspects of the bourgeois revolution
(the declining birthrate and the sexual restraints birth control necessitated;

the breakdown of old customs; the frightening ways of the new cities; the influx of new immigrants; conflict within the medical world; the bourgeois matron's increasingly public persona; the pervasive sense of change out of control) onto the mythologized figure of the aborting matron. They then counterposed her to another of their mythic sexual construction—the True Woman who accepted her biological destiny and gloried in her reproductive sexuality. The aborting matron served as the scapegoat for all that was problematic in the new social order. The dependent and domestic True Woman asserted that, despite its emerging problems, the bourgeois order, rooted in women's biology, was natural and God-ordained. Janus-faced, these two mythic women, male-constructed symbols of order and disorder, defined the bourgeois male order. If, as Roland Barthes argued, the object of bourgeois myth is to make the bourgeois order seem natural, the AMA had constructed a complex and classic bourgeois myth.

I have thus far postulated an essentially sociological explanation for the chronology of the anti-abortion movement. An analysis of its rhetoric reveals equally significant psychosexual components. The image of the lethally powerful aborting woman not only bespoke men's professional anxieties; it expressed far more universal and psychological primitive fears and projections. Indeed, the psychosexual is as revealing as the professional. Each constitutes one pole in a complex bipolar symbolic language. Both meanings were deeply appealing. We must decipher both if we are to understand the mass appeal the anti-abortion movement wielded—or the processes by which emotive language becomes political.

Male physicians overelaborated their insistence on the immorality of abortion in a number of psychologically significant ways. The anti-abortionists based their argument on the fact that the fetus was alive from conception. To kill a fetus was therefore to kill a person, to commit murder.[65] This argument is sufficient in itself, but H. R. Storer and other anti-abortion leaders obsessively embellished it. The mother, they insisted time and again, had no special or even primary influence over the fetus that grew within her—or a closer physical or spiritual relation to it. Certainly her influence on or closeness to the fetus did not exceed that of the father; some gynecologists even claimed that because male genes were stronger than female, the father's influence upon the fetus was greater than the mother's.[66] Nature had given the mother's womb to the fetus to grow in; the mother did nothing herself. In an era that idealized motherhood as perhaps none other did, anti-abortion physicians denigrated and denied its power. Hugh Hodge originated this argument in 1839:

> Facts, in great numbers, can readily be produced, which posi-
> tively prove that there is no direct communication between the
> fetus (even in its earliest embryonic and most imperfect state),
> and the mother whose organs contain it. . . . It derives from its
> mother the material for support and growth, and a nidus, or
> spot, where it shall be protected from physical injury. Similar
> to the chick in the ovo, it is, therefore, not only a living but
> an independent being; and, as it will be universally acknowl-
> edged that the father has no influence over his offspring after
> the moment of conception, the same is true as regards the
> mother. The embryo thus generated by germs from each parent
> has henceforth an independent existence. . . . As the acorn,
> removed from the towering oak, and dropped into the earth,
> is capable of vegetating and producing, in due time, under
> favorable circumstance, by its own inherent powers, another
> oak . . . so the embryo, by its own vital properties, received at
> the moment of fecundation, is gradually developed in utero,
> from its independent state of existence . . . to that of the perfect
> foetus. . . . Physiologically, therefore, the infant after birth,
> while deriving all its nourishment and means of support from
> the breast of its mother, cannot be regarded as more independent
> than the foetus in utero.[67]

Some thirty years later, H. R. Storer repeated this same argument.

> Before the egg has left the woman's ovary, before impregnation
> has been effected, it may perhaps be considered as a part of and
> parcel of herself, but not afterwards when it has reached the
> womb, that nest provided for the little one by kindly nature,
> it has assumed a separate and independent existence, though still
> dependent upon the mother for subsistence. For this end the
> embryo is again attached to its parent's [note the neuter term]
> person, temporarily only. . . .

Storer elaborated on Hodge's comparison of women and lower phyla:

These reasonings are strengthened by the evidence of analogy. The utter loss of direct influence by the female bird upon its offspring from the time the egg has left her and the marked effect originally of the male; the independence in body, in movement, and in life, of young marsupial mammals, almost from the very first moment of their conception, identical analogically with the intra-uterine state of other embryos . . .[68]

This argument permeated the clinical literature as well. One physician, called to assist at the miscarriage of twins, decided to carry on an experiment testing the ability of the fetus to live independent of the mother. His vocabulary is almost identical to that of Hodge and Storer:

Shortly after my arrival a fetus was extruded with the placenta and membranes entire. The circulation went on beautifully for thirty minutes, when I severed the cord, which was still pulsating regular and with good volume. I think it is probable that the circulation might have been kept up for several hours, perhaps days. This and other similar cases that have occurred certainly go very far to prove the independent existence of the fetus in utero, bearing the same relation as the chick in ovo does to the parent bird. . . . P.S. they died immediately after the cord was cut.[69]

Not only was the mother merely a nidus or spot provided "by kindly nature"; she was frequently, and inherently, an irrational, irresponsible, insane spot as well. The influence of the uterus and the ova, Storer and others argued, affected women's rational processes, rendering them incapable of well-reasoned decisions, depriving them of human reason. "Woman's mind is prone to depression and, indeed, to temporary actual derangement under the stimulus of uterine excitation," Storer warned, "and this unlike at the time of puberty and the final cessation of the menses, at the monthly period and at conception, during pregnancy, at labor, and during lactation. . . ."[70] Not surprisingly, Storer was the author of a book claiming that all insanity in women was caused by gynecological disorders and could be cured by hysterectomies or other gynecological surgery.[71] "There can be no doubt but that the chronic forms of uterine disease," E. P. Christian argued, "more especially do exert such an influence even to modifying the affections, judgement and will, which in aggravated forms becomes insanity."[72]

The effect of such arguments was to reduce the awesome reproductive powers of woman to a very manageable level. Gone was woman, source of regeneration, who from her dark interior brought forth life. H. R. Storer and his fellow physicians (one of whom in a letter referred to himself as Storer's "yolkmate")[73] had re-created her as weak and childlike, in need of the guardianship and direction of her male physician.

The physicians' psychological involvement is indicated as well in another aspect of the anti-abortion argument. Physicians unfailingly referred to the fetus as male. He was "the potential male," "the future young man." The fetus's potential life, as described by Hugh Hodge, followed an exclusively male path. Hodge wrote: "the invisible product of conception is developed, grows, passes through the embryotic and foetal stages of existence, appears as the breathing and lovely infant, the active, the intelligent boy, the studious and moral youth, the adult man, rejoicing in the plentitude of his corporeal strength and intellectual powers, capable of moral and spiritual enjoyments; and finally, in this world, as the aged man. ... It seems hardly necessary to repeat," Hodge continued, "that physicians, medical men, must be regarded as the guardians of the rights of infants." The AMA had in effect created a new Oedipal triangle, linking the male physician with the male fetus against the mother. The mother was potentially lethal and insane; only the male physician could protect the male fetus. Especially when the physician actually prevented an abortion, it was he, not the mother, who gave the fetus life. Fetus and physician bonded to thwart the powerful and dangerous mother.[74]

The AMA's legislative campaign, as we have seen, was highly effective. By the 1880s, bourgeois men controlled bourgeois women's access to abortion. Legislative control of the body and behavior of others, however, rarely brings with it the power to silence those who are thus sexually constrained. Marginal, powerless, and rebellious social groups will maintain their own unique symbolic discourses. Often these symbols and metaphors, myths and narratives will exist quite separate from the dominant discourse, at times as secret, in-group languages. In this way dominant and marginal groups construct elaborate symbolic systems which, like the rails of a train, cover the same territory, parallel to each other but never crossing.

Bourgeois women and men developed highly divergent sexual symbols during the second half of the nineteenth century. The AMA's anti-abortion campaign constituted a decidedly male discourse. Male physicians had spoken to each other, to male medical reformers and male politicians —but rarely to women. Victorian women, after all, did not have to acquiesce to the legislative regulation of their own bodies. They could not vote. It is equally significant that Victorian women did not publicly respond to the male anti-abortion discourse. Rather, they developed a distinctive system of sexual images through which they expressed their reactions to economic and institutional changes in the larger society and their response to disparate female-male power relations. Between 1870 and 1900, a growing number of women writers, physicians, political and sexual reformers, moralists, and feminists published sexual and marital advice books addressed exclusively to bourgeois women readers. Despite these women's sharp personal and ideological differences, their fears and exhortations coalesced to form a remarkably harmonious female vision. This fact and the widespread popularity of their books among bourgeois women indicate that their arguments constituted a new symbolic discourse that paralleled and opposed the male anti-abortion discourse. In their pages, images of marital rape, of unwanted pregnancies, of marriage as legalized prostitution replaced male images of unnatural aborting mothers and willful urbane ladies. Women, the authors insisted, must develop their own sexual power within the home, control the frequency of intercourse, dominate the sexual act. Significantly, these women condemned abortion as bitterly as the AMA had. For the women, however, the husband who forced unwanted pregnancies upon his wife, and not the willful and fashionable matron, constituted the dangerous and disorderly figure.[75]

Abortion did not symbolize an increase in personal and sexual freedom for these women, but its reverse. The vaginal penetration the male abortionist perpetrated upon the unwillingly pregnant wife replicated her husband's initial uninvited penetration. Abortion, in this way, doubly violated women's physical integrity. These medical and domestic treatises expressed their audience's real sexual concerns: fear of unwanted pregnancy, complaints that husbands cared little for their wives' sexual pleasure, anxieties about the effectiveness of nineteenth-century birth-control techniques. At the same time, however, these women authors transposed specific sexual and marital concerns into an elaborate metaphoric construction in which male sexual power within the home symbolized male economic and political power outside the home—the raped wife, the economic and legal powerlessness of women, the wife weighed down by many children and domestic chores, the constraints and discontents of domesticity. During the 1860s, 1870s, and 1880s, two warring mythic figures—the women writers' image of the lustful and uncontrollable husband, and the male writers' construction of the unnatural aborting wife— expressed bourgeois women's and men's radically disparate social alarms and angers. The fact that neither women nor men could hear or respond to the others' fears and complaints underscores the difficulty women and men, within the same class, often within the same family, had in communicating.

The New Woman as Androgyne:
Social Disorder and Gender Crisis,
1870–1936[1]

Following the passage of the 1882 New York State law, the issue of abortion faded from the American political stage for a hundred years. Bourgeois men had won the debate. They had successfully defined as "unnatural" the bourgeois matron who avoided motherhood, who separated sex from reproduction and asserted her own will. That same decade, a new social and political drama opened, one that focused on the "naturalness" and legitimacy of another American woman—the single, highly educated, economically autonomous New Woman. The New Woman constituted a revolutionary demographic and political phenomenon. Eschewing marriage, she fought for professional visibility, espoused innovative, often radical, economic and social reforms, and wielded real political power. At the same time, as a member of the affluent new bourgeoisie, most frequently a child of small-town America, she felt herself part of the grass roots of her country. Her quintessentially American identity, her economic resources, and her social standing permitted her to defy proprieties, pioneer new roles, and still insist upon a rightful place within the genteel world. Repudiating the Cult of True Womanhood in ways her mother—the new bourgeois matron—never could, she threatened men in ways her mother never did.

For half a century, American women and men bitterly debated the social and sexual legitimacy of the New Woman. Through her, they argued about the "naturalness" of gender and the legitimacy of the bourgeois social order. They agreed on only one point: The New Woman challenged existing gender relations and the distribution of power. By defining her as physiologically "unnatural," the symptom of a diseased society, those whom she threatened reaffirmed the legitimacy and the "naturalness" of the bourgeois order. By insisting on their own social and sexual legitimacy, the New Women repudiated that order.

In many ways, this battle of words merely rephrased the conflicts Victorians had aired during the AMA campaign against abortion. The battle over the New Woman, however, does suggest another way in which sexual language functions as political metaphor. We see this when, during moments of intense confrontation, politically opposing groups adopt identical metaphors and images. This is a rare but fascinating phenomenon. It characterized the sexual discourse of the 1920s as both women and men transposed the New Woman into a sexually freighted metaphor for social disorder and protest. This fusion of symbolic systems developed slowly. By the 1920s the New Women had begun to debate men in a mythic sexual language that male physicians and sex reformers had originated a generation earlier. Of course, the New Women did not simply assume the male vocabulary. Rather, they invested male images with female political intent. In this way, they sought to use male myths to repudiate male power— to turn the male world upside down. They failed. By the 1930s, women and men alike had disowned the New Woman's brave vision. The New Woman herself, shorn of her political power and public influence, had become a subject of misunderstanding and ridicule.

It is crucial to understand the debate over the New Woman's sexual and political legitimacy. Not only does it exemplify the sexual as political metaphor; it constitutes one of the few times in which women have adopted male language to their own symbolic and political intent. If language reflects social experiences, which differ along gender lines, we must ask how women and men came to speak the same language. Had gender ceased to constitute a critical social force, a major factor in the inequitable distribution of power? If we answer no, then it must follow that male metaphors, no matter how transposed, could not fully express women's experiences and needs. Had New Women relinquished a critical source of identity and political strength—the power to create language? Can embattled social and political groups survive if shorn of that power? On the other hand, if the marginal or powerless wish to challenge the dominant discourse, must they frame their challenge in the language of the dominant mode? The debate over women's sexual and social autonomy that raged throughout the first third of the twentieth century raises many of these tortuous questions. It illustrates as well the dual nature of language as an empowering and a restraining social and psychological agency. We cannot understand the ways in which the physical body enters political discourse, the acquisition and exercise of political power, or, more simply, women's and men's relations between the Great War and the Great Depression, unless we decode the metaphoric languages that developed around the issue of the New Woman. To do so we must first examine the New Woman as a social and political force in Progressive America. We must then trace the complex evolution of the metaphoric languages that translated this flesh-and-blood creature into a condensed symbol of disorder and rebellion.

We identify the New Woman most directly with the new women's colleges. In her own mind and the minds of her contemporaries, education constituted the New Woman's most salient characteristic—and her first self-conscious demand. Complex economic, demographic, and institutional factors, factors that were largely external to the world of women, led to the emergence of the women's college. These factors included the growing need for a literate population; the delayed age of marriage, especially among the affluent bourgeoisie; a quintessentially bourgeois ideology that stressed upward mobility through education; accumulated wealth, which permitted the bourgeoisie the luxury of endowing educational institutions —even ones for women. Young women seized upon this novel institution for reasons of their own and so transformed the women's college into a potentially revolutionary social force.[2] Many young women saw in higher education an opportunity for intellectual self-fulfillment and for an autonomous role outside the patriarchal family. They asserted their right to an education equal to that of men. Since childhood they had dreamed of going to college. Bitterly resenting any restrictions on women's options, they linked college education and self-fulfillment with feminism and glorious achievements.[3] They were daughters of the new bourgeois matrons, and their dreams were heralded by the clubs and organizations their mothers had created and the role expansion those mothers had secured. Yet, ironically, their mothers' achievements only spurred the daughters' determination to create radically different roles for themselves. M. Carey Thomas, daughter of an affluent Quaker family in Baltimore and future president of Bryn Mawr College, was one such angry young woman. Her adolescent diary details her youthful idealism, her intellectual ambition, and her ambivalent attitude toward her mother. She learned her feminism at women's club meetings her mother took her to. At the same time, Thomas experienced her feminism as a revolt against her mother's ways.

January 6 [1871]. . . . After supper we went to Anna Dickinson's lecture. . . . She said one very true thing she said "that if a boy had genious [sic] and tallent [sic] and splendid abilities, and when he had grown to man-hood should come to his parents and tell them he felt it his duty to go out into the world and do his part elevating the human race, they would dry their tears and send him forth with their blessing resting upon him; but if a girl grown up in the same way with the same talent same genious [sic] same splendid abilities should in the same way express her desire, they would put her in her chamber lock the door and put the key in their pocket and then feel they had done their duty. Oh my how terrible how *fearfully* unjust. A girl certainly [should] do what she chooses as well as a boy. When I grow up—we'll see what will happen.

Dr. Morris walked home with us and talked all the while about the "sacred shrine of womanhood" and no matter what splendid talents a woman might have she couldn't use them better than by being a wife and mother and then went off in some high faluting stuff about the strength of women's devotion completely forgetting that all women ain't wives and mothers and they I suppose are to fold their hands and be idle waiting for an *ellgable* [sic] offer. Bah! Stuff and nonsense!

October 1 . . . I ain't good and I ain't bad. I ain't a tomboy but I ain't *ladylike* and I'm everything that's disagreeable and I do want a little excitement and I do want to go to Vassar. . . . I *do so want to,* and I am *perfectly determined* to get a good education. . . .

Oh I think its cruel when a girl wants to go to college and learn and she can't and is laughed at and absolutely kept from it while *a boy* is made to go whether he wants to or not. I don't see why the world is made so unjust and I don't see why all unjustness should be turned against girls in general and me in particular. More and more every day I'm making up my mind to be a doctor for when I grow up I can't be dependent on father and mother and I ain't going to get married and I don't want to teach school, so what can I do? . . . I can't imagine anything worse than living a regular young ladies [*sic*] life. . . . I don't *care* if everybody would cut me. I *despise* society and I *detest* girls. . . . It makes me mad to see everybody so contented. . . .⁴

As women's colleges proliferated in the 1870s and 1880s and as male universities hesitantly opened their doors to women, the New Women set off, doughty late-Victorian pioneers. Laden with hatboxes, ball gowns, and lace antimacassars, they searched for the intellectual excitement of which M. Carey Thomas wrote, for roles that were not ladylike and were fulfilling.⁵ For most of these New Women, college constituted the first time they had left the physical comforts and emotional security of home and kin. For the first time, they found themselves outside conventional institutions and modes of behavior. The large dormitories into which they moved physically represented the changes that were transforming their lives. The freshman no longer nestled in a room in her parents' home; she now lived within an impersonal, institutional structure. The first letters of women students to their families refer to the homesickness and fears that swept through them as they entered those imposing buildings—and to their efforts to transform their rooms into reassuring reconstructions of what they had known at home. While Wellesley freshman Florence Scofield strenuously denied her own homesickness in a letter she wrote her mother that first momentous month in college (September 1876), she did comment at length on the homesickness of her two roommates. Concerning one she wrote: "Poor girl, I fear she is very much homesick. She feels very blue indeed today there being a slow drizzling rain outside which she sits and watches and then wipes her eyes." Concerning her second roommate, she commented in the same letter: "This is her first year away from home also and yesterday when her mother came to see her, I think she would a little rather have gone back with her than remain here." Florence's own longing for home revealed itself when the traditional love token mothers send their college daughters arrived—the box of fruit and other goodies. "I was much pleased with my box," Florence confessed. "It seemed so good to see all the things [with] which I was so familiar, even the box was beautiful in its familiarity. I saw your thoughtfulness in many things for which I had not sent. I ate the pears which were delicious, though it was rather a breach of rules so to do. . . ." M. Carey Thomas, who finally succeeded in convincing her parents to send her to Cornell University as a member of the first class to include women, rented two rooms in Sage Hall, Cornell's women's dormitory. In this way, the rather fastidious and class-conscious Thomas informed her mother, she had acquired two bureaus, two tables, and two bookcases, and lots of room. She sought through pictures of friends and relatives to make her college room look just like her commodious arrangements at home.[6]

New college women sought anxiously for sympathetic faces among the other New Women they found there. Comforting practices, borrowed from the earlier female academies, eased life in the women's colleges as administrators instituted a host of supportive rituals. Junior and senior women adopted their freshmen and sophomore "sisters," brought them fruit and flowers, guided their steps. May Days and Lantern Nights brought the young women together.[7] In a strange and, at times, frightening environment, rituals that drew on traditional female expressions of affection eased the way for the New Women pioneers.

Those women who dared to enter the formerly male strongholds of the newly coeducational universities faced a particularly alien environment. Their presence violated many more taboos than did women's attendance at an all-female college. And the "coeds'" demands were far more radical. They sought not an equal but an identical education. The same ceremonies would mark their acquisition of the same degree. On a daily basis, they would meet with young men to assert their intellectual equality, perhaps to demonstrate their scholarly superiority. And they would do so without any of the protective rituals that surrounded "visiting" between young women and men within the traditional Victorian home. Coeducation threatened the very principle of gender polarity. Parents, administrators, and faculty observed the experiment with concern.[8]

Many male students openly resented this female invasion of their halls and quads. They did little to make the young women's lot easier. "Coeds" reported clinging together tenaciously, waiting for one another after class so as not to have to walk alone past an army of bemused young men. M. Carey Thomas vividly described one such incident. "There are three hundred boys in the present Freshman class," she wrote her parents. "There is nothing disagreeable here about the men except that they collect by fifty's on the steps of different buildings and to pass between them into the lecture rooms is quite an ordeal. They stare so—usually I find myself perfectly crimson by the time I am past them."[9] Ellen Cort Brown, who graduated from Cornell a few years after Thomas, in 1882, described her coeducational experiences in somewhat greater detail.

> We never talked to the men in the halls or the classrooms when coming or going, nor walked anywhere with them—on the campus. In the large lecture halls and the small class rooms, filled mostly with our brothers and cousins and future husbands, we walked demurely as inconspicuously as we could manage, and took seats, always at the front. . . . We were not insulted—only tolerated and ignored.[10]

Indeed, male students' response to the educated woman was far from enthusiastic. Charlotte Williams Conable, who has traced the history of women at Cornell, reports that the men, when among themselves, lampooned their women fellow students—and looked down upon them, sexually and socially. Male student songs included lines such as "I'm glad all the girls are not like Cornell women / They're ugly as sin and there's no good within 'em." Suggesting that women who desired a college education were socially unpolished and frequently from the lower classes, the young men sang, "The coed leads a wretched life / She eats potatoes with a knife." Fraternity rules forbade members to speak to coeds or invite them to fraternity parties. The college woman might be brilliant but she had forfeited her right to a place in fashionable society.[11]

The costs of coeducation were great, Thomas finally admitted. At the end of her senior year she carefully calculated what the experience had cost her emotionally.

> There is much that is very hard for a *lady* in a mixed university and I should not subject any girl to it unless she were determined to have it. The educational problem is a terrible one—girls' colleges are inferior and it seems impossible to get the most illustrious men to fill their chairs, and on the other hand it is

a fiery ordeal to educate a lady by coeducation—it is impossible
to make one who has not felt it understand the living on a
volcano or on a house top—Frank Heath's story and that horri-
ble cartoon were samples—yet it is the only way and learning
is worth it. [12]

To place a woman outside of a domestic setting, to train a woman
to think and feel "as a man," to encourage her to succeed at a career, indeed
to place a career before marriage, violated virtually every late-Victorian
norm. It was literally to take her outside of conventional structures and
social arrangements. No longer a girl, not yet married, the college woman
had withdrawn from the world of bourgeois domesticity, of cooking, child
care, and entertaining, to enter the cloistered environment of the women's
college or dormitory. She thus made herself the intellectual peer of young
men, and rendered herself socially questionable by that very act. College
women were liminal figures locked together in a novel ritual and a novel
place. Conscious of being scrutinized by a dubious world, they reached out
to one another, forming the intense bonds of a shared identity that characterize the liminal experience.[13] Their liminality crossed generational
boundaries. The New Women teachers devoted themselves to their New
Women students, ardently cultivating the future.[14] Crushes—among students for their teachers, between students—Nancy Sahli tells us, abounded;
as did lasting friendships and networks of loving friends woven into the
length and breadth of a woman's life.[15]

Women students, faculty, and administrators had transformed the
college experience into a unique rite of passage. The word "unique" is used
appropriately. Not only did college education constitute a novel experience for nineteenth-century women, it emerged as a highly irregular ritual
from the perspective of modern anthropology, violating many characteristics anthropologists have come to expect of rites of passage. Societies
institute rites of passage to mark off and contain processes of change that
might otherwise threaten social cohesion. Socially dominant groups—not
the liminal initiands—control the rite, seeking to inculcate socially ap-
proved roles.[16] College, in contrast, prepared young women for roles
Victorian society viewed with intense ambivalence. Women educational
reformers frequently controlled the rites, at least within the women's
colleges. In their hands, college education became an agency for social

change rather than for social cohesion. It pitted the liminal figure against the world that created and sustained her rite of passage.

Let us look more carefully at the unresolved conflicts embedded in the college experience. Parents and male college administrators had originally intended the college years to constitute but a pause in a woman's normal progression from girlhood to marriage. From their perspective, the college years constituted a socially contained ritual that prepared the young woman for the predictable and conventional role of educated wife. Within the bourgeoisie, the demographic trend toward later marriage within the bourgeoisie, the high value society placed on education—and not a desire to train their daughters for new roles—had led them to sanction those daughters' college experience. As already suggested, however, women college educators and a few of their male supporters viewed women's education in a far different light. The most radical educators (and many young women students) saw college education as a way to compete with men for a place within the new bourgeois professions and urban bureaucracies. Even conservative women educators, Martha Vicinis claims, sought through college education to teach the impersonal executive skills women would need to function as autonomous professional women in a nondomestic world. College education thus functioned to draw young women out of their mothers' and grandmothers' domestic mindset.[17] These innovative goals coincided with the desires of many college women themselves, who evinced little interest in returning to the world of conventional gender roles and heterosexual marriage. From the 1870s through the 1920s, between 40 and 60 percent of women college graduates did not marry, at a time when only 10 percent of all American women did not.[18] These women had invested college education with their dreams of autonomy and power. It promised them a new identity, equality with men, "the hope," to again quote M. Carey Thomas, "of doing something splendid after all."[19]

College completed, the more adventurous and determined of these educated women experimented with alternative life styles and institutions. Like their mothers, they formed separatist organizations of women to deal with the new problems of an industrial and urbanized world. Unlike their mothers, they used these single-sex institutions to sustain a life lived permanently outside the bourgeois home. The women's college constituted their first haven in a critical world. Many New Women chose to remain there as faculty. The women's college offered them many advantages. Within the institution that had initially fostered their ambitions, they could continue to devote themselves to their own intellectual development. Here, surrounded by like-minded women, supporting themselves financially, they could also nurture the younger women who followed in their footsteps. Early women faculty struggled to improve the quality and status of women's colleges. Some, like Mary Woolley, Vida Scudder, and especially M. Carey Thomas, devoted their lives to creating women's colleges equal in all respects to the best men's colleges.

The settlement house constituted another favorite institution. The New Women transformed the settlement houses, borrowed initially from British male reformers, into predominantly female institutions. Whereas male settlement-house residents averaged a stay of six years, women residents often remained a lifetime. The settlement house represented their home, their fellow women residents, their family.[20] A sororial intensity marked the inner dynamics of the settlement house, just as it did the women's college. College women and settlement-house residents called one another "sister." Teachers and settlement-house founders were loved as "mothers." Certainly Jane Addams was beloved by the other Hull House residents (many of whom had been her classmates at Rockford Female Seminary or came from other women's colleges). Like college students, many of these women settlement-house residents formed passionate relationships with one another. Some felt that they had married for life. Jane Addams and Mary Rozet Smith's relationship spanned forty years. Jeannette Marks and Mary Woolley lived together in the president's house at Mount Holyoke for over a quarter of a century and then entered retirement together. Vida Scudder and Florence Converse, professors at Wellesley, close friends of Marks and Woolley, actively involved in the College Settlement House in New York City, rejoiced when they were finally able to establish joint housekeeping. M. Carey Thomas shared "the Deanery" at Bryn Mawr first with Mamie Gwinn and, after their much-celebrated rupture, with Mary Garrett. These constituted only the most commented-upon examples of a practice common to women's colleges and settlement houses alike.[21]

Significantly, while rejecting the patriarchal family and their mothers' domestic lives, the first generation of New Women did not repudiate the traditional world of female love or the concept of the female family.

It was the male-dominated, not the female-guided, family that restricted women's full development, they insisted. Educated women could develop alternative, single-sex familial institutions which would foster women's autonomy and creative productivity. In radical new environments, on the brink of developing a host of new roles for women, the first generation of New Women wove the traditional ways of their mothers into the heart of their brave new world.

Indeed, the more politically radical of the New Women used the loving world of female bonding and traditional female familial concepts to forge a network of women reformers and social innovators into a singularly effective political machine. Settlement-house women spun out a delicate web of interlocking social-justice organizations led and staffed by militant (and, often, single) New Women. Residents of America's worst slums, familiar with the daily workings of industrial capitalism, they figured prominently within the left wing of the Progressive Movement. Jane Addams's Hull House family included socialist Florence Kelley (the first factory inspector for the state of Illinois); Alice Hamilton (the first woman on the faculty of the Harvard Medical School), who almost single-handedly created the new specialty of industrial medicine; Julia Lathrop, with Jane Addams an alumna of the Rockford Female Seminary, who led in the investigation of state institutions for the insane and pioneered in establishing the juvenile court system; Grace Abbott, another Rockford Female Seminary graduate, who fought to win a place for women within the AFL and who battled long and hard for child-labor legislation; Sophonisha Breckinridge, Wellesley graduate student, holder of a Ph.D. in political science and a law-school degree from the University of Chicago, a woman who led the battle for child-labor legislation and played a key role in the Women's Trade Union League. Women reformers depended on one another for emotional and social succor. Nor did they willingly relinquish their supportive networks. Florence Kelley, moving from Chicago to New York to assume the duties of general secretary of the National Consumers' League, simply shifted her residence from Hull House to the Henry Street Settlement. Here she busily constructed a second dense network of women reformers, which she then wove together with the Hull House "female family." When Jane Addams and Florence Kelley convinced President Taft to establish the Children's Bureau, they also convinced him to appoint Hull House resident Julia Lathrop as director.

When Lathrop retired in 1921, a second Hull House woman, Grace Abbott, replaced her as director. Kelley introduced Lathrop and Abbott to that other warhorse of child-labor legislation and the social-justice movement, Josephine Goldmark. Working together through the Chicago School of Civics and Philanthropy, the graduate program at the University of Chicago, a network of settlement houses which included Hull House, the Henry Street Settlement, Greenwich House, the College Settlement, and Tremont House, and, finally, through the Women's Trade Union League and the National Consumers' League, these women lobbied for the legalization of trade unions and strikes and worked to organize women workers. They fought for workmen's compensation, minimum-wage and maximum-hour legislation, national health insurance, medical care for pregnant women and children, aid for dependent children. They became expert lobbyists and effective manipulators of public opinion. Their vision extended beyond the parochial boundaries of their communities or country. Seeking international peace and racial justice, they founded the Women's International League for Peace and Freedom and played a pivotal role in organizing the NAACP.[22]

Radical causes and loving female friendships constituted the woof and warp of the tapestry of female power and orchestrated social change which the New Women wove between the 1890s and the First World War. Through their efforts to re-form urban America, they created a position of power and legitimacy for themselves. As they had during the Second Great Awakening, liminal and radical women used male radical ideology between the 1890s and the 1920s to build new roles for themselves. Loving and living with other women, within the separatist environment of women's colleges, settlement houses, and reform organizations, dedicating their lives to the advancement of other women, the New Women amassed greater political power and visibility than any other group of women in American experience.

Sadly, their struggle for autonomy often led to estrangement from their own mothers and female kin, who remained within the old female world and who feared the attraction the new world held for their daughters. The mothers of the New Women, of course, had stepped outside the restrictions of domesticity and passivity, constructing active and creative roles through the agency of women's clubs, educational and industrial unions, the YWCA, and the WCTU. They read widely, knew their urban surroundings, and considered themselves highly educated women. Their principal identity, however, remained that of married women. Nor were they college women. M. Carey Thomas's mother hesitated long before permitting Thomas to be one of the first women to attend Cornell University.[23] Jane Addams's stepmother insisted that Addams fulfill all the duties genteel society expected of a young bourgeois girl while Addams was enrolled in the Women's Medical College of Pennsylvania. She bitterly resented Addams's refusal to marry. Addams's sisters could not understand why their unmarried sister did not make herself more available to aid them in the domestic crises of childbirth and illness.[24]

Resentful words, lingering guilt, and consequent alienation divided the New Women from their mothers and their female kin. M. Carey Thomas briefly returned home after college to attend graduate courses at Johns Hopkins University. The painful alienation she had first expressed during adolescence again surfaced in her diary:

> I do believe I shall shoot myself. . . . There is no use living and then mother would see in the morning that she had been cruel. She says that I outrage her every feeling, that it is the greatest living grief to have me in the house . . . that she has ceased to love me except as a child . . . that I am utterly and entirely selfish. . . .[25]

A generation later, Margaret Anderson, newly graduated from college, wrote the author of a young girl's advice column in a Chicago newspaper to ask "how a perfectly nice but revolting girl could leave home."[26] Thus, while replicating the emotional world and single-sex institutional construction of their mothers, the New Women, by rejecting marriage and insisting on careers, had repudiated their mothers' world. The New Woman remained a liminal figure long after college. She stood determinedly outside conventional institutions. Indeed, she had to create alternative institutions and careers for herself, since the normative world offered her no haven other than the role of the spinster aunt or the poorly paid and unmarried schoolteacher. It is in this sense that I see her as a perennially liminal figure—a figure always outside of the existing social structures and with no way of coming in.

The emergence of institutions of higher education for women elicited a hostile and frightened response from traditional-minded men. Not only did higher education open new roles for bourgeois women, it challenged the West's traditional basis for gender differentiation. Since classical Greece, men had insisted that man represented the mind, woman the body, man the creative principle, woman the reproductive impulse, man the heaven-born aspect of human nature, woman its earth-bound component. Put most succinctly, man was the creator and representative of culture, woman of nature. To educate woman would violate each of these binary oppositions and make woman, not man, the mediating figure. Alarmed by the real and the philosophical implications of equal education for women and men, Victorian educators and physicians launched an attack which combined some of the most ancient principles of medicine with the nineteenth century's increasingly deterministic vision.

The human body, Victorian male physicians insisted and male educators readily concurred, was both hierarchical and fragile, its delicate balances easily destroyed by external forces. A closed energy system, the body allocated scarce energy resources governed by rigid, biologically determined and gender-linked priorities. Within the male body, the higher organs—the brain and heart—dominated. Predictably, the reproductive organs dominated the female's body. The woman who favored her mind at the expense of her ovaries—especially the woman who spent her adolescence and early adulthood in college and graduate school—would disorder a delicate physiological balance.[27] Her overstimulated brain would become morbidly introspective. Neurasthenia, hysteria, insanity would follow.[28] Her ovaries, robbed of energy rightfully theirs, would shrivel, and sterility and cancer ensue.[29]

Society, late-nineteenth-century physicians warned, must protect the higher good of racial health by avoiding situations in which adolescent girls taxed their intellectual faculties in academic competition. Pointedly, they compared the robust fertility of early-nineteenth-century women with the relative barrenness of their granddaughters—New Women. "Our great-grandmothers got their schooling during the winter months and let their brains lie fallow for the rest of the year. They knew less about Euclid and the classics than they did about housekeeping and housework. But they made good wives and mothers, and bore and nursed sturdy sons and buxom daughters and plenty of them at that."[30] "Why," as another physician pointedly asked, "spoil a good mother by making an ordinary grammarian?"[31]

Yet, doctors fulminated, where did the daughters of the nation's most virtuous and successful middle-class families spend these years of puberty and adolescence? They spent these years in schools. They sat for long hours each day bending over desks, reading thick books, competing with boys for honors. They flocked to the new colleges. They fought for admission to graduate and professional programs. They journeyed to Germany and Switzerland seeking education equal to that given men. In 1901 a gynecologist projected the diseased life such an intellectually competitive woman would lead:

> The nervous force, so necessary at puberty for the establishment of the menstrual function, is wasted on what may be compared as trifles to perfect health, for what use are they without health? The poor sufferer only adds another to the great army of neurasthenics and sexual incompetents, which furnish neurologists and gynecologists with so much of their material. . . . Bright eyes have been dulled by the brain-fag and sweet temper transformed into irritability, crossness and hysteria, while the womanhood of the land is deteriorating physically.
>
> She may be highly cultured and accomplished and shine in society, but her future husband will discover too late that he has married a large outfit of headaches, backaches and spine aches, instead of a woman fitted to take up the duties of life.[32]

Such medical admonitions, published in ever-growing numbers by America's most eminent physicians (Harvard Professor Edward Clarke, for example, or Philadelphia's elegant society physician S. Weir Mitchell), exerted a strong influence upon educators, even those connected with institutions that admitted women. Throughout the 1870s, state legislators debated the advisability of their universities' offering unrestricted educational programs to women. A number of universities that did admit women prescribed a lighter courseload, or refused to permit women's admission to regular degree programs. "Every physiologist is well aware," the Regents of the University of Wisconsin explained in 1877,

> that at stated times, nature makes a great demand upon the energies of early womanhood and that at these times great caution must be exercised lest injury be done. . . . Education is

greatly to be desired, . . . but it is better that the future matrons
of the state should be without a University training than that
it should be produced at the fearful expense of ruined health,
better that the future mothers of the state should be robust,
hearty, healthy women than that, by over study, they entail
upon their descendants the germs of disease.[33]

This fear for succeeding generations born of educated women was widespread. "We want to have body as well as mind," one commentator noted,
"otherwise the degeneration of the race is inevitable."[34] Such transcendent
responsibilities made the individual woman's personal ambitions seem triv-
ial indeed.

The selfish woman who, despite the pleas of educators, legislators, and
physicians, insisted on placing her own intellectual fulfillment above her
duty to the race, not only risked nervous exhaustion and wasting diseases;
she might also develop dangerously masculine physiological characteristics.
Her breasts might shrivel, her menses become irregular or cease altogether.
Sterility could ensue, facial hair might develop. Many such women began
to wear heavy boots. These women flirted with hermaphroditism, but not
with homosexuality![35] American physicians through the 1870s talked of
women's sexual deviance exclusively in terms of the rejection of motherhood—not of men.

Significantly, male physicians and educators elaborated a parallel but
antithetical argument concerning the interaction between sexual and intellectual development among young men. The young man who stimulated
his reproductive organs at the expense of his brains courted disease as surely
as the young woman who developed her mind at the expense of her
reproductive organs. I refer, of course, to the male anti-masturbation
literature of the early-to-mid-nineteenth century.[36] Within the male medical model, young women and young men constituted happily contrasting
figures, the one the "natural" inversion of the other.

On the level of public policy, the Victorian male medical model was
direct and simple. Nature, not individual caprice, determined women's and
men's social characteristics and roles. State legislators, college administrators, and fond parents must not permit young women to attend college,
nor should men marry women who had thrown away good health and a
fecund future in the foolish pursuit of education.

Behind these efforts at social control lay a far more complicated emotional and symbolic message, one that expressed small-town America's fear of and resistance to social changes that extended far beyond the possibility of new roles for a small elite of women. The Victorian medical model, with Manichean determination, projected a bitter war between the mind and the body, especially between woman's mind and body. Binary opposites, mind and body, men and women, could not be fused. The surety of social order and cohesion rested upon their biological opposition.

This vision did more than rationalize gender relations. It assured small-town Americans, caught in the throes of relentless change, that they in fact lived in a world composed of timeless and unambiguous social categories rooted in absolute physiological laws. Such laws robbed change of its legitimacy—if not of its power. Yet while absolute, these laws were vulnerable to violation: Although insisting that biology was destiny, Victorian physicians had not espoused an absolutist form of biological determinism. Young men, vulnerable to the "unnatural" stimulation of the new cities, might masturbate, displacing to the lower organs energy needed by the brain. Women should subordinate mind to body, yet no physiological force kept them out of college. Once they were there, an irreversible train of exhaustion and disease would follow; biology would destroy determinedly educated women. But mid-Victorian biology could only punish sinners. It could not prevent sin.

Thus we find a medical model of easily violated laws, weakly defended by threats of pollution. An odd system, but one that bespoke the reality experienced by small-town Americans. They had constructed a hierarchical society, shored up by a myriad of social rituals and priorities which none could violate without social punishment. Economic forces beyond their control—or understanding—now threatened that society. They could insist upon the moral superiority and biological "naturalness" of their society, but they could not protect it from destructive external forces. Inhabitants of settled communities beset by change, they invoked laws they could no longer enforce. They fought with the only device open to those powerless to resist change—futile threats of magical punishments against those who violated the old ways.

Victorian male physicians had projected the principal characteristics of small-town America onto the human body. Both were hierarchical systems, composed of a myriad of interdependent parts. Physical and social health rested on the harmonious acceptance of that hierarchy. The brain must not steal energy from the ovaries, just as women must not alter their roles, or the immigrant and the Catholic aspire to political and social dominance. The physical body's closed energy system paralleled the small town's limited markets and modest capital resources. Each was frighteningly vulnerable to external forces, which could disorder its delicate balances. Railroads, finance capitalism, international cartels, massive immigration, and burgeoning industrial cities threatened small-town America in the 1870s and 1880s. Stimulation associated with the new world —college, a wild urban life—could destroy the delicate physiological balance of America's youth. Transposing social into physiological dangers, Victorian physicians and educators had created a medical model that located the etiology of disease in the institutions and social relations of the urban world. Physiological disorder would parallel social disorder as small-town America's daughters abandoned the old sureties and fled to the college and the city.

Developing their own metaphoric language, the New Women denied that they were either physiologically "unnatural" or socially deviant. Rejecting men's insistence upon a closed energy system, they argued that education, exercise, and careers would strengthen women's bodies and minds. The confined and married woman—weakened by frequent pregnancies, burdened with a large family—was far more prone to hysteria, depression, or gynecological diseases than her educated sister.[37]

Late-nineteenth-century women physicians, as might have been expected, helped formulate the New Woman's response. They failed to share the alarm with which their male colleagues contemplated the dangers of coeducation. They emphatically repudiated male physicians' insistence on women's physiological fragility. Mary Putnam Jacobi published a highly influential article refuting male physicians' assertions that menstruation constituted a female disease. Menstruation was a natural process; it did not exhaust a woman's energies or interfere with her other activities. Energy levels differed from individual to individual, but a good diet and exercise, combined with the "natural" exuberance of youth, could take girls as well as boys through a productive and safe college career. Women, in short, could be both female and human. Women physicians thus rejected four of the basic tenets of male Victorian medicine: the closed energy system, hierarchy of bodily functions, female physiological fragility, a female/body–male/mind polarity. Professional women seeking equality with men, they insisted on the similarities that tied men and women together—not on their complementarity. Like that of their male counterparts, their conception of the body reflected their social experiences and their professional needs.

Women physicians pointed out the class hypocrisy present in their male colleagues' arguments. No one, a female physician commented sardonically, worked harder or in unhealthier conditions than the washerwoman; yet would-be saviors of American womanhood did not inveigh against this abuse—washing, after all, was appropriate work for women. Women doctors often did agree with the general male observation that their sisters were too frequently weak and unhealthy. They, however, blamed not education or social activism but the artificiality of dress and the slavery to fashion—aspects of the middle-class woman's life style that they found particularly demeaning. "The fact is that girls and women can bear study," Alice Stockham explained, "but they cannot bear compressed viscera, tortured stomachs and a displaced uterus," the results of fashionable clothing and an equally fashionable sedentary life. Another woman physician, Sarah Stevenson, wrote in a similar vein: " 'How do I look?' is the everlasting story from the beginning to the end of woman's life. Looks, not books, are the murderers of American woman."[38]

Other, more politically active New Women developed complementary arguments. A woman, they argued, did not have to bear children to fulfill her feminine nature. Women who sought to secure the health and happiness of working-class children through child-labor legislation, the public-health movement, visiting-nursing services, and educational reform, Jane Addams and other settlement-house women argued, had assumed the role of public mothers. Indeed, Addams, Wald, and other first-generation New Women reformers vigorously defended their "womanly" natures. Echoing M. Carey Thomas's earlier sentiments, they did not seek to act the male part. Rather, they battled economic and political injustice quite self-consciously as women reformers. Women, they argued, uncorrupted by the world of politics and trade, sexually pure, experienced in the loving care of others, were far better fitted than men to fight for social justice and to advance the well-being of womankind and mankind alike. Women teachers and reformers felt the same devotion for their "children" that biological mothers did. But whereas mothers nurtured only their own, these women cared for hundreds, even thousands, of America's neediest children. "The maternal feeling is as intense and pure in many unmarried women as in their married sisters," Mrs. Horace Mann had argued in 1870, defending women's right to advanced education. "Oppressive husbands, not education and 'single blessedness,' " she added, "stunt growth . . . spoil family life . . . pervert and maim the development of the human being." Indeed, she editorialized, "I believe it is a fact that the higher the state of civilization and refinement, the more unmarried women there are."[39]

And so, Jane Addams, Lillian Wald, and others defended the new ways in an old language. The New Women had not originated these arguments. Their "mothers," fictive and real, had done so, in the 1850s, 1860s, and 1870s, as they had feminized the Cult of True Womanhood. During those decades, bourgeois matrons had transposed the cult's original religious and moral imagery into a female symbolic system that expressed women's attitudes toward family change and justified new roles for women outside the family. Like earlier Female Moral Reformers, these Victorian matrons had contrasted woman's sexual purity and tenderness to man's power and oppressiveness. More pious and domestic than men, the efficient housekeepers of the nation, True Women, they argued, could not confine their efforts to their homes and families. They must extend their "home rule" to encompass the world—wherever children and other women needed their ministrations. With these words they had justified the most ambitious of their women's-club projects and the "Do Everything" policy of Frances Willard and the WCTU.

The New Women of Jane Addams's and M. Carey Thomas's generation had grown up in a world governed by these words and this traditional insistence on women's innate purity and nurturance. Effortlessly, they used these old arguments to justify public roles that, in their eyes, merely carried their "mothers' " ideas to a logical conclusion. The New Women's sense of solidarity with women across class boundaries, which they took with them into the settlement-house and social-justice movements, also drew upon traditional patterns of female intimacy, harmonizing with the emotional and physical love women had long expressed for one another. Ironically, then, the New Women called upon two traditional female languages to phrase their revolt against the confinements of bourgeois domesticity.

By themselves, however, the old languages were not enough. The

New Women first infused them with the Enlightenment's insistence on the individual's right to self-fulfillment—a belief most bourgeois Americans espoused in the nineteenth century. They then embellished these earlier arguments with the language of a new, optimistic, nondeterministic science which reflected the hopes and ambitions of America's new women of science. This uniquely female merger of languages differed radically from the medical model Victorian physicians and educators had developed. Women's language, men's language—each reflected the different traditions, experiences, and dreams of its speakers. In the 1870s and 1880s, linked to Progressive enthusiasm and to most Progressives' belief in the power of the individual to alter her, as well as his, world, within a bourgeois social structure where both the birthrate and the marriage rate were steadily declining, the New Women's language proved the most persuasive—to men as well as to women. The New Women won this first "scientific" debate with the men of the old bourgeoisie. Yet conflicts existed between the older female language and the New Scientific Discourse, conflicts which would prove troublesome later on.

With the 1890s male physicians and social critics initiated a new wave of attacks upon the respectability and legitimacy of the New Woman. The second debate commenced as male asylum directors, doctors, academics, psychiatrists, and psychologists (all members of new bourgeois professions and bureaucracies) shifted the definition of female deviance from the New Woman's rejection of motherhood to their rejection of men. From being "unnaturally" barren, the autonomous woman, outside of heterosexual marriage, emerged as "unnaturally" sexual. Adopting the novel "scientific" categories of the European sexologists, British and American physicians and scientists insisted that unmarried career women and political activists constituted an "intermediate sex." They violated normal gender categories. They fused the female and the male. They were "Mannish Lesbians," the embodiment of social disorder.

A second generation of New Women confronted these new attacks upon their right to enter the "male" world and assume "male" power. They did so, however, in a new and complex manner. Seizing the men's most central symbolic constructs they invested them with female intent and thus inverting, repudiated them. As already postulated, however, the act of adopting another's language can be tricky and costly, even if one does so with a self-conscious, ironic intent. As long as gender remained a major factor in the inequitable distribution of power—a major determiner of women's and men's life experiences—women's assumption of men's symbolic constructs involved women in a fundamental act of alienation. No matter how transposed, male sexual metaphors could not fully express women's social experiences and political needs. In adopting a male symbolic system, rather than further developing their own unique discourse, feminist writers of the 1920s and 1930s may have come close to relinquishing a critical source of self-identity and political strength—the power to create language. Can embattled social and political groups survive shorn of that power? Yet, if the marginal or powerless wish to challenge the dominant discourse, must they not frame their challenge in the language of the dominant mode? The debate over women's sexual and social autonomy that raged throughout the first third of the twentieth century raises many of these questions. It also illustrates the dual nature of language as an empowering and restraining social and psychological agency.

While male homosexuality was a well-recognized behavior throughout Western history, condemned in canon and civil law (indeed, a capital offense in English common law), few discussions of lesbianism predate the late nineteenth century.[40] In fact, a category for genteel lesbian deviance originated only in the 1880s and 1890s. As we have already seen, however, British and American physicians did describe behavior we would now define as lesbian: young women, often schoolgirls or college women, in bed together enjoying genital stimulation accompanied by avowals of passionate emotional attachment.[41] At times one of the women might assume the role of *"liebe Knabe"* or "beloved boy," as M. Carey Thomas described the role she assumed while involved with another young woman at the highly respectable Howland Academy.[42] Though physicians carefully labeled comparable behavior when engaged in by boys and college men as homosexual and perverted, they categorized the women as masturbators.[43] British and American physicians, in fact, insisted that female homosexuality was a rare and exotic phenomenon. French literature, especially mid–nineteenth-century novels (as well as pornography), did discuss female homosexuality in terms far closer to those we use today.[44] But few bourgeois American women would have read such novels. For these women and the men who surrounded them, passion between women was neither disturbing nor deviant.[45]

Beginning at mid–century, medical and scientific discussions of male homosexuality began to increase in number, first in Germany and Austria and then, gradually, in France and Italy. Ultimately British and American medical journals began to reflect this interest. In 1852, a German physician, Johann Ludwig Caspar, argued that male homosexuality resulted from a physical, not a moral, aberration.[46] Later, a Hanoverian lawyer, C. H. Ulrichs, himself a homosexual, undertook a crusade to defend homosexuals against charges of moral degeneracy. Homosexuality, he argued, was not an example of willful moral depravity but a congenital degenerative defect. A woman's soul was trapped in a man's body; the homosexual man deserved sympathy and toleration, not persecution and punishment.[47] By the early 1880s, French physicians, especially neurologists such as Charcot, had accepted the German definition of male homosexuality as a form of hereditary degeneration, rather than a specific isolated sexual (and moral) act. Italian physicians, led by Cesare Lombroso, adopted a similar interpretation.[48]

The study of male homosexuality thus emerged as one of the concerns of that new medico-scientific field of investigation peculiar to the late nineteenth century—sexology. It is important to place the discussion of homosexuality within its historical perspective, that is, to see it as one facet of the overall sexual and scientific discourse of the late nineteenth century. This was the golden age of scientific determinism, of social Darwinism and eugenics. Taxonomy assumed unquestioned scientific centrality as Victorian men traced the precise evolution of their social as well as their natural world. Grammar and political institutions, man, birds, and fish all were categorized, their stages of development carefully distinguished—all placed within a grand evolutionary schema of progressive development or of degenerative decay. The sexologists' fascination with human sexual variations exemplifies this pattern. Now specific sexual acts, fantasies, fetishes, sensations, became the subject of taxonomical scrutiny. Genus and species were assigned. Degrees of abnormality and perversion were carefully charted in much the same spirit as that with which the evolution of the horse and of the dative case were traced. And, I would argue, with the same goal: the reassertion of order in a conflicting and changing world. Within the sexologists' categorical elaboration, the male Victorian imagination had again fused the social and the sexual. The sexologists had transposed the amorphous qualities of the socially disorderly into specific forms of sexual deviance. They then categorized and cross-referenced these forms, carefully defining their progressive states of sexual disorderliness. Thus they fictively contained and controlled social disorder, hedging it in with a sexualized language. The abortion campaign, the medical condemnation of women's education, and finally homosexuality all constituted variations on the nineteenth-century man's mythic discourse.

Michel Foucault argues that the Victorians' sexual discourse constituted a new technology of power. The bourgeois order extended its control over the individual and the family, he argued, through ever more elaborate definitions of sexual deviance.[49] Few would reject Foucault's conclusions. Yet Foucault focuses too narrowly on social control and thus unduly simplifies the process by which language is sexualized and the body politicized. Before the body can exist as an agency of social control, it must exist as an expressive medium. Both through literal body language and through physical metaphor and image, the body provides a symbolic system through which individuals can discuss social realities too complex or conflicted to be spoken overtly. Social, not sexual, disorder lies at the heart of this discourse. The control of literal sexual behavior at all times constitutes a secondary goal. Male sexologists were obsessed not with sex but with imposing order through the elaboration of categories of the normal and the perverted. Perverted behavior did not have to cease. Quite the contrary. A proxy, it existed to be railed against and thus to give the sexologists a sense of power over chaos and reaffirm their faith in their ability to restore order. The pre-eminent function of sexualized discourse, at all times and in all places, is therefore emotive. But it is frequently political as well. As Foucault argues, and as we have already seen in the AMA's anti-abortion rhetoric, when a group establishes its political and economic hegemony, it is able to invest its words with power. It is at this point that the body will be politicized. Then the sexuality of those who threaten order and are marginal to power will be regulated and controlled.

The leading spokesman for sexology in nineteenth-century Europe was the Viennese neurologist Krafft-Ebing. Krafft-Ebing defined sexology as the study of "abnormal" and "perverse" sexual practices, which did not involve a primary interest in reproductive intercourse, and ranged from fetishes and phobias through sado-masochism to bestiality. Prominently among these perversions, Krafft-Ebing listed homosexuality, which, he insisted, was an organic disease, not a moral failing.[50] By affirming the biological base of homosexuality, Krafft-Ebing at the same time legitimized the sexologists' claim to be new men of science. Yet sexology as a biological science continued to stand at the intersection of the physical, the psychological, and the moral. The physiological roots of homosexuality in particular, and of sexual perversions in general (like those of hysteria) remained obscure. For millennia sexual perversions had been the purview of clerics, not physicians. High among the seven deadly sins, unnatural sexuality was central to the Catholic confessional. Sexologists struggled to reverse this vision of sexual perversion as moral license. Arguing for an organic model, they insisted that sexual perversity, especially homosexuality, was a physiological abnormality. It could develop in childhood or puberty as the result of a specific disease-related trauma, but more commonly it constituted a vicious form of congenital degeneracy, a hereditary taint. As such it formed the dark side of evolution, progress reversed, on the way to destruction.[51] Krafft-Ebing's monumental *Psychopathia Sexualis* consisted of elaborate case studies that traced the genetic origins of homosexuality back through generations of hysterical aunts, neurasthenic uncles, insane grandfathers, drunken fathers, and feeble-minded cousins.[52] Homosexuality could constitute as well a specific atavistic response, a sudden throwback to a primitive bisexuality, a tragic freak of nature. As one of Krafft-Ebing's American disciples explained in 1884:

> The original bi-sexuality of the ancestors of the race, shown in the rudimentary female organs of the male, could not fail to occasion functional, if not organic, reversions when mental or physical manifestations were interfered with by disease or congenital defect.[53]

A few years later, Havelock Ellis, the most influential purveyor of sexology in Britain and the United States, expressed the theory of congenital, degenerative homosexuality in its most popular form. He wrote in the *Medico-Legal Journal* of 1895–96:

> Putting the matter in a purely speculative shape, we might say that at conception the organism is provided with fifty percent of male germs, fifty percent of female germs, and that as development proceeds, either the male or female germs get the upper hand, killing out those of the other sex until only a few abortive

germs of the opposite sex are left. In some persons, however, we may imagine that the process has not proceeded normally on account of some peculiarity in the number or character of either the original male germs or female germs or both, the result being that the individual becomes organically twisted into a shape that is fitted for the exercise of the inverted sexual impulse. The same seed of "suggestion" is sown in various soils. In many it dies out, in a few it flourishes; the cause can only lie in a difference in the soil.[54]

Early medical students of the perverse had focused almost exclusively upon male homosexuality. By 1884, twenty-seven clinical cases of homosexuality had been reported in the medical literature of Europe and the United States; only four involved women, and all four were transvestites.[55] By the mid-1880s, however, Krafft-Ebing had begun to alter this discourse by pointedly including lesbianism in his discussion of sexual perversions. True to the sexologists' taxonomical impulses, he divided lesbianism into four categories or degrees of homosexual deviance. Each category fused sexual, physiological, and social characteristics. In his first category he included women who "did not betray their anomaly by external appearance or by mental (masculine) sexual characteristics." They were, however, responsive to the approaches of more masculine-appearing and -behaving women. However, Krafft-Ebing reported, some of this first category of lesbians, when physically examined, did display a masculine formation of the larynx. The second classification of lesbians, which Krafft-Ebing called "virginity," included women with a "strong preference for male garments." These women were the female analogy of effeminate men. By the third stage, "inversion is fully developed, the woman so acting assumes a definitely masculine role." The fourth stage, or "gynandry," represented "the extreme grade of degenerative homosexuality." Krafft-Ebing explained in 1889:

> The woman of this type possesses of the feminine qualities only the genital organs; thought, sentiment, action, even external appearance are those of a man. Often enough does one come across in life such characters whose frame, pelvis, gait, appearance, coarse masculine features, rough, deep voice, etc., betrayed rather the man than the woman.[56]

Krafft-Ebing did not focus on the sexual behavior of the women he categorized as lesbian but, rather, on their social behavior and physical appearance. In every case study, Krafft-Ebing linked lesbianism to the rejection of conventional female roles, to cross-dressing, and to "masculine" physiological traits. The following statement exemplifies his approach:

> Uranism may nearly always be suspected in females wearing their hair short, or who dress in the fashion of men, or pursue the sports and pastimes of their male acquaintances; also in opera singers and actresses who appear in male attire on the stage by preference. . . . The female urning may chiefly be found in the haunt of boys. She is the rival of their play, preferring the rocking-horse, playing at soldiers, etc., to dolls and other girlish occupations. The toilet is neglected, and rough boyish manners affected. Love for art finds a substitute in the pursuits of the sciences. . . . Perfumes and sweetmeats are disdained. The consciousness of being a woman and thus to be deprived of the gay college life, or to be barred from the military career, produces painful reflections. The masculine soul, heaving in the female bosom, finds pleasure in the pursuit of manly sports, and in manifestations of courage and bravado.[57]

The first symptom of *sexual* perversion, Krafft-Ebing argued, usually involved the rejection of conventional feminine behavior in childhood. As Krafft-Ebing reported in another of his numerous and elaborate case studies:

> Even in her earliest childhood she preferred playing at soldiers and other boys' games; she was bold and tom-boyish and tried even to excel her little companions of the other sex. She never had a liking for dolls, needlework or domestic duties. Puberty at fifteen. . . . Her dreams were of a lascivious character . . . with herself in the *rôle* of man.[58]

Krafft-Ebing's lesbians seemed to desire male privileges and power as ardently as, perhaps more ardently than, they sexually desired women. For Krafft-Ebing, social perversion preceded and signaled the onset of sexual perversion. In case study after case study, he focused on social not sexual desires. See, for example, his description of another gynandrous woman:

> At sixteen she thought she possessed the qualities of a man. She bewailed the fact that she was not born a man, as she hated feminine things and dress generally. Would much rather have been a soldier. Sweetmeats she disdained, preferring a cigar. She became convinced that she could not marry a woman and upon promise to conquer her perverse sexual inclinations she was dismissed.[59]

Krafft-Ebing made gender inversion physiologically manifest. The women who "aped" men's roles looked like men. But even more, having rooted social gender in biological sexuality, Krafft-Ebing then made dress analogous to gender. Only the abnormal woman would challenge conventional gender distinctions—and by her dress you would know her. "She was quite conscious of her pathological condition," Krafft-Ebing reported of a third woman. "Masculine features, deep voice, manly gait, without beard, small breasts; cropped her hair short and gave the impression of a man in women's clothes."[60] In this way Krafft-Ebing, through the creation of a new medico-sexual category, the Mannish Lesbian, linked women's rejection of traditional gender roles and their demands for social and economic equality to cross-dressing, sexual perversion, and borderline hermaphroditism. A new metaphoric system was born, in which physical disease again bespoke social disorder.

Early medical discussions of lesbianism in the United States reflected Krafft-Ebing's focus on transvestism and the assumption of male behavior. The first American article on lesbianism, written by an assistant physician in the Willard, New York, Asylum for the Insane, appeared in 1883. Lucy Ann Slater, or, as she called herself, the Reverend Joseph Lobdell, had been institutionalized in 1880, subject to manic-depressive outbreaks. Slater (or Lobdell) had dressed in men's clothing and claimed to be a Methodist minister. Earlier in her life Slater had gained fame as "The Female Hunter of Long Eddy." Having grown up in a mountainous area of New York State, she had chosen, after a short and unhappy marriage, to support herself by hunting; she wore men's clothing and lived in the wild. At one point, ill and destitute, she had entered an almshouse, where she met an attractive, educated young woman who had been abandoned by her husband. The two women left the almshouse together and established a home in the wilderness. Lucy Ann Slater adopted a male persona and supported "his wife" by hunting. The wife called Lucy Ann Slater her husband. The physician reporting the case identified their life together as "lesbian love." They came into contact with the state on only two occasions. Once Slater returned to her home town and was recognized as a woman dressed in male clothing; she was arrested as a vagrant. Slater's wife wrote a petition to the court for the release of her husband. The physician described the petition. "The pen used by the writer was a stick whittled to a point and split; the ink was pokeberry juice. The chirography is faultless and the language used is a model of clear, correct English." The second time was when Slater became manic-depressive.[61] During the next decade the medical journals reported a steady number of lesbian cases, all of which shared two fundamental characteristics: the women were both transvestites and poor. They had been detected when incarcerated in almshouses, insane asylums, or prisons. Through the 1880s, the medical profession agreed: homosexuality, a rarity among American women, existed exclusively among the poor and the marginal. It was either practiced by prostitutes at the request of male patrons or was linked to extreme transvestism.[62]

In 1892 a *cause célèbre* catapulted the discussion of lesbianism, until now quite a minor theme in the medical and asylum journals, into polite and influential circles. A young woman, Alice Mitchell, daughter of a wealthy Memphis family, fell in love with Freda Ward, the daughter of another well-to-do family. Alice planned to assume a male persona; the two women would then be married by a Memphis minister and leave for New Orleans, where Alice hoped to support Freda, wearing men's clothing and securing a job. Freda's family detected the plot and convinced Freda to break off her relationship with Alice. Alice, after months of severe depression, slit Freda's throat. The violent ending of a plan by two women to flee family and friends and live as husband and wife in New Orleans electrified the country and drew popular attention to the existing body of literature on lesbian transvestism.[63]

Thus far, however, nothing in these male medical discussions of lesbianism referred directly to the lives and loves of such bourgeois and educated women as Sarah Orne Jewett, Jane Addams, Vida Scudder, or M. Carey Thomas. These women praised the feminine qualities of the women they loved; they certainly did not practice cross-dressing. None of them reported feeling that a male soul inhabited her female body. While, as we have seen, M. Carey Thomas played with a male persona while "smashed" in high school, by the end of college she emphatically affirmed a primary female identity. She did so even though being a man would have brought all her ambitions within her grasp. Discussing a young male friend, she wrote in her diary in September 1877, "I hope he will persevere and go to Germany and I wish I were a man for that; because *Germany* is shut to ladies along with the J.H.U. [Johns Hopkins University] and a few other of the most glorious things in the world. . . ." Then she added immediately, "Yet I would not be a man."[64] Mary Woolley always discussed her love for Jeannette Marks in the most traditional of romantic terms. The ladylike and religious Woolley loved the feminine in Marks. "A sweeter woman never did draw breath," she wrote Marks, "nor a truer, sincerer, nobler woman! You and your mother are enshrined in my heart as the dearest women God ever made." When Marks spent a summer away from Woolley, Woolley unself-conciously wrote that nightly, following her prayers, she caressed the bed on which they had slept together, pretending it was Marks's body. She placed this passion within a marital context, considering Marks and herself married. Indeed, Woolley experienced the church service marking Jeannette's conversion to the Episcopal Church (from the Quakerism of her parents) as a marriage sacrament during which they gave their hearts to God and to each other.[65] The first generation of New Women, just as their mothers and grandmothers had, merged gentility and eroticism.

Nothing could have been further from the New Woman's genteel self-image than the figure of the female hunter of Long Eddy, hefting her rifle and passing as a man. Krafft-Ebing's fusion of a woman's love for other women with a masculine physiognomy, and with feminist demands for education and new roles, remained an alien concept for this first generation of New Women. Their conceptual systems, their definitions of the natural and the abnormal, still reflected the beliefs and language of their mothers' and fathers' generation. At the height of Progressive romanticism, it seemed to them equally laudable to re-form the world, to re-form gender, and to love women. Even the rejection of heterosexual marriage did not transform these genteel Edwardian women into "unnatural inverts"—in their own eyes or in those of the men of their generation.

Their innocence would not continue much longer. The male sexologist who most directly broke into this female world of love and intimacy, defining it as both actively sexual and as sexually perverted, was Havelock Ellis. Ellis is a complex figure. An innovative—indeed, iconoclastic—student of human sexuality, he insisted that conventional medical and moral approaches failed to recognize the complexity of human sexuality as a physiological, psychological, and sociological phenomenon. An early influence on Freud's theories of sexuality, Ellis reinforced psychoanalysis's radical new vision with anthropological discoveries of the varied and changeable nature of sexuality.[66] His refutation of Krafft-Ebing's and Lombroso's crude biological determinism classifies him as a liberal defender of sexual nonconformity.[67] An enemy of Victorian repression and hypocrisy, he holds a place of honor in our pantheon of sexual liberators. Ellis's interests were far from academic. He defended homosexuals from political and legal attack, and insisted that homosexuals had made important contributions to their society. They were not moral degenerates; they should not be treated as atavistic outcasts. He supported political feminists as well, befriending Margaret Sanger when she fled to England to avoid prosecution for violating the Comstock Law and championing Marie Stopes's birth-control campaign and Ellen Key's demands for marriage reform.[68]

It is ironic, then, that Ellis, not the more deterministic sexologists, provided the theoretical underpinning for conservative attacks upon the New Women as sexually perverted and socially dangerous. Ellis rejected Krafft-Ebing's insistence that a male soul resided in a lesbian's body as physiological nonsense.[69] He thus divorced the definition of sexual inversion from cross-dressing and suspicions of transsexuality. More clearly than any writer before Freud, Ellis insisted that a woman's love for other women was in itself sexual and "inverted." Many active lesbians, Ellis insisted, were genteel, educated, feminine in appearance, thought, and behavior. (He hastened to add, however, that they were usually less attractive than the women who were drawn to men.[70]) Nor did the female sexual invert have to engage in overt genital arousal. Women could experience their love for other women as the most innocent and tender of platonic involvements. The lesbian, Ellis explained, frequently did not understand the nature of her sexual impulses. "She likes to kiss and embrace the women she is attracted to," Ellis wrote in 1895. He went on to define as inverted just the type of schoolgirl and college crush M. Carey Thomas had detailed in her diary some twenty years earlier, and which many New Women had openly discussed.

> A school girl or young woman forms an ardent attachment for another girl, probably somewhat older than herself, often a school fellow, sometimes her school mistress, upon whom she will lavish an astonishing amount of affection and devotion. . . . The girl who expends this wealth of devotion is surcharged with emotion but she is often unconscious or ignorant of the sexual impulse and she seeks for no form of sexual satisfaction. Kissing and the privilege of sleeping with the friend are, however, sought, and at such times it often happens that even the comparatively unresponsive friend feels more or less definite sexual emotion (pudendal turgescence with secretion of mucus and involuntary twitching of neighboring muscles), though little or no attention may be paid to this phenomenon; and in the common ignorance of girls in sex matters it may not be understood. In some cases there is an attempt, either intuitional or instinctive, to develop the sexual feeling by close embraces and kissing. This rudimentary kind of homosexual relationship is, I believe, more common among girls than among boys. These passionate friendships, of a more or less unconsciously sexual character, are certainly common.[71]

"Inversion," Ellis continued, was biological, hereditary, and irreversible. The "invert" was powerless to change her inclination. Had lesbianism been limited to the "congenital invert," women born to the "intermediate sex," Ellis advised, society would have no grounds for alarm. Genetic anomalies, these women constituted a small percentage of the population. Although chromosomally aberrant, they should be tolerated and allowed to live out their sexual impulses. But, Ellis cautioned, the situation was not that simple. The existence of a second group of abnormal women—a group Ellis called homosexuals—transformed the "congenital invert" into a socially threatening figure. Many women, Ellis argued, though not genetically inverted, possessed a genetic predisposition—a weakness—for the advances of other women. For such women homosexuality was an acquired characteristic—preventable and curable. Placed in an unwholesome environment—a woman's boarding school or college, a settlement house, a women's club, or a political organization—the homosexual woman could succumb to the blandishments of the "congenital invert" who sought her as a partner. Kept within a heterosexual world, she would overcome her predisposition and grow up to be a "normal" woman.[72]

How can we explain Ellis's espousal of a theory so fraught with conservative social and political implications? When Ellis had defined male homosexuality (or, to use his term, "inversion") as a congenital anomaly, a genetic "sport," he had acted to defend a group already condemned as morally polluted and physiologically degenerate. Male homosexuality had been a capital offense in England; Ellis wrote during Oscar Wilde's trial. Ellis elaborated upon the contribution male homosexuals had made to human history, listing the great male homosexuals of times past. Homosexual men were not effeminate, Ellis insisted, but as brave and honorable as any other group of men.[73] Homosexual men hailed Ellis as their advocate.[74] But the medical discourse and political realities surrounding female homosexuality, as we have seen, differed dramatically from those surrounding male homosexuality. Before Havelock Ellis no one had questioned the "naturalness" of the New Women's genteel passions. Ellis did not write to defend the New Women from criminal prosecution and allegations of moral and physical degeneracy. He initiated those allegations. Even more significantly, Ellis phrased them as an attack upon political feminism. Why? The answer may lie in Ellis's commitment to a biological explanation for human behavior and in the ambivalent attitude toward the New Women which followed from that commitment.

Ellis, while politically liberal and psychologically sensitive, remained a *man* of his time. He could not abandon the nineteenth century's organic model for human behavior. Ellis, Jeffrey Weeks reminds us, had been born the year Darwin published *The Origin of Species*. "He was born, that is," Weeks continues, "of a generation which, as George Bernard Shaw put it, 'began by hoping more from science than perhaps any generation ever hoped before.' "[75] Ellis could not conceptualize sex except as part of a biological model. He insisted, as we have already seen, that sexual inversion was rooted in chromosomal and genetic irregularities. The invert was not a normal woman or man.[76]

Ellis's biologically deterministic vision extended beyond simple sexual behavior to embrace gender relations and especially women's role in the perfection of the race. Ellis was above all a eugenicist. The stereotypic definitions of masculinity and femininity (the complementarity of the genders), he argued, were rooted in genetic difference. Women, the mothers of the race, were by nature modest, sexually passive and responsive, sensitive, and emotional, because these emotions were essential to good mothering and thus to the perpetuation of the race. And so, while repudiating Krafft-Ebing's physiological metaphor of a male soul trapped in a female body, Havelock Ellis continued to insist on the complementarity of gender and the ancient polarity of woman/body–man/mind. From this perspective, Ellis's rather startling assertion that women's brains are "to a certain extent in their wombs" makes sense if read metaphorically.[77] Ellis had simply restated, with poetic succinctness, the Victorian medical thesis that in woman's physiological hierarchy, her womb transcended her brain.

Ellis's biological vision led him also to repudiate Freud's theories concerning the original polymorphous nature of human sexuality. Freud had gone too far in abandoning a biological model for heterosexuality. By insisting on humans' initial bisexuality, Ellis argued, Freud had separated the sexual drive from the drive to perpetuate the human race—that is, from reproductive sexuality. Ellis, the child of Darwin, could not accept such a radical separation.[78]

Ellis's commitment to a male/mind–female/body polarity informed his response to feminism in general and to the determinedly unmarried New Women in particular. In the 1880s, Ellis had applauded feminist denunciations of Victorian injustices toward women. As feminists began to demand absolute equality, and as New Women followed careers and rejected marriage, Ellis re-evaluated his own feminist convictions. Women's responsibilities to the race made them primarily child-bearers and -rearers and only secondarily public figures. The feminists, Ellis concluded, had gone too far. The New Women—unmarried, career-oriented, politically active, often lovingly involved with one another—emerged within Ellis's model as "unnatural" and selfish women. Their "unnaturalness" extended beyond the social to envelop the sexual realm as well. Having tied female sexuality to reproduction and to a gentle and loving personality, Ellis logically concluded that women were by nature sexually passive, waiting for the sexually active male to claim them. The female invert, therefore, had to act like a man sexually. She denied the boundaries that separated the genders and "unnaturally" inverted traditional femininity, both sexually and socially.[79]

By dichotomizing lesbians into "true inverts" and potential hetero-sexuals, Ellis depicted the female invert not as a genetic anomaly and a helpless victim but as a woman on the make, sexually and racially danger-ous. Seeking a more feminine partner, she sexually rivaled men. Education, feminist ideology, the new women's colleges and settlement houses, all freed the "female invert" from the restraints of family, permitting her to reach out to young girls, drawing them into lesbianism. Ellis insisted that the numbers of lesbians had steadily increased since the expansion of women's roles and institutions. The connections Ellis drew between what he believed was a rising incidence of middle-class lesbianism and feminist political and educational advances reveal a man troubled by changes he could not in principle oppose. Feminism, lesbianism, equality for women, all emerge in Ellis's writings as problematic phenomena. All were unnatu-ral, related in disturbing and unclear ways to increased female criminality, insanity, and "hereditary neurosis." Ellis continued:

> The modern movement of emancipation—the movement to obtain the same rights and duties, the same freedom and respon-sibility, the same education and the same work, must be re-garded as on the whole a wholesome and inevitable movement. But it carries with it certain disadvantages. It has involved an increase in feminine criminality and in feminine insanity, which are being elevated towards the masculine standard. In connec-tion with these, we can scarcely be surprised to find an increase in homosexuality which has always been regarded as belonging to an allied, if not the same, group of phenomena. Having been taught independence of men and disdain for the old theory which placed women in the moated grange of the home to sigh for a man who never comes, a tendency develops for women to carry this independence still further and to find love where they find work. I do not say that these unquestionable influences of modern movements can directly cause sexual inversion, though they may indirectly, in so far as they promote hereditary neurosis; but they develop the germs of it, and they probably cause a spurious imitation. This spurious imitation is due to the fact that the congenital anomaly occurs with special frequency in women of high intelligence who, voluntarily or involun-tarily, influence others.[80]

Ellis went on to describe as classically inverted a female personality that was suspiciously "masculine" and decidedly like that many of the new college women aspired to. "The brusque energetic movements, the attitude of the arms, the direct speech, the inflexions of the voice, the masculine straight-forwardness and sense of honor," he told a medical audience, "and especially the attitude towards men, free from any suggestion either of shyness or audacity, will often suggest the underlying psychic abnormality to a keen observer."[81]

And so Havelock Ellis transformed the New Woman into a sexual anomaly and a political pariah. Citing Ellis as an unimpeachable scientific expert, American physicians and educators launched a political campaign against the New Woman, the institutions that nurtured her, and her feminist and reform programs. "Female boarding schools and colleges are the great breeding grounds of artificial [acquired] homosexuality," R. N. Shufeldt wrote in the *Pacific Medical Journal* in 1902.[82] William Lee Howard, in the respectable *New York Medical Journal* of 1900, commented acidly:

> The female possessed of masculine ideas of independence, the virago who would sit in the public highways and lift up her pseudo-virile voice, proclaiming her sole right to decide questions of war or religion, or the value of celibacy and the curse of woman's impurity, and that disgusting antisocial being, the female sexual pervert, are simply different degrees of the same class—degenerates.[83]

As Progressive women reformers increased their political power in the years immediately preceding the First World War, and as the suffrage movement reached its crescendo, articles complaining of lesbianism in women's colleges, clubs, prisons, and reformatories—wherever women gathered—became common. While feminist leaders were not directly attacked as lesbians, the political climate began to change in significant if subtle ways. College administrators, for example, wary of changing professional and public attitudes, adopted restrictive dormitory policies. Warning young women of the dangers inherent in intense female friendships, they prohibited women from spending the night in one another's rooms.[84] Physicians as well as educators had begun to counsel women they now defined as "latent homosexuals." Forcefully drawing the young women's attention to their dangerous predisposition for "inversion," doctors pressed them to marry quickly and have children. One St. Louis physician described a case he felt ended successfully.

> Direct accusation, in a confidential and kindly way, was the next step. . . . A free confession . . . followed. . . . She was really an honest, well-disposed person, and, convinced of only kind intentions, and shown the evil of perversion and the way to better her health, cooperation was at once gained. . . . She married soon afterward and now has an apparently healthy child. . . .[85]

By the 1920s, charges of lesbianism had become a common way to discredit women professionals, reformers, and educators—and the feminist political, reform, and education institutions they had founded. Plays appeared depicting the dangers of lesbianism in women's schools and colleges. (M. Carey Thomas attended one such play in the 1920s, her niece and Barnard College President Millicent McIntosh reported. Keenly aware of the effect such a dramatic presentation could have, Thomas "was grieved that this sort of thing . . . would make it difficult for women to develop the warm and close relationships some of them needed so very much."[86])

Medical arguments and sensationalist literature began to exert an influence upon young women. The percentage of women college graduates who married increased significantly in the 1910s and 1920s. The percentage who attended graduate and professional schools and who pursued careers dropped proportionately. Between 1889 and 1908, 55 percent of Bryn Mawr women had not married; 62 percent entered graduate school. Of those women who married, 54 percent continued in a career and remained economically autonomous. (In fact, during these years only 10 percent of Bryn Mawr graduates did not work.) Between 1910 and 1918, as warnings against lesbianism proliferated, these figures reversed: 65 percent of Bryn Mawr women now married, only 49 percent went on for further training. Wellesley and other women's colleges mirrored the Bryn Mawr trend. The retreat from professional prominence and economic autonomy had begun —foreshadowing a decline in women's political power. Many factors contributed to this trend; but the campaign against "masculine straightforwardness" and independence played its part.[87]

The repression of women's loving relations and of female economic autonomy, Rayna Rapp and Ellen Ross have argued, also played a central role in conservative economic and political movements of the 1920s. Business leaders feared that in the years following the First World War, America's industrial capacity would exceed Americans' consumption patterns. The educated, career-oriented woman, they also feared, would be too busy to consume with the enthusiasm America's industrial capacity required. Big business, Rapp and Ross argue, carefully orchestrated a campaign to return women to the home and transform the redomesticated woman into the bulwark of America's new consumer economy.[88]

Male companionate-marriage sex reformers and psychoanalysts provided the ideological underpinning and scientific legitimization for this campaign. In doing so, the male sex reformers portrayed the lesbian in one of two ways. She could surface within their literature as a "Mannish Lesbian," a sexually atavistic and ungovernable woman, associated with the 1920s bar culture and with European decadence. In this guise, she appeared as the aggressive seducer of other women, the ruthless, perverted competitor of the male suitor. She became man's enemy—fearful because she was sexually powerful, yet ultimately defeated and impotent. She stalked the pages not only of popular sexual treatises, novels, and short stories, but of the 1920s avant-garde literature as well. James Joyce and D. H. Lawrence created a number of such characters, whom Lawrence especially then proceeded self-righteously to humiliate and destroy.[89]

The autonomous woman assumed a second, alternative, persona in the male literature of the 1920s—that of the aging Lady in Lavender. As a schoolteacher, settlement-house worker, or college professor, she was the mentor, not the suitor, of the young woman. Having "unnaturally" denied her own sexual impulses, she sought emotional release through man-hating and bellicose and outdated feminist rhetoric. She preyed upon the innocence of young girls, teaching them to fear men and their own sexual impulses.[90] This vision of the New Woman constitutes a final, ironic inversion of the sexologists' original attack. From being the dangerous, sexual competitor of the New Man, the New Woman had become a repressed, at times ludicrous, figure. As such she no longer threatened the New Man. Rather, he had made her the enemy of the "liberated" woman of the 1920s—the flapper.

The New Man could portray the New Woman as the enemy of liberated women because he had redefined the issue of female autonomy in sexual terms. He divorced women's rights from their political and economic context. The daughter's quest for heterosexual pleasures, not the mother's demand for political power, now personified female freedom. Linking orgasms to chic fashion and planned motherhood, male sex reformers, psychologists, and physicians promised a future of emotional support and sexual delights to women who accepted heterosexual marriage —and male economic hegemony. Only the "unnatural" woman continued to struggle with men for economic independence and political power.[91]

Christina Simmons has sensitively unraveled the mixed message the New Men sought to disseminate. Companionate-marriage advocate J. W. Meagher, writing in 1929, Simmons points out, echoed the sentiments implicit in Havelock Ellis's linking of feminism, women's education, and lesbianism. His tone came closer, however, to the harsher statements of conservative popularizers of sexology, physicians such as R. N. Shufeldt and William Lee Howard. "The driving force in many agitators and militant women who are always after their rights," Meagher informed his fellow marriage reformers, "is often an unsatisfied sex impulse, with a homosexual aim. Married women with a completely satisfied libido rarely take an active interest in militant movements." Even heterosexual experiments of the most moderate type (the wife requesting the superior position during intercourse) smacked of latent homosexuality, Meagher continued. "A homosexual woman often wants to possess the male and not to be possessed by him. . . . With them orgasm is often only possible in the superior position."[92]

How did women respond to this new male discourse? The first generation of New Women, who had so effectively repudiated the attacks of the Victorian physicians, remained strangely silent. They seemed unable to respond to Krafft-Ebing's and Havelock Ellis's redefinition of their loving relations as sexually perverted and of their desire for political equality as "unnatural gender ape-ing." Nor did they attempt to counter the alternative image of themselves as repressed old maids. One possible explanation for such politically costly silence may be rooted in sexual rather than political considerations. Sexual issues had caused a serious rift within the ranks of the New Women, eroding their social cohesion and political effectiveness. As the rising percentage of women college graduates who married indicates, male sexual promises had found a responsive audience. Unlike the first generation, the New Women who came to maturity in the first three decades of the twentieth century thought of sexual autonomy not as freedom from marital oppression but, in positive terms, as the right to sexual experimentation and self-expression. Bohemian Greenwich Village attracted radical New Women who, a generation earlier, would have flocked to women's settlement houses. Margaret Sanger's sex-education lectures attracted scores of these young women. So did the Heterodoxy Club, which Mabel Dodge Luhan tells us was "for unorthodox women, women who did things and did them openly."[93] Edna St. Vincent Millay's famous "First Fig" epitomized their flamboyant rejection of sexual conventions earlier New Women had simply not questioned.

> My candle burns at both ends;
> It will not last the night;
> But ah, my foes, and oh, my friends—
> It gives a lovely light![94]

New Women of the second and third generations needed to discuss their sexual identity in a new sexual language. The New Women of the first generation did not. In their fifties and sixties by the 1920s, the first generation with few exceptions would not or could not alter their Victorian romantic vocabulary. Sexual liberation emphatically was not *their* political issue. Strains developed between the successive generations of autonomous women. Jane Addams's and Lillian Wald's political alienation from Crystal Eastman—a cofounder of the Women's International League for Peace and Freedom and a co-worker in social-justice causes—because of what they considered Eastman's sexual flamboyance illustrates the split's serious political consequences.[95] Addams and Wald, Eastman and Millay spoke increasingly hostile languages. To the later generations of New Women the new sexual vocabulary offered by Havelock Ellis and other liberal male sex reformers appeared as congenial—at times more congenial than the rallying cries of the older political feminists. This was true even for some women who came of age in the late nineteenth century. Mary Austin, folklorist and feminist writer for *The Nation*, referred to these problems in 1927.

> That sexual desire was something to which God in his inscrutable wisdom had sacrificed all women, was so certainly believed

by my mother's generation that it was never even successfully camouflaged by preachers and teachers with blague about the sanctity of motherhood. But my own generation still lacked even a vocabulary by which measures of escape could be intelligently discussed. As for the convenient and illuminating terminology of "sex psychology" with which modern youth mitigates its own confusion, everyone knows that it was still some twenty years ahead.

(As Elaine Showalter points out, Austin's words masked Austin's own experience with a venereal-diseased husband and the birth of a child who was consequently severely retarded.)[96] It was just that "illuminating terminology of 'sex psychology' " that British feminist Frances Wilder wrote British sexologist and homosexual Edward Carpenter to thank Carpenter for providing. As she explained to Carpenter, women in the 1920s needed an overtly sexual conceptual system into which to place their desires—even though this conceptual system carried with it a very costly political price tag.

Wilder wrote Carpenter that she had loved other women (yearned to "caress" and "fondle" them) since adolescence, yet she had not defined her feelings as sexual or acted upon them. After reading Carpenter's discussion of "sexual inversion" she "realize[d] that I was more closely related to the intermediate sex than I had hitherto imagined. . . ." Now, she reported, she could admit her sexual feelings and reach beyond a loneliness rooted in sexual repression. To accept a medical definition of sexual abnormality, however, did not mean that Wilder, as a feminist, had accepted a definition of political or social deviance. Wilder ended her letter with a bitter attack upon the enslavement of women in heterosexual marriage.[97]

To explain the New Woman's adoption of the new male vocabulary by focusing primarily on her sexual needs or on her presumed internalization of deviance oversimplifies an extremely complex phenomenon. If nothing else, the intellectual sophistication of so many of the women involved—Virginia Woolf, Djuna Barnes, Natalie Barney, Gertrude Stein, for example—precludes such an approach. Once more we must explore sexual vocabulary as a multifocal language that speaks simultaneously of sexual experiences, social realities, and political desires. The symbolically laden phrases that the New Women and the New Men chose during these years—"the intermediate sex," "sexual inversion," "a male soul trapped in a female body," "the Mannish Lesbian"—do not describe literal sexual acts. They are spatial and hierarchical images, concerned with issues of order, structure, and difference. The term "intermediate sex" does not conjure up images of sexual passion or of physical desire. It refers, rather, to space, to the state of being between categories—that is, outside of order. "Inversion" inverts. It turns "normal," predictable order and hierarchies upside down. Linked by the sexologists to transvestism, it invokes earlier metaphors, "The-Woman-on-Top," for instance, or "The-World-Upside-Down," so popular in Europe during the economic and intellectual upheavals of the early modern period. "The-Woman-on-Top" iconography customarily portrayed a burly, "heroically" large woman beating her frail husband on his bare buttocks.[98] "The-World-Upside-Down" imagery featured women in armor and men spinning, as well as the violence of the oppressed—including women—against those on top.[99] "The Invert," "The-Woman-on-Top," and "The-World-Upside-Down" all link "irregular" sexuality to challenges to social (and, of course, domestic) order. The image of a male soul trapped in a female body, the "Mannish Lesbian," is even more emotionally laden. It makes graphic the male/mind–female/body polarity inherent in all the other metaphors. Yet it remains a highly ambiguous political image. On one level, the "Mannish Lesbian" fused, and thus denied, that polarity. But the converse is equally true. The image of the "Mannish Lesbian" held immiscible essences in an eternal tension of differences.

These metaphors departed radically from earlier female imagery. They again force us to speculate concerning the difference between the successive generations of New Women. Certainly their social experiences and sexual expectations differed. Had their political demands changed as well? Feminists can espouse one of two quite distinct objectives. They can fight for *women's* rights or they can demand equality with men. Did the New Women who adopted the male metaphors demand equality with men, while other feminists, who sought rights for *women,* continued to speak the traditional female languages? To deepen our understanding of generational differences among the New Women, to extend our understanding of gender relations and of language, let us trace the evolution of this new metaphoric language, which spoke so ambiguously of male fears and female desire. To do so, let us commence with the original male constructions.

Krafft-Ebing's novel construct, the Mannish Lesbian, the male soul trapped in a female body, constituted a condensed symbol of great complexity. An intermediate sex, neither male nor female, she literally embodied the New Women's demand for a role beyond conventional gender. Male commentators, from the sexologists of the 1880s to the companionate-marriage reformers and modernist writers of the 1920s, had deliberately used her to stand for a freak of nature, a logical impossibility. These "New Men," far more than their Victorian predecessors, sexualized their biological determinism and social conservatism. They rooted gender distinctions in genital differences. The genitals were biologically observable, unchangeable, uncontestable—and above all "natural." To protest gender, therefore, was to deny the genitals—to war with nature. The woman who would be a man, the man who assumed the female role—homosexuals, transvestites, hermaphrodites—symbolized social chaos and decay. Sandra Gilbert, in a brilliant article contrasting men and women modernist writers, proposes this thesis.[100] For the male modernists, Gilbert argues, the male transvestite or hermaphrodite symbolized the emasculation of both man's sexual and his social powers, for society had fused the two. A sport of nature, he represented cognitive and social disarray. In the distorted, nightmarish world of Night Town in Joyce's *Ulysses*, the cross-dressed Bella mirrors the corseted Bloom; the unnatural woman complements the unnatural man. Sterile, ghoulish repudiations of gender, they personify a disordered world, as does Eliot's Tiresias, his dry dugs a metaphor for the modern waste land.[101]

As with the hermaphroditic man, the Mannish Lesbian's fusion of the male and the female suggested only decay and ultimate powerlessness. Male modernists, like Victorian physicians, did not use androgyny as a metaphor for accumulated power or for full human potential. Again the woman who would be a man emerged as a sterile and ludicrous hermaphrodite. When challenged by powerful, gender-confident men—Joyce, Lawrence, the sexologists all reassured themselves—her power would fade. She would disappear as Bella/Bello did into a haze of unreality with the coming of the dawn. She would crumble, as in Lawrence's *The Fox*, before man's phallic strength.[102]

Women writers of the 1920s and 1930s deliberately transposed the male sexual metaphors into a feminist language. Both male and female modernists used the concept of an "intermediate sex" to symbolize an intermediate social role. The "Mannish Lesbian"—the woman who stood between and thus outside of conventional sexual categories—represented the New Women's repudiation of conventional gender distinctions and restrictions. In contrast to the male modernists' denunciation of the "Mannish Lesbian" as an unnatural hermaphrodite, Gilbert argues, feminist modernists insisted that woman's assertion of "male" power and ambition was "natural." Gender distinctions were artificial, man–made constructions. Gender, not the New Woman, was "unnatural." Gender distinctions twisted the *human* spirit, deforming men as well as women. Gender conventions lay at the heart of the confining traditions they, as modernists, fought against. Androgyny was their ideal.[103]

Feminist modernists turned to dress and to body imagery to repudiate gender and to assert a new order. Susan Gubar argues that women writers and artists in the 1910s and 1920s adopted male dress as a self-conscious political statement. She points to Stein's creation of an "intermediate" and unconventional costume; to the expatriate Paris lesbians' adoption of male fashion; and, much earlier, to American physician and feminist Alice Walker's use of Victorian male clothing to protest the oppression of the conventional female role.[104]

Not content with fabricating gender and costume into a personal statement of self, feminist modernists wove them into the heart of their creative—and political—imagery. Take, for example, Virginia Woolf's *Orlando.* [105] In *Orlando,* Woolf created a mad, surrealistic *Bildungsroman* or perhaps, one could argue, a female novel of initiation. Orlando seeks identity and fulfillment first through the guidance of corrupt male literary advisers, next through an exotic romance set in a frozen carnival, and, finally, through public service in foreign lands. Each experience increases his alienation and confusion until, suddenly, Orlando awakes from a dream (have we here a play on Sleeping Beauty?), female. Thereafter gender becomes amorphous and time irrelevant. Centuries pass like days. A shimmering creature, Orlando as woman maintains the characteristics she displayed when a man, to which she simply adds, as if she were donning another layer of clothing, her sensibility of being female and the ironic distance that experience gives her. Indeed, throughout Orlando, clothes, not genitals or personality, symbolize gender change. The body remains amorphous, Orlando's character beyond gender. Her husband, Marmaduke Bonthrop Shelmerdine, Sandra Gilbert points out, proves to be "as strange and subtle as a woman."[106] Both glory in androgyny, the confusion of categories, the options that extend beyond social proprieties. Tying gender to dress rather than dress to gender, Woolf inverts Krafft-Ebing's dark vision of the "Mannish Lesbian." Her joyous androgyne counterposes Krafft-Ebing's decadent hermaphrodite.

Feminist modernists, lampooning the sexologists' obsession with cross-dressing, caustically reproved the male modernists' rapture with biological determinism. Their self-conscious political imagery, however, had even broader implications. It inverted the very process of bourgeois myth formation so central to the construction of the bourgeois social order and to the male sexual discourse which had begun in the nineteenth century precisely to defend gender conventions. We have already examined Roland Barthes's argument that bourgeois myth clothes the bourgeoisie—a politically and economically self-interested class, the product of concrete historical forces—in the aura of timeless human nature.[107] Expressed more generally, Barthes maintains that through metaphor and symbol, bourgeois myth invests the sociologically contingent with the characteristics of the biologically inevitable and unquestionable. What is bourgeois becomes "natural," all else "unnatural." Male modernists, by fusing gender and genitals, by insisting that to repudiate gender conventions was to war against nature, had joined with sexologists in constructing a classic bourgeois myth. They had clothed gender distinctions specific to late-nineteenth-century industrial countries in the unchangeability of human biology. Feminist modernists, by rejecting the "naturalness" of gender, insisted that society's most fundamental organizational category—gender —was artificial, hence "unnatural," as changeable as dress. From this first principle, it then followed that nothing social or political was "natural." Institutional structures, values, behavior, all were artifact, all relative, all reflective not of nature but of power.

Repudiating the "natural," feminist modernists set their novels in "unnatural" worlds and unstructured situations, beyond the threshold of conventional order. Their plots violate the restrictions of time (*Orlando*), of day and night (*Nightwood*), of conventional literary forms (Gertrude Stein's novels), of national loyalties (*The Well of Loneliness*).[108] In surrealistic and expatriate worlds, New Women float between genders and violate divisions between appearance and reality. We have already examined Orlando, whose life encompassed four centuries, two genders, and a number of countries. Stephen Gordon, Radclyffe Hall's classic Mannish Lesbian, though she has none of Orlando's surrealism, ends the novel as a romantic figure in a darkened house, an expatriate in an alien land. Having discovered the intermediate nature of her sexuality, Stephen must flee the structured security of Morton, her family home, the conventions of the English gentry, and England itself to live a creative life in the "no man's land" of lesbian Paris in the 1920s. Here Stephen, Mary, and a score of Hall's other lesbian figures, locked out of the "normal world" of families and their native England, wander in an unnatural night world of transvestite bars.[109]

Djuna Barnes also chose the unstructured world of transvestite Paris for her novel. Barnes's title, *Nightwood,* tells all, for a wood at night is a world without structure, a haunted place, invested with primitive magic. The epitome of disordered nature, the night wood inverts the ordered "natural world" of Darwinian evolution and of social Darwinism. Barnes signals the "un-naturalness" of the night wood in her opening scene: the death of a widowed mother in childbirth. Basic natural processes have been disrupted in this scene. A newborn infant has killed its mother; the mother, through death, has abandoned her child; a child in need of parents is orphaned. All these events depict the inhumanity of nature and the uncertainty of human existence. They also signal the demise of woman as mother and family member.[110] Barnes then leads us further into her surrealistic night world. Her characters embody social, geographic, and gender disorder. Everyone in *Nightwood* is homeless, afloat between expatriate Paris and Berlin and a dreamlike America. Not one can claim a certain identity, few a clear gender. Their existence denies the inevitability of all structure and categories. They are liminal.

Long before Barnes's time, the human imagination had already created a character who specifically embodies the disorder and the creative power we associate with liminality, a creature who exists to break taboos, violate categories, and defy structure. I refer, of course, to the Trickster. We have already met one American trickster, the Davy Crockett of the comic almanacs.[111] A wild youth, Crockett escaped old values, institutions, and modes of social control to live in a boundless wood, half man, half animal, of ambiguous sexuality, given to violence and disorder. These characteristics epitomize the Trickster, for the Trickster is disorderly, libidinous, scatological, of indeterminate sex and changeable gender. Both Crockett and the classic tricksters of folklore (the Winnebago Trickster, the African spider Anani, Ulysses from classic mythology, perhaps, Dionysus) ritually violate taboos.[112] They dress as women; the Winnebago Trickster even becomes female for a time and bears children, only to remember suddenly that he is also a man and to move on.[113] Their creators use tricksters to demonstrate the contingency of order, the fragility of social custom. Youthful heroes on a journey of discovery, they float within a structureless world—Crockett on the Mississippi, Ulysses on his Odyssey, the Winnebago Trickster on mythic rivers and lakes. Their lives, as their stories, are episodic. They live outside the home and the family, unconfined by social categories or real communities. Disorder defines the Trickster, but so does power. The Trickster continually alters her/his body, creates and re-creates a personality. A creative force at war with convention, beyond gender, the Trickster personifies unfettered human potential.[114] She/he constitutes the ideal feminist hero.

Certainly, Orlando is a trickster par excellence. She floats across time, through unbelievable settings. Creating her/himself out of fancy, farce, and finery, she tricks us into abandoning all that we know: that sex is unchangeable, gender distinctions "natural," time confining, and patriarchy invincible. For a brief moment, as Orlando frees us, we revel in the headiness of what might be.

Barnes's *Nightwood* is filled with tricksters who have draped their lives in borrowed fancies and wear the whole cloth of illusion. Take Frau Mann, for instance: her name is an oxymoron that calls forth both the androgyne and Krafft-Ebing's "Mannish Lesbian." A trapeze artist, Frau Mann escapes the confines of earth (society). The single, autonomous woman, she violates all social categories and gender restraints. Yet to do so she must live in a world beyond the "natural" order of the day, gender and propriety. Indeed, Frau Mann's very body denies the distinction between reality and illusion. She seemed, Barnes tells us, "to have a skin that was the pattern of her costume. . . . The stuff of the tights was no longer a covering, it was herself."[115] Illusion freed her from gender restraints. At the same time it robbed her of her sexuality.

"The span of the tightly stitched crotch was so much her own flesh that she was as unsexed as a doll. The needle that had made one the property of the child made the other the property of no man."[116]

Sexuality was the critical issue for this generation of New Women. They linked it with identity and with freedom. Yet Barnes's imagery is ambiguous. Has the defiance of gender restrictions made Frau Mann (and thus all women who define themselves as beyond conventional gender) "as unsexed as a doll"—that is, without a true identity? Or is Barnes's implication far more positive: that the woman beyond gender is beyond being owned? Frau Mann embodies one of the critical dilemmas of modern feminism: in rejecting gender as an artificial construction, does one lose one's identity as a woman? Beyond gender, what is one? Frau Mann remains enigmatic.[117]

Classically, the Trickster is a comic character, a joke that *momentarily* turns the world upside down. But as we saw with Crockett, the joke is not serious. Its inversion of order is transitory. It suggests but does not effect an alternative order. Woolf uses Orlando to expose the absurdity of rigid gender rules and the pomposity of the male literary canon. But Orlando changes neither England nor literature. She/he merely suggests what might be.

Not all tricksters are comic. The fools in Shakespeare's tragedies are tragic figures who cry out against the cruelty of an "unnatural" and an "inhuman" world. So are the tragic tricksters that inhabit Djuna Barnes's *Nightwood.* They exist not merely as Orlando does, to comment upon the absurdity of social arrangements and thus trick us into thinking in unconventional ways. They have declared war against social convention and live out the consequences of their actions. Sadly, in defeat, they have retreated, to a mad night wood of inversion and of pain. They speak to a critical new aspect of the New Women's experiences—the price paid by those who literally use their bodies and their emotions to invert received order. We are reminded of M. Carey Thomas's comments on the cost to her (a well-to-do and well-connected young woman) of attending a coeducational college: "It is impossible to make one who has not felt . . . the fiery ordeal . . . understand the living on a volcano or on a house top," she wrote in the 1870s.[118] Society meted out far harsher penalties against the sexual deviant in the 1920s than it had against the gender deviant of the 1870s. The New Women of the 1920s and 1930s—Barnes and Hall, especially— were among the first to challenge publicly the new sexual taboos against female love. They belonged to the first generation to bear the full brunt of social ostracism and legal censorship. It may well be that it is to these feelings that "Dr." O'Connor refers when he describes the forces that transformed him into a liar—and a tragic trickster. " 'Look here,' the doctor said to Nora, 'Do you know what has made me the greatest liar this side of the moon, telling my stories to people like you, to take the mortal agony out of their guts, and to stop them from . . . screaming, with their eyes staring over their knuckles with misery which they are trying to keep off, saying, "Say something, Doctor, for the love of God!" and me talking away like mad. Well, that, and nothing else, has made me the liar I am.' "[119] The tragic Nora's pain is the reverse side of the coin of Orlando's escape from gender. It is the coin levied by society as payment for such actual gender reversal.

Metaphor by metaphor, feminist modernists of the 1920s and 1930s had inverted men's language. The ultimate inversion, of course, is to transform male masterpieces into feminist statements. *Orlando* and *Nightwood* both constitute self-conscious transformations of male forms. As feminist works they differ radically, of course, presenting two distinct visions of a world beyond gender. *Orlando,* Esther Newton suggests, is more a political attack upon male gender structures than an exposition of female experiences.[120] *Nightwood,* while condemning conventional order, speaks eloquently of the experience of marginality and of deviance. As their messages differed, so too did the masterpieces they reworked.

Orlando, a surrealistic spoof, constitutes a feminist transmogrification of *As You Like It.* This delicate play on love and gender suited Woolf's purposes admirably. The title itself both empowers the individual and insists on the relativity of order. In a wild and unstructured wood, Shakespeare endlessly inverts gender. Rosalind, Orlando's love in *As You Like It,* assumes a male disguise as the shepherd Ganymede (the youth Jove desired and abducted). As Ganymede, Rosalind is pursued by the love-stricken Phebe. She also persuades Orlando to make mock love to Ganymede, as if Ganymede were the beloved Rosalind. Gender reversal and outright gender denial escalate to the point where gender and dress cease to constitute significant categories. Witty, intelligent, wise, Rosalind is the triumphant trickster. The plot revolves around her elaborate tricks. Setting up the riddle that ends the play, she tells the assembled characters: "[To Phe.] I will marry you if ever I marry woman, and I'll be married tomorrow. [to Orl.] I will satisfy you, if ever I satisfied man, and you shall be married tomorrow. [to Sil.] I will content you, if what pleases you contents you, and you shall be married tomorrow.[121]

Gender inversion leads to role inversion. Not only does the cross-dressed Rosalind dominate the plot; she also presents the epilogue. As Rosalind points out in the opening line of the epilogue, for a woman to presume such a public role and a degree of equality with men is highly unusual. "It is not the fashion to see the lady the epilogue; but it is no more unhandsome than to see the lord the prologue." The play ends with the greatest gender trick of all. Shakespeare's audience knew full well that the female character Rosalind, who, dressed as Ganymede, was wooed by Orlando, was, in reality, a young male actor.[122] The epilogue ends as the young man playing Rosalind flirts with his male audience, calling their attention simultaneously to his inversion of gender and to his power as a woman/man to determine his own actions. "If I were a woman I would kiss as many of you as had beards that pleased me, complexions that liked me and breaths that I defied not. . . ."[123] Shakespeare's *As You Like It* and Woolf's *Orlando* invest androgyny with power and wit.

Djuna Barnes, concerned with judgment, the New Women's expulsion from the world of legitimacy and power, and with suffering, chose a very different male creation to invert. Barnes modeled *Nightwood* on Dante's *Divine Comedy*. Dr. O'Connor, that enigmatic teller of truths, twice announces himself as Dante Alighieri.[124] The *Divine Comedy* begins in a dark wood where Dante stumbles as lost and fearful as the characters in *Nightwood*.

> *I woke to find my self in a dark wood,*
> *Where the right road was wholly lost and gone,*
> *Ay me! how hard to speak of it—that rude*
> *And rough and stubborn Forest! the mere breath*
> *Of memory stirs with old fear in the blood;*
> *It is so bitter, it goes nigh to death. . . .*[125]

Dante stated in a letter to his patron that the *Divine Comedy* was a grand allegory in which "Man, as by good or ill deserts, in the exercise of his free choice, . . . becomes liable to rewarding or punishing justice."[126] *Nightwood* is an allegory of judgment and damnation. Barnes's characters, by exercising their free will, have entered a night wood beyond gender and conventional order. Here they are judged by the conventional world, which refuses to readmit them on their own terms—their assertion of personal and sexual freedom. The torments of hell follow Nora, Robin, Jenny, Felix, and Dr. O'Connor. Each in turn cries out to God for mercy.

This is a somber but not an inaccurate vision of the experience of the New Woman/Lesbian in the dark years of the 1930s.

The New Women of the 1920s and 1930s, imbuing male imagery with feminist meaning, transformed the sexologists' symbolic system. Boldly, they asserted their right to participate in male discourse, to function in a public (male) arena, and to act as men did—both in and out of bed. Female images of women beyond gender, however, did not simply affirm the individual's transcendence of social constructions. As the debate between the New Women and the New Men wore on without a feminist victory, their symbols acquired a second, darker message. *The Well of Loneliness* and, even more starkly, *Nightwood* bespoke the pain that accompanied public condemnation, social ostracism, and legal censorship.

These women's deliberate adaptation of male symbols in order to engage in political debate raises many philosophical and political questions. I have based my analysis on the premise that words are rooted in experience. If this is so, can male symbols accurately represent female experiences? Or, rather, by enveloping women's experiences in male forms, do we distort—indeed, deny—those experiences? Clothes are cultural artifacts, lightly donned or doffed, but words are rooted in our earliest and most profound experiences of social location and of the distribution of power. In stripping their discourse of female-originated metaphors and images, did the feminist modernists come dangerously close to denuding themselves of a female identity? And of female authority? Images and metaphors are the tools of authorship—a power to create that Gilbert and Gubar have persuasively argued is intimately linked to authority.

The issue of identity frames the dilemma. The feminist modernists rejected an older, Victorian or Edwardian female identity, tied as it was to sexual purity and sacrifice. They did not wish to be the Housekeepers of America, or to justify their political activities as Home Protection (a device chosen by Frances Willard and the Women's Christian Temperance Union). They wished to free themselves completely from considerations of gender, to be autonomous and powerful individuals, to enter the world as if they were men. Hence they spoke with men's metaphors and images. (Yet, we must never forget, they simultaneously invested those images and metaphors with a condemnation of gender and demands for equality quite alien, even threatening, to the male originators of the discourse.)

Their words echoed their experiences. Both words and experiences defied traditional gender categories. The educated bourgeois women who came to political and creative maturity in the 1910s and 1920s had grown up in a uniquely androgynous world. They *assumed* their right to exist outside of gender, in the public arena. The victories won by earlier cohorts of New Women in professional and educational areas had made their androgynous world possible. Yet, ironically, this greater freedom did not bond women across the generations. It alienated them. The New Women of the 1920s were unique—and isolated. They could speak meaningfully only to other women so uniquely situated. Neither the earlier generations, who had lived and fought in a far more separatist world, nor later women less advantageously situated than they in terms of access to professional advancement and economic autonomy shared their perspective, or their language.[127] The political solidarity of the successive generations of New Women slipped away as their discourses became more disjointed and conflicted. In this process, the New Women lost much of their political power and many of their economic and institutional gains.

The brave and unique generation of the 1920s confronted a profound dilemma. They shed their primary identity as women before the world they inhabited accepted the legitimacy of androgyny. Despite their brilliant inversions of male metaphors, men refused to share power with them. In fact, the public world was increasingly closed to the New Women. Divested of their primary alliance with the older feminists, they had few resources with which to challenge this reassertion of male power. And so the androgynous language through which they sought to affirm their legitimacy and centrality only confirmed their increasing marginality—to the world of women as well as that of men. Like Robin Vote, Dr. O'Connor, and Nora Flood, they wandered, baffled, in a night wood of broken promises and thwarted expectations.

Words are active as well as reflective agents. When heard and understood, they can revolutionize their world. The New Women of the 1920s, through the deft construction of androgynous dreams and ironic inversions, sought to create an androgynous world. But words, unallied to material sources of power, become like spirits divorced from corporeal form—shades, fantasies, brave but sad illusions. The New Women of the 1920s did not fail because they chose the wrong discourse. They failed because they lacked the real economic and institutional power with which to wrest hegemony from men and so enforce their vision of a gender-free world. We can learn much from their errors—and their successes. Our very first lesson must be to understand and not to blame them.

NOTES *and* INDEX

Notes

HEARING WOMEN'S WORDS

1. I do not intend this to be a definitive survey of the past fifteen years of women's history. Rather, I will discuss those aspects of women's history which most influenced or paralleled my own work. I have also limited my review to American analyses.

For general surveys of the field see, among others, Mary P. Ryan, "The Explosion of Family History," *Reviews in American History* 10 (December 1982); Estelle Freeman, "Sexuality in Nineteenth-Century America: Behavior, Ideology and Politics," ibid.; Elaine Tyler May, "Expanding the Past: Recent Scholarship on Women in Politics and Work," ibid. See also Martha Vicinis, "Sexuality and Power: A Review of Current Work in the History of Sexuality," *Feminist Studies* VIII (Spring 1982): 133–56.

2. See, for example, Alice Kessler Harris, *Out to Work* (New York: Oxford University Press, 1982); W. Elliot Brownlee and Mary M. Brownlee, "Introduction," in *Women in the American Economy*, ed. W. Elliot Brownlee and Mary M. Brownlee (New Haven: Yale University Press, 1976); Leslie Woodcock Tentler, *Wage-Earning Women: Industrial Work and Family Life in the United States, 1900–1930* (New York: Oxford University Press, 1979); Susan Reverby, "From Aide to Organizer: The Oral History of Lillian Roberts," in *Women of America*, ed. Mary Beth Norton and Carol Berkin (Boston: Houghton Mifflin, 1976); Claudia Goldin and Kenneth Sokoloff, "Women, Children and Industrialization in the Early Republic: Evidence from the Manufacturing Censuses," *Journal of Economic History*

XLII (December 1982): 741–74; Claudia Goldin, "The Changing Economic Role of Women: A Quantitative Approach," *Journal of Interdisciplinary History* XIII (1983): 707–33. For a survey of recent economic history analyses see Joan Smith, "The Way We Were: Women and Work," *Feminist Studies* VIII (Summer 1982): 437–56; Judith McGaw, "Women's Work in the American Past: Historians' Insights and Oversights," in *Women and the Workplace*, ed. Valerie Gill Couch (Norman: University of Oklahoma Press), pp. 39–51; Joan Wallach Scott, "The Mechanization of Women's Work," *Scientific American* (September 1982): 67–87. For a classic discussion of the effect of industrialization on women and the family, albeit based on European sources, see Louise Tilly and Joan Scott, *Women, Work and the Family* (New York: Holt, Rinehart and Winston, 1978).

3. Susan Hirsch's *The Roots of the American Working Class: The Industrialization of Crafts in Newark, 1800–1860* (Philadelphia: University of Pennsylvania Press, 1978) raises these general issues, examining them against the backdrop of industrialization of the crafts in Newark.

4. Elizabeth H. Pleck, "A Mother's Wages: Income Earning Among Married Italian and Black Women, 1896–1911," in *The American Family in Social-Historical Perspective*, ed. Michael Gordon, 2nd ed. (New York: St. Martin's Press, 1978), pp. 490–510; Jacqueline Jones, "My Mother Was Much of a Woman: Black Women, Work and the Family Under Slavery," *Feminist Studies* VIII (Summer 1982): 235–70; Suzanne Lebsock, "Free Black Women and the Question of Matriarchy:

Petersburg, Virginia, 1784–1820," ibid., pp. 271–92.

5. Theodore Dreiser, *Sister Carrie* (Philadelphia: University of Pennsylvania Press, 1981); Anzia Yezierska, *Bread Givers* (New York: George Braziller, 1975).

6. Barbara Welter, "The Cult of True Womanhood: 1820–1860," *American Quarterly* XVIII (Summer 1966).

7. See especially Azel Ames, Jr., *Sex in Industry: A Plea for the Working Girl* (Boston: James R. Osgood, 1875). Carroll Wright, in his classic *Working Girls of Boston* (New York: Arno Press, 1969), defended the "naturalness" and morality of women in Boston's needle trades and sales force. It is even more significant, of course, that he felt called upon to do so.

8. See, for example, Nancy Cott, *The Bonds of Womanhood: "Woman's Sphere" in New England, 1780–1835* (New Haven: Yale University Press, 1977); Kathryn Kish Sklar, *Catherine Beecher: A Study in American Domesticity* (New Haven: Yale University Press, 1973).

9. For a fascinating analysis of this process see Gloria Melnick Moldow, *The Gilded Age: Promise and Disillusionment, Women Doctors and the Emergence of the Professional Middle Class* (Urbana: University of Illinois Press, in press). See as well Paul Star, *The Social Transformation of American Medicine* (New York: Basic Books, 1983). For earlier studies see Linda Gordon, *Women's Bodies, Women's Rights* (New York: Viking Press, 1976); Mary Walsh, *Doctors Wanted, No Women Need Apply: Sexual Barriers in the Medical Profession 1835–1875* (New Haven: Yale University Press, 1977); John S. Haller and Robin M. Haller, *The Physician and Sexuality in Victorian America* (Urbana: University of Illinois Press, 1974). Barbara Dudden has explored this phenomenon in nineteenth-century Germany (personal communication). For Great Britain see Judith Walkowitz, *Prostitution and Victorian Society* (Cambridge: Cambridge University Press, 1980).

10. Eleanor Flexner, *Century of Struggle* (Cambridge, Mass.: Harvard University Press, 1959); Ann Firor Scott, *The Southern Lady: From Pedestal to Politics* (Chicago: University of Chicago Press, 1970); Ann Firor Scott and Andrew Mackay Scott, *One Half the People: The Fight for Women's Suffrage* (Urbana: University of Illinois Press, 1975); Gerda Lerner, *The Grimké Sisters from South Carolina* (New

York: Schocken Books, 1971); Ellen DuBois, *Feminism and Suffrage* (Ithaca, N.Y.: Cornell University Press, 1978).

11. Blanche Glassman Hersch, *The Slavery of Sex: Feminist Abolitionists in America* (Urbana: University of Illinois Press, 1978); Carroll Smith-Rosenberg, "Beauty, the Beast and the Militant Woman," *American Quarterly* XXIII (1971), and *Religion and the Rise of the American City* (Ithaca, N.Y.: Cornell University Press, 1971); Mary Ryan, "The Power of Women's Networks: A Case Study of Female Moral Reform in Antebellum America," *Feminist Studies* V (Spring 1979), and *Womanhood in America, from Colonial Times to the Present* (New York: Watts Press, 1975).

For a superb study of late-Victorian female reform efforts see Mari Jo Buhle, *Women and American Socialism, 1870–1920* (Urbana: University of Illinois Press, 1981), especially chaps. 2 and 3. Blanche Cook has pointed to the centrality of female support networks within the left wing of the Progressive Movement in her excellent essay "Female Support Networks and Political Activism: Lillian Wald, Crystal Eastman, Emma Goldman," *Chrysalis* III (1977). For an examination of Southern white women and reform see Jacquelyn Dowd Hall, *Revolt Against Chivalry: Jessie Daniel Ames and the Women's Campaign Against Lynching* (New York: Columbia University Press, 1979).

12. The chief spokeswoman for this position is Joan Hoff Wilson, "The Illusion of Change: Women and the American Revolution," in *The American Revolution*, ed. Alfred Young (DeKalb: Northern Illinois University Press, 1976). Gerda Lerner addresses these issues in "The Lady and the Mill Girl: Changes in the Status of Women in the Age of Jackson, 1800–1840," *Midcontinent American Studies Journal* X (Spring 1969): 5–14. Lois Green Carr and Lorena S. Walsh examine the ways in which the harshness of first settlement experiences enhanced the economic resources and legal status of women who survived, in "The Planter's Wife: The Experience of White Women in Seventeenth-Century Maryland," *William and Mary Quarterly*, 3rd ser. XXXIV (1977): 542–71.

13. Leading spokeswoman for this school is Mary Beth Norton; see her "Eighteenth-Century American Women in Peace and War: The Case of the Loyalists," *William and Mary Quar-*

terly, 3rd ser. XXXIII (July 1976): 386–409, and "Colonial Women to 1800: The Myth of the Golden Age," in *Women of America,* ed. Norton and Berkin. See also Norton, *Liberty's Daughters: The Revolutionary Experience of American Women, 1750–1800* (Boston: Houghton Mifflin, 1980); Linda Kerber, *Women of the Republic* (Chapel Hill: University of North Carolina Press, 1980), and "Daughters of Columbia: Educating Women for the Republic, 1787–1805," in *The Hofstadter Aegis: A Memorial,* ed. Stanley Elkins and Eric McKitrick (New York: Alfred A. Knopf, 1974), pp. 36–59. The situation is extremely complex. Marylynn Salmon, in her fine essay "Equality or Submersion? Female Covert Status in Early Pennsylvania," in *Women of America,* traces the ways in which land scarcity and other commercial pressures eroded the protection British common law had given women at the same time that other commercial needs encouraged equity law's protection of propertied women.

14. Lerner, "The Lady and the Mill Girl"; Ryan, "Power of Women's Networks." This argument constitutes a subspecies of the more general social-control argument. For a recent male analysis of male religious efforts at social control, see Paul E. Johnson, *Shopkeepers' Millennium: Society and Revivals in Rochester, New York, 1815–1837* (New York: Hill and Wang, 1978).

15. Hersch, *Slavery of Sex;* Buhle, *Women and American Socialism.*

16. Philip Greven's pathbreaking study of New England families and communities, *Four Generations: Population, Land and Family in Colonial Andover, Massachusetts* (Ithaca, N.Y.: Cornell University Press, 1970), is severely flawed by his failure to discuss women's family experience, other than in terms of birthrate and age of first marriage. His analysis of child-rearing practices and personality development in the nineteenth century, *The Protestant Temperament: Patterns of Child-Rearing, Religious Experience and the Self* (New York: Alfred A. Knopf, 1977), demonstrates a similar gender blindness and subsequent serious distortion. See as well Joseph Kett's *Rites of Passage* (New York: Basic Books, 1977).

17. Gayle Rubin, "Traffic in Women," in *Towards an Anthropology of Women,* ed. Rayna Reiter (New York: Monthly Review Press, 1975).

18. Roland Barthes, *Mythologies,* sel. and trans. Annette Lavers (New York: Hill and Wang, 1972).

19. Smith-Rosenberg, *Religion.*

20. See, for example, *The Maternal Physician: A Treatise on the Nurture and Management of Infants, by an American Matron* (New York: Isaac Riley, 1811; Reprinted New York: Arno Press, 1972); *Advice to Young Mothers on the Physical Education of Children by a Grandmother* (Boston: Hilliard, Gray and Co., 1833); William Buchan, *Advice to Mothers on the Subject of Their Own Health, and of the Means of Promoting the Health, Strength and Beauty of Their Offspring* (Boston: Joseph Bumstead, 1809); Hugh Smith, *Letters to Married Ladies . . . by an American Physician* (New York: E. Bliss and E. White and G. and G. Carvell, 1827); S. Cancoast, *The Ladies' Medical Guide* (Philadelphia: John E. Patterson Company, 1859).

21. See, for example, Alexander Walker, *Woman Physiologically Considered* (New York: J. and H. G. Langley, 1840); Alfred H. Hayes, *Physiology of Woman* (Boston: Peabody Medical Institute, 1869); George H. Napheys, *The Physical Life of Woman* (Philadelphia: H. C. Watts Co., 1885).

22. M. D. T. De Bienville, *Nymphomania, or a Dissertation Concerning the Furor Uterinus,* trans. Edward Sloan Wilmot (London: J. Bew, 1775); Thomas Hersey, *Midwives' Practical Directory* (Baltimore: Sands and Neilson, 1836); Eugene Becklard, *"Know Thyself": The Physiologist or Sexual Physiology* (Boston: Bela Marsh, 1859); James Ashton, *The Book of Nature* (New York: Wallis and Ashton, 1861); Wesley Grindle, *New Medical Revelations* (Philadelphia, 319 South Thirteenth Street, 1857).

23. Sarah B. Elliott, *Aedology;* W. W. Bliss, *Woman's Life: A Pen Picture of Woman's Functions, Frailties and Follies* (Boston: A. W. Lovering, 1879); Robert La Grange, *Premature Decay* (Philadelphia, 1879); Charles Meigs, *Lecture on Some of the Distinctive Characteristics of the Female* (Philadelphia: Collins, 1847); Russell T. Trall, *Sexual Physiology* (New York: Miller, Wood, 1866); Mrs. Mary Wood-Allen, *What a Young Woman Ought to Know* (Philadelphia: The Vir Publishing Co., 1905). I disagree with the analysis of shifts in medical attitudes toward female sexuality which Nancy Cott posits in "Passionlessness: An Interpretation of Victorian Sexual Ideol-

ogy, 1790–1850," *Signs* IV (1978): 219–36, that the repression of women's sexuality was greatest in the opening decades of the century and gradually diminished as the century went on. On the contrary, virtually the only medical writers who emphasized women's innate asexuality during the first half of the nineteenth century were medical reformers such as Sylvester Graham, C. B. Woodward, Samuel Gregory, and William Alcott. More prestigious physicians maintained the eighteenth century's far more "modern" view of woman's innate sexuality. We must also remember that the male reformers were not especially interested in female sexuality and discussed it only to suggest that pure women would help young men to act in a pure way. See Carroll Smith-Rosenberg, "Sex as Symbol in Victorian Purity: An Ethnohistorical Analysis of Jacksonian America," *American Journal of Sociology* LXXXIV Supplement (1978): 212–47. In all events, the reformers constituted a group quite separate from, and self-consciously at war with, the medical establishment. The establishment considered their ideas absolutely bizarre. It was only with mid-century that the establishment began to adopt the reformers' repressive ideology.

24. See, for example, Carroll Smith-Rosenberg and Charles Rosenberg, "The Female Animal: Medical and Biological Views of Woman and Her Role in Nineteenth-Century America," *Journal of American History* LX (September 1973): 332–56.

25. See "The Abortion Movement and the AMA, 1850–1880" in this volume.

26. For a lengthy discussion of the way prostitution was used to expand the power of the state (and of the medical profession) into the lives of women, see Ruth Rosen's excellent *The Lost Sisterhood: Prostitution in America, 1900–1918* (Baltimore: Johns Hopkins University Press, 1980). Judith Walkowitz, *Prostitution and Victorian Society: Women, Class and the State* (Cambridge and New York: Cambridge University Press, 1980), provides a brilliant analysis of women, sex, and class in Victorian Britain.

27. See James Mohr, *Abortion in America: The Origins and Evolution of National Policy* (New York and Oxford: Oxford University Press, 1978). See also Star, *Social Transformation of American Medicine*.

28. See, for example, *New England Primer Enlarged* (Boston: printed by D. and J. Knee-

land, 1761); J[ohn] Wright, *Spiritual Songs for Children* (Boston: printed and sold by Zacharia Fowle, 1764); Sir Matthew Hale, *Affectionate Epistles to His Children* (Philadelphia: printed by William Spotswood, 1790); *Exhibition of Tom Thumb* (Boston: Ebenezer Battelle, 1787); *Juvenile Poems* (Windsor, State of Vermont: printed by Alden Spooner, 1792); Rufus Adams, *The Young Gentleman's and Lady's Explanatory Monitor* (Zanesville, Ohio: D. Chambers, 1815); [John Taylor], *Verbum Sempiternum* (Boston: printed for and sold by N. Procter, 1765).

29. [James Ridley], *The Adventures of Urad* (Boston: Mein & Fleeming, 1767).

30. See, for example, Margaret Coxe, *The Young Ladies' Companion* (Columbus, Ohio: Isaac N. Whiting, 1845); Rev. Daniel C. Eddy, *The Young Woman's Friend* (Boston: Thayer & Eldridge, 1869); Frances Power Cobbe, *The Duties of Women* (Boston: George H. Ellis, 1881); Adrien Sylvain, *The Virtues and Defects of a Young Girl* (New York: D. & J. Sadlier & Co., 1872).

31. William A. Alcott, *The Young Wife; or Duties of Woman in the Marriage Relation* (New York: Arno Press, 1972; [c. 1837]).

32. See "Puberty to Menopause: The Cycle of Femininity in Nineteenth-Century America" and "The Hysterical Woman: Sex Roles and Role Conflict in Nineteenth-Century America," in this volume.

33. Mary Hallock Foote to Richard Gilder, December 13, 1873, Mary Hallock Foote Papers, Department of Special Collections, Stanford University.

34. Manigault Family Papers, Southern Historical Collection, Duke University; Harriet Manigault Diary, Historical Society of Pennsylvania; Charlotte Wilcox McCall Diary, Historical Society of Pennsylvania.

35. For a spectrum of different responses to this article, see Ellen DuBois in "Politics and Culture in Women's History: A Symposium," *Feminist Studies* VI (Spring 1980): 28–36; Lillian Faderman, *Surpassing the Love of Men* (New York: William Morrow and Co., 1981); Cook, "Female Support Networks."

36. Adrienne Rich, *Of Woman Born* (New York: W. W. Norton and Co., 1976). See also Gayle Rubin, "Traffic in Women," in *Towards an Anthropology of Women*, ed. Rayna Reiter (New York: Monthly Review Press, 1975), pp. 157–210.

37. This position is strongly implied in Marjorie Housepian Dobkin, *The Making of a Feminist: Early Journals and Letters of M. Carey Thomas* (Kent, Ohio: Kent State University Press, 1979). For a similar position, see Anna Mary Wells, *Miss Marks and Miss Woolley* (Boston: Houghton Mifflin Co., 1978).

38. For examples of female-female and male-male bonding in working-class and ethnic families, see Michael Young and Peter Wilmott, *Family and Kinship in East London,* rev. ed. (Baltimore: Penguin Books, 1964); Elizabeth Botts, *Family and Social Networks* (London: Tavistock Publications, 1957); Mirra Komarovsky, *Blue Collar Marriage* (New York: Random House, 1964).

39. See "The Female World of Love and Ritual: Relations Between Women in Nineteenth-Century America" in this volume.

40. For examples of mother-daughter conflict, see M. Carey Thomas's girlhood journals, with their detailed accounts of such stress, in Dobkin, *Making of a Feminist,* pp. 49, 55, 57–58, 61, 63. On the other hand, mothers also encouraged daughters, which made the relationship highly ambivalent (p. 100). Jane Addams also comments upon the phenomenon in her autobiography, *Twenty Years at Hull House* (New York: Macmillan, 1910), and in a short article, "The College Woman and the Family Claim," *The Commons* IV (September 1898).

41. For an example of a mother and daughter giving birth literally in the same bed, see *The Memoirs of Gluckel of Hameln*, trans. Marvin Lowenthal (New York: Schocken Books, Inc., 1977). Ann Bradstreet is a good example of a woman who continued to bear children after her own children had married, and whose father had sired a large family after her own marriage and the beginning of her child-bearing career. Her half-sisters were therefore younger than her own children (their nieces and nephews). For a quick sketch of Ann Bradstreet's life, see Ola Elizabeth Winslow's entry in *Notable American Women, 1607–1950: A Biographical Dictionary,* ed. Edward James and Janet James (Cambridge, Mass.: Belknap Press of Harvard University, 1971).

42. See "The Female World of Love and Ritual: Relations Between Women in Nineteenth-Century America" in this volume.

43. Mari Jo Buhle, *Women and American Socialism.*

44. See, for example, the writings of Crystal Eastman: Crystal Eastman, *On Women and Revolution,* ed. Blanche Weissen Cook (New York: Oxford University Press, 1978), and, especially, Cook's excellent introduction, pp. 1–38.

45. See "The New Woman as Androgyne: Social Disorder and Gender Crisis, 1870–1936," in this volume.

46. Mary Hallock Foote to Helena DeKay Gilder, n.d. [1890s], Mary Hallock Foote Collection, Manuscript Division, Stanford University. See also quotations in Cook, "Female Support Networks," and Faderman, *Surpassing the Love of Men,* pp. 190–203.

47. See, for example, Dobkin, *Making of a Feminist,* pp. 17–88, and Wells, *Miss Marks and Miss Woolley,* p. 56.

48. John Boswell, "Revolutions, Universals, Categories," *Salmagundi* LVIII–LIX (Fall 1982–Winter 1983): 89–114.

49. It is not that he is unaware of the multiple forces that influence sexual ideology, but only that in the end Boswell is primarily interested in using ideology to trace patterns of sexual behavior, not interaction of behavior, ideology, and socioeconomic forces.

50. Boswell, "Revolutions," pp. 107–9.

51. This picks up one of Gayle Rubin's basic points in "Traffic in Women."

52. William Rounseville Alger, *Friendships of Women,* 12th ed. (Boston: Roberts Brothers, 1890). The first edition appeared in 1869. A copy of the 1890 edition in the Schlesinger Library, Radcliffe College, was once owned by Frances Willard and contains her inter-linear notes.

53. Denis Diderot, *La Religieuse* (New York: French and European Publications, Inc., 1972); Honoré de Balzac (3 épisode), "La Fille aux yeux d'or," in *Oeuvres complètes de M. de Balzac,* vol. 9 (Paris: Bibliophiles de l'Originale, 1965–76); Théophile Gautier, *Mademoiselle de Maupin and One of Cleopatra's Nights* (New York: Modern Library, n.d.); Emile Zola, *Nana,* ed. Henri Mitterrand (New York: French and European Publications, Inc., 1977; original date of publication in France, 1835). Others who discussed female homosexuality in the nineteenth century include Maupassant, Bourget, Daudet, Lamartine, Swinburne, and Verlaine.

54. For an expanded discussion see "The New Woman as Androgyne: Social Disorder and Gender Crisis, 1870–1936," in this volume.

55. George Chauncey, "Female Deviance," *Salmagundi* LVIII–LIX (Fall 1982–Winter 1983): 114–46; Faderman, *Surpassing the Love of Men,* pp. 239–53.

56. Michel Foucault, *The History of Sexuality* (New York: Pantheon Books, 1978).

57. See an unpublished manuscript by Myra Jehlen, "Against Human Wholeness. A Suggestion for a Feminist Epistemology."

58. I refer to scholars such as Sandra Gilbert and Susan Gubar [*The Mad Woman in the Attic* (New Haven: Yale University Press, 1980)]; Jane Gallup [*The Daughter's Seduction: Feminism and Psychoanalysis* (Ithaca: Cornell University Press, 1982)]; Carol Gilligan [*In a Different Voice: Psychological Theory and Women's Development* (Cambridge, Mass.: Harvard University Press, 1982)]; Susan C. Bourque and Kay Barbara Warren [*Women of the Andes: Patriarchy and Social Change in Two Peruvian Towns* (Ann Arbor, Mich.: University of Michigan Press, 1981)]; Elaine Showalter [*Women's Liberation and Literature* (New York: Harcourt Brace Jovanovich, 1971)]. Mikhail M. Bakhtin may well offer the most useful definition of language as a social entity. "At any given moment," he argued, "a language is stratified not only into dialects in the strict sense of the word (i.e., dialects that are set off according to formal linguistic markers), but is . . . stratified as well into languages that are socio-ideological: languages belonging to professions, to genres, languages peculiar to particular generations." M. M. Bakhtin, *The Dialogic Imagination: Four Essays,* ed. Michael Holquist (Austin: University of Texas Press, 1981), XIX, and, especially, "Discourse in the Novel," pp. 259–422.

59. For a discussion of the construction of metaphor and myth, see Roland Barthes, "Myth Today," in *Mythologies,* and Victor Turner, *Dramas, Fields and Metaphors* (Ithaca, N.Y.: Cornell University Press, 1974), pp. 24–32.

60. This work will appear in a book of mine tentatively entitled "The Body Politic," to be published by Alfred A. Knopf, Inc.

61. See, for example, "The Cross and the Pedestal: Women, Anti-Ritualism, and the Emergence of the American Bourgeoisie," in this volume.

62. See, for example, "Beauty, the Beast, and the Militant Woman: A Case Study in Sex Roles and Social Stress in Jacksonian America," in this volume.

63. Mrs. E. B. Duffey, *What Women Should Know* (Philadelphia: J. M. Stoddart, 1873); Elizabeth Edson Evans, *The Abuse of Maternity* (Philadelphia: J. B. Lippincott, 1875).

64. See discussions of the Women's Christian Temperance Union in Buhle, *Women and American Socialism,* pp. 60–87, and of the women involved in the antiprostitution movement in Rosen, *The Lost Sisterhood,* chapter 4.

65. Kate Chopin, *The Awakening* (New York: Bard Books, 1972; originally published 1889); Edith Wharton, *House of Mirth* (New York: Signet Classic, 1964; originally published 1905).

66. Alice B. Stockham, *Karezza* (Chicago: Alice B. Stockham, 1896).

67. See Carroll Smith-Rosenberg, "Sex as Symbol," and "Davy Crockett as Trickster: Pornography, Liminality, and Symbolic Inversion in Victorian America," in this volume.

68. See especially "The Abortion Movement and the AMA, 1850–1880," and "The New Woman as Androgyne: Social Disorder and Gender Crisis, 1870–1936," in this volume.

69. See "Puberty to Menopause: The Cycle of Femininity in Nineteenth-Century America," in this volume, as well as Carroll Smith-Rosenberg and Charles Rosenberg, "The Female Animal: Medical and Biological Views of Woman and Her Role in Nineteenth-Century America," *Journal of American History* LX (September 1973): 332–56.

70. Mary Douglas, *Natural Symbols: Explorations in Cosmology* (New York: Vintage Books, 1973); see especially chaps. 1, 5, 12, 16.

71. Ibid., chap. 5, especially pp. 93–94, 96–97, 101.

72. Ibid., chap. 1, and pp. 97–99, 111, 114, 124–25, 191.

73. Ibid., chaps. 5, 6, 10.

74. Ibid., p. 132.

75. Victor Turner, *Forests of Symbols* (Ithaca, N.Y.: Cornell University Press, 1967), pp. 28, 29–47.

76. Barthes, *Mythologies,* pp. 109–31.

77. Ibid., pp. 141, 137–45.

78. Ibid., pp. 145–48. For a specific feminist criticism of Barthes, see Jehlen.

79. Turner, *Dramas,* chaps. 6, 7.

80. Roland Barthes, *Image, Music, Text,* translated by S. Heath (New York: Hill and

Wang, 1977), pp. 156–59. For a highly suggestive application of Barthesian concepts to the interpretation of religious rituals, see James A. Boon, "Symbols, Sylphs and Siwa: Allegorical Machineries in the Text of Balinese Culture (and History)," unpublished paper, presented to the Ethnohistory Seminar, University of Pennsylvania, March 10, 1983.

. . .

THE FEMALE WORLD OF LOVE AND RITUAL

1. Research for this chapter was supported in part by a grant from the Grant Foundation, New York, and by a National Institutes of Health trainee grant. I would like to thank several scholars for their assistance and criticism in preparing this chapter: Erving Goffman, Roy Schafer, Charles E. Rosenberg, Cynthia Secor, Anthony Wallace. Judy Breault, who has just completed a biography of an important and introspective nineteenth-century feminist, Emily Howland, served as a research assistant for this chapter, and her knowledge of nineteenth-century family structure and religious history proved invaluable.

2. The most notable exception to this rule is now eleven years old: William R. Taylor and Christopher Lasch, "Two 'Kindred Spirits': Sorority and Family in New England, 1839–1846," *New England Quarterly* 36 (1963): 25–41. Taylor has made a valuable contribution to the history of women and the history of the family with his concept of "sororial" relations. I do not, however, accept the Taylor-Lasch thesis that female friendships developed in the mid-nineteenth century because of geographic mobility and the breakup of the colonial family. I have found these friendships as frequently in the eighteenth century as in the nineteenth, and would hypothesize that the geographic mobility of the mid-nineteenth century eroded them as it did so many other traditional social institutions. Helen Vendler (Review of *Notable American Women, 1607–1950,* ed. Edward James and Janet James, *New York Times,* November 5, 1972, sec. 7) points out the significance of these friendships.

3. I do not wish to deny the importance of women's relations with particular men. Obviously, women were close to brothers, husbands, fathers, and sons. However, there is evidence that, despite such closeness, relationships between men and women differed in both emotional texture and frequency from those between women. Women's relations with one another, although they played a central role in the American family and American society, have been so seldom examined either by general social historians or by historians of the family that I wish in this essay simply to examine their nature and analyze their implications for our understanding of social relations and social structure. I have discussed some aspects of male-female relationships in two articles: "Puberty to Menopause: The Cycle of Femininity in Nineteenth-Century America," *Feminist Studies* 1 (1973): 58–72, and, with Charles Rosenberg, "The Female Animal: Medical and Biological Views of Woman and Her Role in 19th-Century America," *Journal of American History* LX (1973): 332–56.

4. See Freud's classic paper on homosexuality, "Three Essays on the Theory of Sexuality," in *The Standard Edition of the Complete Psychological Works of Sigmund Freud,* trans. James Strachey (London: Hogarth Press, 1953), 7:135–72. The essays originally appeared in 1905. Professor Roy Schafer, Department of Psychiatry, Yale University, has pointed out that Freud's view of sexual behavior was strongly influenced by nineteenth-century evolutionary thought. Within Freud's schema, genital heterosexuality marked the height of human development (Schafer, "Problems in Freud's Psychology of Women," *Journal of the American Psychoanalytic Association* 22 [1974]: 459–85).

5. For a novel and most important exposition of one theory of behavioral norms and options and its application to the study of human sexuality, see Charles Rosenberg, "Sexuality, Class and Role," *American Quarterly* 25 (1973): 131–53.

6. See, e.g., the letters of Peggy Emlen to Sally Logan, 1768–72, Wells Morris Collection, box 1, Historical Society of Pennsylvania; the Eleanor Parke Custis Lewis Letters, Historical Society of Pennsylvania, Philadelphia.

7. Sarah Butler Wistar was the daughter of Fanny Kemble and Pierce Butler. In 1859 she married a Philadelphia physician, Owen Wistar. The novelist Owen Wistar was her son. Jeannie Field Musgrove was the half-orphaned daughter of constitutional lawyer and New

York Republican politician David Dudley Field. Their correspondence (1855–98) is in the Sarah Butler Wistar Papers, Wistar Family Papers, Historical Society of Pennsylvania.

8. Sarah Butler, Butler Place, S.C., to Jeannie Field, New York, September 14, 1855.

9. See, e.g., Sarah Butler Wistar, Germantown, Pa., to Jeannie Field, New York, September 25, 1862, October 21, 1863; Jeannie Field, New York, to Sarah Butler Wistar, Germantown, July 3, 1861, January 23 and July 12, 1863.

10. Sarah Butler Wistar, Germantown, to Jeannie Field, New York, June 5, 1861; Jeannie Field to Sarah Butler Wistar, November 22, 1861. See also, Sarah Butler Wistar, Germantown, to Jeannie Field, New York, February 29, 1864; Jeannie Field to Sarah Butler Wistar, January 4 and June 14, 1863.

11. Sarah Butler Wistar, London, to Jeannie Field Musgrove, New York, June 18. See also August 3, 1870.

12. See, e.g., two of Sarah's letters to Jeannie: December 21, 1873, July 16, 1878.

13. This is the 1868–1920 correspondence between Mary Hallock Foote and Helena DeKay Gilder, a New York friend (the Mary Hallock Foote Papers are in the Manuscript Division, Stanford University). Wallace E. Stegner has written a fictionalized biography of Mary Hallock Foote (*Angle of Repose* [Garden City, N.Y.: Doubleday & Co., 1971]). See, as well, her autobiography: Mary Hallock Foote, *A Victorian Gentlewoman in the Far West: The Reminiscences of Mary Hallock Foote,* ed. Rodman W. Paul (San Marino, Calif.: Huntington Library, 1972). In many ways these letters are typical of those that women wrote to other women. Women frequently began letters to each other with salutations such as "Dearest," "My Most Beloved," "You Darling Girl," and signed them "tenderly" or "to my dear dear sweet friend, good-bye." Without the least self-consciousness, one woman in her frequent letters to a female friend referred to her husband as "my other love." She was by no means unique. See, e.g., Annie to Charlena Van Vleck Anderson, Appleton, Wis., June 10, 1871, Anderson Family Papers, Manuscript Division, Stanford University; Maggie to Emily Howland, Philadelphia, July 12, 1851, Howland Family Papers, Phoebe King Collection, Friends Historical Library, Swarthmore College; Mary Jane Bur-

leigh to Emily Howland, Sherwood, N.Y., March 27, 1872, Howland Family Papers, Sophia Smith Collection, Smith College; Mary Black Couper to Sophia Madeleine DuPont, Wilmington, Del., n.d. [1834] (two letters), Samuel Francis DuPont Papers, Eleutherian Mills Foundation, Wilmington, Del.; Phoebe Middleton, Concordville, Pa., to Martha Jefferis, Chester County, Pa., February 22, 1848; and see in general the correspondence (1838–49) between Rebecca Biddle of Philadelphia and Martha Jefferis, Chester County, Pa., Jefferis Family Correspondence, Chester County Historical Society, West Chester, Pa.; Phoebe Bradford Diary, June 7 and July 13, 1832, Historical Society of Pennsylvania; Sarah Alden Ripley to Abba Allyn, Boston, n.d. [1818–20], and Sarah Alden Ripley to Sophia Bradford, November 30, 1854, in the Sarah Alden Ripley Correspondence, Schlesinger Library, Radcliffe College; Fanny Canby Ferris to Anne Biddle, Philadelphia, October 11 and November 19, 1811, December 26, 1813, Fanny Canby to Mary Canby, May 27, 1801, Mary R. Garrigues to Mary Canby, five letters, n.d. [1802–8], Anne Biddle to Mary Canby, two letters n.d., May 16, July 13, and November 24, 1806, June 14, 1807, June 5, 1808, Anne Sterling Biddle Family Papers, Friends Historical Society, Swarthmore College; Harriet Manigault Wilcox Diary, August 7, 1814, Historical Society of Pennsylvania. See as well the correspondence between Harriet Manigault Wilcox's mother, Mrs. Gabrielle Manigault, Philadelphia, and Mrs. Henry Middleton, Charleston, S.C., between 1810 and 1830, Cadwalader Collection, J. Francis Fisher Section, Historical Society of Pennsylvania. The basis and nature of such friendships can be seen in the comments of Sarah Alden Ripley to her sister-in-law and long-time friend, Sophia Bradford: "Hearing that you are not well reminds me of what it would be to lose your loving society. We have kept step together through a long piece of road in the weary journey of life. We have loved the same beings and wept together over their graves" (Mrs. O. J. Wistar and Miss Agnes Irwin, eds., *Worthy Women of Our First Century* [Philadelphia: J. B. Lippincott & Co., 1877], p. 195).

14. Mary Hallock [Foote] to Helena, n.d. [1869–70], n.d. [1871–72], folder 1, Mary Hallock Foote Letters, Manuscript Division, Stanford University.

15. Mary Hallock [Foote] to Helena, September 15 and 23, 1873, n.d. [October 1873], October 12, 1873.

16. Mary Hallock [Foote] to Helena, n.d. [January 1874], n.d. [Spring 1874].

17. Mary Hallock [Foote] to Helena, September 23, 1873; Mary Hallock [Foote] to Richard Gilder, December 13, 1873. Throughout the rest of their lives, Molly's letters are filled with tender and intimate references, as when she wrote, twenty years later and from two thousand miles away: "It isn't because you are good that I love you—but for the essence of you which is like perfume" (n.d. [1890s?]).

18. I am in the midst of a larger study of adult gender roles and gender-role socialization in America, 1785–1895. For a discussion of social attitudes toward appropriate male and female roles, see Barbara Welter, "The Cult of True Womanhood: 1800–1860," *American Quarterly* 18 (Summer 1966): 151–74; Ann Firor Scott, *The Southern Lady: From Pedestal to Politics, 1830–1930* (Chicago: University of Chicago Press, 1970), chaps. 1, 2; Smith-Rosenberg and Rosenberg, "The Female Animal."

19. See, e.g., the letters of Peggy Emlen to Sally Logan, 1768–72; the Eleanor Parke Custis Lewis Letters.

20. See especially Elizabeth Botts, *Family and Social Network* (London: Tavistock Publications, 1957); Michael Young and Peter Willmott, *Family and Kinship in East London,* rev. ed. (Baltimore: Penguin Books, 1964).

21. This pattern seemed to cross class barriers. A letter that an Irish domestic wrote in the 1830s contains seventeen separate references to women but only seven to men, most of whom were relatives and two of whom were infant brothers living with her mother and mentioned in relation to her mother (Ann McGrann, Philadelphia, to Sophie M. DuPont, Philadelphia, July 3, 1834, Sophie Madeleine DuPont Letters, Eleutherian Mills Foundation).

22. Harriet Manigault Diary, June 28, 1814, and passim; Jeannie Field, New York, to Sarah Butler Wistar, Germantown, April 19, 1863; Phoebe Bradford Diary, January 30, February 19, March 4, August 11, and October 14, 1832, Historical Society of Pennsylvania; Sophie M. DuPont, Brandywine, to Henry DuPont, Germantown, July 9, 1827, Eleutherian Mills Foundation.

23. Martha Jefferis to Anne Jefferis Sheppard, July 9, 1843; Anne Jefferis Sheppard to Martha Jefferis, June 28, 1846; Anne Sterling Biddle Papers, passim; Eleanor Parke Custis Lewis, Virginia, to Elizabeth Bordley Gibson, Philadelphia, November 24 and December 4, 1820, November 6, 1821.

24. Phoebe Bradford Diary, January 13, November 16–19, 1832, April 26 and May 7, 1833; Abigail Brackett Lyman to Mrs. Catling, Litchfield, Conn., May 3, 1801, collection in private hands; Martha Jefferis to Anne Jefferis Sheppard, August 28, 1845.

25. Lisa Mitchell Diary, 1860s, passim, Manuscript Division, Tulane University; see also Eleanor Parke Custis Lewis to Elizabeth Bordley [Gibson], February 5, 1822; Jeannie McCall, Cedar Park, to Peter McCall, Philadelphia, June 30, 1849, McCall Section, Cadwalader Collection, Historical Society of Pennsylvania.

26. Peggy Emlen to Sally Logan, May 3, 1769.

27. For prime examples of this type of letter, see Eleanor Parke Custis Lewis to Elizabeth Bordley Gibson, passim; Fanny Canby to Mary Canby, Philadelphia, May 27, 1801; Sophie M. DuPont, Brandywine, to Henry DuPont, Germantown, February 4, 1832.

28. Place of residence is not the only variable significant in characterizing family structure. Strong emotional ties and frequent visiting and correspondence can unite families that do not live under one roof. Demographic studies based on household structure alone fail to reflect such emotional and even economic ties between families.

29. Eleanor Parke Custis Lewis to Elizabeth Bordley Gibson, April 20 and September 25, 1848.

30. Maria Inskeep to Fanny Hampton Correspondence, 1823–60, Inskeep Collection, Tulane University Library.

31. Eunice Callender, Boston, to Sarah Ripley [Stearns], September 24 and October 29, 1803, February 16, 1805, April 29 and October 9, 1806, May 26, 1810.

32. Sophie DuPont filled her letters to her younger brother Henry (with whom she had been assigned to correspond while he was at boarding school) with accounts of family visiting (see, e.g., December 13, 1827, January 10 and March 9, 1828, February 4 and March 10, 1832; also Sophie M. DuPont to Victorine Du-

Pont Bauday, September 26 and December 4, 1827, February 22, 1828; Sophie M. DuPont, Brandywine, to Clementina B. Smith, Philadelphia, January 15, 1830; Eleuthera DuPont, Brandywine, to Victorine DuPont Bauday, Philadelphia, April 17, 1821, October 20, 1826; Evelina DuPont [Biderman] to Victorine Du-Pont Bauday, October 18, 1816). Other examples, from the Historical Society of Pennsylvania, are Harriet Manigault [Wilcox] Diary, August 17, September 8, October 19 and 22, December 22, 1814; Jane Zook, West Town School, Chester County, Pa., to Mary Zook, November 13, December 7 and 11, 1870, February 26, 1871; Eleanor Parke Custis [Lewis] to Elizabeth Bordley [Gibson], March 30, 1796, February 7 and March 20, 1798; Jeannie McCall to Peter McCall, Philadelphia, November 12, 1847; Mary B. Ashew Diary, July 11 and 13, August 17, summer and October 1858; and, from a private collection, Edith Jefferis to Anne Jefferis Sheppard, November 1841, April 5, 1842; Abigail Brackett Lyman, Northampton, Mass., to Mrs. Catling, Litchfield, Conn., May 13, 1801; Abigail Brackett Lyman, Northampton, to Mary Lord, August 11, 1800. Mary Hallock Foote vacationed with her sister, her sister's children, her aunt, and a female cousin in the summer of 1874; cousins frequently visited the Hallock farm in Milton, N.Y. In later years Molly and her sister Bessie set up a joint household in Boise, Idaho (Mary Hallock Foote to Helena, July [1874?] and passim). Jeannie Field, after initially disliking her sister-in-law, Laura, became very close to her, calling her "my little sister" and at times spending virtually every day with her (Jeannie Field [Musgrove], New York, to Sarah Butler Wistar, Germantown, March 1, 8, and 15, and May 9, 1863).

33. Martha Jefferis to Anne Jefferis Sheppard, January 12, 1845; Phoebe Middleton to Martha Jefferis, February 22, 1848. A number of other women remained close to sisters and sisters-in-law across a long lifetime (Phoebe Bradford Diary, June 7, 1832, and Sarah Alden Ripley to Sophia Bradford, cited in Wistar and Irwin, *Worthy Women*, p. 195).

34. Rebecca Biddle to Martha Jefferis, 1838–49, passim; Martha Jefferis to Anne Jefferis Sheppard, July 6, 1846; Anne Jefferis Sheppard to Rachel Jefferis, January 16, 1865; Sarah Foulke Farquhar [Emlen] Diary, September

22, 1813, Friends Historical Library, Swarthmore College; Mary Garrigues to Mary Canby [Biddle], 1802–8, passim; Anne Biddle to Mary Canby [Biddle], May 16, July 13, and November 24, 1806, June 14, 1807, June 5, 1808.

35. Sarah Alden Ripley to Abba Allyn, n.d.

36. Phoebe Bradford Diary, July 13, 1832.

37. Mary Hallock [Foote] to Helena DeKay Gilder, December 23 [1868 or 1869]; Phoebe Bradford Diary, December 8, 1832; Martha Jefferis and Anne Jefferis Sheppard letters, passim.

38. Martha Jefferis to Anne Jefferis Sheppard, August 3, 1849; Sarah Ripley [Stearns] Diary, November 12, 1808, January 8, 1811. An interesting note of hostility or rivalry is present in Sarah Ripley's diary entry. Sarah evidently deeply resented the husband's rapid remarriage.

39. Martha Jefferis to Edith Jefferis, March 15, 1841; Mary Hallock Foote to Helena, n.d. [1874–75?]; see also Jeannie Field, New York, to Sarah Butler Wistar, Germantown, May 5, 1863; Emily Howland Diary, December 1879, Howland Family Papers.

40. Anne Jefferis Sheppard to Martha Jefferis, September 29, 1841.

41. Frances Parke Lewis to Elizabeth Bordley Gibson, April 29, 1821.

42. Mary Jane Burleigh, Mount Pleasant, S.C., to Emily Howland, Sherwood, N.Y., March 27, 1872; Emily Howland Diary, September 16, 1879, January 21 and 23, 1880; Mary Black Couper, New Castle, Del., to Sophie M. DuPont, Brandywine, April 7, 1834.

43. Harriet Manigault Diary, August 15, 21, and 23, 1814, Historical Society of Pennsylvania; Polly [Simmons] to Sophie Madeleine DuPont, February 1822; Sophie Madeleine DuPont to Victorine Bauday, December 4, 1827; Sophie Madeleine DuPont to Clementina Beach Smith, July 24, 1828, August 19, 1829; Clementina Beach Smith to Sophie Madeleine DuPont, April 29, 1831; Mary Black Couper to Sophie Madeleine DuPont, December 24, 1828, July 21, 1834. This pattern appears to have crossed class lines. When a former Sunday-school student of Sophie DuPont's (and the daughter of a worker in her father's factory) wrote to Sophie, she discussed her mother's health and activities quite naturally (Ann McGrann to Sophie Madeleine DuPont, August 25, 1832; see also Elizabeth Bordley to Martha, n.d. [1797]; Eleanor Parke Custis

[Lewis] to Elizabeth Bordley [Gibson], May 13, 1796, July 1, 1798; Peggy Emlen to Sally Logan, January 8, 1786. All but the Emlen/Logan letters are in the Eleanor Parke Custis Lewis Correspondence, Historical Society of Pennsylvania).

44. Mrs. L. L. Dalton, "Autobiography," Circle Valley, Utah, 1876, pp. 21–22, Bancroft Library, University of California, Berkeley; Sarah Foulke Emlen Diary, April 1809; Louisa G. Van Vleck, Appleton, Wis., to Charlena Van Vleck Anderson, Göttingen, n.d. [1875], Anderson Family Papers; Harriet Manigault Diary, August 16, 1814, July 14, 1815; Sarah Alden Ripley to Sophy Thayer [early 1860s], quoted in Wistar and Irwin, *Worthy Women*, p. 212. The Jefferis family papers are filled with empathetic letters between Martha and her daughters, Anne and Edith. See, e.g., Martha Jefferis to Edith Jefferis, December 26, 1836, March 11, 1837, March 15, 1841; Anne Jefferis Sheppard to Martha Jefferis, March 17, 1841, January 17, 1847; Martha Jefferis to Anne Jefferis Sheppard, April 17, 1848, April 30, 1849. A representative letter is this of March 9, 1837, from Edith to Martha: "My heart can fully respond to the language of my own precious Mother, that absence has not diminished our affection for each other, but has, if possible, strengthened the bonds that have united us together & I have had to remark how we had been permitted to mingle in sweet fellowship and have been strengthened to bear one another's burdens. . . ."

45. Abigail Brackett Lyman, Boston, to Mrs. Abigail Brackett (daughter to mother), n.d. [1797], June 3, 1800; Sarah Alden Ripley wrote weekly to her daughter Sophy Ripley Fisher after the latter's marriage (Sarah Alden Ripley Correspondence, passim); Phoebe Bradford Diary, February 25, 1833, passim, 1832–33; Louisa G. Van Vleck to Charlena Van Vleck Anderson, December 15, 1873, July 4, August 15 and 29, September 19, and November 9, 1875. Eleanor Parke Custis Lewis's long correspondence with Elizabeth Bordley Gibson contains evidence of her anxiety at leaving her foster mother's home at various times during her adolescence and at her marriage, and her own longing for her daughters, both of whom had married and moved to Louisiana (Eleanor Parke Custis [Lewis] to Elizabeth Bordley [Gibson], October 13, 1795, November 4, 1799,

passim, 1820s and 1830s). Anne Jefferis Sheppard experienced a great deal of anxiety on moving two days' journey from her mother at the time of her marriage. This loneliness and sense of isolation persisted through her marriage until, finally a widow, she returned to live with her mother (Anne Jefferis Sheppard to Martha Jefferis, April 1841, October 16, 1842, April 2, May 22, and October 12, 1844, September 3, 1845, January 17, 1847, May 16, June 3, and October 31, 1849; Anne Jefferis Sheppard to Susanna Lightfoot, March 23, 1845, and to Joshua Jefferis, May 14, 1854). Daughters evidently frequently slept with their mothers—into adulthood (Harriet Manigault [Wilcox] Diary, February 19, 1815; Eleanor Parke Custis Lewis to Elizabeth Bordley Gibson, October 10, 1832). Daughters also frequently asked mothers to live with them and professed delight when they did so. See, e.g., Sarah Alden Ripley's comments to George Simmons, October 6, 1844, in Wistar and Irwin, *Worthy Women*, p. 185: "It is no longer 'Mother and Charles came out one day and returned the next,' for mother is one of us: she has entered the penetratice [*sic*], been initiated into the mystery of the household gods, . . . Her divertissement is to mend the stockings . . . whiten sheets and napkins, . . . and take a stroll at evening with me to talk of our children, to compare our experiences, what we have learned and what we have suffered, and, last of all, to complete with pears and melons the cheerful circle about the solar lamp. . . ." We did find a few exceptions to this mother-daughter felicity (M. B. Ashew Diary, November 19, 1857, April 10 and May 17, 1858). Sarah Foulke Emlen was at first very hostile to her stepmother (Sarah Foulke Emlen Diary, August 9, 1807), but they later developed a warm, supportive relationship.

46. Sarah Alden Ripley to Sophy Thayer, n.d. [1861].

47. Mary Hallock Foote to Helena [winter 1873] (no. 52); Jossie, Stevens Point, Wis., to Charlena Van Vleck [Anderson], Appleton, Wis., October 24, 1870; Pollie Chandler, Green Bay, Wis., to Charlena Van Vleck [Anderson], Appleton, Wis., n.d. [1870]; Eleuthera DuPont to Sophie DuPont, September 5, 1829; Sophie DuPont to Eleuthera DuPont, December 1827; Sophie DuPont to Victorine Bauday, December 4, 1827; Mary Gilpin to Sophie DuPont,

September 26, 1827; Sarah Ripley Stearns Diary, April 2, 1809; Jeannie McCall to Peter McCall, October 27 [late 1840s]. Eleanor Parke Custis Lewis's correspondence with Elizabeth Bordley Gibson describes such an apprenticeship system over two generations—that of her childhood and that of her daughters. Indeed, Eleanor Lewis's own apprenticeship was quite formal. She was deliberately separated from her foster mother so that she could spend a winter of domesticity with her married sisters and her remarried mother. It was clearly felt that her foster mother's (Martha Washington) home at the nation's capital was not an appropriate place to develop domestic talents (October 13, 1795, March 30, May 13, and [summer] 1796, March 18 and April 27, 1797, October 1827).

48. Education was not limited to the daughters of the well-to-do. Sarah Foulke Emlen, the daughter of an Ohio Valley frontier farmer, for instance, attended day school for several years during the early 1800s. Sarah Ripley Stearns, the daughter of a shopkeeper in Greenfield, Massachusetts, attended a boarding school for but three months, yet the experience seemed very important to her. Mrs. S. S. Dalton, a Mormon woman from Utah, attended a series of poor country schools and greatly valued her opportunity, though she also expressed a great deal of guilt for the sacrifices her mother accepted to make her education possible (Sarah Foulke Emlen Journal, Sarah Ripley Stearns Diary, Mrs. S. S. Dalton, "Autobiography").

49. Maria Revere to her mother [Mrs. Paul Revere], June 13, 1801, Paul Revere Papers, Massachusetts Historical Society. In a letter to Elizabeth Bordley Gibson, March 28, 1847, Eleanor Parke Custis Lewis from Virginia discussed the anxiety her daughter felt when her granddaughters left home to go to boarding school. Eleuthera DuPont was very homesick when away at school in Philadelphia in the early 1820s (Eleuthera DuPont, Philadelphia, to Victorine Bauday, Wilmington, Del., April 7, 1821; Eleuthera DuPont to Sophie Madeleine DuPont, Wilmington, Del., February and April 3, 1821).

50. Elizabeth Bordley Gibson, a Philadelphia matron, played such a role for the daughters and nieces of her lifelong friend, Eleanor Parke Custis Lewis, a Virginia planter's wife (Eleanor Parke Custis Lewis to Elizabeth

Bordley Gibson, January 29, 1833, March 19, 1826, and passim through the collection). The wife of Thomas Gurney Smith played a similar role for Sophie and Eleuthera DuPont (see, e.g., Eleuthera DuPont to Sophie Madeleine DuPont, May 22, 1825; Rest Cope to Philema P. Swayne [niece], West Town School, Chester County, Pa., April 8, 1829, Friends Historical Library, Swarthmore College). For a view of such a social pattern over three generations, see the letters and diaries of three generations of Manigault women in Philadelphia: Mrs. Gabrielle Manigault, her daughter, Harriet Manigault Wilcox, and granddaughter, Charlotte Wilcox McCall. Unfortunately, the papers of the three women are not in one family collection (Mrs. Henry Middleton, Charleston, S.C., to Mrs. Gabrielle Manigault, n.d. [mid-1800s]; Harriet Manigault Diary, vol. 1; December 1, 1813, June 28, 1814; Charlotte Wilcox McCall Diary, vol. 1, 1842, passim; all in Historical Society of Philadelphia).

51. Frances Parke Lewis, Woodlawn, Va., to Elizabeth Bordley Gibson, Philadelphia, April 11, 1821, Lewis Correspondence; Eleuthera DuPont, Philadelphia, to Victorine DuPont Bauday, Brandywine, December 8, 1821, January 31, 1822; Eleuthera DuPont, Brandywine, to Margaretta Lammont [DuPont], Philadelphia, May 1823.

52. Sarah Ripley Stearns Diary, March 9 and 25, 1810; Peggy Emlen to Sally Logan, March and July 4, 1769; Harriet Manigault [Wilcox] Diary, vol. 1, December 1, 1813, June 28 and September 18, 1814, August 10, 1815; Charlotte Wilcox McCall Diary, 1842, passim; Fanny Canby to Mary Canby, May 27, 1801, March 17, 1804; Deborah Cope, West Town School, to Rest Cope, Philadelphia, July 9, 1828, Chester County Historical Society, West Chester, Pa.; Anne Zook, West Town School, to Mary Zook, Philadelphia, January 30, 1866, Chester County Historical Society, West Chester, Pa.; Mary Gilpin to Sophie Madeleine DuPont, February 25, 1829; Eleanor Parke Custis [Lewis] to Elizabeth Bordley [Gibson], April 27, July 2, and September 8, 1797, June 30, 1799, December 29, 1820; Frances Parke Lewis to Elizabeth Bordley Gibson, December 20, 1820.

53. Anne Jefferis Sheppard to Martha Jefferis, March 17, 1841.

54. Peggy Emlen to Sally Logan, Mount

Vernon, Va., March 1769; Eleanor Parke Custis [Lewis] to Elizabeth Bordley [Gibson], Philadelphia, April 27, 1797, June 30, 1799; Jeannie Field, New York, to Sarah Butler Wistar, Germantown, July 3, 1861, January 16, 1863; Harriet Manigault Diary, August 3 and 11–13, 1814; Eunice Callender, Boston, to Sarah Ripley [Stearns], Greenfield, May 4, 1809. I found one exception to this inhibition of female hostility toward other women: the diary of Charlotte Wilcox McCall, Philadelphia (see, e.g., her March 23, 1842, entry).

55. Sophie M. DuPont and Eleuthera DuPont, Brandywine, to Victorine DuPont Bauday, Philadelphia, January 25, 1832.

56. Sarah Ripley [Stearns] Diary and Harriet Manigault Diary, passim.

57. Sophie Madeleine DuPont to Eleuthera DuPont, December 1827; Clementina Beach Smith to Sophie Madeleine DuPont, December 26, 1828; Sarah Foulke Emlen Diary, July 21, 1808, March 30, 1809; Annie Hethroe, Ellington, Wis., to Charlena Van Vleck [Anderson], Appleton, Wis., April 23, 1865; Frances Parke Lewis, Woodlawn, Va., to Elizabeth Bordley [Gibson], Philadelphia, December 20, 1820; Fanny Ferris to Debby Ferris, West Town School, Chester County, Pa., May 29, 1826. An excellent example of the warmth of women's comments about one another and the reserved nature of their references to men is seen in two entries in Sarah Ripley Stearns's diary. On January 8, 1811, she commented about a young woman friend: "The amiable Mrs. White of Princeton . . . one of the loveliest most interesting creatures I ever knew, young fair and blooming . . . beloved by everyone . . . formed to please & to charm . . ." She referred to the man she ultimately married always as "my friend" or "a friend" (February 2 or April 23, 1810).

58. Jeannie Field, New York, to Sarah Butler Wistar, Germantown, April 6, 1862.

59. Elizabeth Bordley Gibson, introductory statement to the Eleanor Parke Custis Lewis Letters [1850s], Historical Society of Pennsylvania.

60. Sarah Foulke [Emlen] Diary, March 30, 1809.

61. Harriet Manigault Diary, May 26, 1815.

62. Sarah Ripley [Stearns] Diary, May 17 and October 2, 1812; Eleanor Parke Custis Lewis to Elizabeth Bordley Gibson, April 23,

1826; see also, Rebecca Ralston, Philadelphia, to Victorine DuPont [Bauday], Brandywine, September 27, 1813.

63. Anne Jefferis to Martha Jefferis, November 22 and 27, 1840, January 13 and March 17, 1841; Edith Jefferis, Greenwich, N.J., to Anne Jefferis, Philadelphia, January 31, February 6 and February 1841.

64. Edith Jefferis to Anne Jefferis, January 31, 1841.

65. Eleanor Parke Custis Lewis to Elizabeth Bordley, November 4, 1799. Eleanor and her daughter Parke experienced similar sorrow and anxiety when Parke married and moved to Cincinnati (Eleanor Parke Custis Lewis to Elizabeth Bordley Gibson, April 23, 1826). Helena DeKay visited Mary Hallock the month before her marriage; Mary Hallock was an attendant at the wedding; Helena again visited Molly about three weeks after her marriage; and then Molly went with Helena and spent a week with Helena and Richard in their new apartment (Mary Hallock [Foote] to Helena DeKay Gilder [Spring 1874] [no. 61], May 10, 1874 [May 1874], June 14, 1874, [Summer 1874]). See also Anne Biddle, Philadelphia, to Clement Biddle (brother), Wilmington, March 12 and May 27, 1827; Eunice Callender, Boston, to Sarah Ripley [Stearns], Greenfield, Mass., August 3, 1807, January 26, 1808; Victorine DuPont Bauday, Philadelphia, to Evelina DuPont [Biderman], Brandywine, November 25 and 26, December 1, 1813; Peggy Emlen to Sally Logan, n.d. [1769–70?]; Jeannie Field, New York, to Sarah Butler Wistar, Germantown, July 3, 1861.

66. Mary Hallock to Helena DeKay Gilder [1876] (no. 81); n.d. (no. 83), March 3, 1884; Mary B. Ashew Diary, vol. 2, September-January 1860; Louisa Van Vleck to Charlena Van Vleck Anderson, n.d. [1875]; Sophie DuPont to Henry DuPont, July 24, 1827; Benjamin Ferris to William Canby, February 13, 1805; Benjamin Ferris to Mary Canby Biddle, December 20, 1825; Anne Jefferis Sheppard to Martha Jefferis, September 15, 1884; Martha Jefferis to Anne Jefferis Sheppard, July 4, 1843, May 5, 1844, May 3, 1847, July 17, 1849; Jeannie McCall to Peter McCall, November 26, 1847, n.d. [late 1840s]. A graphic description of the ritual surrounding a first birth is found in Abigail Lyman's letter to her husband, Erastus Lyman, October 18, 1810.

67. Fanny Ferris to Anne Biddle, November 19, 1811; Eleanor Parke Custis Lewis to Elizabeth Bordley Gibson, November 4, 1799, April 27, 1827; Martha Jefferis to Anne Jefferis Sheppard, January 31, 1843, April 4, 1844; Martha Jefferis to Phoebe Sharpless Middleton, June 4, 1846; Anne Jefferis Sheppard to Martha Jefferis, August 20, 1843, February 12, 1844; Maria Inskeep, New Orleans, to Mrs. Fanny G. Hampton, Bridgeton, N.J., September 22, 1848; Benjamin Ferris to Mary Canby, February 14, 1805; Fanny Ferris to Mary Canby [Biddle], December 2, 1816.

68. Eleanor Parke Custis Lewis to Elizabeth Bordley Gibson, October-November 1820, passim.

69. Emily Howland to Hannah, September 30, 1866; Emily Howland Diary, February 8, 11, and 27, 1880; Phoebe Bradford Diary, April 12 and 13, and August 4, 1833; Eunice Callender, Boston, to Sarah Ripley [Stearns], Greenwich, Mass., September 11, 1802, August 26, 1810; Mrs. H. Middleton, Charleston, to Mrs. Gabrielle Manigault, Philadelphia, n.d. [mid-1800s]; Mrs. H. C. Paul to Mrs. Jeannie McCall, Philadelphia, n.d. [1840s]: Sarah Butler Wistar, Germantown, to Jeannie Field [Musgrove], New York, April 22, 1864; Jeannie Field [Musgrove] to Sarah Butler Wistar, August 25, 1861, July 6, 1862; S. B. Randolph to Elizabeth Bordley [Gibson], n.d. [1790s]. For an example of similar letters between men, see Henry Wright to Peter McCall, December 10, 1852; Charles McCall to Peter McCall, January 4, 1860, March 22, 1864; R. Mercer to Peter McCall, November 29, 1872.

70. Mary Black [Couper] to Sophie Madeleine DuPont, February 1827, [November 1, 1834], November 12, 1834, two letters, n.d. [late November 1834]; Eliza Schlatter to Sophie Madeleine DuPont, November 2, 1834.

71. For a few of the references to death rituals in the Jefferis papers, see Martha Jefferis to Anne Jefferis Sheppard, September 28, 1843, August 21 and September 25, 1844, January 11, 1846, summer 1848, passim; Anne Jefferis Sheppard to Martha Jefferis, August 20, 1843; Anne Jefferis Sheppard to Rachel Jefferis, March 17, 1863, February 9, 1868. For other Quaker families, see Rachel Biddle to Anne Biddle, July 23, 1854; Sarah Foulke Farquhar [Emlen] Diary, April 30, 1811, February 14, 1812; Fanny Ferris to Mary Canby, August 31, 1810. This is not to argue that men and women did not mourn together. Yet in many families women aided and comforted women, and men, men. The same-sex death ritual was one emotional option available to nineteenth-century Americans.

72. Sarah Foulke [Emlen] Diary, December 29, 1808.

73. Eunice Callender, Boston, to Sarah Ripley [Stearns], Greenfield, Mass., May 24, 1803.

74. Katherine Johnstone Brinley [Wharton] Journal, April 26, May 29, and May 30, 1856, Historical Society of Pennsylvania.

75. A series of fourteen letters written by Peggy Emlen to Sally Logan (1768-71) has been preserved in the Wells Morris Collection, box 1, Historical Society of Pennsylvania (see especially May 3 and July 4, 1769, January 8, 1768).

76. The Sarah Alden Ripley Collection, the Schlesinger Library, Radcliffe College, contains a number of Sarah Alden Ripley's letters to Mary Emerson. Most of these are undated, but they extend over a number of years and contain letters written both before and after Sarah's marriage. The eulogistic biographical sketch appeared in Wistar and Irwin, *Worthy Women*. It should be noted that Sarah Butler Wistar was one of the editors who sensitively selected Sarah's letters.

77. See Sarah Alden Ripley to Mary Emerson, November 19, 1823. Sarah Alden Ripley routinely, and, one must assume, ritualistically, read Mary Emerson's letters to her infant daughter, Mary. Eleanor Parke Custis Lewis reported doing the same with Elizabeth Bordley Gibson's letters, passim. Eunice Callender, Boston, to Sarah Ripley [Stearns], October 19, 1808.

78. Mary Black Couper to Sophie M. DuPont, March 5, 1832. The Clementina Smith–Sophie DuPont correspondence of 1,678 letters is in the Sophie DuPont Correspondence. The quotation is from Eliza Schlatter, Mount Holly, N.J., to Sophie DuPont, Brandywine, August 24, 1834. I am indebted to Anthony Wallace for informing me about this collection.

79. Mary Grew, Providence, R.I., to Isabel Howland, Sherwood, N.Y., April 27, 1892, Howland Correspondence, Sophia Smith Collection, Smith College.

80. Helena Deutsch, *Psychology of Women* (New York: Grune & Stratton, 1944), vol. 1,

chaps. 1–3; Clara Thompson, *On Women,* ed. Maurice Green (New York: New American Library, 1971).

. . .

BOURGEOIS DISCOURSE AND THE AGE OF JACKSON

1. Philip Greven, *Four Generations: Population, Land and Family in Colonial Andover, Massachusetts* (Ithaca, N.Y.: Cornell University Press, 1970), is the most cited study of a family-based, kin-enmeshed, and static New England village. See, as well, John Waters, "The Traditional World of the New England Peasants: A View from Seventeenth-Century Barnstable," *New England Historical and Genealogical Register*; Michael Zuckerman, *The Peaceable Kingdom: Massachusetts Towns in the Eighteenth Century* (New York: Alfred A. Knopf, 1970); Susan Hirsch, *The Roots of the American Working Class: The Industrialization of Crafts in Newark, 1800–1860* (Philadelphia: University of Pennsylvania Press, 1978), chap. 1; Sam Bass Warner, *Private City: Philadelphia in Three Periods of Its Growth* (Philadelphia: University of Pennsylvania Press, 1968), sect. I.

2. For a particularly interesting presentation of this thesis, see Roland Berthoff, *An Unsettled People: Social Order and Disorder in American History* (New York: Harper and Row, 1971), pp. 177–234.

3. James Henretta, *The Evolution of American Society, 1700–1815* (Lexington, Mass.: Heath, 1973); Charles S. Grant, *Democracy in the Connecticut Frontier Town of Kent* (New York: W. W. Norton & Co., 1972); Jackson Turner Main, *The Social Structure of Revolutionary America* (Princeton, N.J.: Princeton University Press, 1965). John K. Alexander, "The City of Brotherly Fear: The Poor in Late Eighteenth Century Philadelphia," in *Cities in America,* ed. Kenneth T. Jackson and Stanley K. Schultz (New York: Alfred A. Knopf, 1972), pp. 13–35; Diane Lindstrom, *Economic Development in the Philadelphia Region, 1810–1850* (New York: Columbia University Press, 1978); Anthony J. Wallace, *Rockdale* (New York: Alfred A. Knopf, 1978).

4. Lindstrom, *Economic Development,* pp. 100–19, see as well chap. 5; Herbert M. Cummings, "Pennsylvania: Network of a Canal Port," *Pennsylvania History* XXI (1954): 160–73; George Rogers Taylor, *The Transportation Revolution 1815–1860* (New York: Holt, Rinehart and Winston, 1951), and "American Economic Growth Before 1840: An Explanatory Essay," in Ralph Andreano, ed., *New Views on American Economic Development* (New York: Schenkman, 1965), pp. 379–98; Stuart Bruchey, *The Roots of American Economic Growth, 1607–1861* (New York: Harper and Row, 1965).

5. Robert G. Albion, *The Rise of the Port of New York,* reprint ed. (Hampden, Conn.: Archon Books, 1961); Taylor, *Transportation Revolution,* pp. 32–37; Whitney R. Cross, *The Burned-over District* (Ithaca, N.Y.: Cornell University Press, 1950), chaps. 4, 5; W. Freeman Galpen, *Central New York: An Island Empire* (New York: Lewis Historical Publishing Company, 1941); Paul Johnson, *Shopkeepers' Millennium: Society and Revivals in Rochester, New York, 1815–1837* (New York: Hill and Wang, 1879), chap. 1; Mary Ryan, *Cradle of the Middle Class* (Cambridge: Cambridge University Press, 1981), chap. 1.

6. Kenneth Lockridge, "Land, Population and the Evolution of New England Society, 1630–1790," *Past and Present* XXXIX (1968): 62–80; James Henretta, "The Morphology of New England Society," *Journal of Interdisciplinary History* II (1971–72): 379–98; Grant, *Democracy in the Frontier Town,* pp. 97–103; Robert Gross, *The Minute Men and Their World* (New York: Hill and Wang, 1976), chaps. 6, 7; Kenneth Lockridge, *A New England Town: The First Hundred Years and Dedham* (New York: W. W. Norton, 1970), sect. II.

7. David Allmendinger, *Paupers and Scholars* (New York: St. Martin's Press, 1975), chap. 1; Berthoff, *An Unsettled People,* chap. 10.

8. James Henretta, "Famines and Farms: Mentalité in Pre-industrial America," *William & Mary Quarterly* XXXV, third series (1978): 3–32; Paul W. Gates, *The Farmer's Age: Agriculture 1815–1860* (New York: Holt, Rinehart and Winston, 1960), chap. 2.

9. For a discussion of the flow of young people along the Erie Canal, see Ryan, *Cradle,* chap. 2, and Johnson, *Shopkeepers' Millennium,* chap. 1.

10. Allan S. Horlick, *Country Boys and Merchant Princes* (Louisburg, Pa.: Bucknell University Press, 1975).

11. Robert Wells, "Women's Lives Trans-

formed: Demographic and Family Patterns in America, 1600–1970," in *Women of America,* ed. Mary Beth Norton and Carol Berkin (Boston: Houghton Mifflin, 1976).

12. Kathryn Kish Sklar, "The Founding of Mount Holyoke College," in *Women of America,* ed. Norton and Berkin, pp. 177–201; Nancy Cott, *The Bonds of Womanhood: "Woman's Sphere" in New England, 1780–1835* (New Haven: Yale University Press, 1977), pp. 30–35. For a dated but encyclopedic study of women and education see Thomas Woody, *The History of Women's Education,* 2 vols. (New York and Lancaster, Pa.: The Science Press, 1929).

13. Thomas Dublin, *Women at Work: The Transformation of Work and Community in Lowell, Massachusetts, 1826–1860* (New York: Columbia University Press, 1981); Cott, *Bonds of Womanhood,* pp. 36–40.

14. Women domestics and seamstresses constituted an economically insecure and frequently destitute segment of the urban work force of pre–Civil War America. They came primarily from rural Protestant backgrounds. Not infrequently they swelled the ranks of America's urban prostitutes. For some contemporary descriptions of the "class" of women, see New York Magdalen Society, *First Annual Report of the New York Magdalen Society, Instituted January 1, 1830* (New York, 1831); John R. McDowall, *Magdalen Facts* (New York, 1832). Johnson, in *Shopkeepers' Millennium* (p. 39), refers to women employed in Rochester's shoe industry doing piecework, sewing uppers and lowers together.

15. For descriptions of the position of the servant in the preindustrial family, see Edmund Morgan, *The Puritan Family, Religion and Domestic Relations in Seventeenth Century New England* (Westport, Conn.: Greenwood Press, 1980). Elizabeth Drinker commented at length on her attitude toward a young woman who, while a servant in her home, became pregnant and bore an illegitimate child. Drinker cared for the servant during her pregnancy, assisted in the childbirth, and took responsibility for raising the child afterward. At the same time, she permitted herself some highly judgmental comments concerning the mother's parents and the father of the child. See this portion of the Drinker diary reproduced in Cecil Drinker, *Not So Very Long Ago: A Chronicle of Medicine and Doctors in Colonial Philadelphia* (New

York: Oxford University Press, 1937). The Elizabeth Drinker Diary consists of 40 volumes, and is at the Historical Society of Pennsylvania.

16. For the beginning of this trend, see Douglas Lamar Jones, "Poverty and Vagabondage: The Process of Servitude in 18th Century Massachusetts," paper presented at the Organization of American Historians Convention, April 1979. Dismissal of servants who had been seduced had become a common event (and, from women's point of view, a problem) by the 1830s, according to the American Female Moral Reform Society's *Advocate of Moral Reform,* passim. See "Beauty, the Beast, and the Militant Woman: A Case Study in Sex Roles and Social Stress in Jacksonian America," in this volume. The movement of immigrant Catholic women into domestic service in the 1850s further strained mistress-servant ties.

17. For a contemporary description of these practices, see Mathew Carey, *A Plea for the Poor: An Enquiry How Far the Charges Against Them of Improvidence, Idleness and Dissipation Are Founded in Truth, by a Citizen of Philadelphia* (Philadelphia, 1831). For secondary sources, see Jesse Eliphalet Pope, *The Clothing Industry in New York,* University of Missouri Studies I (Columbia: University of Missouri Press, 1903); Egal Feldman, *Fit for Men: A Study of New York's Clothing Trade* (Washington, D.C.: Public Affairs Press, 1960); Robert Ernst, *Immigrant Life in New York City, 1825–63* (New York: King's Crown Press, 1949).

18. Hirsch, *Roots of the American Working Class,* chap. 1.

19. Ibid., chaps. 2–5; Bruce Laurie, *Working People in Philadelphia* (Philadelphia: Temple University Press, 1980).

20. Hirsch, *Roots of the American Working Class,* chap. 4, especially pp. 55–76.

21. Ibid., chaps. 3 and 4. For a discussion of the family wage economy, see Stephen Thernstrom, *Progress and Poverty: Social Mobility in a Nineteenth-Century City* (Cambridge, Mass.: Harvard University Press, 1965). Chapters 1 and 2 of Louise Tilly and Joan Scott, *Women, Work and the Family* (New York: Holt, Rinehart & Winston, 1978), place the family wage economy in the overall framework of women's relation to the wage economy. See also Bernard Farbes, *Guardian of Virtue: Salem Families in 1800* (New York: Basic Books, 1972).

22. Hirsch, *Roots of the American Working Class*, chaps. 3 and 4.

23. Johnson, *Shopkeepers' Millennium*, chap. 2; Ryan, *Cradle*, chap. 4, especially pp. 145–46; Horlick, *Country Boys*, introduction, chaps. 1, 2; Stuart Blumin, "Residential Mobility Within the 19th Century City," ed. Stephen Thernstrom and Peter Knight, and "Mobility and Change in Ante-Bellum Philadelphia," in *Nineteenth Century Cities*, ed. Stephen Thernstrom and Richard Sennett (New Haven: Yale University Press, 1969); Warner, *Private City*, chaps. 3 and 4. Contemporaries commented dolefully upon these changes: Philip Hone, *The Diary of Philip Hone, 1828–1851*, 2 vols. in 1, ed. Allan Nevins (New York: Ayer Co., 1970; reprint of 1927 ed.).

24. For the classic description of the Cult of True Womanhood see Barbara Welter, "The Cult of True Womanhood: 1800–1860," *American Quarterly* 18 (Summer 1966). For discussions of women's philanthropic activism, see Carroll Smith-Rosenberg, *Religion and the Rise of the American City* (Ithaca, N.Y.: Cornell University Press, 1971), chaps. 3, 4, 5, 7; Ryan, "The Power of Female Networks: A Case Study of Female Moral Reform in Antebellum America," *Feminist Studies* V (Spring 1979), and *Cradle*, chaps. 3–5; Barbara Berg, *The Remembered Gate: Origin of American Feminism* (New York: Oxford University Press, 1978); Blanche Glassman Hersch, *The Slavery of Sex: Feminist Abolitionists in America* (Urbana: University of Illinois Press, 1978), chaps. 1, 5; Eleanor Flexner, *Century of Struggle* (Cambridge, Mass.: Harvard University Press, 1959), chaps. 2, 3, 4.

25. George Templeton Strong, *The Diary of George Templeton Strong*, ed. Allan Nevins and Milton Halsey Thomas, 4 vols. (New York: Macmillan, 1952); John Pintard, *Letters from John Pintard to His Daughter, Eliza Noel Pintard Davidson, 1816–1833*, ed. Dorothy C. Barck, 4 vols. (New York: New York Historical Society, 1940).

26. Blumin, "Residential Mobility"; Michael Katz, Michael J. Doucet, and Mark J. Stern, *The Social Organization of Early Industrial Capitalism* (Cambridge, Mass.: Harvard University Press, 1982); Edward Pressen, *Riches, Class and Power Before the Civil War* (New York: Heath, 1973).

27. Smith-Rosenberg, *Religion*; Ryan, *Cradle*, chaps. 3, 5; Johnson, *Shopkeepers' Millennium*, chap. 4; Bruce Laurie, "Fire Companies and Gangs in Southwark: the 1840s," ed. Allen F. Davis and Mark H. Haller, *The Peoples of Philadelphia* (Philadelphia: Temple University Press, 1973).

28. Johnson, in *Shopkeepers' Millennium* (pp. 59–61, 79–83), discusses the functions that participation in the early temperance movement served new members of the male bourgeoisie: a reaffirmation of their social status, a bond across new class divides. Chapter 6 discusses later bourgeois efforts to use religious institutions to create a sense of order and cohesion in a fragmenting world.

29. See Welter, "Cult of True Womanhood."

30. See, especially, Louis J. Kern, *An Ordered Love* (Chapel Hill: University of North Carolina Press, 1981), and "The Cross and the Pedestal: Women, Anti-Ritualism, and the Emergence of the American Bourgeoisie," in this volume.

31. Arthur Eugene Bestor, Jr., *Backwoods Utopias: The Sectarian and Owenite Phases of Communitarian Socialism in America, 1663–1829* (Philadelphia: University of Pennsylvania Press, 1950).

32. Carroll Smith-Rosenberg, "Sex as Symbol in Victorian Purity: An Ethnohistorical Analysis of Jacksonian America," *American Journal of Sociology* LXXXIV Supplement (1978): 212–47; see also "Davy Crockett as Trickster: Pornography, Liminality, and Symbolic Inversion in Victorian America," in this volume.

33. See, for example, Kathryn Kish Sklar, *Catherine Beecher: A Study in American Domesticity* (New Haven: Yale University Press, 1973); Ryan, "Power of Female Networks"; Hersch, *Slavery of Sex*, chap. 5.

34. Smith-Rosenberg, *Religion*, chaps. 3 and 4; Berg, *The Remembered Gate*.

35. See "Beauty, the Beast, and the Militant Woman: A Case Study in Sex Roles and Social Stress in Jacksonian America," in this volume.

. . .

DAVY CROCKETT AS TRICKSTER

1. This article was supported by a Rockefeller Foundation Humanities Fellowship. I am especially indebted to Catherine Albanese for first calling the mythic and symbolic significance of Davy Crockett to my attention.

2. My perspective has been informed by symbolic anthropology's contention that the physical body frequently serves as a symbol for the body politic. See especially Mary Douglas, *Natural Symbols: Explorations in Cosmology* (New York: Pantheon Books, 1970), and *Purity and Danger: An Analysis of Concepts of Pollution and Taboo* (New York: Routledge & Kegan Paul, 1966); Victor Turner, *Ritual Process* (Chicago: Aldine Pub. Co., 1969). For another example of my use of these theories, see Carroll Smith-Rosenberg, "Sex as Symbol in Victorian Purity: An Ethnohistorical Analysis of Jacksonian America," *American Journal of Sociology*, LXXXIV Supplement (1978): 212–47.

3. Michel Foucault presents this argument most persuasively in *The History of Sexuality*, vol. I, *An Introduction* (New York, 1978). Jacques Donzelots, *The Policing of Families* (New York: Pantheon Books, 1979), incorporates a similar argument. As this essay indicates, I feel it is important to take Foucault's argument much further. We must recognize and account for the diversity of sexual attitudes during the nineteenth century: the bitterness of the century's sexual debates, the antistructural, at times almost whimsical character of some forms of nineteenth-century sexual experimentation. We must follow through Foucault's admonition that we carefully distinguish author and audience far more rigorously than he himself has done thus far. In the United States, at least, there was a great diversity among sexual discussants, and consequently in their imagery and concerns. The sexual discourse, with its at times stridently conflicting voices, serves as a mirror for conflicting responses to social change. It provides the historian with a window, albeit deliberately distorted, into the emotional experience of change. For an earlier but quite influential interpretation of Victorian sexual repression, see Peter Cominos, "Late Victorian Sexual Repression and the Social System," *International Review of Social History* VIII (1963): 18–48, 216–50.

4. Sylvester Graham, William Alcott, and O. S. Fowler were probably the most widely read and influential of the male moral reformers. Examples of their books include William Alcott, *The Young Man's Guide* (Boston, 1833), and *Physiology of Marriage* (Boston, 1866); O. S. Fowler, *Love and Parentage* (New York, 1844), and *Amativeness* (New York, 1856); Sylvester Graham, *Lecture to Young Men on*

Chastity (Boston, 1834). For an analysis of this group see Smith-Rosenberg, "Sex as Symbol." Significantly, during the same years that the male moral reform movement flourished, from the 1830s to the 1860s, a female moral reform movement quite distinct in membership and goals burgeoned as well. The women were concerned with the double standard, prostitution, the seduction of farm girls and domestics in a rapidly industrializing world. They sought ways to curtail male autonomy and male power within the bourgeois family. They constitute a third voice in this sexual dialogue.

5. *Davy Crockett's Almanac 1835–1841* (Nashville, Tenn., 1835–41). There seems to be some dispute over whether the almanacs after 1838, although bearing a Nashville imprint, were published in Tennessee, or whether they were actually published in New York City.

6. *Crockett's Yaller Flower Almanac for '36* (New York, 1835).

7. David Crockett, *An Account of Col. Crockett's Tour to the North and Down East . . .* (Philadelphia, 1835); Richard Penn Smith, *Col. Crockett's Exploits and Adventures in Texas . . .* (Philadelphia, 1836); David Crockett, *A Narrative of the Life of David Crockett* (Philadelphia, 1834). For a scholarly history of the almanac in the United States, see Milton Drake, *Almanacs of the United States* (New York, 1962). For a modern reproduction of the Nashville, Tennessee, Davy Crockett series with an interpretive introduction and discussion of the publishing history of the Crockett almanacs, see Franklin J. Meine, *The Crockett Almanacs Nashville Series, 1835–1838*, ed. with an intro. by Franklin J. Meine, and with a note on their humor by Harry J. Owens (Chicago, 1955).

8. Meine, "Introduction," especially p. v.

9. The content of the Crockett comic almanacs, all published in the major Eastern cities after the early Nashville series, contrasts sharply with farmers' almanacs actually published in the West. I surveyed farmers' almanacs published in both the Southwest and the Northwest from the 1810s through the 1850s, none of which is comic. They either address practical agricultural problems (e.g., Kellogg & Co.'s *Alabama Almanac, 1839* [Mobile, 1839]; or R. Goudy, Jr., *The Illinois Farmer's Almanac and Repository of Useful Knowledge for the Year 1840* [Jacksonville, Ill., and St. Louis, 1839]); the needs and interests of farm women (e.g., *The Housewife's Almanac, or*

the Young Wife's Oracle for 1840! [New York, 1840]); or were political, religious, or reforming in nature (e.g., *The Christian Almanac for the Western Reserve, Ohio, 1837* [Cleveland, 1836]; *Applegates Whig Almanac for 1835* [New York, 1835]; or *The American Anti-Slavery Almanac for 1840* [New York, 1839]). Private publishers in the major Eastern seaports and in a few Midwestern *entrepôts* such as Cincinnati published comic almanacs, cheap comiclike pamphlets, humorous, somewhat scatological, and racist. These publications attacked the educated religious reformers, women, and the elderly. They were antiblack and anti-immigrant. They violated virtually all Victorian proprieties. It is within this tradition that the Crockett almanacs belong. Why did the comic publishers invert the drama and values of the male moral reformers? Unfortunately we know little about the actual authors and publishers of the Crockett almanacs. Did they also have their roots sunk deeply in a Calvinist New England and Greater New England heritage? Were they new men from the South or from rural mid-Atlantic areas relatively free from Puritan influences? Or were they longtime urban dwellers, amused at the experiences of rural newcomers to the cosmopolitan world? I cannot answer these questions. I suspect that the answers would tell us a great deal.

10. *Davy Crockett's Almanac for 1835* (Nashville, 1835).

11. Ibid., pp. 4, 3–8. The theme of tyrannical father and assertive, autonomous son in righteous flight into an unstructured world is repeated in the original story of Davy Crockett's alter ego, Ben Harding, who hates his apprenticeship, flees a tyrannical master, and escapes to a region as unordered as the forest— the sea. *Davy Crockett's Almanac 1836* (Nashville, 1836), p. 13, and *Davy Crockett's Almanac for 1840* (Nashville, 1840), pp. 18–19.

12. *Davy Crockett's Almanac 1835*, pp. 6–8.

13. *Davy Crockett's Almanac 1845* (Boston, 1844), n. p.

14. See, for example, ibid., n. p.; *Davy Crockett's Almanac 1850*; three separate volumes were published in 1850, in New York City, Boston, and Philadelphia, all of which mention daughters. *Davy Crockett's Almanac 1835*, p. 18, does mention the existence of a son, who has no name and who does not take any role in the story.

15. R. G. A. Levinge, *Echoes from the Back-woods* (London, 1849), II: 11–13; *Davy Crockett's Almanac 1835*, p. 3.

16. *Davy Crockett's Almanac 1837*, p. 19.

17. *Davy Crockett's Almanac 1838* (Nashville, 1837), n. p.

18. *Davy Crockett's Almanac 1835*, pp. 27, 12–38; *Davy Crockett's Almanac 1836*, pp. 22, 30, 46–47. All the Crockett almanacs are filled with stories of violent fights between Westerners and the mythic animals of the forest.

19. *Davy Crockett's Almanac 1836*, p. 39; *Davy Crockett's Almanac 1847* (Boston, New York, and Philadelphia, 1846), n. p.; *Crockett's Almanac 1850* (New York, 1850), n. p.; *Crockett's Yaller Flower Almanac '36* (New York, 1835), pp. 9, 19–20.

20. *Davy Crockett's Almanac 1837*, p. 19.

21. *Davy Crockett's Almanac 1845* (Boston, 1845), n. p.

22. *Davy Crockett's Almanac 1836*, p. 39.

23. *Crockett Awl-man-ax 1839* (New York, 1839), p. 21.

24. *Crockett Almanac 1846* (Boston, 1846), n. p.

25. *Crockett Almanac 1849* (Boston, 1849), n. p.

26. Douglas, *Purity and Danger*, p. 94.

27. Turner, *Ritual Process*, pp. 125, 108–30.

28. *Davy Crockett's Almanac 1835*, p. 3.

29. Roland Barthes, "Myth Today," in *Mythologies*, sel. and trans. Annette Lavers (New York: Hill and Wang, 1972), especially pp. 142–43.

30. Mary Douglas, "The Social Control of Cognition: Some Factors in Joke Perception," *Man* III (1968): 361–76, especially pp. 364, 368–69.

31. Ibid., p. 371.

32. See, for example, *Davy Crockett's Almanac 1836* (Nashville, 1836), pp. 7–8, 18, 37, 43–44; *Davy Crockett's Almanac for 1837* (Nashville, 1837), p. 17; *Davy Crockett's Almanac for 1838* (Nashville, 1838), pp. 141, 146–48; *Davy Crockett's Almanac for 1839* (Nashville, 1839), p. 19; *Davy Crockett's Almanac 1845* (Boston, 1845), n. p.

33. *Davy Crockett's Almanac 1836*, pp. 28–201.

34. Ibid., p. 49.

35. *Davy Crockett's Almanac 1836*, p. 16; *Crockett Almanac 1846*, n. p.

36. See, for example, *Davy Crockett's Almanac 1835*, p. 8; *Davy Crockett's Almanac 1836*, p. 12; *Davy Crockett Almanac 1839*, pp. 21, 28, 32;

Davy Crockett's 1847 Almanac (New York, 1847), n. p.; *Crockett Almanac 1850,* n. p.

37. *Davy Crockett Almanac 1839,* p. 14.

38. *Davy Crockett's Almanac 1835,* p. 21.

39. *Davy Crockett's Almanac 1844* (New York, 1844), n. p.

40. *Davy Crockett's Almanac 1845* (Boston, 1845), n. p.

41. *The Crockett Almanac 1846,* n. p.

42. *Davy Crockett's Almanac 1836,* p. 32.

43. Allusions to themes of buggery, *vagina dentata* exhibition, and male homosexuality occur in virtually every Crockett almanac. These frequently take the form of bizarre illustrations: the face of a baby seen within a reptile's open mouth framed by a circle of teeth. In another illustration Crockett leans against Ben Harding, both wear ecstatic grins, both have their legs spread. From between Harding's legs come two rays of lightning that pass between Crockett's legs. Crockett holds an upturned bottle with liquid flowing down between his legs, and over the rays of lightning in the background is a tall ship's smokestack with smoke billowing out. There is an exaggeratedly long knife in Crockett's belt directly over his genitals (*Crockett's Almanac 1846,* n. p.; *Elton's Comic All-My-Nack 1847* [New York, 1847], cover). For *vagina dentata* theme see *Davy Crockett's Almanac 1836,* p. 16; *Crockett's Almanac 1846,* n. p.; *Crockett Almanac 1849,* n. p.

44. Douglas, "The Social Control of Cognition," p. 365.

45. Ibid., p. 372.

46. Barthes's analysis of the significance and function of myth for the bourgeoisie is particularly suggestive for understanding one of the functions of the Crockett myth (*Mythologies,* pp. 131–48).

. . .

BEAUTY, THE BEAST, AND THE MILITANT WOMAN

1. "Minutes of the Meeting of the Ladies' Society for the Observance of the Seventh Commandment Held in Chatham Street Chapel, May 12, 1834," and "Constitution of the New York Female Moral Reform Society," both in ledger book entitled "Constitution and Minutes of the New York Female Moral Reform Society, May 1834 to July 1839," deposited in the archives of the American Female Guardian Society (hereinafter referred to as AFGS),

Woodycrest Avenue, Bronx, New York. (The Society possesses the executive committee minutes from May 1835 to June 1847, and from January 7, 1852, to February 18, 1852.) For a more detailed institutional history of the Society, see Carroll Smith-Rosenberg, *Religion and the Rise of the American City* (Ithaca, N.Y.: Cornell University Press, 1971), chaps. 4, 7. The New York Female Moral Reform Society changed its name to American Female Guardian Society in 1849. The Society continues today, helping children from broken homes. Its present name is Woodycrest Youth Service.

2. John R. McDowall, *Magdalen Report,* reprinted *McDowall's Journal* 2 (May 1834): 33–38. For the history of the New York Magdalen Society see *First Annual Report of the Executive Committee of the New York Magdalen Society, Instituted January 1, 1830.* See also Rosenberg, *Religion,* chap. 4.

3. Flora L. Northrup, *The Record of a Century* (New York: American Female Guardian Society, 1934), pp. 13–14; cf. *McDowall's Defence* 1, no. 1 (July 1836): 3; *The Trial of the Reverend John Robert McDowall by the Third Presbytery of New York in February, March, and April, 1836* (New York, 1836); [Thomas Hastings, Sr.], *Missionary Labors Through a Series of Years among Fallen Women by the New York Magdalen Society* (New York: New York Magdalen Society, 1870), p. 15.

4. Northrup, *Record of a Century,* pp. 14–15; only two volumes of *McDowall's Journal* were published, covering the period January 1833 to December 1834. Between the demise of the New York Magdalen Society and the organization of the New York Female Moral Reform Society (hereafter, NYFMRS), McDowall was connected, as agent, with a third society, the New York Female Benevolent Society, which he had helped found in February 1833. For a more detailed account see Carroll S. Rosenberg, "Evangelicalism and the New City," Ph.D. dissertation, Columbia University, 1968, chap. 5.

5. *McDowall's Journal* 2 (January 1834): 6–7.

6. "Minutes of the Meeting of the Ladies' Society . . . May 12, 1834," and "Preamble," in "Constitution of the New York Female Moral Reform Society."

7. *The Advocate of Moral Reform* (hereafter, *Advocate*) 1 (January–February 1835): 6. The *Advocate* was the Society's official journal.

8. Close ties connected the NYFMRS with

the Finney wing of American Protestantism. Finney's wife was the Society's first president. The Society's second president, Mrs. William Green, was the wife of one of Finney's closest supporters. The Society's clerical support in New York City came from Finney's disciples. Their chief financial advisers and initial sponsors were Arthur and Lewis Tappan, New York merchants who were also Charles Finney's chief financial supporters. For a list of early "male advisers" to the NYFMRS see Joshua Leavitt, *Memoir and Select Remains of the Late Reverend John R. McDowall* (New York: Joshua Leavitt, Lord, 1838), p. 248, also pp. 99, 151, 192. See as well L. Nelson Nichols and Allen Knight Chalmers, *History of the Broadway Tabernacle of New York City* (New Haven: Tuttle, Morehouse & Taylor, 1940), pp. 49–67; William G. McLoughlin, Jr., *Modern Revivalism* (New York: Ronald Press, 1959), pp. 50–53.

9. For an excellent modern analysis of Finney's theology and his place in American Protestantism, see McLoughlin, *Modern Revivalism.* McLoughlin has also edited Finney's series of New York revivals, which were first published in 1835: Charles Grandison Finney, *Lectures on Revivals of Religion,* ed. William G. McLoughlin (Cambridge, Mass.: Harvard University Press, 1960). McLoughlin's introduction is excellent.

10. Smith-Rosenberg, *Religion,* chaps. 2 and 3.

11. These reforms were by no means mutually exclusive. Indeed, there was a logical and emotional interrelation between evangelical Protestantism and its missionary aspects and such formally secular reforms as peace, abolition, and temperance. The interrelation is demonstrated in the lives of such reformers as the Tappan brothers, the Grimké sisters, Theodore Dwight Weld, and Charles Finney, and in the overlapping membership of the many religious and "secular" reform societies of the Jacksonian period. On the other hand, the overlap was not absolute, some reformers rejecting evangelical Protestantism, others pietism or another of the period's reforms.

12. *Advocate* 1 (January–February 1835): 4; Northrup, *Record,* p. 19.

13. *Advocate* 1 (March 1835): 11–12; 1 (November 1835): 86; NYFMRS, "Executive Committee Minutes, June 6, 1835 and April 30, 1836." These pious visitors received their most

polite receptions at the more expensive houses, whereas the girls and customers of lower-class, slum brothels met them almost uniformly with curses and threats.

14. NYFMRS, "Executive Committee Minutes, Jan. 24, 1835."

15. *Advocate* 1 (January–February 1835): 7.

16. For a description of one such incident see *Advocate* 4 (January 15, 1838): 15.

17. *Advocate* 1 (September 1, 1835): 72; Northrup, *Record,* p. 19.

18. *Advocate* 1 (March 1835): 11; NYFMRS, "Executive Committee Minutes, Apr. 5, 1836, May 30, 1835."

19. NYFMRS, "Executive Committee Minutes, Oct. 4, 1836."

20. NYFMRS, "Executive Committee Minutes, June 6 and June 25, 1835, June [n.d.], 1836"; NYFMRS, *The Guardian or Fourth Annual Report of the New York Female Moral Reform Society Presented May 9, 1838* (New York: pp. 4–6).

21. "Budding," "lovely," "fresh," "joyous," "unsuspecting lamb" were frequent terms used to describe innocent women before their seduction. *The Advocate* contained innumerable letters and editorials on this theme. See, for example, *Advocate* 4 (January 1, 1838): 1; *Advocate* 10 (March 1, 1844): 34; *Advocate and Guardian* [the Society changed the name of its journal in 1847] 16 (January 1, 1850): 3.

22. Letter in *Advocate* 1 (April 1835): 19.

23. "Murderer of Virtue" was another favorite and pithy phrase. For a sample of such references see *Advocate* 4 (February 1, 1838): 17; *Advocate* 10 (January 1, 1844): 19–20; *Advocate* 10 (January 15, 1844): 29; *Advocate* 10 (March 1, 1844): 33.

24. *Advocate* 1 (January–February 1835): 3; *Advocate* 1 (April 1835): 19; *Advocate and Guardian* 16 (January 1, 1850): 3.

25. Letter in *McDowall's Journal* 2 (April 1834): 26–27.

26. Many subscribers wrote to *The Advocate* complaining of the injustice of the double standard. See, for example, *Advocate* 1 (April 1835): 22; *Advocate* 1 (December 1835): 91; *Advocate and Guardian* 16 (January 1, 1850): 5.

27. *Advocate* 1 (January–February 1835): 6–7.

28. Resolution passed at the Quarterly Meeting of the NYFMRS, January 1838, printed in *Advocate* 4 (January 15, 1838): 14.

29. This was one of the more important functions of the auxiliaries, and their members

uniformly pledged themselves to ostracize all offending males. For an example of such pledges see *Advocate* 4 (January 15, 1838): 16.

30. *Advocate and Guardian* 16 (January 1, 1850): 3.

31. McDowall urged his rural subscribers to report any instances of seduction. He dutifully printed all the details, referring to the accused man by initials but giving the names of towns, counties, and dates. Male response was on occasion bitter.

32. *Advocate* 1 (January-February 1835): 2.

33. Throughout the 1830s virtually every issue of *The Advocate* contained such letters. *The Advocate* continued to publish them throughout the 1840s.

34. For detailed discussions of particular employment agencies and the decision to print their names, see NYFMRS, "Executive Committee Minutes, Feb. 12, 1845, July 8, 1846."

35. NYFMRS, "Executive Committee Minutes, Mar. 1, 1838, Mar. 15, 1838"; *Advocate* 4 (January 15, 1838): 15.

36. The Society appears to have begun its lobbying crusade in 1838. NYFMRS, "Executive Committee Minutes, Oct. 24, 1838, Jan. 4, 1842, Feb. 18, 1842, Apr. 25, 1844, Jan. 8, 1845"; American Female Moral Reform Society (the Society adopted this name in 1839), *Tenth Annual Report for . . . 1844*, pp. 9–11; American Female Moral Reform Society, *Fourteenth Annual Report for . . . 1848*.

37. The NYFMRS's executive-committee minutes for the years 1837, 1838, 1843, and 1844 especially are filled with instances of the committee's instituting suits against seducers for damages in the case of loss of services.

38. *Advocate* 1 (January-February 1835): 6–7; 4 (January 1, 1838): 1.

39. *Advocate* 10 (February 1, 1844): 17–18: *Advocate and Guardian* 16 (January 1, 1850): 3–4.

40. *Advocate* 10 (January 1, 1844): 7–8.

41. *Advocate* 2 (January 1836): 3; *Advocate* 4 (January 15, 1838): 13.

42. *Advocate* 4 (January 1, 1838): 1–2; *Advocate* 10 (February 15, 1844): 26; *Advocate and Guardian* 16 (January 15, 1850): 15.

43. *Advocate* 1 (January-February 1835): 5–6.

44. An editorial in *The Advocate* typified the Society's emphasis on the importance of child-rearing and religious education as an exclu-

sively maternal role. "To a mother—You have a child on your knee. . . . It is an immortal being; destined to live forever! . . . And who is to make it happy or miserable? You—the mother! You who gave it birth, the mother of its body, . . . its destiny is placed in your hands" (*Advocate* 10 [January 1, 1844]: 8).

45. NYFMRS, "Executive Committee Minutes, June 25, 1835."

46. NYFMRS, "Executive Committee Minutes, Oct. 4, 1836, and May 22, 1837, and Sept. 11, 1839." Indeed, as early as 1833 a substantial portion of John McDowall's support seemed to come from rural areas. See, for example, *McDowall's Journal* 1 (August 1833): 59–62.

47. NYFMRS, "Executive Committee Minutes, Oct. 4, 1838"; Northrup, *Record,* p. 22.

48. NYFMRS, "Executive Committee Minutes, May 10, 1839"; NYFMRS, "Quarterly Meeting, July, 1839." Power within the new national organization was divided so that the president and the board of managers were members of the NYFMRS, while the vice presidents were chosen from the rural auxiliaries. The annual meeting was held in New York City, the quarterly meetings in one of the towns of Greater New England.

49. Virtually every issue of *The Advocate* is filled with letters and reports from the auxiliaries discussing their many activities.

50. The view that many women held of their role is perhaps captured in the remarks of an editorialist in *The Advocate* in 1850. Motherhood was unquestionably the most correct and important role for women. But it was a very hard role. "In their [mothers'] daily rounds of duty they may move in a retired sphere—secluded from public observation, oppressed with many cares and toils, and sometimes tempted to view their position as being adverse to the highest usefulness. The youthful group around them tax their energies to the utmost limit—the wants of each and all . . . must be watched with sleepless vigilance; improvement is perhaps less marked and rapid than is ardently desired. . . . Patience is tried, faith called into exercise; and all the graces of the Spirit demanded, to maintain equanimity and exhibit a right example. And *such* with all its weight of care and responsibility is the post at which God in his providence has placed the mothers of our

land." The ultimate reward of motherhood which the writer held out to her readers, significantly, was that they would be the ones to shape the character of their children. *Advocate and Guardian* 16 (January 15, 1850): 13.

51. NYFMRS, *Guardian*, p. 8.

52. NYFMRS, "Executive Committee Minutes, Oct. 24, 1836."

53. See two letters, for example, to *The Advocate* from rural subscribers. Although they are written fifteen years apart and from quite different geographic areas (the first from Hartford, Connecticut, the second from Jefferson, Illinois), the sentiments expressed are remarkably similar. Letter in *Advocate* 1 (April 1835): 19; *Advocate and Guardian* 16 (January 15, 1850): 14.

54. Letter in *Advocate* 4 (January 1, 1838): 6.

55. Letters and reports from rural supporters expressing such sentiments dotted every issue of *The Advocate* from its founding until the mid-1850s.

56. The editors of *The Advocate* not infrequently received (and printed) letters in which a rural subscriber would report painfully how some young woman in her family had suffered social censure and ostracism because of the machinations of some lecher—who emerged from the affair with his respectability unblemished. This letter to *The Advocate* was the first opportunity to express the anguish and anger she felt. For one particularly pertinent example, see an anonymous letter in *Advocate* 1 (March 1835): 15–16.

57. NYFMRS, "Executive Committee Minutes, Oct. 4, 1836"; *Advocate* 1 (April 1835): 19–20; *Advocate* 3 (January 15, 1837): 194; *Advocate* 4 (January 1, 1838): 5, 7–8; *Advocate* 4 (April 1838): 6–7. An integral part of this expression of power was the women's insistence that they had the right to investigate male sexual practices and norms. No longer would they permit men to tell them that particular questions were improper for women's consideration. See, for example, NYFMRS, "Circular to the Women of the United States," reprinted in *Advocate* 1 (January–February 1835): 6–7, 4.

58. NYFMRS, "Executive Committee Minutes, June 28, 1837."

59. Letter in *Advocate* 1 (April 1835): 19.

60. *Advocate and Guardian* 16 (January 15, 1850): 9.

61. *Advocate* 1 (May 1835): 38; NYFMRS,

Guardian, pp. 5–6. The Society initially became concerned with the problems of the city's poor and working women as a result of efforts to attack some of the economic causes of prostitution. The Society feared that the low wages paid seamstresses, domestics, or washerwomen (New York's three traditional female occupations) might force otherwise moral women to turn to prostitution. The Society was, for example, among the earliest critics of the low wages and bad working conditions of New York's garment industry.

62. Significantly, the Society's editors and officers placed the responsibility for the low wages paid seamstresses and other female workers on ruthless and exploitative men. Much the same tone of antimale hostility is evident in their economic exposés as in their sexual exposés.

63. NYFMRS, "Executive Committee Minutes, Feb. 20, 1835, Oct. 4 and Oct. 5, 1836"; NYFMRS, *Fifth Annual Report*, p. 5.

64. AFGS, *Eleventh Annual Report*, pp. 5–6. For details of replacing male employees with women and the bitterness of the male reactions, see the NYFMRS executive-committee minutes for early 1843, passim. Nevertheless, even these aggressively feminist women did not feel that women could with propriety chair public meetings, even those of their own Society. In 1838, for instance, when the ladies discovered that men expected to attend their annual meeting, they felt that they had to ask men to chair the meeting and read the women's reports. Their decision was made just after the Grimké sisters had created a storm of controversy by speaking at large mixed gatherings of men and women. Northrup, *Record*, pp. 21–25. For the experiences of the Grimké sisters with this same problem, see Gerda Lerner's excellent biography, *The Grimké Sisters from South Carolina* (Boston: Houghton Mifflin, 1967), chaps. 11–14.

65. NYFMRS, "Executive Committee Minutes, Aug. 3, 1837."

66. NYFMRS, "Executive Committee Minutes, June 2, 1847, Mar. 28, 1849." *The Advocate* regularly reviewed her books, and made a point of reviewing books by women authors in general.

67. *Advocate and Guardian* 16 (January 15, 1850): 10.

68. *Advocate* 4 (February 15, 1838): 28.

69. See Lerner, *The Grimké Sisters.*

70. *Advocate* 4 (January 1, 1838): 3–5.

71. Ibid., p. 5.

72. See, for example, *Advocate* 4 (April 1, 1838): 55; 4 (July 16, 1838): 108.

73. For examples of the glorification of the maternal role, see *Advocate* 10 (March 15, 1844): 47, and *Advocate and Guardian* 16 (January 15, 1850): 13–14.

. . .

THE CROSS AND THE PEDESTAL

1. This essay assumed its present form as a result of an ongoing intellectual exchange and the thoughtful criticisms of a group of scholars who meet regularly to discuss class and gender perspective on the analysis of culture. I am deeply indebted to the suggestions and criticisms of Judith Friedlander, Suzanne Hoover, Myra Jehlen, Esther Newton, Judith Walkowitz, and Daniel Walkowitz. The essay began life as a paper presented to a National Endowment for the Humanities seminar on revolution organized by Sacvan Bercovitch at Columbia University.

2. The phrase "New Men and New Measures" refers to new (and usually young) revival ministers who had not risen to religious prominence through orthodox routes, and to their new revivalistic measures—praying for sinners by name, all-night revival meetings, the "anxious seat." For an overall discussion of the Second Great Awakening revivals, and especially of Charles G. Finney, see William G. McLoughlin, *Modern Revivalism* (New York: Ronald Press, 1959), and *Revivals, Awakenings, and Reforms: An Essay on Religion and Social Change in America, 1607–1977* (Chicago: University of Chicago Press, 1980); T. Scott Miyakawa, *Protestants and Pioneers* (Chicago: University of Chicago Press, 1964); Whitney R. Cross, *The Burned-over District* (Ithaca, N.Y.: Cornell University Press, 1950); Donald G. Matthews, "The Second Great Awakening as an Organizing Progress," *American Quarterly* 21 (1969): 23–43.

3. Mary Ryan, in *Cradle of the Middle Class* (Cambridge: Cambridge University Press, 1981), chap. 2, presents a superb community study of women's participation in revivals, demonstrating this pattern of women's numerical dominance.

4. Cross, *Burned-over District*, chaps. 3, 14, 16, especially pp. 176–78.

5. Ryan, *Cradle*, pp. 71–72; Cross, *Burned-over District*, p. 177.

6. Ryan, *Cradle*, pp. 88–89, 92. McLoughlin, *Revivals, Awakenings, and Reforms,* found that women played a central role in revivals throughout the Second Great Awakening, Southern as well as Northern, rural as well as urban. He sees women's religious intensity as part of women's response to a life that was in many ways harder than that of men. Concerning Southern women, McLoughlin wrote: "Women in particular were drawn to camp meetings, for they bore the heaviest burdens of pain, sickness, sorrow, unremitting labor and old age. For their labors there were few social rewards and no public victories." "Christian fellowship . . ." McLoughlin continues, "offered a different but equally important source of security for men and children. It gave regularity and order to life, it offered a source of strength beyond the self" (pp. 132–33; see also pp. 120–22). Whitney Cross offers a similar explanation in *Burned-over District*, pp. 84–89. Cross described women's revival participation as typically beginning each morning with meetings of the revivalist and "a little band of sisters" whose "agonizing supplication" helped spark the revival. See *Burned-over District*, pp. 176–77.

7. For a discussion of women's route from religious revivals to the inner city, see Carroll Smith-Rosenberg, *Religion and the Rise of the American City* (Ithaca, N.Y.: Cornell University Press, 1971). Evangelist Charles Finney was one of the male religious radicals who encouraged this new role for women. See his comments upon his second New York City revival in 1832, Charles G. Finney, *Memoirs* (New York: AMS Press, 1876), p. 321.

8. Ryan states, "Contrary to all the rhetoric about brotherhood, women dominated the temperance ranks." Ryan found, for instance, that 61 percent of the Oneida County Temperance Society members were women (*Cradle,* pp. 135, 140). See "Beauty, the Beast, and the Militant Woman: A Case Study in Sex Roles and Social Stress in Jacksonian America," in this volume. See also Cross, *Burned-over District,* pp. 215, 237. The early feminists saw temperance as a crucial stage in a woman's coming to a feminist consciousness and in the develop-

ment of her organizational skills. Many early feminists, most notably Susan B. Anthony and Matilda Joslyn Gage, came to feminism from the temperance movement. See Elizabeth Cady Stanton, Susan B. Anthony, and Matilda Joslyn Gage, *History of Women Suffrage* (New York: Arno Press, 1969), vol. I.

9. Blanche Glassman Hersch, *The Slavery of Sex: Feminist Abolitionist Women in America* (Urbana: University of Illinois Press, 1978), passim.

10. For a description of Myrtilla Miner's efforts to establish a school for young black women, see Eleanor Flexner, *Century of Struggle* (Cambridge, Mass.: Harvard University Press, 1959), pp. 38–40, 98–101.

11. William McLoughlin posits a parallel analysis. Conventional evangelical churches provided women with restricted and domestic religious roles. Only in the unstructured and mystical new denominations could women hope to exert power. "Only as a cultic Goddess, as Father-Mother God or as female incarnation of Jesus, could women have significant leadership roles outside the home. . . . [This] occurred in Shakerism, in Christian Science, in Jemima Wilkinson's Society of the Universal Friend, to some extent in Quakerism, and above all in Spiritualism, where female 'mediums' or mediators easily bridged the mystical gap between this world and the next" (McLoughlin, *Revivals, Awakenings, and Reforms*, p. 121).

12. Herbert A. Wiskey, Jr., *Pioneer Prophetess: Jemima Wilkinson, the Public Universal Friend* (Ithaca, N.Y., 1964); Cross, *Burned-over District*, pp. 33–36.

13. Edward Andrews, *The People Called Shakers* (New York: Oxford University Press, 1953); Cross, *Burned-over District*, p. 302. For a discussion of Shaker attitudes toward sex, women, and family structures, see Louis J. Kern, *An Ordered Love* (Chapel Hill: University of North Carolina Press, 1981), pt. II, pp. 71–134.

14. Cross, *Burned-over District*, chap. 14. For ties between Perfectionism and the American Female Moral Reform Society, see Cross, *Burned-over District*, pp. 230–31; Kern, *An Ordered Love*, pt. IV. For studies of the Oneida experiment itself see *The Family, Communes and Utopian Societies*, ed. Sallie TeSelle (New York: Harper & Row, 1972); Maren Lock-

wood Carden, *Oneida: Utopian Community to Modern Corporation* (Baltimore: Johns Hopkins University Press, 1969); Constance Noyes Robertson, *Oneida Community* (Syracuse: Syracuse University Press, 1970).

15. For the latest study of spiritualism, see Ruth Brandon's *The Spiritualists* (New York: Alfred A. Knopf, 1983).

16. Horace Bushnell, *Christian Nurture* (New Haven: Yale University Press, 1967). See also Barbara Cross's brilliant analysis, *Horace Bushnell* (Chicago: University of Chicago Press, 1958).

17. For the pioneer analysis of the Cult of True Womanhood, see Barbara Welter, "The Cult of True Womanhood: 1800–1860," *American Quarterly* 18 (Summer 1966). See as well Mary Ryan's recent study, "The Power of Female Networks: A Case Study of Female Moral Reform in Antebellum America," *Feminist Studies* V (Spring 1979).

18. Gerda Lerner, in *The Grimké Sisters from South Carolina* (Boston: Houghton Mifflin, 1967), discusses standard male opposition to women who violate the gender conventions of Christianity; see especially chaps. 8–12. See also Jill Conway, "Perspectives on the History of Women's Education in the United States," *History of Education Quarterly* IV (Spring 1974): 1–12; Robert S. Fletcher, *A History of Oberlin College from Its Foundation Through the Civil War* (Oberlin: Oberlin College, 1953), 2 vols., especially I: 377 ff. and II: 643 ff.; Robert Fletcher, "The First Coeds," *American Scholar* VII (Winter 1938): 76–86; Ronald Hogland, "Co-education of the Sexes at Oberlin College," *Journal of Social History* VI (Winter 1972–73): 160–76.

19. Cross, *Burned-over District*, pp. 230–31; Ryan, *Cradle*, pp. 83–98; Ryan, "Power of Female Networks."

20. Hersch, *Slavery of Sex*, chaps. 1, 4; see also Elizabeth Cady Stanton, *The Woman's Bible* (New York: Arno Press, 1972).

21. See, for example, Mary Douglas, *Natural Symbols: Explorations in Cosmology* (New York: Vintage Books, 1973), passim, but especially chap. 1 and pp. 27, 40–41, 104.

22. For a highly suggestive article concerning women's religious anti-ritualism and periods of violent political and economic upheaval, see Keith Thomas, "Women and the Civil War Sects," *Past and Present* XIII (1968): 41–62. See

as well Christopher Hill, *The World Turned Upside Down* (New York, 1972); Nancy L. Rolker, "The Appeal of Calvinism to French Noblewomen in the Sixteenth Century," *Journal of Interdisciplinary History* II (1972): 391–418; Lyle Koehler, "The Case of the American Jezebels: Anne Hutchinson and Female Agitation during the Antinomian Turmoil, 1636–40," *William and Mary Quarterly* XXXI, 3rd ser. (1974): 55–78; Mary Maples Dunn, "Saints and Sisters: Congregational and Quaker Women in the Early Colonial Period," *American Quarterly* XXVIII (1976); Barbara Taylor, "Religious Heresy and Feminism in Early English Socialism," in *Tearing the Veil*, ed. Susan Lipshitz (London: Routledge & Kegan Paul, 1978), pp. 120–25.

23. For a discussion of the function of hypotheses in social-science analysis, see William Goode and Paul Hatt, *Methods in Social History* (New York: McGraw-Hill, 1952), chap. 6.

24. Ibid., pp. 62–64. For a discussion of the relation between individual and collective properties in the analysis of groups, see Paul F. Lazarsfeld, "Evidence and Inference in Social Research," in *Readings in the Philosophy of the Social Sciences*, ed. May Brodbeck, pp. 617–24.

25. Ryan, *Cradle*, chaps. 2 and 3; Paul Johnson, *Shopkeepers' Millennium: Society and Revivals in Rochester, New York, 1815–1837* (New York: Hill and Wang, 1879); Cross, *Burned-over District*; Hersch, *The Slavery of Sex*, chap. 4. See also biographical sketches in Edward T. James and Janet James, *Notable American Women, 1607–1950: A Biographical Dictionary* (Cambridge, Mass.: Belknap Press of Harvard University Press, 1971).

26. Two notable exceptions to the statement that students of American religious enthusiasm ignore women are Whitney Cross and Keith Thomas. Otherwise historians have studied either the relation between religious enthusiasm and political revolution (see the recent review article by John M. Murrin, "No Awakening, No Revolution? More Counterfactual Speculations," *Reviews in American History* XI [1983]). For the most recent example of the old social-control analysis see Paul Johnson, *Shopkeepers' Millennium*. Neither group seeks to further its understanding of the interchange between religious and social disorder by exploring differences in the male-female experience—or differences within even the same group of men over time.

27. McLoughlin, *Revivals*.

28. Anthony Wallace, *The Death and Rebirth of the Seneca* (New York: Alfred A. Knopf, 1970); see also Wallace, "Revitalization Movements," *American Anthropology* LVIII (1956): 264–81.

29. McLoughlin, *Revivals*, p. 12.

30. Ibid., pp. 9–23.

31. Ibid. This explanation would go far to explain the career of both Charles G. Finney and Lyman Beecher, often conflicted male leaders of the Second Great Awakening.

32. Ibid., p. 13.

33. Victor Turner is especially concerned with adding movement and action to the traditional structuralist approach of anthropologists. See his *Dramas, Fields and Metaphors* (Ithaca, N.Y.: Cornell University Press, 1974), chaps. 1, 6.

34. Douglas, *Natural Symbols*, pp. 32, 57, and chaps. 12, 16.

35. Ibid., pp. 33, 44, 52, 104, 109–10, 195.

36. Ibid., pp. 34–35, 40, 91, 179–81.

37. Ibid., pp. 40, 114, 182–88.

38. For a highly sophisticated discussion of shifts in theology, see Sidney E. Mead, *Nathaniel W. Taylor* (Chicago: University of Chicago Press, 1942).

39. Ann Douglas, *The Feminization of American Religion* (New York: Alfred A. Knopf, 1977).

40. Miyakawa, *Protestants and Pioneers*; Cross, *Burned-over District*, especially bks. IV, V; William G. McLoughlin, *Modern Revivalism* (New York: Ronald Press, 1959), chaps. 1–3; John L. Thomas, "Romantic Reform in America," *American Quarterly* XVII (1965); David B. Davis, "The Emergence of Immediatism," *Mississippi Valley Historical Review* (1962).

41. Marylynn Salmon, "Equality or Submersion? Female Covert Status in Early Pennsylvania," in *Women of America*, ed. Mary Beth Norton and Carol Berkin (Boston: Houghton Mifflin, 1976); Mary Beth Norton, "The Myth of the Golden Age," in *Women of America*, ed. Norton and Berkin. Linda E. Speth and Alison Duncan Hirsch, "Women, Family, and Community in Colonial America: Two Perspectives," *Women & History* IV (1982), differ somewhat from Salmon's and Norton's positions. See also Philip Greven, *Four Generations: Population, Land and Family in Colonial Andover, Massachusetts* (Ithaca, N.Y.: Cornell

University Press, 1970), passim; Ryan, *Cradle,* chaps. 1, 2.

42. Robert Wells, "Women's Lives Transformed: Demographic and Family Patterns in America, 1600–1970," in *Women of America,* ed. Norton and Berkin.

43. See, for example, Kathryn Kish Sklar, *Catherine Beecher: A Study in Domesticity* (New Haven: Yale University Press, 1973).

44. Susan Hirsch, *The Roots of the American Working Class: The Industrialization of Crafts in Newark, 1800–1860* (Philadelphia: University of Pennsylvania Press, 1978); Thomas Dublin, *Women at Work: The Transformation of Work and Community in Lowell, Massachusetts, 1826–1860* (New York: Columbia University Press, 1981).

45. For this argument see, among others, Edward Pessen, *Jacksonian America: Society, Personality and Politics* (New York: Dorsey Press, 1969); Stuart Blumin, "Residential Mobility within the Nineteenth Century City," *The Peoples of Philadelphia,* ed. Allen F. Davis and Mark H. Haller (Philadelphia: Temple University Press, 1973); Bruce Laurie, *Working People of Philadelphia* (Philadelphia: Temple University Press, 1980). James Henretta, "Economic Development and Social Structure in Colonial Boston," *William and Mary Quarterly* XXII (1965), shows the beginnings of this trend toward increasing economic inequality in the eighteenth century. See Johnson, *Shopkeepers' Millennium,* chap. 2; Allan S. Horlick, *Country Boys and Merchant Princes* (Lewisburg, Pa.: Bucknell University Press, 1975); and David Allmendinger, *Paupers and Scholars* (New York: St. Martin's Press, 1975), for corroborative information about youthful male rootlessness.

46. See, for example, Welter, "Cult of True Womanhood"; Douglas, *The Feminization of American Religion*; or the role Horace Bushnell molded for the Christian mother in *Christian Nurture.* See as well Ryan, *Cradle,* chap. 3, and "Power of Female Networks."

47. Ryan, *Cradle*; Johnson, *Shopkeepers' Millennium.*

48. Ryan, *Cradle,* chap. 2.

49. To their social marginality, young women added a biological factor. A significant number, though far from a majority, of female revival converts were pregnant at the time of their conversion (Ryan, *Cradle,* pp. 82–83); Rosemary Reuther, among others, argued that

revival enthusiasm marked a biological rite of passage, that of first pregnancy and motherhood.

50. Ryan, *Cradle,* p. 80.

51. Ryan, *Cradle,* p. 78. Cross, *Burned-over District,* pp. 239–40, gives similar examples among Methodists in other New York State communities.

52. Ryan, *Cradle,* p. 79.

53. Ibid., pp. 82–83.

54. Victor Turner, *Ritual Process* (Chicago: Aldine Pub. Co., 1969), pp. 44–45.

55. Ibid., pp. 94, 106–11.

56. Ibid., p. 103.

57. Ibid., pp. 100, 102.

58. See, for example, McLoughlin, "Introduction," in Charles Grandison Finney, *Lectures on Revivals of Religion,* ed. McLoughlin (Cambridge, Mass.: Harvard University Press, 1960), pp. xxxvi–xxxviii, and McLoughlin, *Revivals,* pp. 123–27.

59. Finney, *Lectures on Revivals of Religion,* Lecture I and passim.

60. See Johnson, *Shopkeepers' Millennium,* passim, and Burtram Wyatt-Brown, "Partners in Piety: Lewis and Arthur Tappan, Evangelical Abolitionists, 1828–41," unpublished doctoral dissertation, Johns Hopkins University, 1963.

61. Cited by Nancy Hewitt in "An Ethnohistorical Approach to Women's Activism in Rochester, New York, 1820–1860," unpublished paper, presented by History Workshop, Department of History, University of Pennsylvania, March 1980.

62. Turner, *Dramas, Fields and Metaphors,* Preface and chap. 1.

63. Ibid., chaps. 6 and 7.

64. Ibid., chap. 6.

65. Nancy Hewitt, *Women's Activism and Social Change, Rochester, New York, 1822–1872* (Ithaca, N.Y.: Cornell University Press, 1984), chaps. 4 and 5.

66. Laurie, *Philadelphia* pp. 33–52.

. . .

BOURGEOIS DISCOURSE AND THE PROGRESSIVE ERA

1. Robert Wiebe, *The Search for Order, 1877–1920* (New York: Hill and Wang, 1967), p. 4. I have derived my vision of the gradual transference of power and leadership from a small-

town, commercially based bourgeoisie to a new, far more complex bourgeois economic and social structure in large part from Wiebe.

2. Wiebe, *Search for Order*, chap. 1.

3. Paul Johnson, *Shopkeepers' Millennium: Society and Revivals in Rochester, New York* (New York: Hill and Wang, 1879), chaps. 1 and 2, describes this phase as it appears in Rochester. In the 1830s and 1840s, Rochester appeared on the surface to be a wild boom town. Underneath, Rochester's industrial and mercantile elite demonstrated the strong cultural and economic ties they felt to their agrarian hinterland. The farming community they served imposed its values, schedules, and needs upon them. Michael Katz, Michael J. Doucet, and Mark J. Stern, *The Social Organization of Early Industrial Capitalism* (Cambridge, Mass.: Harvard University Press, 1982), found the economy of Buffalo and of Hamilton, Ontario, also closely tied to an agricultural hinterland (pp. 3–4). Wiebe (chaps. 1 and 2) finds this pattern to be characteristic of the commercial *entrepôts* that dotted agrarian America.

4. Wiebe, *Search for Order*, pp. 3–4. See also Mary Ryan, *Cradle of the Middle Class* (Cambridge: Cambridge University Press, 1981), chaps. 3 and 4.

5. Ann Filor Scott, "Jane Addams," in *Notable American Women, 1607–1950: A Biographical Dictionary*, ed. Edward James and Janet James (Cambridge, Mass.: Belknap Press of Harvard University), I: 16–22; Allen Davis, *The American Heroine: The Life and Legend of Jane Addams* (New York: Oxford University Press, 1973). Jane Addams, in her autobiography, *Twenty Years at Hull House* (New York: Macmillan, 1910), lovingly describes the world of Cedarville, Illinois, and her father's devotion to Abraham Lincoln (chaps. 1 and 2). One gets the sense of a simple, timeless, and sure world, a world remarkably unlike the London and Chicago that settlement-house workers such as Addams chose to live in.

6. Katz et al., *Social Organization*, pp. 10–11 and especially chap. 3.

7. Stephen Thernstrom, *Progress and Poverty: Social Mobility in a Nineteenth-Century City* (Cambridge, Mass.: Harvard University Press, 1965), pp. 31 and 84–90; Stephen Thernstrom and Peter R. Knight, "Men in Motion: Some Data and Speculations About Urban Popula-

tion Mobility in Nineteenth-Century America," *Journal of Interdisciplinary History* I (1970); Stephen Thernstrom, *The Other Bostonians: Poverty and Progress in an American Metropolis, 1880–1970* (Cambridge, Mass.: Harvard University Press, 1973).

8. Katz et al., *Social Organization*, pp. 113, 119, and chap. 3.

9. Ibid., p. 29.

10. Ibid., pp. 31–35.

11. Wiebe, *Search for Order*, chap. 1.

12. Ibid., chap. 2; Seymour Mandelbaum, *Boss Tweed's New York* (Westport, Conn.: Greenwood Press, 1982).

13. For the classic literary description of the railroad's destruction of small-town and agrarian America, see Frank Norris, *The Octopus* (Laurel, N.Y.: Lightyear Press, 1976). Many of the rural and agrarian reform movements of the 1870s, 1880s, and 1890s expressed a romantic fear of the dangerous city: the Grange, the early Farmer's Alliance and Populist movement, the Women's Christian Temperance Union (Wiebe, *Search for Order*, chaps. 3, 4).

14. Theodore Dreiser, *Sister Carrie* (Philadelphia: University of Pennsylvania Press, 1981).

15. Katz et al., *Social Organization*, p. 104.

16. Mandelbaum, *Boss Tweed's New York*, passim; Wiebe, *Search for Order*, chap. 2.

17. Wiebe, *Search for Order*, p. 45. For a classic example of the bourgeois fascination with and horror of the alien city, see Jacob A. Riis, *How the Other Half Lives* (New York: Garrett Press, 1970; first published in 1890).

18. Wiebe, *Search for Order*, pp. 12–13.

19. Ibid.

20. Ibid., p. 14.

21. Jane Addams, *Twenty Years at Hull House*, refers to the small-town resentment and fear of the divisive new class structure of the industrial cities (pp. 41–42, 66–71). For other contemporary comments, see Robert A. Woods et al., *The Poor in Great Cities* (New York: Charles Scribner's Sons, 1895), and Charles Loring Brace, *The Dangerous Classes of New York and Twenty Years Among Them* (New York: Wynkoop and Hallenbeck, 1880). See also John Higham, *Strangers in the Land: Patterns of American Nativism* (New Brunswick, N.J.: Rutgers University Press, 1955), chaps. 3, 4; Robert H. Bremner, *From the Depths: The Discovery of Poverty in the United*

States (New York: New York University Press, 1956).

22. Wiebe, *Search for Order,* chap. 5.

23. Mari Jo Buhle, *Women and American Socialism, 1870–1920* (Urbana: University of Illinois, 1981), pp. 49–53.

24. Ibid.

25. Ibid., pp. 53–58.

26. Carroll Wright, *The Working Girls of Boston* (New York: Arno Press, 1969).

27. Buhle, *Women and American Socialism,* pp. 58–60.

28. Mari Jo Buhle, unpublished paper presented at Boston College, Women's Studies Conference, Spring 1983.

29. Eleanor Flexner, *Century of Struggle* (Cambridge, Mass.: Harvard University Press, 1959), chap. XIII. For the perspective of some of the founders of the women's-club movement, see Jennie C. Croly, *History of the Woman's Club Movement in America* (New York: H. G. Allen and Co., 1898), and Frances E. Willard, *Home Protection Manual: Continuing an Argument for the Temperance Ballot for Women* (New York: "The Independent" office, 1879). See also Mary Earhart, *Frances Willard: From Prayer to Politics* (Chicago: University of Chicago Press, 1944); [Women's Press Club of New York City], *Memories of Jane Cunningham Croly, "Jennie June"* (New York: Putnam, 1904).

30. Buhle, *Women and American Socialism*, pp. 57–59.

31. See "The Abortion Movement and the AMA, 1850–1880," in this volume.

32. Henry James, *Daisy Miller* (New York: Harper & Brothers, 1879), and *Portrait of a Lady* (London: Macmillan and Co., 1881).

33. The adolescence of Baltimorean M. Carey Thomas (future president of Bryn Mawr College) offers an excellent example of this pattern. See her journal, *The Making of a Feminist: Early Journals and Letters of M. Carey Thomas*, ed. Marjorie Housepian Dobkin (Kent, Ohio: Kent State University Press, 1979). M. Carey Thomas's youth was by no means unique. See Vida Scudder's remarks in her autobiography, *On Journey* (New York: E. P. Dutton & Co., Inc., 1937), or Mary Kingsbury Simkhovitch, *Neighborhood: My Story of Greenwich House* (New York: W. W. Norton and Co., 1938).

34. Edward James and Janet James, eds., *Notable American Women,* contains highly suggestive biographical sketches of these women.

35. Gertrude Stein's fictional account of M. Carey Thomas in *Fernhurst* is a good example of the "second generation's" criticisms of the "first generation" (*Fernhurst, QED and Other Early Writings* [New York: Liveright, 1971]).

36. Typical of the "first generation" are: Jane Addams, born 1860, graduated from college 1881; Vida Scudder, born 1858; Florence Kelley, born 1859, graduated from college 1882; Lillian Wald, born 1867, graduated from nursing school 1891; Grace Dodge, born 1856; Julia Lathrop, born 1858, graduated from college 1880.

37. Typical of the "second generation" are: Gertrude Stein, born 1874, graduated from college 1897; Willa Cather, born 1873, graduated from college 1895; Crystal Eastman, born 1881, graduated from college 1903; Mary Kingsbury Simkhovitch, born 1867, graduated from college 1890; Isadora Duncan, born 1878, London dancing debut 1900; Natalie Barney, born 1876, first novel published 1900; Margaret Sanger, born 1879, graduated from nursing school 1902.

· · ·

PUBERTY TO MENOPAUSE

1. This is not to say that the question of adolescence and aging in women did not appear in nineteenth-century fiction; quite the contrary. Fictional discussions, however, lack the explicit physiological and sexual detail that characterized medical accounts. There were indeed so many popular nineteenth-century medical guides for women that they may be said to constitute a specific genre; all discussed such issues with varying degrees of explicitness. This article is based on a study of popular women's medical guides and of medical literature written for a professional medical audience: gynecological textbooks, monographs, and journal articles.

2. For an expanded study of this metaphor and its implications for woman's social role see Carroll Smith-Rosenberg and Charles Rosenberg, "The Female Animal: Medical and Biological Views of Women in Nineteenth-

Century America," *Journal of American History* 60 (September 1973), in press.

3. Charles West, *Lectures on the Diseases of Women*, 2 vols. (London: John Churchill, 1861), vol. I, no. I; A. J. C. Skene, *Education and Culture as Related to the Health and Diseases of Women* (Detroit: George S. Davis, 1889), p. 22.

4. John Wiltbank, *Introductory Lecture for the Session, 1853–54* (Philadelphia: Edward Grattan, 1854), p. 7.

5. This changing ideology reflected, of course, more than a simple improvement in medical knowledge. It reflected both a rapid growth in the prestige of science as a reference area in the mid- and late nineteenth century, as well as the growing conflict that centered on women's role. As the traditional role of wife and mother seemed increasingly under attack, the medical and biological defenses of that role increased proportionately. For a general discussion of the role of scientific language and metaphor and the growing emotional relevance of science in dealing with such social problems see Charles E. Rosenberg, "Science and American Social Thought," in *Science and Society in the United States*, eds. David D. Van Tassel and Michael G. Hall (Homewood, Ill.: The Dorsey Press, 1966), pp. 135–62.

6. William Pepper, "The Change of Life in Women," *Clinical News* I (1880): 505; J. H. Kellogg, *Ladies' Guide in Health and Disease* (Battle Creek, Mich.: Modern Medicine Publishing Co., 1895), p. 371. See as well Edward H. Dixon, *Woman and Her Diseases* (New York: author, 1846), p. 71; Charles Meigs, *Females and Their Diseases* (Philadelphia: D. G. Brinton, 1879), p. 332. A number of women physicians disagreed. Disease in women originated not in diseased ovaries, they argued, but in the unhealthy and restrained way women lived—without exercise, fresh air, or serious employment to occupy their minds. For a classic example of this "feminist" argument see Alice Stockham, *Tokology*, rev. ed. (Chicago: Sanitary Publishing Co., 1887), p. 257. With this particular exception, however, I found a remarkable uniformity in medical opinions on the specific issues discussed in this essay both in terms of chronology, that is, between the late eighteenth century and the late nineteenth, and between representatives of the medical establishment and so-called quack doctors.

7. Edward Tilt, *The Change of Life in Health and Disease*, 4th ed. (New York: Bermingham & Co., 1882), p. 14; P. Henry Chavasse, *Physical Life of Man and Woman* (Cincinnati: National Publishing Co., 1871), p. 155; Caleb Ticknor, *Philosophy of Living* (New York: Harper & Bros., 1836), pp. 304–5.

8. Alexander Hamilton, *A Treatise on the Management of Female Complaints* (New York: Samuel Campbell, 1792), pp. 98–99; Gunning Bedford, *Lecture Introductory to a Course on Obstetrics and Diseases of Women and Children* (New York: Jennings, 1847), p. 8; Meigs, *Females and Their Diseases*, p. 334; George J. Englemann, "The American Girl To-day: The Influence of Modern Education on Functional Development," *Transactions of the American Gynecological Society* 25 (1900): 9–10.

9. [W. W. Bliss], *Woman and Her Thirty Year Pilgrimage* (New York: William M. Littell, 1869).

10. This was a pattern that remained constant throughout the century. See for example: Joseph Brevitt, *The Female Medical Repository* (Baltimore: Hunter & Robinson, 1810), p. 39; John Burns, *Principles of Midwifery*, 2 vols. (Philadelphia: Edward Parker), p. 138; J. Smedley, "The Importance of Making a Physical Exploration during the Climacteric Period," *Hahnemannean Monthly* 8 (1886): 487; William Capp, *The Daughter* (Philadelphia: F. A. Davis, 1891), p. 65; Kellogg, *Ladies' Guide*, p. 371.

11. A. M. Longshore-Potts, *Discourses to Women on Medical Subjects* (San Diego, Calif.: author, 1890), pp. 32, 94.

12. Dixon, *Woman and Her Diseases*, p. 21; William P. Dewees, *A Treatise on the Diseases of Females* (Philadelphia: H. C. Carey & J. Lea, 1826), p. 56. Again, this pattern can be found in medical literature throughout the nineteenth century. See for example: William Buchan, *Domestic Medicine Adapted to the Climate and Diseases of America*, 2nd ed. (Philadelphia: R. Folwell, 1801), pp. 356–57; Samuel Bard, *A Compendium of the Theory and Practice of Midwifery* (New York: Collins & Co., 1819), p. 39; Albert Hayes, *Physiology of Woman* (Boston: Peabody Medical Institute, 1869), pp. 86–87; Longshore-Potts, *Discourses to Women*, p. 67.

13. Michael Ryan, *Philosophy of Marriage*, 4th ed. (London: J. Bailliere, 1843), p. 143; Frederick Hollick, *The Marriage Guide, or Natural History of Generation* (New York: T. W.

Strong, c. 1860), p. 111; Dewees, *Treatise*, pp. 20–21; William Alcott, *The Young Woman's Book of Health* (Boston: Tappan, Whittemore & Mason, 1850), pp. 120–21.

14. [Dr. Porter], *Book of Men, Women and Babies* (New York: De Witt & Davenport, 1855), p. 90; Hayes, *Physiology of Women*, p. 86; Meyer Solis-Cohen, *Girl, Wife and Mother* (Philadelphia: The John C. Winston Co., c. 1911), p. 27; Capp, *The Daughter*, p. 55.

15. Edward Clarke, *Sex in Education* (Boston: James R. Osgood & Co., 1873), p. 47; J. H. Kellogg, *Plain Facts about Sexual Life* (Battle Creek, Mich.: Office of the Health Reformer, 1877), pp. 52–53; Buchan, *Domestic Medicine*, p. 357; Meigs, *Females and Their Diseases*, p. 165; Hayes, *Physiology of Women*, p. 79.

16. For two classic expositions of this argument see: Clarke, *Sex in Education*, and Azel Ames, Jr., *Sex in Industry* (Boston: James R. Osgood, 1875). See as well: T. A. Emmet, *The Principles and Practice of Gynecology* (Philadelphia: Henry C. Lea, 1879), p. 21; Rebecca Crumpler, *A Book of Medical Discourses, In Two Parts* (Boston: Cashman, Keating & Co., 1883), p. 121; and Smith-Rosenberg and Rosenberg, "The Female Animal."

17. Hamilton, *Treatise*, p. 100; John See, *A Guide to Mother and Nurses* (New York: author, 1833), pp. 13–14; Tulio Suzzara Verdi, *Maternity, A Popular Treatise for Young Wives and Mothers* (New York: J. B. Ford and Co., 1870), p. 347; Mrs. E. R. Shepherd, *For Girls: A Special Physiology*, 20th ed. (Chicago: Sanitary Publishing Co., 1888), pp. 132–37; Stockham, *Tokology*, p. 254.

18. Shepherd, *For Girls*, pp. 8–9; Dixon, *Woman and Her Diseases*, p. 75; M. K. Hard, *Woman's Medical Guide* (Mt. Vernon, Ohio: W. H. Cochran, 1848), p. 6; Augustus K. Gardner, *Conjugal Sins* (New York: G. J. Moulton, 1874), p. 22; Henry B. Hemenway, *Healthful Womanhood and Childhood* (Evanston, Ill.: V. T. Hemenway & Co., 1894), p. 16.

19. See *Guide to Mothers*, p. 12; Lydia Maria Child, *The Family Nurse* (Boston: Charles J. Hendee, 1837), p. 43; Calvin Cutter, *The Female Guide* (West Brookfield, Mass.: Charles A. Mirick, 1844), p. 49; Potter, *How Should Girls Be Educated?*, p. 5; Capp, *Daughter*, vol. 2, 3.

20. Clarke, *Sex in Education*, p. 27; Elizabeth Evans, *The Abuse of Maternity* (Philadelphia: J. B. Lippincott and Co., 1875), p. 26. There was a lengthy medical debate over the nature of menstrual blood, in which these popular beliefs were discussed. See note 23.

21. Henry C. Wright, *Marriage and Parentage* (Boston: Bela Marsh, 1854), p. 32; Stockham, *Tokology*, p. 252.

22. Meigs, *Females and Their Diseases*, p. 53; Charles E. Warren, *Causes and Treatment of Sterility in Both Sexes* (Boston: International Medical Exchange, 1890), pp. 58–59. Until quite late in the nineteenth century some physicians doubted whether menstrual blood was in fact blood, or if it was not a special discharge which drew off germs and waste from the circulatory system and thus each month cleansed a woman's system. See for example: Samuel Pancoast, *The Ladies' Medical Guide*, 6th ed. (Philadelphia: John E. Potter, c. 1859), pp. 154–55; Longshore-Potts, *Discourses to Women*, p. 69; Shepherd, *For Girls*, pp. 137–38, for this argument. For refutations see A. M. Mauriceau, *The Married Woman's Medical Companion* (New York: author, 1855), pp. 30–31, and T. R. Trall, *Sexual Physiology* (New York: Miller, Wood & Co., 1866), p. 58.

23. An excellent example of this formula is found in Hayes, *Physiology of Woman*, pp. 84–85. In this passage Hayes significantly refers to menstruation as "an internal wound, the real cause of all this tragedy." For a male physician to refer to menstruation as a "tragedy" seems a bit disproportionate unless Hayes is referring unconsciously to some other primitively perceived tragedy, as for instance castration or death. For an interesting discussion of male fear of menstruation and female genitalia see Karen Horney, "Denial of the Vagina," in *Feminine Psychology*, and with an introduction by Harold Kelman (New York: Norton, 1967). The common medical argument and folk belief that menstruation spoiled the milk of a nursing mother and indeed that such milk could cause convulsions or death in the infant may also be related to a general fear of menstrual blood.

24. George Robert Rowe, *On Some of the Most Important Disorders of Women* (London: John Churchill, 1844), pp. 27–28; William Carpenter, *Principles of Human Physiology*, 4th American ed. (Philadelphia: Lea and Blanchard, 1850), p. 698; Hollick, *Marriage Guide*, p. 95.

25. Tilt, *Change of Life,* p. 13; Horatio R. Storer and Franklin Fiske Heard, *Criminal Abortion* (Boston: Little, Brown and Company, 1868), p. 90 n.; Verdi, *Maternity,* p. 345.

26. Dixon, *Woman and Her Diseases,* p. 101; Tilt, *Change of Life,* pp. 10–12; Bard, *Compendium,* pp. 78–79.

27. Tilt, *Change of Life,* pp. 12–16; Dewees, *Treatise,* p. 94; Hayes, *Physiology of Women,* p. 95.

28. Joseph Ralph, *A Domestic Guide to Medicine* (New York: author, 1835), p. 130; L. H. Mettler, "Menopause," *Medical Register* 2 (1887): 323.

29. Tilt, *Change of Life*, contains the classic list of menopausal diseases—118 in all, pp. 106–246. See, as well, B. F. Baer, "The Significance of Menorrhagia Recurring about or after the Menopause," *American Journal of Obstetrics* 17 (1884): 461–62; Lawson Tait, "Climacteric Diabetes in Women," *The Practitioner* 36 (June 1886): 401–8; William Pepper, "The Change of Life in Women," pp. 505–6; Dewees, *Treatise,* pp. 94–103; Denman, *Introduction to Midwifery,* pp. 192–93; Sara E. Greenfield, "The Dangers of Menopause," *Woman's Medical Journal* (Toledo) 12 (1902): 183–85.

30. See, for example, C. J. Aldrich, "The Role Played by Intestinal Fermentation in the Production of the Neurosis of Menopause," *Physician and Surgeon* (Detroit) 19 (1897): 438–44; Philander Harris, "The Dangers of Certain Impressions Regarding the Menopause," *Transactions of the Medical Society of New Jersey* (1898), pp. 317–25; Dewees, *Treatise,* p. 103.

31. Buchan, *Domestic Medicine,* p. 360. This was the most popular physiological explanation of menopausal problems. See as well: West, *Diseases of Women,* p. 44; Hayes, *Physiology of Women,* p. 96; Tilt, *Change of Life,* pp. 54, 85.

32. Denman, *Midwifery,* pp. 189–91; Dixon, *Woman and Her Diseases,* p. 103; Shepherd, *For Girls,* pp. 138–39; Mettler, "Menopause," p. 323; Longshore-Potts, *Discourses to Women,* pp. 94–95; "Change of Life in Women," pp. 505–6.

33. Dewees, *Treatise,* pp. 92, 95; Rowe, *On Some Common Disorders,* p. 36; George Woodruff Johnston, "Certain Facts Regarding Fertility, Utero-Gestation, Parturition and the Puerperium in the So-Called 'Lower' or 'Laboring' Classes," *American Journal of Obstetrics and Dis-*

eases of Women and Children 21 (May 1888): 19.

34. Tilt also reported giving menopausal women anaphrodisiacs to control their sexual impulses. *Change of Life,* pp. 79, 93–94; Kellogg, *Plain Facts,* p. 80.

35. Taylor, *A Physician's Counsels to Women,* pp. 93–94.

36. See *Guide to Mothers and Nurses,* p. 18; Brevitt, *Woman's Medical Repository,* pp. 52–53; Longshore-Potts, *Discourses to Women,* p. 95.

37. Tilt, *Change of Life,* pp. 16, 39, 94–95; Taylor, *Physician's Counsels to Women,* pp. 85, 90–92; Bard, *Compendium,* p. 80; Burns, *Principles of Midwifery,* p. 162.

38. Ann Preston, *Valedictory Address to the Graduating Class, Female Medical College of Pennsylvania at the Twelfth Annual Commencement, March 16, 1864* (Philadelphia: William S. Young, Printer, 1864), p. 9.

39. Dewees, *Treatise,* p. 92; Aldrich, "Neuroses of Menopause," pp. 153–54; Baer, "Menorrhagia . . . Menopause," p. 451; Hal C. Wyman, "The Menopause-Gangliasthenia: A Clinical Lecture in the Michigan College of Medicine," *Michigan Medical News* 5 (1882): 313; Mauriceau, *Married Woman's Private Medical Companion,* p. 7.

40. This quote as well as many other lengthy excerpts from Elizabeth Drinker's diary are reprinted in Cecil K. Drinker, *Not So Long Ago: A Chronicle of Medicine and Doctors in Colonial Philadelphia* (New York: Oxford University Press, 1937), pp. 59–60.

41. Meigs, *Females and Their Diseases,* p. 55; Longshore-Potts, *Discourses to Women,* pp. 98–102.

42. Eliza W. Farnham, *Woman and Her Era,* 2 vols. (New York: A. J. Davis & Co., 1864), pp. 56–57.

43. Horney, *Feminine Psychology.* See especially her essays on "Fear of Woman," "Denial of the Vagina," and "Female Masochism."

44. For a discussion of such issues see Charles E. Rosenberg, "Sexuality, Class and Role in Nineteenth-Century America," *American Quarterly* (May 1973): in press.

· · ·

THE HYSTERICAL WOMAN

1. The writing of this chapter was supported in part by a grant from the National Institutes of

Health and by a grant from the Grant Foundation, New York. I would like to thank Renée Fox, Cornelia Friedman, Erving Goffman, Charles E. Rosenberg, and Paul Rosenkrantz for having read and criticized this essay. I would also like to thank my clinical colleagues Philip Mechanick, Henry Bachrach, and Ellen Berman, of the Psychiatry Department of the University of Pennsylvania for similar assistance. Versions of this essay were presented to the Institute of the Pennsylvania Hospital, the Berkshire Historical Society, and initially, in October 1971, at the Psychiatry Department of Hahnemann Medical College, Philadelphia.

2. For a review of the recent psychiatric literature on hysteria see Aaron Lazare, "The Hysterical Character in Psychoanalytic Theory: Evolution and Confusion," *Archives of General Psychiatry* XXV (August 1971): 131–37; Barbara Ruth Easser and S. R. Lesser, "Hysterical Personality: A Reevaluation," *Psychoanalytic Quarterly* XXXIV (1965): 390–405; Marc H. Hollander, "Hysterical Personality," *Comments on Contemporary Psychiatry* I (1971): 17–24.

3. Elizabeth Zetzel, *The Capacity for Emotional Growth: Theoretical and Clinical Contributions to Psychoanalysis, 1943–1969* (London: Hogarth Press, 1970), chap. 1-f, "The So-Called Good Hysteric."

4. David Shapiro, *Neurotic Styles* (New York: Basic Books, 1965).

5. The argument can be made that hysteria exists among men and therefore is not exclusively related to the female experience; the question is a complex one. There are, however, four brief points concerning male hysteria that I would like to make. First, to this day hysteria is still believed to be principally a female "disease" or behavior pattern. Second, the male hysteric is usually seen by physicians as somehow different. Today it is a truism that hysteria in males is found most frequently among homosexuals; in the nineteenth century, men diagnosed as hysterics almost exclusively had a lower socioeconomic status than their physicians—immigrants, especially "new immigrants," miners, railroad workers, blacks. Third, since it was defined by society as a female disease, one may hypothesize that there was some degree of female identification among the men who assumed a hysterical role. Lastly, we must recall

that a most common form of male hysteria was battle fatigue and shell shock. I should like to thank Erving Goffman for the suggestion that the soldier is in a position analogous to women's regarding autonomy and power.

6. The word "choose," even in quotation marks, is value-laden. I do not mean to imply that hysterical women consciously chose their behavior. I feel that three complex factors interacted to make hysteria a real behavioral option for American women: first, the various experiences that caused a woman to arrive at adulthood with significant ego weaknesses; second, certain socialization patterns and cultural values that made hysteria a readily available alternate behavior pattern for women; and third, the secondary gains conferred by the hysterical role in terms of enhanced power within the family. Individual cases presumably represented their own peculiar balance of these factors, all of which will be discussed in this essay.

7. Nineteenth-century hysteria has attracted a good number of students; two of the most important are Henri F. Ellenberger, *The Discovery of the Unconscious* (New York: Basic Books, 1970), and Ilza Veith, *Hysteria: The History of a Disease* (Chicago: University of Chicago Press, 1965). Ellenberger and Veith approach hysteria largely from the framework of intellectual history. For a review of Veith see Charles E. Rosenberg, "Historical Sociology of Medical Thought," *Science* CL (October 15, 1965): 330. For two studies that view nineteenth-century hysteria from a more sociological perspective, see Esther Fischer-Homberger, "Hysterie und Misogynie: Ein Aspekt der Hysteriegeschichte," *Gesnerus* XXVI (1969): 117–27, and Marc H. Hollander, "Conversion Hysteria: A Post-Freudian Reinterpretation of Nineteenth-Century Psychosocial Data," *Archives of General Psychiatry* XXVI (1972): 311–14.

8. These conclusions are drawn from a larger study of male and female gender roles and gender-role socialization in the United States from 1785 to 1895 on which I am at present engaged. This research has been supported by both the Grant Foundation, New York City, and the National Institute of Child Health and Human Development, N.I.H. For a basic secondary source see Barbara Welter, "The Cult of True Womanhood," *American Quarterly* XVIII (1966): 151–74.

9. For the daily activities of a nineteenth-century American housewife, see, for example, *The Maternal Physician: By an American Matron* (New York: Isaac Riley, 1811; reprinted New York: Arno Press, 1972); Hugh Smith, *Letters to Married Ladies* (New York: Bliss, White and G. & C. Carvill, 1827); John S. C. Abbott, *The Mother at Home* (Boston: Crocker and Brewster, 1833); Lydia H. Sigourney, *Letters to Mothers* (New York: Harper & Brothers, 1841); Mrs. C. A. Hopkinson, *Hints for the Nursery or the Young Mother's Guide* (Boston: Little, Brown & Company, 1836); Catherine Beecher and Harriet Beecher Stowe, *The American Woman's Home* (New York: J. B. Ford & Company, 1869). For an excellent secondary account of the Southern woman's domestic life, see Anne Firor Scott, *The Southern Lady: From Pedestal to Politics, 1830–1930* (Chicago: University of Chicago Press, 1970).

10. Nineteenth-century domestic medicine books, gynecology textbooks, and monographs on the diseases of women provide a detailed picture of women's diseases and health expectations.

11. S. Weir Mitchell, *Doctor and Patient* (Philadelphia: J. B. Lippincott Company, 1887), pp. 84, 92.

12. See, among others, Edward H. Dixon, *Woman and Her Diseases* (New York: Charles H. Ring, 1846), pp. 135–36; Alice Stockham, *Tokology: A Book for Every Woman* (Chicago: Sanitary Publishers, 1887), p. 83; Sarah A. Stevenson, *Physiology of Women*, 2nd ed. (Chicago: Cushing, Thomas & Co., 1881), p. 91; Henry Pye Chavasse, *Advice to a Wife and Counsel to a Mother* (Philadelphia: J. B. Lippincott, 1891), p. 97. A Missouri physician reported the case of a twenty-eight-year-old middle-class woman with two children. Shortly after the birth of her second child, she missed her period, believed herself to be pregnant for a third time, and succumbed to hysterical symptoms: depression, headaches, vomiting, and seizures. Her doctor concluded that she had uterine disease, exacerbated by pregnancy. He aborted her and reported a full recovery the following day. George J. Engelmann, "A Hystero-Psychosis Epilepsy Dependent upon Erosions of the Cervix Uteri," *St. Louis Clinic Record*, 1878, pp. 321–24. For similar cases, see A. B. Arnold, "Hystero-Hypochondriasis," *Pacific Medical Journal* XXXIII

(1890): 321–24, and George J. Engelmann, "Hystero-Neurosis," *Transactions of the American Gynecological Association* II (1877): 513–18.

13. For studies of declining nineteenth-Century American birthrates, see Yasukichi Yasuba, *Birth Rates of the White Population in the United States, 1800–1860* (Baltimore: Johns Hopkins University Press, 1962); J. Potter, "American Population in the Early National Period," in *Proceedings of Section V of the Fourth Congress of the International Economic History Association*, ed. Paul Deprez (Winnipeg, 1970), pp. 55–69.

14. William A. Hammond, *On Certain Conditions of Nervous Derangement* (New York: G. P. Putnam's Sons, 1881), p. 42; S. Weir Mitchell, *Lectures on the Diseases of the Nervous System, Especially in Women*, 2nd ed. (Philadelphia: Lea Brothers & Co., 1885), pp. 110, 114; Charles K. Mills, "Hysteria," in *A System of Practical Medicine by American Authors*, ed. William Pepper, assisted by Louis Starr, vol. V, "Diseases of the Nervous System" (Philadelphia: Lea Brothers & Co., 1883), p. 213; Charles E. Lockwood, "A Study of Hysteria and Hypochondriasis," *Transactions of the New York State Medical Association* XII (1895): 340–51. E. H. Van Deusen, superintendent of the Michigan Asylum for the Insane, reported that nervousness, hysteria, and neurasthenia were common among farm women and resulted, he felt, from the social and intellectual deprivation of their isolated lives (Van Deusen, "Observations on a Form of Nervous Prostration," *American Journal of Insanity* XXV [1869]: 447). Significantly, most English and American authorities on hysteria were members of a medical elite who saw the wealthy in their private practices and the very poor in their hospital and dispensary work. Thus the observation that hysteria occurred in different social classes was often made by the very same clinicians.

15. Thomas Sydenham, "Epistolary Dissertation," in *The Works of Thomas Sydenham, M.D. . . . with a Life of the Author*, ed. R. G. Latham, 2 vols. (London: New Sydenham Society, 1850), II: 85.

16. Some women diagnosed as hysterics displayed quite bizarre behavior—including self-mutilation and hallucinations. Clearly a certain percentage of these women would be diagnosed today as schizophrenic. The majority of the women diagnosed as hysterical, however,

did not display such symptoms, but, rather, appear from clinical descriptions to have had a personality similar to that considered hysterical by mid-twentieth-century psychiatrists.

17. For three typical descriptions of such seizures, see Buel Eastman, *Practical Treatise on Diseases Peculiar to Women and Girls* (Cincinnati: C. Cropper & Son, 1848), p. 40; Samuel Ashwell, *A Practical Treatise on the Diseases Peculiar to Women* (London: Samuel Highley, 1844), pp. 210–12; William Campbell, *Introduction to the Study and Practice of Midwifery and the Diseases of Children* (London: Longman, Rees, Orme, Brown, Green & Longman, 1833), pp. 440–42.

18. Dixon, *Woman and Her Diseases*, p. 133.

19. For examples of mid-nineteenth-century hysterical symptoms see Colombat de L'Isère, *A Treatise on the Diseases and Special Hygiene of Females*, trans. with additions by Charles D. Meigs (Philadelphia: Lea and Blanchard, 1815), pp. 522, 527–30; Gunning S. Bedford, *Clinical Lectures on the Diseases of Women and Children* (New York: Samuel S. & W. Wood, 1855), p. 373.

20. Robert B. Carter, *On the Pathology and Treatment of Hysteria* (London: John Churchill, 1853), p. 3.

21. See, for example, F. C. Skey, *Hysteria* (New York: A. Simpson, 1867), pp. 66, 71, 86; Mary Putnam Jacobi, "Hysterical Fever," *Journal of Nervous and Mental Disease* XV (1890): 373–88; Landon Carter Grey, "Neurasthenia: Its Differentiation and Treatment," *New York Medical Journal* XLVIII (1888): 421.

22. See, for example, George Preston, *Hysteria and Certain Allied Conditions* (Philadelphia: P. Blakiston, Son & Co., 1897), pp. 31, 53; Lockwood, "Hysteria and Hypochondriasis," p. 346; Buel Eastman, *Practical Treatise*, p. 39; Thomas More Madden, *Clinical Gynecology* (Philadelphia: J. B. Lippincott, 1895), p. 472.

23. See W. Symington Brown, *A Clinical Handbook on the Diseases of Women* (New York: William Wood & Company, 1882); Charles L. Dana, "A Study of the Anaesthesias of Hysteria," *American Journal of the Medical Sciences* (October 1890): 1; William S. Playfair, *The Systematic Treatment of Nerve Prostration and Hysteria* (Philadelphia: Henry C. Lea's Son & Co., 1883), p. 29.

24. For a discussion of the importance of creating such organic etiologies in the legitimization of an increasingly large number of such "functional" ills, see Charles E. Rosenberg, "The Place of George M. Beard in Nineteenth-Century Psychiatry," *Bulletin of the History of Medicine* XXXVI (1962): 245–59. See also Owsei Temkin's discussion, in his classic history of epilepsy, *The Falling Sickness*, 2nd rev. ed. (Baltimore: Johns Hopkins University Press, 1971), of the importance placed by neurologists in the late nineteenth century upon the differentiation of epilepsy and hysteria.

25. Campbell, *Midwifery and the Diseases of Children*, pp. 440–41; Walter Channing, *Bed Case: Its History and Treatment* (Boston: Ticknor and Fields, 1860), pp. 41–42, 49; Charles L. Mix, "Hysteria: Its Nature and Etiology," *New York Medical Journal* LXXII (August 1900): 183–89.

26. Preston, *Hysteria*, pp. 96–97.

27. Ashwell, *Practical Treatise*, p. 226.

28. Mills, "Hysteria," p. 258.

29. Mitchell, *Diseases of the Nervous System*, p. 66.

30. Madden, *Clinical Gynecology*, p. 474. The uterine origin of hysteria was by far the most commonly held opinion throughout the eighteenth and nineteenth centuries. Some believed it to be the exclusive cause, others to be among the most important causes. For three typical examples see: Alexander Hamilton, *A Treatise on the Management of Female Complaints and of Children in Early Infancy* (Edinburgh: Peter Hill, 1792), pp. 51–53; George J. Engelmann, "Hystero-Neurosis"; Augustus P. Clarke, "Relations of Hysteria to Structural Changes in the Uterus and its Adnexa," *American Journal of Obstetrics* XXXIII (1891): 477–83. The uterine theory came under increasing attack during the late nineteenth century. See Hugh J. Patrick, "Hysteria; Neurasthenia," *International Clinics* III (1898): 183–84; Skey, *Hysteria*, p. 68.

31. Robert Barnes, *Medical and Surgical Diseases of Women* (Philadelphia: H. C. Lea, 1874), p. 101; S. D. Hopkins, "A Case of Hysteria Simulating Organic Disease of the Brain," *Medical Fortnightly* XI (July 1897): 327; Mills, "Hysteria," p. 218; J. Leonard Corning, *A Treatise on Hysteria and Epilepsy* (Detroit: George S. Davis, 1888), p. 2; August A. Eshner, "Hysteria in Early Life," read before the Philadelphia County Medical Society, June 23, 1897.

32. For examples of such concern and complexity, see A. A. King, "Hysteria," *The American Journal of Obstetrics* XXIV (May 1891): 513–15; Marshall Hall, *Commentaries Principally on the Diseases of Females* (London: Sherwood, Gilbert and Piper, 1830), p. 118; L'Isère, *Diseases and Special Hygiene*, p. 530.

33. Robert B. Carter, *On the Pathology and Treatment of Hysteria* (London: John Churchill, 1853), p. 140; J. Leonard Corning, *A Treatise on Hysteria and Epilepsy* (Detroit: George S. Davis, 1888), p. 70; Mills, "Hysteria," p. 218.

34. Preston, *Hysteria*, p. 36.

35. See, for example, Mitchell, *Diseases of the Nervous System*, p. 170; Rebecca B. Gleason, M.D., of Elmira, New York, quoted by M. L. Holbrook, *Hygiene of the Brain and Nerves and the Cure of Nervousness* (New York: M. L. Holbrook & Company, 1878), pp. 270–71.

36. S. Weir Mitchell, *Fat and Blood* (Philadelphia: J. B. Lippincott, 1881), pp. 30–31.

37. Lockwood, "Hysteria and Hypochondriasis," pp. 342–43; virtually every authority on hysteria echoed these sentiments.

38. Hamilton, *A Treatise on the Management of Female Complaints and of Children in Early Infancy* (Edinburgh: Peter Hill, 1792), p. 52; Dixon, *Woman and Her Diseases*, pp. 142–43; Ashwell, *Practical Treatise*, p. 217; Mills, "Hysteria," p. 230.

39. Channing, *Bed Case*, p. 28.

40. Robert B. Carter, *Pathology and Treatment*, p. 113.

41. Jacobi, "Hysterical Fever," pp. 384–88; M. E. Dirix, *Woman's Complete Guide to Health* (New York: W. A. Townsend & Adams, 1869), p. 24; E. B. Foote, *Medical Common Sense* (New York: published by the author, 1864), p. 167.

42. Reuben Ludlum, *Lectures, Clinical and Didactic, on the Diseases of Women* (Chicago: C. S. Halsey, 1872), p. 87; Robert Barnes, *Medical and Surgical Diseases of Women* (Philadelphia: H. C. Lea, 1874), p. 247. In 1847, the well-known Philadelphia gynecologist Charles D. Meigs had asked his medical-school class the rhetorical question "What is her erotic state? What the protean manifestations of the life force developed by a reproductive irritation which you call hysteria?" (*Lectures on the Distinctive Characteristics of the Female, delivered before the Class of Jefferson Medical College, January*

5, *1847* [Philadelphia: T. K. & P. G. Collins, 1847], p. 20).

43. Thomas Laycock, *An Essay on Hysteria* (Philadelphia: Haswell, Barrington, and Haswell, 1840), pp. 76, 103, 105. See also Graham J. Barker-Benfield, "The Horrors of the Half-Known Life," Ph.D. thesis, University of California at Los Angeles, 1969, and Ann Douglas Wood, "The Fashionable Diseases: Women's Complaints and Their Treatment in Nineteenth Century America," *Journal of Interdisciplinary History* IV:1 (Summer 1973): 25–52, for a speculative psychoanalytic approach to gynecological practice in nineteenth-century America.

44. Dixon, *Woman and Her Diseases*, p. 134; Corning, *Hysteria and Epilepsy*, p. 70; William Murray, *A Treatise on Emotional Disorders of the Sympathetic System of the Nerves* (London: John Churchill, 1866). An extensive nineteenth-century masturbation literature exists. See, for example, Samuel Gregory, *Facts and Important Information for Young Women on the Self-Indulgence of the Sexual Appetite* (Boston: George Gregory, 1857), and Calvin Cutter, *The Female Guide: Containing Facts and Information upon the Effects of Masturbation* (West Brookfield, Mass.: Charles A. Mirick, 1844). Most general treatises on masturbation refer to its occurrence in females.

45. Preston, *Hysteria*, p. 37; Carter, *Pathology and Treatment*, pp. 46, 90. Nineteenth-century physicians maintained a delicate balance in their view of the sexual etiology of hysteria. Any deviation from moderation could cause hysteria or insanity: habitual masturbation, extended virginity, overindulgence, prostitution, or sterility.

46. Skey, *Hysteria*, p. 63.

47. Mitchell, *Diseases of the Nervous System*, p. 266; Mitchell, *Fat and Blood*, p. 37.

48. Carter, *Pathology and Treatment*, p. 58.

49. For an exposition of this argument, see Erving Goffman, "Insanity of Place," *Psychiatry* XXXII (1969): 357–88.

50. Such complaints are commonplace in the medical literature. See Mitchell, *Diseases of the Nervous System*, p. 67; Mitchell, *Doctor and Patient*, p. 117; Robert Thornton, *The Hysterical Women: Trials, Tears, Tricks and Tantrums* (Chicago: Donohue & Henneberry, 1893), pp. 97–98; Channing, *Bed Case*, pp. 35–37; Colombat de L'Isère, *A Treatise on the Diseases and*

Special Hygiene of Females, trans. with additions by Charles D. Meigs (Philadelphia: Lea and Blanchard, 1815), p. 534.

51. The fact that the physician was at the same time employed and paid by the woman or her family—in a period when the profession was far more competitive and economically insecure than it is in the mid-twentieth century —implied another level of stress and ambiguity.

52. Channing, *Bed Case,* p. 22; Thomas A. Emmett, *Principles and Practices of Gynecology* (Philadelphia: H. C. Lea, 1879), p. 107; L. C. Grey, "Clinical Lecture," p. 132.

53. Carter, *Pathology and Treatment,* p. 119; Ashwell, *Practical Treatise,* p. 227.

54. Skey, *Hysteria,* p. 60.

55. Thornton, *The Hysterical Woman.*

56. Thomas A. Emmett, *Incidents of My Life* (New York: G. P. Putnam's Sons, 1911), p. 210. These are Emmett's recollections at the end of a long life. It is interesting that decades earlier Emmett, in discussing the treatment of hysterical women, had confessed in hostile frustration, "In fact the physician is helpless. . . ." (Emmett, *Principles and Practices,* p. 107.)

57. Mitchell, *Doctor and Patient,* pp. 99–100.

58. Samuel Guze, "The Diagnosis of Hysteria: What Are We Trying to Do," *American Journal of Psychiatry* CXXIV (1967): 494–98; Otto Kernberg, "Borderline Personality Organization," *Journal of the American Psychoanalytic Association* XV (1967): 641–85. For a critical discussion of the entire problem of diagnosis, see Henry Bachrach, "In Defense of Diagnosis," *Psychiatry* (in press).

59. I base these statements on an ongoing study of children's literature in which I am engaged. The American Antiquarian Society's collection of eighteenth- and nineteenth-century children's books is particularly rich. See also Charles Carpenter, *History of American School Books* (Philadelphia: University of Pennsylvania Press, 1963), and Nigel Temple, ed., *Seen and Not Heard: A Garland of Fancies for Victorian Children* (London: Hutchinson & Co. Ltd., 1970), which offers a pleasant sample of nineteenth-century children's literature.

60. Anna Freud, *The Ego and the Mechanisms of Defense,* trans. Cecil Bains (New York: International Universities Press, Inc., 1946), chap. 10.

61. Ibid., p. 111. See also chap. 8.

62. For a study of nineteenth-century male child-rearing practices see Joseph Kett, *Rites of Passage, Adolescence in America, 1790 to the Present* (New York: Basic Books, 1977). For a study of the effect of traditional gender-based child-rearing practices on girls see Judith M. Bardwick and Elizabeth Douvan, "Ambivalence: The Socialization of Women," in *Women in a Sexist Society,* eds. Vivian Gornick and Barbara K. Moran (New York: Basic Books, 1971), pp. 147–59. Carol Gilligan's *In a Different Voice* (Cambridge, Mass.: Harvard University Press, 1982) challenges the negative vision implied in the Bardwick and Douvan study, placing in a new light the entire issue of a daughter's identification with her mother.

63. Karen Horney, "The Problem of Feminine Masochism," in Horney, *Feminine Psychology,* ed. Harold Kelman (New York: W. W. Norton, 1967), pp. 214–44. See also her essays, "The Overvaluation of Love" and "The Neurotic Need for Love," in Horney, *Feminine Psychology.*

64. Horney, "Feminine Masochism," pp. 229 and passim.

· · ·

THE ABORTION MOVEMENT AND THE AMA, 1850–1880

1. The research for this essay was supported by a faculty research grant from the National Endowment for the Humanities, 1975–76. I would like to thank James Henretta and Diana Hall for their careful reading of this manuscript and their many valuable suggestions. Richard Wolfe and Saul Bennison were generous in their suggestions as well.

2. For an excellent analysis of the social and medical history of abortion in America, see James Mohr, *Abortion in America: The Origins and Evolution of National Policy* (New York and Oxford: Oxford University Press, 1978). For the legal history of abortion, see Lawrence Lader, *Abortion* (New York: Bobbs-Merrill Co., 1966); David T. Smith, *Abortion and the Law* (Cleveland: Press of Case Western Reserve University, 1973). For a clear statement of the history of the Roman Catholic Church's position, see Robert J. Huser, *The Crime of Abortion in Common Law* (Washington, D.C.: Catholic University of America Press, 1942);

John Noonan, *Contraception: A History of Its Treatment by Catholic Theologians and Canonists* (Cambridge, Mass.: Belknap Press of Harvard University, 1965).

3. The leader of this lobbying campaign was Harvard Medical School Professor Horatio R. Storer. The letters written and received by Storer during this campaign are in the Rare Book Room, Countway Medical Library, Harvard Medical School.

4. Mohr, *Abortion in America,* pp. 4–16.

5. Quoted by Lader, *Abortion,* p. 78.

6. Walbert and Butler, *Abortion, Society and the Law* (Cleveland: Press of Case Western Reserve University, 1973), pp. 327–28.

7. For forty-five years following independence, no state passed any law on abortion. By 1840 only eight states had passed any legislation regulating abortion in any way. Glenn Koopersmith, in "A Comparison of Early and Later Abortion Laws in 19th Century America," unpublished manuscript, University of Pennsylvania, has surveyed the statutes of Connecticut, New York, Iowa, Illinois, Arkansas, Missouri, Indiana, Oregon, California, New Jersey, Massachusetts, Vermont, New Hampshire, Maine, Wisconsin, Ohio, Michigan, Virginia, West Virginia, Mississippi, and Alabama. See also R. Sauer, "Attitudes Towards Abortion in America, 1800–1973," *Population Studies* XXVIII (March 1974): 53–67; Alfred S. Taylor, *Medical Jurisprudence,* 2nd American ed., from 3rd London ed., with notes and additions by R. Eglesfeld Griffith (Philadelphia: Lea and Blanchard, 1850); Alfred S. Taylor, *A Manual of Medical Jurisprudence,* 8th ed. (Philadelphia: J. B. Lippincott and Co., 1866); Alfred S. Taylor, *The Principles and Practice of Medical Jurisprudence,* 2nd ed. (Philadelphia: Henry C. Lea, 1973), vol. II; Mohr, *Abortion in America,* pp. 5–6 and chap. 2.

8. Koopersmith, "Comparison"; Mohr, *Abortion in America,* pp. 20–45. The Storer papers contain reports by local physicians concerning abortion legislation in their particular states. These are interesting not only because they present a survey of the legislation, but because they give local physicians' responses to that legislation and, indeed, indicate the extent of medical knowledge about the legal situation relating to abortion in their particular states. See, for example, D. B. [illegible], Chicago, to H. R. Storer (hereafter HRS), March 23, 1857; R. A. Cameron, Valparaiso, Ind., to HRS,

March 25, 1857; Thomas W. Blatchford, Troy, N.Y., to HRS, March 23, 1857; Charles Hooker, New Haven, to HRS, April 2, 1857; John Keith, Esq., Boston, to HRS, February 18, 1857; Edward E. Phelps, Windsor, Vt., to HRS, March 28, 1857; Edward H. Barton, New Orleans, to HRS, April 2, 1857; Ohio Statute, February 27, 1834.

9. A Maine physician reported as late as 1873, "As to the courts, it is about impossible to get an attorney to prosecute or a jury to convict an abortionist" (P. S. Haskell, "Criminal Abortion," *Transactions, Maine Medical Association* IV [1873]: 463–73). Levin Smith Joynes, a Richmond, Virginia, doctor, reported, "It is . . . doubtful whether the induction of abortion prior to quickening if done with the mother's consent and without injury to her could have been punished" (Levin S. Joynes, Richmond, to HRS, May 4, 1859). Charles H. Porter, an Albany physician, was quoted by Storer as coming to a similar conclusion (Storer, "Proceedings of the Gynaecological Society, Boston," *Journal of the Gynaecological Society, Boston* II [1870]: 284–85). H. R. Storer and Franklin Fiske Heard, in *Criminal Abortion* (Boston: Little, Brown & Co., 1868), p. 54, report that in Massachusetts between 1849 and 1858, thirty-two trials occurred involving charges of abortion, with not one conviction. In 1860, an Irishman professing to be an English surgeon had performed two abortions, killing both women. After a nine-day jury trial in which he argued that although he had performed two abortions there was no evidence that the fetuses were still alive at the time of the abortion—they might have died of the mothers' shame and melancholy—he was convicted of producing abortions but not of manslaughter. He was sentenced to a two-year jail sentence. (C. P. Frost, "Report of a Trial for Criminal Abortion," *American Medical Monthly* XIV [1860]: 196–202.) See also John B. Beck, "Infanticide," in *Elements of Medical Jurisprudence,* 11th ed., ed. Theodore Romeyn Beck and John B. Beck (Philadelphia: J. B. Lippincott & Co., 1860), I: 488, 488n.

10. James William Hoyte, Nashville, to HRS, March 20, 1857; James H. Dickson, Wilmington, N.C., to HRS, March 20, 1857; Alexander Jenkens Semmes, Washington, D.C., to HRS, March 24, 1857; A. Lopez, Mobile, to HRS, April 2, 1857; L. I. Joynes to HRS.

11. J. W. Thomson, Wilmington, Del., to HRS, March 18, 1857.

12. Thomas W. Blatchford, Troy, N.Y., to HRS, March 25, 1859; Simon M. Landis, *A Stricktly Private Book . . . on the Secrets of Generation*, 20th ed. (Philadelphia: Landis Publishing Society, 1872).

13. H. R. Storer, *Why Not? A Book for Every Woman, the Prize Essay* . . . (Boston: Lea and Shepard, 1866), p. 83; J. M. Toner, "Abortion in Its Medical and Moral Aspects," *Medical and Surgical Reporter* V (1861): 443; Walter Coles, "Abortion—Its Causes and Treatment," *St. Louis Medical and Surgical Journal* (1875): 252–53; M. M. Eaton, "Four and a Half Inches of Whalebone in the Uterus: Abortion," *Chicago Medical Examiner* IX (1868): 218; E. M. Buckingham, "Criminal Abortion," *Cincinnati Lancet and Obstetrician* n.s. X (1867): 139–43; Andrew Nebinger, *Criminal Abortion* (Philadelphia: Collins, printer, 1870), pp. 4–5, 7. Mohr, *Abortion in America*, discusses the physicians' campaign in his chap. 6.

14. For a discussion of the Michigan findings see William D. Haggard, *Abortion: Accidental, Essential, Criminal. Address Before the Nashville Academy of Medicine, Aug. 4, 1898* (Nashville, Tenn., 1898), p. 10. See, as well, Ely Van De Warker, *The Detection of Criminal Abortion, and A Study of Foeticidal Drugs* (Boston, 1872); A. K. Gardner, *Conjugal Sins Against the Laws of Life and Health* (New York: Moulton, 1874), p. 131; Alexander C. Draper, *Observations on Abortion: With an Account of the Means both Medicinal and Mechanical, Employed to Produce that Effect* . . . (Philadelphia, 1839); Hugh Hodge, *On Criminal Abortion* (Philadelphia: T. K. and P. G. Collins, printers, 1854). Advocates of birth control routinely used the dangers and prevalence of abortion as one argument justifying their cause (H. R. Storer, *Report of the Suffolk District Medical Society on Criminal Abortion and Ordered Printed . . . May 9 [1857]* [Boston, 1857]; [N. F. Cook,] *Satan in Society: By a Physician* (Cincinnati: C. F. Vent, 1876); H. C. Ghent, "Criminal Abortion or Foeticide," *Transactions of the Texas State Medical Association at the Annual Session 1888–89*, 1888–89. Certainly much of this literature was devoted to the task of convincing middle-class women not to use abortion as a form of family limitation (Mohr, *Abortion in America*, chaps. 3 and 4).

15. Koopersmith, "Comparison"; Mohr, chap. 8.

16. Horatio Robinson Storer and Franklin Fiske Heard, *Criminal Abortion: Its Nature, Evidence and Its Law* (Boston: Little, Brown and Company, 1865), p. 72.

17. See H.R.S. papers, Countway Medical Library, Harvard University.

18. For two modern analyses of Storer's lobbying campaign, see Frederick Carpenter Irving, *Safe Deliverance* (Boston: Houghton Mifflin, 1942), pp. 104–19; Mohr, *Abortion in America*, chap. 6.

19. Storer, *Why Not?*

20. Lader, *Abortion*, pp. 86–91.

21. For recent discussions of Anthony Comstock's career, see David Pivar, *Purity Crusade: Sexual Morality and Social Control, 1868–1900* (Westport, Conn.: Greenwood Press, 1973); R. Christian Johnson, "Anthony Comstock: Reform, Vice and the American Way," Ph.D. thesis, University of Wisconsin, 1973; Mohr, *Abortion in America*, pp. 196–99.

22. Lader, *Abortion*, p. 64.

23. This was the case in which the admitted abortionist and killer of two women received a two-year jail sentence; see above, n. 9.

24. Mohr, *Abortion in America*, p. 100. See also Wendell H. Bash, "Changing Birth Rates in Developing America: New York State, 1840–75," *Milbank Memorial Fund Quarterly* XLI (1963); Colin Forster and G. S. L. Tucker, *Economic Opportunity and White American Fertility Ratios, 1800–1860* (New Haven: Yale University Press, 1972).

25. G. J. Barker-Benfield, "The Spermatic Economy: A Nineteenth-Century View of Sexuality," *Feminist Studies* I (1972): 45–74; and *The Horrors of the Half Known Life: Male Attitudes Toward Women and Sexuality in 19th Century America* (New York: Harper & Row, 1976). For somewhat less psychological interpretations, see Daniel Scott Smith, "Family Limitation, Sexual Control and Domestic Feminism in Victorian America," *Feminist Studies* I (1973): 40–57; Carroll Smith-Rosenberg and Charles Rosenberg, "The Female Animal: Medical and Biological Views of Woman and Her Role in Nineteenth-Century America," *Journal of American History* LX (1973): 332–56; Edward Shorter, "Female Emancipation, Birth Control and Fertility in European History," *American Historical Review* LXXVIII (1973): 605–40.

26. See introductions to Parts II and III of the volume. See, as well, Eleanor Flexner, *Century of Struggle* (Cambridge, Mass.: Harvard

University Press, 1959), chaps. 3, 4, 6, 8; Blanche Glassman Hersch, *The Slavery of Sex: Feminist Abolitionists in America* (Urbana: University of Illinois Press, 1978), chap. 2; Barbara Berg, *The Remembered Gate: Origin of American Feminism* (New York: Oxford University Press, 1978); Mari Jo Buhle, *Women and American Socialism, 1870–1920* (Urbana: University of Illinois Press, 1981), chap. 2.

27. For two rather different studies of the history of newspapers see Raymond Ross, *Slavery and the New York City Newspapers, 1850–1860* (Ann Arbor, Mich.: University Microfilms, 1962), and Anthony Smith, *The Newspaper: An International History* (London: Thames and Hudson, 1979).

28. See Mohr, *Abortion in America,* for a description of the growing commercialization of drugs in America. See also Glenn Sonnedecker, ed., *Kremer's and Urdang's History of Pharmacy,* 3rd ed. (Philadelphia: J. B. Lippincott, 1963).

29. See Mohr, *Abortion in America,* pp. 47–65.

30. Cover, *National Police Gazette* II (March 13, 1847): 209 (reprinted in Mohr, *Abortion in America,* p. 127). See also articles in the *National Police Gazette* for 1845 and 1846, passim. I am indebted to James Mohr's fine study for suggesting this source of popular male opinion on women and abortion.

31. See "Beauty, the Beast, and the Militant Woman: A Case Study of Sex Roles and Social Stress in Jacksonian America," in this volume.

32. Mohr, *Abortion in America,* p. 122. Mohr failed to place this campaign within the overall framework of the American Female Moral Reform Society's work and vision.

33. Mohr, *Abortion in America,* p. 32. See, as well, Richard Harrison Shryock, *Medicine and Society in America, 1660–1860* (New York: New York University Press, 1960), and *Medicine in America: Historical Essays* (Baltimore: Johns Hopkins University Press, 1972); William G. Rothstein, *American Physicians in the Nineteenth Century* (Baltimore: Johns Hopkins University Press, 1972). Starr, *Social Transformation,* pp. 39–49; Mohr, *Abortion in America,* pp. 32–33; Whitefield J. Bell, Jr., *The Colonial Physicians and Other Essays* (New York: Science History Publications, 1975), pp. 6–16; Julia Cherry Spruill, *Women's Life and Work in the Southern Colonies* (New York: W. W. Nor-

ton & Co., 1972; originally published 1938); Joseph Kett, *Formation of the American Medical Profession* (New Haven: Yale University Press, 1968), p. 108; Mary R. Walsh, *Doctors Wanted: No Women Need Apply* (New Haven: Yale University Press, 1978), pp. 3–6, 14–16; John Blake, "Women and Medicine in Ante-Bellum America," *Bulletin of the History of Medicine* XXXIX (1965): 99–123.

34. See the superb cook-book collection at the Schlesinger Library. Beginning in the late eighteenth century, an increasing number of domestic-medicine books aided women and their male fellow amateurs. See, for example, William Buchan, *Domestic Medicine, or a Treatise on the Prevention and the Cure of Diseases by Regimen and Simple Medicines,* 2nd ed. (Philadelphia: John Dunlap, for R. Aitken, 1772); William Buchan, *Advice to Mothers* . . . (Boston: Joseph Bumstead, 1809; reprinted New York: Arno Press, 1972); *The Maternal Physician: A Treatise on the Nurture and Management of Infants* . . . *by an American Matron* (New York: Arno Press, 1972; originally published 1811); Hugh Smith, *Letters to Married Ladies* (New York: E. Bliss and E. White and G. and G. Carvell, 1827). For a slightly later-nineteenth-century domestic-medicine book, see John C. Gunn, *Domestic Medicine* . . . (New York: Saxton, Barker & Co., 1860). For an overview of the domestic-medicine phenomenon, see Starr, *Social Transformation,* pp. 32–37.

35. Starr, *Social Transformation,* pp. 43–44, and, more generally, 40–44. For biographical information concerning William A. Alcott, see Herbert Thoms's sketch in *Dictionary of American Biography,* ed. Allen Johnson and Dumas Malone (New York: Scribner's, 1931). For more recent discussion of medical education in the Age of Jackson, see Starr, pp. 40–44; William F. Norwood, *Medical Education in the United States Before the Civil War* (Philadelphia: University of Pennsylvania Press, 1944). For a study of several of these medical reformers, albeit in a different context, see Carroll Smith-Rosenberg, "Sex as Symbol in Victorian Purity," *American Journal of Sociology* LXXXIV Supplement (1978): 212–47.

36. As early as 1800, two-thirds of America's urban physicians had not graduated from regular medical schools. Over the next few decades these figures would steadily increase (Starr, *So-*

cial Transformation, pp. 44, 47, 64, chap. 2; Kett, *Formation*, pp. 185–86; J. M. Toner, "Tabulated Statistics of the Medical Profession of the United States," *Transactions of the American Medical Association* XXII [1871]). I am indebted to Paul Starr for this last reference.

37. Starr, *Social Transformation*, pp. 51–54, 96–102; Harris Coulter, *Divided Legacy: A History of Schism in Medical Thought* (Washington, D.C.: McGrath Publishing Co., 1973); Martin Kaufman, *Homeopathy in America: The Rise and Fall of a Medical Heresy* (Baltimore: Johns Hopkins University Press, 1971); Kett, *Formation*, pp. 185–86; Alex Berman, "The Impact of the Nineteenth-Century Botanico-Medical Movement in American Pharmacy and Medicine, Ph. D. dissertation, University of Wisconsin, 1954; Richard Shryock, "Sylvester Graham and the Popular Health Movement, 1830–1870," in *Medicine in America: Historical Essays*.

38. Starr, *Social Transformation*, pp. 54–59, and chap. 2.

39. Peter Dobkin Hall, "Population, Patriarchy, and the Occupational Structure: The Institutional Crisis of the Late Eighteenth Century," unpublished paper, Institute for Social and Policy Studies, Yale University, April 1978.

40. Starr, *Social Transformation*, pp. 57–59, and chap. 3; Kett, *Formation*, p. 112; Mohr, *Abortion in America*, chap. 5.

41. Herbert Thoms, *Chapters in American Obstetrics* (Baltimore: Charles C. Thomas, 1933), p. 48 and passim; Alick W. Bourne, *A Synopsis of Obstetrics and Gynecology* (Baltimore: Williams & Wilkin Company, 1949).

42. Samuel Gregory was the principal publicist in the attack against male midwives. Samuel Gregory, *Letters to Ladies in Favor of Female Physicians* (Boston: George Gregory, 1848); George Gregory, *Medical Morals* (New York: published by the author, 1853). For recent reprints of the major documents in the debate, see Charles Rosenberg and Carroll Smith-Rosenberg, *The Male Midwife and the Female Doctor: The Gynecology Controversy in Nineteenth-Century America* (New York: Arno Press, 1974). Women attacked the notion of male midwives far into the nineteenth century; even such socially conservative women as Sarah Josepha Hale, editor of *Godey's Ladies Book*, and Catherine Beecher, the leading female opponent of feminism, opposed male gynecologists. Opposition to male midwives constituted an important motive in the establishment of women's medical colleges in the mid-nineteenth century. For female practice that differed sharply from female rhetoric (probably along class lines), see Scholten, "Obstetrick Art."

43. Irving, *Safe Deliverance*, pp. 104–19.

44. John Blake, "Women and Medicine in Ante-Bellum America," *Bulletin of the History of Medicine* XXXIX (1965): 99–123.

45. William Henry Brisbane, Arena, Wis., to HRS, March 19, 1859; R. H. Barton, Columbia, S.C., to HRS, April 12, 1859.

46. Draper, *Observations on Abortion*, p. 110; Coles, "Abortion," p. 255; Toner, "Medical and Moral Aspects," pp. 443–44.

47. S. Weir Mitchell, *Doctor and Patient* (Philadelphia: J. B. Lippincott, 1888), pp. 48–49, 52–54; E. P. Christian, "Pathological Consequences Incident to Induced Abortion," *Detroit Review of Medicine and Pharmacy* II (April 1867): 147; Toner, "Medical and Moral Aspects," pp. 443–46; Walter Channing, "Effects of Criminal Abortion," *Boston Medical and Surgical Journal* LX (1859): 139; Storer, *Why Not?*, pp. 12–13, 85.

48. See "The Hysterical Woman: Sex Roles and Role Conflict in Nineteenth-Century America," in this volume.

49. Mohr, *Abortion in America*, chaps. 3 and 4.

50. For Hippocrates' significantly different influence on Islamic medicine, see Basim F. Musallam, "Why Islam Permitted Birth Control," *Arab Studies Quarterly* III, no. 2 (1981): 181–97; Musallam, *Sex and Society in Islam* (Cambridge: Cambridge University Press, 1983), chap. 3.

51. "Criminal Abortion," an editorial, *The Buffalo Medical Journal*, pp. 247–51. See, as well, letters from Blatchford to HRS, March 25, 1859; E. H. Barton to HRS, April 12, 1859; Wm. Henry Brisbane to HRS, April 6, 1859; Draper, *Observations on Abortion*, pp. 5–6; Christian, "Pathological Consequences Incident to Induced Abortion," p. 147; Toner, "Medical and Moral Aspects," pp. 443–46; Channing, "Effects of Criminal Abortion," p. 139; Storer, *Why Not?*, pp. 12–13, 85. See also Mohr, *Abortion in America*, pp. 33–40, 160–61. Certainly abortion was a profitable business. The medical literature indicates that fifty to a hundred dollars was not an unusual

fee for a physician to charge during the 1840s and 1850s. Those who specialized in abortions, whether trained physicians or not, seemed to do very well financially—that is, if they were located in a commercial urban environment (Mohr, pp. 95–98).

52. G. H., "Held for Murder," p. 138; H. Gibbons, "On Feticide," *Pacific Medical and Surgical Journal* XXI (1878): 111.

53. Gibbons, *Observations on Abortion*, p. 6; Christian, "Pathological Consequences," pp. 145–53; Haskell, "Criminal Abortion," pp. 468–69.

54. Gibbons, "On Feticide," p. 111.

55. Hugh Hodge, *Foeticide, or Criminal Abortion; A Lecture Introductory to the Course on Obstetrics and Diseases of Women and Children, University of Pennsylvania, Session 1839–40* (Philadelphia: Lindsay and Blakiston, 1869), pp. 35, 23. Significantly, high-prestige physicians rejected the anti-abortion movement and strongly resisted the right of legislators to dictate their surgical options. Henry Ingersoll Bowditch, an eminent Boston physician, wrote to H. R. Storer attacking Storer's efforts to use the AMA committee to secure legislation dictating medical practice to respected physicians. Bowditch wanted neither the Massachusetts legislature nor H. R. Storer telling him what to do. On the other hand, he applauded Storer's efforts to make the woman who sought an abortion criminally liable. Only the physician could decide when to abort a woman; neither the state legislature nor the woman herself could assume that right, Bowditch contended (Henry Ingersoll Bowditch to HRS, April 20, 1857).

56. Storer, *Why Not?*, p. 83.

57. A. Lopez to HRS, April 2, 1857; Joynes to Storer, May 4, 1859.

58. E. M. Buckingham, "Criminal Abortion," *Cincinnati Lancet and Observer*, n.s. X (1867): 139–43. A psychological explication of men's fear of women's reproductive powers might be helpful here. See Karen Horney's classic essays "The Dread of Woman," *International Journal of Psycho-Analysis* XIII (1933): 348–60, and "The Denial of the Vagina: A Contribution to the Problem of the Genital Anxieties Specific to Women," *International Journal of Psycho-Analysis* XIV (1933): 57–70.

59. W. L. Atlee and D. A. O'Donnell, "Report of the Committee on Criminal Abortion,"

Transactions of the American Medical Association XXII (1871): 241.

60. Channing, "Effects of Criminal Abortion," pp. 134–35, 138.

61. E. Frank Howe, *Sermon on Ante-Natal Infanticide Delivered at the Congregational Church in Terre Haute, on Sunday Morning, March 28, 1869* (Terre Haute, Ind., 1869), pp. 2–3. Howe also quotes a typical editorial in *Harper's Magazine*, February 1859, which asserted that married women increasingly sought abortions because "women have become altogether immersed in pursuit of mere pleasure and fashion. Nothing must stand in the way of these objects" (p. 3). Storer, *Why Not?*, p. 85; Toner, "Medical and Moral Aspects," pp. 443–46; D. H., "On Producing Abortion: A Physician's Reply to the Solicitations of a Married Woman to Produce a Miscarriage for Her," *Nashville Journal of Medicine and Surgery* XVII (1876): 200–3.

62. Channing, "Effects of Criminal Abortion," pp. 134–35. See also Toner, "Medical and Moral Aspects," p. 445; J. Gailler Thomas, *Abortion and Its Treatment* (New York: D. Appleton and Company, 1894), p. 11. The editor of the *Buffalo Medical Journal* in 1858 complained that one of the most annoying aspects of abortion was the attitude of the woman who very casually entered the physician's office and demanded an abortion. If refused, she informed the physician that he was wrong to turn her down and disdainfully took her business elsewhere ("Criminal Abortion," *Buffalo Medical Journal* XIV [1858]: 249). H. R. Storer, exemplifying Carol Gilligan's argument that men focus on abstract morality while women insist on the importance of considering the effect that abstract morality will have on human relationships and feelings [see Carol Gilligan, *In a Different Voice: Psychological Theory and Women's Development* (Cambridge, Mass.: Harvard University Press, 1982)], complained, "Abstract morality is here comparatively powerless; our American women arrogate to themselves the settlement of what they consider . . . purely an ethical question," Storer and Heard, *Criminal Abortion*, p. 74n.

63. Gibbons, "On Feticide," pp. 110–11; Haskell, "Criminal Abortion," p. 467.

64. Storer, *Why Not?*, p. 85; Storer and Heard, *Criminal Abortion*, pp. 41–50; Gibbons, "On Feticide," *Pacific Medical and Surgical Jour-*

nal XXI (1878): 11; Nebinger, *Criminal Abortion,* pp. 7–9; Obstetrical Society of Boston, "Minutes, November 14, 1874," Manuscript Division, Countway Medical Library.

65. D.H., "On Producing Abortion," pp. 200–3; Beck, "Infanticide," p. 140; John S. Streeter, *Practical Observations on Abortions* (London: Sherwood, Gilbert & Piper, 1840), pp. 5–6; Storer and Heard, *Criminal Abortion,* pp. 9–10. Storer, not surprisingly, stated the anti-abortion position with great clarity: "The whole question of the criminality of the offense turns on this one fact—the real nature of the foetus *in utero.* If the foetus be a lifeless excretion, however soon it might have received life, the offense is comparatively as *nothing*; if the foetus be already, and from the very outset, a human being alive, however early its stage of development, and existing independently of its mother . . . the offense becomes, in every stage of pregnancy, MURDER" (p. 9).

66. Storer went so far as to argue that the father's genetic influence on the fetus was far greater than the mother's. He also took great pleasure in asserting that women were quite ignorant of the fetal development within themselves. The male obstetrician, not the mother, detected fetal life first, and was best equipped, because of his scientific training and rational, calm nature, to preserve that fetus's health (Storer, *Why Not?,* pp. x, 33). An analysis of the vocabulary used in mid-nineteenth-century obstetrical texts shows that physicians thought of the mother as completely passive during childbirth. One particularly popular image was of the male obstetrician as the captain, guiding the boat, the fetus, to a safe birth—the male medical and nautical metaphors reinforcing each other and excluding women. The mother in the medical metaphor is not passive: she is inert, totally objectified, and often simply absent altogether. In these texts the male physician, not the mother, gives birth to the child.

67. Hodge, *On Criminal Abortion,* pp. 9–10.

68. Storer, *Why Not?,* p. 30; Storer and Heard, *Criminal Abortion,* p. 11.

69. J. F. Grant, "Extrusion of an Ovum at the Fifth Month of Utero Gestation with the Membrane Entire," *American Journal of the Medical Sciences,* n.s. XXXIV (1857): 554. Implicit in these arguments was the equation of women with the lower animals. Woman, with all her reproductive powers, did not pose a real threat to man, because while man was linked to God in the great chain of being, woman was linked to the animals. If anything, Darwinian concepts of evolution, rather than weakening this equation, were used to strengthen it. As late as 1878, H. Gibbons, a California physician, could write in a medical journal, "What a blessing that God has made woman, in this respect, like the brute creation, and forced upon her the animal instinct of love of offspring! But for this, so prevalent is the hatred of family increase, that I verily believe that child murder would be tenfold more common in our Christian land than it is in China." Nowhere is the analogy of man to culture, woman to nature, or the attempt to explain the sociological in physiological terms made more boldly! ("On Feticide," p. 99.) Implicit in this is also a dread of woman's power to kill; the magical, all-powerful mother of childhood emerges in her very denial.

70. Storer, *Why Not?,* pp. 74–75. See also Storer, "Peculiar Pain or Pressure at the Top of the Head," *Journal of the Gynecological Society of Boston* II (1870): 261.

71. H. R. Storer, *The Causation, Course, and Treatment of Reflex Insanity in Women* (Boston: Lee and Shepard, 1871).

72. Christian, "Pathological Consequences," pp. 152–53.

73. Levin Smith Joynes to HRS, May 4, 1859.

74. Coles, "Abortion," p. 256; Toner, "Medical and Moral Aspects," p. 444; Streeter, *Practical Observations,* p. 6; Storer and Heard, *Criminal Abortion,* pp. 72, 14; Hodge, *Foeticide,* p. 35. Adrienne Rich, "The Theft of Childhood," *New York Review of Books* XXXII, no. 15 (October 2, 1975): 25–30, gives a classic example of the male physicians' continued view of the mother as the enemy, or as the murderer, of the fetus. The fetus in this view is always conceived (the pun is virtually unavoidable here!) as male. Rich cites Frederick Leboyer, *Birth Without Violence* (New York: Alfred A. Knopf, 1975), p. 26, where he describes the birth experience of a fetus: "An intransigent force—wild, out of control—has gripped the infant. . . . The prison has gone berserk, demanding its prisoner's death. . . . This monstrous unremitting pressure that is crushing the baby, pushing it out toward the

world—and this blind wall, which is holding it back, containing it. These things are all one: the mother! It is *she* who is the enemy, she who stands between the child and life. . . . The infant is like one possessed. Mad with agony and misery, alone, abandoned, it fights with the strength of despair. The monster drives the baby lower still. And not satisfied with crushing, it twists it in a refinement of cruelty. . . . And the infant's head—bearing the brunt of the struggle . . . why doesn't the head give way? The monster drives it down one more time. . . ." Leboyer's identification is clear, and it is not with the mother, who also experiences the pain of childbirth.

75. These women writers include figures as disparate as: Alice B. Stockham, *Karezza: Ethics of Marriage* (Chicago: Alice B. Stockham & Co., 1896); Elizabeth Blackwell, *Essays in Medical Sociology* (London: Ernest Bell, 1902); Victoria Woodhull, *The Elixir of Life, or Why Do We Die?* (New York: Woodhull & Claflin, 1873); Mrs. L[ucinda] B. Chandler, *The Divineness of Marriage* (New York: Great American Printing Company, 1872).

. . .

THE NEW WOMAN AS ANDROGYNE

1. The history of this essay is even longer than the essay itself. It first took form as a talk, "Male Mythologies and the Female Ego: Some Notes on the Internalization of Deviance," at a conference on women and psychotherapy, held at City University of New York Graduate Center in February 1981. An altered version formed the first half of a joint paper that Esther Newton and I delivered at the Fifth Bi-Annual Berkshire Conference on Women's History, Vassar College, 1981: "The Mythic Lesbian and the New Woman: Power, Sexuality and Legitimacy." Revised yet again, the joint article was published, as "La Femme nouvelle, l'homme nouveau et la lesbienne mythique (fin XIXe, début XXe siècle)," in *Femmes: Représentations, sexualités, pouvoirs* (Paris: Editions Tierce, 1984). In order to develop our separate insights and interests further, Newton and I then separated our halves. Newton's appears as "The Mythic Mannish Lesbian: Radclyffe Hall and the New Woman," *Signs* (Summer 1984), pp. 557–75, mine in this present guise. Newton's and my halves existed for so long as Siamese

twins that it is difficult now to tease out which ideas I can claim as originally my contribution, which are hers, and which constitute the creation of two minds working in harmony. Let me say, simply, that in writing this essay I am deeply indebted to Esther Newton's insights and understanding of the "New Woman." Though our perspectives and interpretations differ at times, I could not have written this essay without her. I also wish to thank Phyllis and Donald Rackin, Lucienne Frappier-Mazur, Sandra Gilbert, Susan Gubar, and Elaine Showalter for their suggestions and assistance.

2. For studies of the beginnings of women's higher education in the post–Civil War years in America, see Mabel Newcomer, *A Century of Higher Education for American Women* (New York: Harper and Row, 1959); Thomas Woody's encyclopedic *A History of Women's Education in the United States* (New York: Science Press, 1929), 2 vols.; Keith Melder, "Mask of Oppression: The Female Seminary Movement in the United States," *New York History* LV (1974): 261–79; Dorothy McGuigan, *The Dangerous Experiment: 100 Years of Women at the University of Michigan* (Ann Arbor: Center for the Continuing Education of Women, 1970); Charlotte Williams Conable, *Women at Cornell: The Myth of Equal Education* (Ithaca, N.Y.: Cornell University Press, 1977); Edward Potts Cheyney, *History of the University of Pennsylvania, 1740–1940* (Philadelphia: University of Pennsylvania Press, 1940); Dorothy A. Plumb and George B. Dowell, *The Magnificent Enterprise: A Chronicle of Vassar College* (Poughkeepsie, N.Y., 1961); Arthur Charles Cole, *A Hundred Years of Mount Holyoke College: The Evolution of an Educational Ideal* (New Haven: Yale University Press, 1940); Cornelia Lynde Meigs, *What Makes a College? A History of Bryn Mawr* (New York: Macmillan and Co., 1956).

3. For some New Women's discussions of what college education meant to them, see Vida Scudder, who commented in her autobiography, *On Journey* (New York: E. P. Dutton and Co., 1937), that she had harbored "a private fairy tale wherein, disguised as a boy, she crept into Harvard" (p. 58). Education was as critical to Florence Kelley: see Josephine Goldmark's biography, *Impatient Crusader* (Urbana: University of Illinois Press, 1953), chap. 2. "Entering College," Kelley told Goldmark, "was for me almost a sacramental experience." Commenting specifically on her years at Cornell,

she wrote: "Little did we care that there was no music, no theater . . . that the stairs to the lecture halls were wooden and the classrooms heated with coal stoves. No one, so far as I know, read a daily paper, or subscribed for a monthly or a quarterly. Our current gossip was Froude's life of Carlyle. We read only bound volumes." Florence Kelley, *Survey Graphic* (February 1, 1927), p. 559, reprinted in Goldmark, *Impatient Crusader,* pp. 11–12. Mary Kingsbury Simkhovitch reported similar feelings in her autobiography, *Neighborhood: My Story of Greenwich House* (New York: W. W. Norton and Co., 1938), to Alice and Edith Hamilton—see Madeleine P. Grant, *Alice Hamilton: Pioneer Doctor in Industrial Medicine* (New York: Abelard-Schuman, 1967), pp. 35–55. See women's bitter response to Edward Clarke's *Sex in Education; or, A Fair Chance for the Girls* (Boston: J. R. Osgood & Co., 1873) in Julia Ward Howe, *Sex and Education: A Reply to Dr. E. H. Clarke's "Sex in Education"* (New York: Arno Press, 1972; reprint of 1874 ed.).

4. M. Carey Thomas, in Marjorie Housepian Dobkin, *The Making of a Feminist: Early Journals and Letters of M. Carey Thomas* (Kent, Ohio: Kent State University Press, 1979), pp. 48–49, 57–58.

5. See, for example, Conable, *Women at Cornell,* chap. 3; Thomas, in Dobkin, *Making of a Feminist,* pp. 66–67, 103–6, 109. In the 1930s, Vida Scudder maintained the enthusiastic, reforming vision of women's education that she had taken with her to Smith College as an entering freshman in 1880: "I must regard the success of colleges for women as one of the few triumphs of idealism, in an age when the shipwreck of former standards and the disintegration of older cultures have precipitated society into a chaos before which men are helpless. I do not know for what reason this throng of educated women has been released into the larger life, just in the period when an old order of civilization is passing away, and the new order emerges in confusion. . . . But I recognize that in general they mean for civilization the introduction of a new element; and for women, a change not only of social opportunity but of psychological make-up, resulting from a transformation of status, actual and prospective, which is no less than epoch-making" (*On Journey,* pp. 63–64).

6. Florence M. Scofield, Wellesley College, to her mother, Madilia Scofield, Worcester, Mass., September 1875 (two letters not otherwise dated) and September 22, 1976; see, as well, her letter to her cousin, also Madilia Scofield, Worcester, Mass., October 19, 1876; in American Antiquarian Society, Worcester, Mass. College women obsessed about the genteel appearance of their rooms, negotiating for additional furniture, taking double rooms. For an example of this pattern, see Thomas, in Dobkin, *Making of a Feminist,* pp. 87–89, 103–6, 109.

7. For a detailed folkloric study of rituals in women's colleges, see Virginia Wolf Briscoe, "Bryn Mawr College Traditions: Women's Rituals as Expressive Behavior," Ph.D. thesis, University of Pennsylvania, 1981, vols. 1 and 2.

8. See, for example, the concern over coeducation expressed by all connected with Cornell. Conable, *Women at Cornell,* chaps. 2 and 3.

9. Thomas, in Dobkin, *Making of a Feminist,* p. 103.

10. Quoted by Conable, *Women at Cornell,* p. 117.

11. Ibid., pp. 116–26.

12. Thomas, in Dobkin, *Making of a Feminist,* p. 121.

13. Victor Turner, *Ritual Process* (Chicago: Aldine Pub. Co., 1969), chaps. 3 and 4.

14. Martha Vicinis, " 'One Life to Stand Beside Me': Emotional Conflicts in First-Generation College Women in England," *Feminist Studies* VIII, no. 3 (Fall 1982): 603–28.

15. Nancy Sahli, "Smashing: Women's Relations Before the Fall," *Chrysalis* VIII (1979): 17–22.

16. Turner, *Ritual Process.*

17. Martha Vicinis, "Distance and Desire: English Schoolgirl Friendships, 1870–1920," paper delivered at "Among Men, Among Women," an international conference on the history of sexuality, University of Amsterdam, June 22–26, 1983.

18. Robert Wein, "Women's Colleges and Domesticity, 1875–1918," *History of Education Quarterly* XIV (Spring 1974): 31–47.

19. Dobkin, *Making of a Feminist,* p. 66; see also pp. 50–52, 60.

20. Conversation with Allen Davis.

21. Anna Mary Wells, *Miss Marks and Miss Woolley* (Boston: Houghton Mifflin Company, 1978). Vida Scudder dedicates her au-

tobiography (as she did her first book) to Florence Converse, "Comrade and Companion."
See also Nan Bauer Magler's fine article concerning Vida Scudder and Florence Converse,
"Vida to Florence, Comrade and Companion,"
Frontiers IV (1979): 13–20. For Scudder's more
general comments on friendships between
women, see *On Journey,* pp. 104–15. Blanche
Wiesen Cook presents a detailed study of this
pattern in her excellent *Women and Support
Networks* (New York: Out & Out Books,
1978); Liela Rupp traces this phenomenon to
women politically active in the suffrage movement and later, in the 1920s, 1930s, and 1940s,
in Alice Paul's Women's Party. See her sophisticated analysis, "'Imagine My Surprise':
Women's Relationships in Historical Perspective," *Frontiers* V (1981): 61–70 (I am indebted
to Sarah Begus for first drawing my attention
to this article). See also Grant, *Alice Hamilton,*
chap. 4, especially pp. 66–68; Scudder, *On
Journey,* chap. 3; Allen Davis, *The American
Heroine: The Life and Legend of Jane Addams*
(New York: Oxford University Press, 1973),
pp. 85–91.

22. Grant, *Alice Hamilton*; Goldmark, *Impatient Crusader*; Mari Jo Buhle, *Women and
American Socialism, 1870–1920* (Urbana: University of Illinois Press, 1981), chaps. 2 and 3;
Allen F. Davis, *Spearheads of Reform: Social
Settlements and the Progressive Movement, 1890–
1914* (New York: Oxford University Press,
1967), passim; Ellen Lagemann, *A Generation of
Women* (Cambridge, Mass.: Harvard University Press, 1979).

23. Thomas, in Dobkin, *Making of a Feminist,* pp. 99, 100–1.

24. Davis, *American Heroine,* pp. 30–31, 41–
43, 83; Antler, "After College, What?" presents
a sophisticated analysis of this phenomenon,
which is the epitome of ambivalence. Jane Addams carefully presented her generation's experience of the mother-daughter tension, "The
College Woman and the Family Claim," *The
Commons* IV (September 1898). M. Carey
Thomas stated this ambivalence in the clearest
terms when, after years of adolescent struggle
against a domestic mode, she wrote her mother
from college: "I love you very dearly and in
spite of my desires after independence, I am
rather glad I have such a home to go to instead
of having to make my own."

25. Thomas, quoted by Antler.

26. Anderson, quoted by Antler.

27. For its most famous male explication, see
Clarke, *Sex in Education.* See, as well, Victorian women's response to Clarke in Howe's *Sex
and Education.*

28. Thomas Addis Emmett, *The Principles
and Practice of Gynecology* (Philadelphia: H. C.
Lea, 1879), p. 21; Thomas Smith Clouston, *Female Education from a Medical Point of View*
(Edinburgh: Macniven & Wallace, 1882),
p. 20.

29. Consider Clarke's statement: "The results [of higher education for women] are
monstrous brains and puny bodies; abnormally
active cerebration, and abnormally weak diges-
tion; flowing thought and constipated bowels;
lofty aspirations and neuralgic sensations"
(p. 41). The body (female/lower)–mind
(male/higher) polarity that was central to Victorian medical thought is clear in this quote:
women torn between male intellectual achievement and female reproductive achievement
literally tore their bodies in half. For other
pleas against education for women, see Lawrence
Irwell, "The Competition of the Sexes and
Its Results," *American Medico-Surgical Bulletin*
X (September 19, 1896): 319–20. All the doy-
ens of American gynecology in the late nineteenth century—Emmett, J. Marion Sims, T.
Gaillard Thomas, Charles D. Meigs, William
Goodell, and S. Weir Mitchell—shared the
conviction that higher education and excessive
development of the nervous system might
interfere with woman's proper performance
of her maternal functions. Mitchell was especially pointed in his attacks on women's colleges, and specifically his criticisms of Vassar
(Mitchell, *Fat and Blood* [Philadelphia: J. B.
Lippincott Co., 1885], and *Doctor and Patient*
[Philadelphia: J. B. Lippincott Co., 1888],
passim).

30. William Goodell, *Lessons in Gynecology*
(Philadelphia: D. G. Brinton, 1879), p. 353.

31. William Warren Potter, *How Should
Girls Be Educated? A Public Health Problem for
Mothers, Educators, and Physicians* (New York:
New York Medical Journal, 1891), p. 9.

32. William Edgar Darnall, "The Pubescent
Schoolgirl," *American Gynecological and Obstetrical Journal* XVIII (June 1901): 490.

33. Board of Regents, University of Wisconsin, *Annual Report for the Year Ending September 30, 1877* (Madison, 1877), p. 45.

34. Clouston, *Female Education*, p. 19.

35. Clarke, *Sex in Education*, passim. For specific references to hermaphroditism, see pp. 44, 93, 115.

36. Carroll Smith-Rosenberg, "Sex as Symbol in Victorian Purity: An Ethnohistorical Analysis of Jacksonian America," *American Journal of Sociology* LXXXIV Supplement (1978): 212–47; Sylvester Graham, *Lecture to Young Men on Chastity*, 3rd ed. (Boston: Light & Stearns, 1837; originally published 1834); S. B. Woodward, *Hints for the Young in Relation to the Health of Mind and Body* (Boston: Light & Stearns, 1856; originally published 1837); R. T. Trall, *Home-Treatment for Sexual Abuses: A Practical Treatise* (New York: Fowlers and Wells, 1856).

37. For an elaborate feminist refutation of Clarke by a variety of bourgeois women born during the first third of the nineteenth century, all educated before the Civil War, all schoolteachers or writers, see Howe, *Sex and Education*. The women include Julia Ward Howe herself; Mrs. Horace Mann (Mary Tyler Peabody, sister of Elizabeth Peabody and of Sophia Peabody Hawthorne, a teacher until she married Mann at the age of thirty-seven); Reverend Olympia Brown (feminist and minister, graduate of Antioch, 1860); Elizabeth Stuart Phelps (best-selling novelist); Caroline H. Dall (feminist, abolitionist, and writer, born 1822); Mercy B. Jackson; Maria A. Elmore; Ada Shepart Badger. Howe also includes official endorsements of women's higher education from Vassar, Antioch, and Oberlin colleges and from the University of Michigan.

38. Sarah H. Stevenson, *The Physiology of Woman, Embracing Girlhood, Maternity and Mature Age*, 2nd ed. (Chicago: Cushing, Thomas & Company, 1881), pp. 68, 77; Alice Stockham, *Tokology: A Book for Every Woman*, rev. ed. (Chicago: Sanitary Publishing Co., 1887), p. 257. Stevenson noted acidly that "the unerring instincts of woman have been an eloquent theme for those who do not know what they are talking about" (p. 79). The dress-reform movement held, of course, far more significant implications than one would gather from the whimsical attitude with which it is normally approached; clothes were very much a part of woman's role. Health reformers, frequently critical as well of the medical establishment whose arguments I have been describing, were often sympathetic to women's claims that not too much, but too little, mental stimulation was the cause of their ills, especially psychological ones. See Martin Luther Holbrook, *Hygiene of the Brain and Nerves and the Cure of Nervousness* (New York: U.S. Book Co., 1878); James C. Jackson, *American Womanhood: Its Peculiarities and Necessities* (Dansville, N.Y.: Austin, Jackson & Co., 1870).

39. Mrs. Horace Mann, in Howe, *Sex and Education*, pp. 52–71.

40. Lillian Faderman, *Surpassing the Love of Men* (New York: William Morrow and Co., 1981); Sahli, "Changing Patterns"; "The Female World of Love and Ritual" in this volume; George Chauncey, Jr., "From Sexual Inversion to Homosexuality: Medicine and the Changing Conceptualization of Female Deviance," *Salmagundi* LVIII–LIX (Fall 1982/Winter 1983): 114–46.

41. Samuel Gregory, *Facts and Important Information for Young Women on the Subject of Masturbation* (Boston: George Gregory, 1857); Gross and Co., *Hygieana: A Non-Medical Analysis of the Complaints Incidental to Females* (London: G. Booth, 1829), see especially pp. 64 and 66.

42. Thomas, in Dobkin, *Making of a Feminist*, pp. 90–93, 69.

43. Graham, *Lecture*, pp. 83–84; O. S. Fowler, *Amativeness or Evils and Remedies of Excessive and Perverted Sexuality* (New York: Fowlers and Wells, 1856), pp. 28–29.

44. See "Hearing Women's Words: A Feminist Reconstruction of History," note 55.

45. "The Female World of Love and Ritual," in this volume. In the various collections of women's personal papers, I found no reference to women reading any of these French novels—even, or perhaps especially, among those women who seemed most sensually involved with other women.

46. See reference to Caspar and his influences on late-nineteenth-century European sexologists in Arno Karlan, *Sexuality and Homosexuality* (London: Macdonald Ltd., 1975), p. 185, and in Jeffrey Weeks, *Sex, Politics and Society: The Regulation of Sexuality Since 1800* (New York and London: Longman Group Limited, 1981), p. 104 and chap. 6 passim.

47. For Carl Ulrichs's influence, ibid.

48. Faderman, *Surpassing the Love of Men*, pt. II, B, chap. 2.

49. Michel Foucault, *The History of Sexuality* (New York: Pantheon Books, 1978).

50. Richard von Krafft-Ebing, *Psychopathia Sexualis with Especial Reference to the Antipathic Sexual Instinct,* trans. F. J. Rebman (Brooklyn: Physicians and Surgeons Book Co., 1908), p. 333. This book was originally published in Stuttgart in 1886.

51. For three excellent analyses of the sexologists' attitudes toward homosexuality, see Chauncey, "From Sexual Inversion to Homosexuality"; Jane Caplan, "Sexuality and Homosexuality," in *Women in Society,* ed. Cambridge Women's Studies Group (London: Virago, 1980), pp. 149–67; Sheila Rowbotham and Jeffrey Weeks, *Socialism and the New Life: The Personal and Sexual Politics of Edward Carpenter and Havelock Ellis* (London: Pluto Press Limited, 1977).

52. Krafft-Ebing, *Psychopathia Sexualis,* pp. 342, 345–46, 351, 353, 355, provides examples of Krafft-Ebing's concern with hereditary patterns.

53. J. C. Kiernan, "Sexual Perversion in the White Chapel Murders," *Medical Standard* (Chicago) IV (1888): 170–72.

54. Havelock Ellis, "Sexual Inversion with an Analysis of Thirty-three New Cases," *Medico-Legal Journal* XIII (1895–96): 263. See pp. 255–61, as well.

55. "Perverted Sexual Instincts: Notes on a Paper read by J. C. Kiernan, M.D.," *Chicago Medical Journal and Examiner* XLVIII (1884): 263–65.

56. Krafft-Ebing, *Psychopathia Sexualis,* pp. 333–36.

57. Ibid., pp. 334–35.

58. Ibid., p. 351.

59. Ibid., p. 355.

60. Ibid.

61. P. M. Wise, "Case of Sexual Perversion," *Alienist and Neurologist* IV (1883): 87–91.

62. E.J.H., Letter to the Editor, *Alienist and Neurologist* V (1884): 351–52; G. Frank Lydston, "Sexual Perversion, Satyriasis and Nymphomania," *Medical and Surgical Reporter* (Philadelphia) LXI (September 7, 1889): 253–58; Kiernan, "Sexual Perversion," pp. 170–72; P. Leidy and C. K. Mills, "Sexual Perversion," *Journal of Nervous and Mental Disease* (New York), n.s. IX (1886): 712; Oliver Penfeld, "A Case of Man-Personification by a Woman," *Australian Medical Journal* n.s. II (April 15, 1880): 145–47.

63. T. Griswold Comstock, "Alice Mitchell of Memphis: A Case of Sexual Perversion or 'Urning' (a Paranoiac)," *New York Medical Times* XX (1892–93): 170–73; "Alice Mitchell the 'Sexual Pervert,' and Her Crime," editorial, *Alienist and Neurologist* XIII (1892): 554–57.

64. Thomas, in Dobkin, *Making of a Feminist,* p. 121.

65. Mary Woolley to Josephine Marks, May 11, July 9, and July 11, 1900.

66. Sigmund Freud, "Contribution I, the Sexual Aberrations," in *Three Contributions to the Theory of Sex* (New York: E. P. Dutton & Co., 1962; originally published 1905) pp. 1, 6.

67. See Jane Caplan's discussion of Havelock Ellis, "Sexuality and Homosexuality," pp. 153, 155–57.

68. Jeffrey Weeks, "Havelock Ellis and the Politics of Sex Reform," in Rowbotham and Weeks, *Socialism and the New Life,* pp. 151–55, 160, 163, 172, 178; David Kennedy, *Birth Control in America: The Career of Margaret Sanger* (New Haven: Yale University Press, 1970), pp. 29–35. Jonathan Katz cites Emma Goldman's letter to Magnus Hirschfeld, praising Havelock Ellis's work in behalf of male homosexuals. Ellis also wrote an introduction to Radclyffe Hall's *Well of Loneliness* (Katz, *Gay American History: Lesbians and Gay Men in the U.S.A., A Documentary* [New York: Thomas Y. Crowell Company, 1976], pp. 379, 403).

69. Ellis, "Sexual Inversion with an Analysis of Thirty-three New Cases," p. 262.

70. Ellis, "Sexual Inversion in Women," *Alienist and Neurologist* XVI (1895): 147–48, states that women who are attracted to true inverts and who, in turn, attract them are "the pick of the women whom the average man would pass by."

71. Ibid., pp. 145–46.

72. Ibid., pp. 146–48, 152–53, 155–57. For his distinction between "homosexuality" and "inversion," see, as well, Ellis, "Sexual Inversion with an Analysis of Thirty-three New Cases," pp. 262–64.

73. Ibid.; Ellis, *Sexual Inversion* (Philadelphia: F. A. Davis Co., 1901), p. 283. For an early article by Ellis specifically attacking European sodomy laws, see Ellis, "Sexual Inversion in Relation to Society and the Law," *Medico-Legal Journal* XIV (1896–97): 279–88. See Weeks's analysis of Ellis's position on male homosexuality, "Havelock Ellis," pp. 160–61.

74. Weeks, "Havelock Ellis," pp. 153–55.

75. Ibid., p. 142.

76. Ellis, "Sexual Inversion with an Analysis of Thirty-three New Cases," passim. Caplan offers an insightful analysis of this part of Ellis's thought in "Sexuality and Homosexuality," p. 156.

77. Ellis, quoted by Weeks, "Havelock Ellis," p. 171.

78. Caplan, "Sexuality and Homosexuality," pp. 156–57.

79. Weeks presents a forceful analysis of Ellis's essentially conservative attitude toward women in "Havelock Ellis," pp. 169–80. For Ellis on the biological and social polarity of women and men, see *Man and Woman* (London: Walter Scott, 1894).

80. Ellis, "Sexual Inversion in Women," pp. 155–56.

81. Ibid., p. 153. For a series of case studies detailing these characteristics among educated and intelligent women, see pp. 148–53.

82. R.W. Shufeldt, "Dr. Havelock Ellis on Sexual Inversion," *Pacific Medical Journal* XLV (1902): 199–207.

83. William Lee Howard, "Effeminate Men and Masculine Women," *New York Medical Journal* LXXI (1900): 687.

84. For a discussion of Alice Stone Blackwell and of Wellesley College's changing politics, see Sahli, "Smashing." See, as well, Margaret Otis, "A Perversion Not Commonly Noted," *Journal of Abnormal Psychology* (1913). Kate Richards O'Hare's article, "Prison Lesbianism" (1919–20), and Charles A. Ford's article, "Homosexual Practices of Psychology" (1929), are both cited and abstracted in Jonathan Katz's invaluable *Gay American History*, pp. 65–74, where there is also an abstract of the Otis article.

85. William S. Barker, "Two Cases of Sexual Contrariety," *St. Louis Courier of Medicine* XXVIII (1903): 269–71.

86. Thomas, in Dobkin, *Making of a Feminist*, pp. 86–87. Lorine Pruette makes a similar observation, commenting that the sexual reformers had now made impossible the easy flow back and forth between homosexual and heterosexual relations that had previously characterized female adolescence (Pruette, "The Flapper," ed. Victor F. Calverton and Samuel D. Schmalhausen, *The New Generation: The Intimate Problems of Modern Parents and Children* [New York: Macaulay, 1930], pp. 574–77). Christina Simmons opens her pathbreaking article on the companionate-marriage movement with this point (Simmons, "Companionate Marriage and the Lesbian Threat," *Frontiers* IV [1979]: 54–59).

87. Wein, "Women's Colleges and Domesticity, 1875–1918," pp. 38–39, 44.

88. Ellen Ross and Rayna Rapp, "Sex and Society: A Research Note from Social History and Anthropology," *Comparative Studies in Society and History* XXIII (1981): 51–72.

89. Sandra Gilbert analyzes the male modernists' attitudes toward the New Woman in "Costumes of the Mind: Transvestism as Metaphor in Modern Literature," *Critical Inquiry* (Winter 1980): 391–417. For an early and important analysis of the companionate-marriage literature, see Simmons, "Companionate Marriage and the Lesbian Threat."

90. F. W. Stella Browne, "Studies in Feminine Inversion," *Journal of Sexology and Psychoanalysis* I (1923): 51–58. See Sheila Rowbotham's analysis of Browne: *A New Word for Women: Stella Browne, Socialist Feminist* (London: Pluto Press, 1977). Browne, Rowbotham argues, was strongly influenced by Ellis.

91. The list of companionate-marriage advocates and sex reformers who denigrated the woman who was hostile or indifferent to heterosexual relations as infantile, repressed, ludicrous includes: Floyd Dell, "Sex in Adolescence," in *Sex Education: Facts and Attitudes* (New York: Child Study Association of America, 1934), p. 49; Dorothy Dunbar Bromley and Florence Haxton Britten, *Youth and Sex: A Study of 1300 College Students* (New York: Harper and Row, 1938), p. 129; John F. W. Meagher, "Homosexuality: Its Psychobiological and Psychopathological Significance," *The Urologic and Cutaneous Review* XXXIII (1929): 508, 512; Edward Podolsky, " 'Homosexual Love' in Women," *Popular Medicine* I (February 1935): 375; Floyd Dell, *Love in the Machine Age: A Psychological Study of the Transition from Patriarchal Society* (New York: Farrar, 1930), pp. 238, 308; Ralph Hay, "Mannish Women or Old Maids?," *Know Yourself* I (July 1938).

92. Meagher, "Homosexuality," pp. 511, 513, cited in Simmons, "Companionate Marriage," p. 57. For companionate-marriage advocacy of the pleasures of heterosexual relations between men and women who treated each other as equals (albeit without necessarily challenging existing sex-role differentiation), see Ben Lindsey and Wainwright Evans, *The*

Companionate Marriage (New York: Boni and Liveright, 1927); Horace Coon, *Coquetry for Men* (New York: Amour Press, 1932); S. D. Schmalhausen, "The Sexual Revolution," in *Sex in Civilization,* ed. V. F. Calverton and S. D. Schmalhausen (New York: Macaulay, 1929). For a position similar to Meagher's, see George K. Pratt, "Accepting One's Sexual Role," in *Sex-Education: A Series of Lectures Concerning Knowledge of Sex in Its Relation to Human Life,* ed. Maurice Bigelow (New York: Macmillan, 1916), and Ernest Groves et al., *Sex Fulfillment in Marriage* (New York: Emerson, 1942).

93. Buhle, *Women and American Socialism,* chap. 4; Elaine Showalter, "Introduction," *These Modern Women* (Old Westbury, N.Y.: Feminist Press, 1978), pp. 3–29; Luhan, quoted in Judith Schwarz, *Radical Feminists of Heterodoxy: Greenwich Village, 1912–1940* (Lebanon, N.H.: Victoria Publishers, Inc., 1982), p. 1. See Gertrude Stein's attacks on M. Carey Thomas for being a single-minded feminist and sexually forbidding: *Fernhurst,* in *Fernhurst, QED and Other Early Writings* (New York: Liveright, 1971; originally written 1904?).

94. Millay, "First Fig," in *The Norton Anthology of Modern Poetry,* ed. Richard Ellmann and Robert O'Clair (New York: W. W. Norton & Company, 1973), p. 492. See, as well, Millay's "Love Is Not All: It Is Not Meat Nor Drink"—"Love is not all: it is not meat nor drink / nor slumber nor a roof against the rain / . . . It well may be that in a difficult hour, / Pinned down by pain and moaning for release, / Or nagged by want past resolution's power, / I might be driven to sell your love for peace, / Or trade the memory of this night for food. / It well may be. I do not think I would" (p. 494)—for this generation's view of the centrality of sexuality and love to their life aims.

95. Blanche Cook, personal communication.

96. Showalter, "Introduction," pp. 15, 78–79.

97. Frances Wilder to Edward Carpenter, reprinted by Ruth F. Claus, "Confronting Homosexuality: A Letter from Frances Wilder," *Signs* II (1977): 928–33.

98. For a provocative and highly influential analysis of "The Woman-on-Top" rituals and iconography of the Middle Ages and early modern period, see Natalie Zemon Davis,

"Woman on Top," in *Society and Culture in Early Modern France* (Stanford, Calif.: Stanford University Press, 1975), pp. 124–51.

99. For a superb anthology on the subject of symbolic inversion, see *The Reversible World: Symbolic Inversion in Art and Society,* ed. Barbara A. Babcock (Ithaca, N.Y.: Cornell University Press, 1978), and especially Babcock's "Introduction," pp. 13–36, and David Kunzle, "World Upside Down: The Iconography of a European Broadsheet Type," pp. 39–94.

100. Sandra Gilbert, "Costumes of the Mind: Transvestism as Metaphor in Modern Literature," *Critical Inquiry* (Winter 1980): 391–417.

101. Ibid.

102. D. H. Lawrence, *The Fox,* in Lawrence, *Four Short Novels* (London: Penguin Books, 1976).

103. Gilbert, "Costumes."

104. Susan Gubar, "Blessings in Disguise: Cross-Dressing as Re-Dressing for Female Modernists," *Massachusetts Review* (Autumn 1981): 477–508.

105. Virginia Woolf, *Orlando: A Biography* (New York: Harcourt Brace Jovanovich, 1956; originally published 1928).

106. Gilbert, "Costumes," pp. 404–7, proposes this vision of Orlando. I am indebted to Lucienne Frappier-Mazur for bringing the European literary tradition (male) of the novel of initiation to my attention. Frappier-Mazur has explored George Sand's *The Countess of Rudolstadt* as a feminist inversion of that form. See Frappier-Mazur's article in the special issue on psycho-poetics in *Poetics* (Spring/Summer 1984), "Desire, Writing and Identity in the Romantic Mystical Novel: Notes for a Definition of the Feminine."

107. Roland Barthes, *Mythologies,* sel. and trans. Annette Lavers (New York: Hill and Wang, 1972), pp. 137–45.

108. Djuna Barnes, *Nightwood* (New York: New Directions, 1961; originally published 1937); Radclyffe Hall, *The Well of Loneliness* (New York: Coucici-Friede, 1934). For other suggestive analyses of these novels, see Catharine Stimpson, "Zero Degree Deviance: The Lesbian Novel in English," *Critical Inquiry* (Winter 1981): 363–79, and Kenneth Burke, "Version, Con-, Per-, and In- (Thoughts on Djuna Barnes's Novel *Nightwood*)," in *Language as Symbolic Action* (Berkeley: University of California Press, 1966), pp. 240–53.

109. See Newton's interpretation of *The Well of Loneliness*: "The Mythic Mannish Lesbian," *Signs* IX (Fall 1984): 557–75.

110. Barnes, *Nightwood*, pp. 1–7.

111. See "Davy Crockett as Trickster," in this volume.

112. For a superb analysis of the Trickster, see Barbara Babcock-Abrahams, " 'A Tolerated Margin of Mess': The Trickster and His Tales Reconsidered," *Journal of the Folklore Institute* XI (1975): 147–86.

113. For a detailed (and somewhat psychoanalytic) interpretation of the Winnebago Trickster, see Paul Radin, *The Trickster: A Study in American Indian Mythology* (New York: Philosophical Library, 1956).

114. Babcock-Abrahams, " 'Tolerated Margin of Mess,' " pp. 153–60. See, as well, Laura Makarius, "Ritual Clowns and Symbolic Behavior," *Diogenes* LXIX (1970): 44–73, especially p. 66; Katherine Luomala, *Maui-of-a-Thousand-Tricks* (Bernice P. Bishop Museum Bulletin 198, 1949), cited by Babcock-Abrahams.

115. For Barnes's presentation of Frau Mann and her fellow circus characters, see *Nightwood*, pp. 11–13, 113.

116. Ibid., p. 113.

117. Babcock-Abrahams, " 'Tolerated Margin of Mess,' " pp. 153–54.

118. Thomas, in Dobkin, *Making of a Feminist*, p. 121.

119. Barnes, *Nightwood*, p. 135.

120. Newton, personal communication.

121. William Shakespeare, *As You Like It*, Act V, scene 2.

122. I am indebted to Phyllis Rackin for emphasizing the importance of this play. It illustrates the way Renaissance playwrights used gender as a metaphor for social order— or disorder. See Phyllis Rackin, "Androgyny, Marriage and Mimesis: The Marriage of the Boy Heroine in Five Renaissance Comedies," paper presented at the International Conference "After the Second Sex: New Directions," University of Pennsylvania, April 6, 1984.

123. *As You Like It*, Epilogue.

124. Barnes, *Nightwood*, p. 80.

125. Dante Alighieri, *The Divine Comedy*, canto I, lines 2–7.

126. Quoted by Dorothy Sayers, "Introduction" to *The Comedy of Dante Alighieri, the Florentine*, trans. Dorothy L. Sayers (London: Penguin Books, 1949), pp. 14–15.

127. The women of the 1920s' inability to reach out to successive generations of women is critical. The women of the 1930s, 1940s, and 1950s, cut off from both the androgynous dream of the 1920s and from the earlier sense of a female rooted identity, did not realize that the feminist modernists, inverting male symbols, had created a new female discourse. These later women heard only the male metaphors. They felt they lived in a world devoid of women's words—in a world of female isolation. They had lost the knowledge of both the first and the second generations of New Women. It is only since the women's movement of the 1960s, 1970s, and 1980s that we have regained a knowledge of our political and literary foremothers.

Index

A NOTE ON THE TYPE

The text of this book was set in a digitized version of Bembo, a well-known Monotype face named for Pietro Bembo, the celebrated Renaissance writer and humanist scholar. The original cutting of Bembo was made by Francesco Griffo, of Bologna, only a few years after Columbus discovered America.

Sturdy, well-balanced, and finely proportioned, Bembo is a face of rare beauty, extremely legible in all of its sizes.

Composed by The Haddon Craftsmen, Inc.,
Scranton, Pennsylvania

Printed and bound by
R. R. Donnelley, Inc., Harrisonburg, Virginia

Designed by Tasha Hall